D1737646

EDITORIAL THINKING
AND WRITING

In the council room of the "New York Times" the editorial
and executive staffs meet daily to discuss the day's news

EDITORIAL THINKING AND WRITING

A TEXTBOOK WITH EXERCISES

BY

CHILTON R. BUSH

ASSOCIATE PROFESSOR OF JOURNALISM, UNIVERSITY OF WISCONSIN

GREENWOOD PRESS, PUBLISHERS
WESTPORT, CONNECTICUT

Originally published in 1932 by
Appleton and Company, New York

First Greenwood Reprinting 1970

Library of Congress Catalogue Card Number 74-98826

SBN 8371-3078-6

Printed in United States of America

TO THE MEMORY OF

FRANK I. COBB

WHO ALWAYS

—AS MR. BABE RUTH WOULD SAY—

HAD SOMETHING ON THE BALL

PREFACE

I have had the opportunity of watching certain intelligent men's minds work—have observed their habits of thinking—and I have been left with the conviction that one thinks better if he becomes conscious of his method of thinking. Thinking, of course, is the perception of relations; and some men of keen insight appear to have an unconscious perception of right relations. Yet the ordinary thinker will profit greatly from a discipline. I do not mean a sterile discipline such as the old-fashioned course in logic used to provide, but an analysis of the thinking process consciously applied within the thinker's field of primary interest—an analysis which accustoms the thinker to seek for principles in a mass of data, compels him to be cautious in accepting his tentative hypotheses, and moves him to canvass all of the possibilities in a given situation.

Some students, of course, acquire such a method along with their major study—the law student, for example, and the medical and engineering student, and, to some extent, the student of economics. The student of journalism, however, often learns the technique of presenting his thought in writing and acquires a considerable amount of information about the social sciences without going deep enough into any subject to acquire a habit of disciplined thinking. This book, therefore—although it discusses the editorial as a literary form, the editor's relation to his readers, and a few other matters of importance to the editorial writer—tries mainly to provide the student of journalism with an explanation of the thinking process in terms of modern social problems, together with a considerable amount of practice material. The material has usually dealt with social problems that will be of importance to the editorial writer during the next decade and, to a great extent, with the half-truths encountered in connection with public policy; it has not often dealt with out-of-date and "settled" questions or with such obvious truths as the older textbooks in logic discussed. Throughout the discussion, moreover, it has been the purpose of the author to present a problem as it would be envisaged by the editorial writer voicing the opinion of a responsible institution, not as it would be looked at by the layman who has no fiduciary relation to the public.

In the teaching of any content subject, the instructor has little difficulty in adapting the textbook to his own method of teaching; provided the book contains an adequate amount of content material and is organized in a logical manner, the instructor has only to assign readings and, in lectures, elaborate and supplement the material in the book. In the teaching of a "tool" subject, however, the teacher is more important than the textbook. The course in "Editorial Writing" belongs to the latter category of subjects because its purpose is to teach the student how to perform certain processes—the process of analyzing social data and the process of presenting thought in writing. This book, which proceeds on the assumption that the first-named process is the more important of the two, tries to provide the student with a kind of material that will enable him not only to understand the process of editorial analysis but to learn how to perform it reasonably well. In this sense, the *material is not content to be learned, but method to be applied.* The student is given the formula for editorial analysis, along with certain directions, supplies, and equipment, and is sent to the laboratory to work through the formula with different sets of data for each type of problem.

This being the method, it is important that the individual teacher be under no compulsion to adhere slavishly to the minutiæ. If the best use of the book is to be made, the instructor should take pains to adapt the material to his own conditions and his own point of view. In these respects he may desire to omit certain readings and assignments, to substitute certain points of view, to correct certain statements, and to emphasize or expand certain sections.

A cursory examination of the book is sufficient to show the method of its organization. The formula for editorial analysis is first explained (Chapters I to III). The remainder of the book, except for two or three chapters, is merely an elaboration of this formula. But the elaborative part, I think, is equally important: it is here that the student may practice the formula in a realistic way. That is to say, he learns to analyze those questions with which newspaper editorials for the next decade or so will be concerned, such as taxation, public utility economics, unemployment insurance, international relations, etc. The book, therefore, contains a certain amount of repetition which is deliberate on the part of the author. In case it seems necessary to omit some of the material, the instructor will find it feasible to do so.

The method of organization requires that a compromise be made between logic and pedagogy. Because the course deals with two different processes—thinking and writing—one process (thinking) has first been treated in entirety and is followed by the other process (writing). Since the character of editorial style cannot be understood apart from the practical purpose of the editorial writer, it seems logical to explain first the editorial writer's purpose and his relation to his readers, for these are the factors that condition his style. To present the material in this logical order, however, is to encounter a serious pedagogical difficulty, namely, the fact that students in the course begin writing editorials during the first week and ought, of course, to learn at the beginning something about the structure and style of editorials. The author's recommendation, therefore—and this will be his own practice in using the book—is to *assign Chapters XV ("The Structure of the Editorial") and XVI ("Editorial Style") immediately after Chapter I, and later in the course return to a more thorough examination of these chapters in their logical place.*

Underlying the whole method of the book is the deeper purpose of aiding the student to articulate his journalistic studies with the social studies in the curriculum. It is the author's hope that not only will the student's interest be enlisted in the social studies (these are the substance of journalism), but that he will perceive the relation between the art of his profession and the subject matter with which journalism deals. The author, naturally, has selected for illustrative purposes the material with which he is most familiar, and this implies that the individual instructor who is unfamiliar with parts of the material will make appropriate substitutions. For the most part, however, the material selected is deemed to be essential for the prospective editorial writer to know, and, in order that he may have more data than the textbook discussion presents, numerous footnotes have been supplied. The aim has been to provide reasonably difficult rather than easy problems.

In the same connection it ought to be noted that the illustrative material is often too meager to provide the student with a thorough understanding of the specific question, and this implies that he do a certain amount of outside reading and investigation. This, it seems to the author, is one of the chief aims of the course in "Editorial Writing." The exercises appended to the text have been carefully selected for the purpose of elaborating the textbook discussions, and it is recommended that they be used as much as possible.

Teachers who perceive the absence in the text of certain aspects of the subject (for example, a treatment of the science of epistemology) will probably find references to them in the exercises.

There remains to say, by way of apology, that this course is in no respect a substitute for the course in logic as that course is usually presented in the universities. A good course in logic succeeds in teaching the student an approach to moral evaluation and provides him with a truer sense of ethical values and with some knowledge of speculative science. This book, although it does not entirely ignore the aims of the course in logic, has only a practical purpose. The individual instructor, however, who can teach his students how to think about group morality certainly ought to do so. The author, who is an incurable idealist, regrets that the textbook discussion could not represent precisely his own attitude toward life. He hopes, nevertheless, that those instructors who make use of the book will feel less conditioned by circumstances and will not be too eager to condemn in class discussion the current radical theories and proposals as being "logically unsound."

If the preceding paragraph, by inference, seems to have minimized the importance of the recent textbooks in logic, the author disavows in this place any such interpretation. In the preparation of the manuscript, the author has leaned heavily on some of the new books, especially the Columbia Associates in Philosophy, *An Introduction to Reflective Thinking,* and E. A. Burtt's *Principles and Problems of Right Thinking.* The debt that all teachers and investigators owe to John Dewey's *How We Think* is shared by this author, and grateful acknowledgment is made. An acknowledgment is also due to some of the writers on argumentation, and to Genung's *The Working Principles of Rhetoric* for the help that it afforded in the preparation of the chapter on editorial style.

In the revision of the manuscript the author has had the excellent advice and aid of Professor and Mrs. Willard Grosvenor Bleyer; Professor M. C. Otto, of the Department of Philosophy of the University of Wisconsin; Professor L. N. Flint of the University of Kansas; and Professors F. L. Mott and F. J. Lazell of the University of Iowa. None of these counselors, however, is responsible for any of the erroneous statements and interpretations that the manuscript may still contain. The author acknowledges with particular gratitude the encouragement and assistance given by Professor Bleyer, whose ideas and points of view he absorbs and afterwards undesignedly attributes to his own originality.

C. R. B.

CONTENTS

EDITORIAL THINKING AND WRITING

CHAPTER I

WHY AND HOW EDITORIALS ARE WRITTEN

Definition of the Editorial.—The term *editorial,* as it is now used in the United States, is an elliptical form of *editorial article,* the modifier of the substantive having come to stand for the substantive itself. The term means simply the editor's comment as distinguished from the news stories written by reporters and the "letters" contributed by readers.

In most European newspapers the distinction between opinion and news is not sharply drawn; this is as it was in American newspapers of an earlier day. In the modern American newspaper, however, opinion is more distinctly separated from news, for political and educational influences have traditionally decreed that opinion be confined to the editorial column. The pragmatic American has great regard for "facts," and his naïve theory of public opinion presumes that if he only be possessed of the "true facts" involved in a social or political controversy he will be able, as a consequence, to arrive at an infallible conclusion. The Frenchman, on the other hand, being more attracted by a point of view, is not so eager to obtain a set of objective facts: he prefers that the facts published in the newspaper be compounded with the opinion of the writer. Many of the so-called news stories in French newspapers, therefore, are articles prepared and signed by specialists and embodying both fact and opinion; they are usually called *articles de fond,* and are placed in the usual news columns.

Signed articles that combine both news and opinion appear also in the best British newspapers, but a special department is reserved nevertheless for editorial opinion. The editorial articles are called "leaders." The term *leader* implies that the editorial article is a discussion of the leading news of the day, as, for example, when Parliament is debating the revision of the prayer-book the editor discusses "The Prayer-Book Controversy"; he explains the points at issue and usually takes a stand on one side of the controversy. The best British, American, and French newspapers adhere to the traditional practice of publishing comprehensive articles of comment about the leading news story of the day,[1] but many of the more popular newspapers of all countries frequently ignore the socially significant news and instead discuss either inconsequential matters or pet policies.

Editorials that discuss the important news of the day and that exert an intellectual leadership in public affairs are the only ones that require study. It is this type of editorial to which this book refers whenever the term *editorial* is used.[2]

The First Editorials.—Newspapers at the end of the eighteenth century were printed and sold by entrepreneurs who had learned the trade of printing. These journals reported facts and gossip about events, and served as mediums for the expression of opinion. At first these newspapers had no editors. The entrepreneur-printer called himself a "printer." He gathered and clipped news, printed the paper, and attended to the business of what we now call advertising, circulation, and job printing; but he made only a feeble effort to interpret events or to exert editorial leadership. Although the paper contained expressions of opinion about public affairs, these were usually contributed by outsiders in the form of "letters." The contributors were agitators or political philosophers who possessed a talent for marshaling arguments and for appealing to the members of the body politic, and they made use of pamphlets as well as newspapers. Under such *noms de plumes* as "Cato," "Junius," and "A Farmer in Pennsylvania" they wrote long polemical arguments which frequently were printed

---

[1] Notable, among French newspapers, is the *bulletin du jour* on the front page of *le Temps*.

[2] So-called entertaining and inspirational editorials are discussed in Chapter XVII.

a section at a time in the successive issues of a newspaper whose "printer" was agreeable to their publication.[3]

During the period of the struggle for independence and for a short time after the founding of the Republic, opinion in the newspaper was almost exclusively contributed by outsiders, but afterward, during the period when the political parties were forming, the political leaders found it advisable to establish or to subsidize newspapers for the special purpose of organizing public thought and mobilizing public will. To some of these newspapers the political leaders themselves contributed, as, for example, Alexander Hamilton, who wrote the series of "Camillus" letters in the New York *Minerva* in defense of the Jay treaty.[4]

Gradually there developed the prototype of the modern editor —a printer who did his own thinking and writing. John Fenno, of the *Gazette of the United States* (1789-1798), a New England school teacher whose "literary achievements" were "handsome," who always referred to himself as the "editor," was representative of the newer type of editor. Although he published numerous "letters" written by Hamilton and by Hamilton's Federalist associates, Fenno himself wrote most of the opinion that appeared in his paper. Contemporary editors of Fenno who supported the Federalist party were Noah Webster, of the *Minerva;* William Coleman, of the New York *Evening Post;* and William Cobbett, of *Porcupine's Gazette.* Opposing these partisan journalists were such Jeffersonian editors as Philip Freneau, of the *National Gazette;* James Cheetham, of the *American Citizen;* Benjamin Franklin Bache, of the Philadelphia *Aurora;* and others.

The practice of publishing daily short articles which embodied the editor's opinion coincided with the era of violent partisan controversy at the dawn of the nineteenth century.

---

[3] The series of articles written by Hamilton, Madison, and Jay under the pseudonym of "Publius," for the purpose of urging ratification of the Constitution, were first published in the New York *Independent Journal* and the New York *Packet,* and reprinted by other papers throughout the states. They were also gathered together in pamphlet form and distributed. We refer to them to-day as *The Federalist.*

[4] See H. C. Lodge, *The Works of Alexander Hamilton* (Federal Edition), Vols. IV and V.

These were the first real editorials, and the editor who first began
the practice of publishing editorials regularly was James
Cheetham, the English radical who became editor of the *American
Citizen* in 1800.[5]

Until recent times, editorials have dealt almost exclusively
with controversial subjects; but increasing mobility in modern
society, political apathy, and certain other factors have changed
the character of editorials so that today their chief function is
interpretative.[6] Although the influence of pamphleteer journalism still survives in editorials—and, indeed, ought to survive
—the editorial writer is more of an interpreter and less of a
leader than were the pamphleteer and "personal" editors.

Types of Editorials.—In studying the editorial as a literary
form, it is desirable that we classify editorials on the basis of
the writer's purpose. The obvious classification on this basis
would be a differentiation of informative, argumentative, and
entertaining editorials, and combinations of these types.[7]

Interpretative and Controversial Types.—Since here, however, we are dealing with editorial "thinking" rather than with
editorial "writing," it is not necessary that we pay any attention
to editorials of the entertaining type; these are discussed in a
subsequent chapter. For the purpose of our analysis, though,
it is desirable that we observe the difference between editorials
that are merely interpretative and those that are controversial.
In the interpretative type, the writer aims merely to give
meaning to the data of an event—to provide the reader with
an explanation of an occurrence or a situation. In the controversial editorial, the writer adopts a specific point of view
with reference to the event or the condition that he is discussing and tries to convince the reader of the soundness or the

---

[5] Although since that date editorials had appeared with some regularity
in several American and British papers, Nathan Hale, who became editor
of the Boston *Daily Advertiser* in 1814, followed the practice of publishing editorials with so much regularity that he has frequently been called
the first editorial writer. W. G. Bleyer corrects this impression in *Main
Currents in the History of American Journalism*, pp. 132-133, 141-143.

[6] For a discussion of the influence of some of these factors on editorial
manner and style, see Chapters XIV and XVI.

[7] Each of these types would also be subject to differentiation. For
example, one would differentiate argumentative editorials on the basis
of whether they were written to convince or to persuade the reader.

desirability of his point of view. In the one case, the purpose of the writer is to help the reader to think; in the other, his purpose is to make the reader agree with the writer's opinion. Controversial editorials usually are arguments which affirm or deny the rightness of a specific *principle,* the desirability of a specific *objective,* or the expediency or wisdom of a specific *policy.* That is to say, controversial editorials usually concern the application of a principle or a policy to a concrete situation or condition, whereas interpretative editorials do not consider the rightness, desirability, or expediency of a principle, objective, or policy, but merely define, explain, diagnose, or predict.[8]

Many controversial editorials, of course, perform some of the functions that we usually identify with interpretative editorials, and we shall not try to make any sharp distinction between the two types. The discussion in Chapters II and III will deal with those processes in editorial analysis which are most closely identified with interpretative editorials. The processes discussed in Chapters V-XIII are concerned chiefly with argumentation. The final chapter deals with miscellaneous types of editorials which, for the most part, reflect the self-expression of the individual writer rather than the opinion of the newspaper itself.

Editorials That Explain Events.—An event, of course, is anything that happens, but for the purposes of this study we shall define an event as a reported occurrence which has social consequence in small or great degree. The following events, for example, have social consequence of high degree: the proposal, enactment, or veto of a legislative measure; the dispatch or receipt of a diplomatic note; the negotiation, ratification, or abrogation of a treaty; the assassination of a high government official; the enunciation of an official policy. Other events may have less social consequence, yet be of some importance in so far as they reflect a participation by the general body of newspaper readers in community life. When events are reported in the newspapers, they frequently require editorial interpretation. Sometimes the reader desires to know what has motivated the event; sometimes he wants to know what is

---

[8] Interpretative editorials also review. See Chapter XVII.

likely to be the effect of the event; sometimes he only wants to know more about the place at which the event occurred, or he wants to know more about the actors who participated in the event. In any case, the task of the editorial writer is to derive meaning from the data and to communicate the meaning to the reader.[9]

The news story, in its conventional form, seldom does more than "signalize" an event.[10] For the newspaper, in its method, is episodic: it reports "spot" news. That is to say, it illuminates the public scene not by bathing it in a constant floodlight, but by flashing on it an erratic searchlight. The hiatuses of darkness between the flashes of light, both in time and space, are of no significance to the ordinary reader. Were it not for the interpretative editorial, the light of understanding, so far as the ordinary newspaper reader is concerned, would seldom touch the dark spots.

News, moreover, is not mere information: it is information that is interesting. The chief quality that makes news interesting is the dramatic: the ordinary reader requires that events—and even ideas—be dramatized. The newspaper, to a great extent, is compelled to submit to this principle of psychology. It must present the news in a pattern that is specially made to fit the "interests" of the reader; and it must consider that the ordinary reader is both uninformed and indifferent as regards data that lacks emotional content.

Much news, therefore, lacks meaning. Its significance to the ordinary reader is simply that something unusual has happened, that somebody has accomplished something unusual, that somebody has made a grievous error, that somebody has called another person a liar, that somebody has threatened somebody else. This sort of narrative is called a "news story." It pos-

---

[9] " 'News', " says John Dewey, "signifies something which has just happened, and which is new just because it deviates from the old and regular. But its *meaning* depends upon relation to what it imports, to what its social consequences are. This import cannot be determined unless the new is placed in relation to the old, to what has happened and been integrated into the course of events. Without coördination and consecutiveness, events are not events; but mere occurrences, intrusions; an event implies that out of which a happening proceeds."—*The Public and Its Problems*, pp. 179-180.

[10] See Walter Lippmann, *Public Opinion*, Chap. XXIII.

sesses some of the elements of a plot: it exhibits a central figure involved in a struggle, or it presents a small section of an epic. The ultimate meaning of the event, therefore, cannot always be presented in the news story. For dramatization of an event, personification of an issue, and symbolization of an idea result in oversimplification. What is necessary, then, to give meaning to an event is interpretation.

The editorial writer, in his relation to life, is both a critic and a teacher. He refines the half-truths annunciated by his artist colleagues who write dramatically and episodically for the first page. He trims down the sharp and jagged pieces of episodic and dramatic news to smoother nuggets of fact so they will fit into the reader's scheme of understanding. He gives proportion to events by lifting them out of the tumult of the moment and setting them down in the calmer background of the past.

The process of interpretation involves the use of various techniques. Sometimes it requires the recital of additional facts to furnish the event with a setting; sometimes it requires a penetrating analysis which seeks to bring forth a concealed motive or a nonapparent policy; sometimes it requires merely the connecting of a series of disconnected news stories. In all cases, the purpose of the editorial writer is to give meaning to the event so that the reader may have a more perfect understanding of the environment in which he lives and a more intelligent participation in society.

Whose Opinion Is Expressed?—So far as the large newspapers are concerned, neither the editorial interpretation of an event nor the editorial policy in general is determined by the whim or prejudice of one editor. Nor is it usually determined by the *reasoning* of one editor. It is more often determined by several editors after conference and discussion. Until recent times, editorial expression in the great newspapers was personal: whatever was written was taken by the readers as the opinion of a single personality. But today editorial expression is anonymous and institutional: it is the product of several men's thought, and it represents the opinion of an entity—"The Times," "The Herald," or "The Globe." Even in the days of the great personal editors, much of the editorial expression —even the expression of opinion as regards politics—was not the opinion of a single editor. It was not possible for even Greeley to formulate the viewpoint of the *Tribune* as regards every important question about which the editorial writers commented, and he had considerable disagreement with his associates, Dana and Reid.

The reasons why editorials in the larger newspapers represent an institutional rather than a personal expression are summarized cogently in an editorial in the Chicago *Tribune* in reply to a reader's query as to why editorials are not signed:

> . . . There is no evasion of responsibility, but merely recognition of the complexity of the authorship. The larger newspapers are not of recent establishment. They contain generations of work, represented by straight descent or by combinations retaining something of the older days.
>
> There have not been many editors who were highly regarded in their day who have not left something of their ideas to their successors. They may be imponderable or specific, but a man of force does not wash out of the institution continuing after him. It is not inevitable, but it is probable that the standards of a paper will have received a valuation and its ideas a direction which will have influence. That is one factor in an editorial.
>
> In the arrival at comment and expression in matters which the newspaper may consider important there is seldom one unmodified opinion. That of the owner, publisher, or editor may be paramount, but it generally is influenced by the opinion of subordinates. What results is the expression of the paper as an institution serving the interests of a community, directed particularly to that part of the community which has shown its interest in that newspaper by buying it.
>
> The editorial expression of a responsible newspaper is not the work of one man, although the writing of it may be. It reflects many things other than his personality, and this held good even in the case of such individualistic writing editors as Henry Watterson of recent activity and of Greeley, Dana, Medill, and others of early days. When the personality of the writer overbalanced that of his institution it was then "Greeley says" and not "the Tribune says." The difference is essential. On one side there is a man in public affairs; on the other an institution which may survive the lives of several men successively.
>
> Public discussion is full of personal, individual statements. They probably make up the bulk of it. Many of them are irrelevant

to any material responsibility. The pleasure or displeasure of the hearers may be inconsequential to the speaker or writer. In the course of time newspaper opinion is held accountable by the body which makes its existence possible, its readers. They take it or they leave it. They make it or they destroy it. There is no irresponsibility in the unsigned editorial, either in or outside of law.[11]

The Editorial Council.—Prior to the preparation of an editorial about an event or a public question, the matter is analyzed by the editorial writers in conference. The group of men who select the subjects about which editorials shall be written and who decide the attitude that their newspaper shall adopt with reference to a matter deserving of comment is referred to as the "editorial council." This body is sometimes composed of only the staff of editorial writers, but more frequently it includes the editor-in-chief, the managing editor, the political cartoonist, the general manager or publisher, and the staff of editorial writers.[12]

The function of the editorial council varies in different newspapers. In some newspapers the council decides the news as well as the editorial policy; in others the council makes decisions only as to what shall appear on the editorial page.

The authority of the council also varies in different newspapers. In thoroughly independent newspapers the council is not bound by the partisan or doctrinaire policies of the proprietors; on the other hand, there are newspapers, especially those whose proprietors are politically ambitious or extremely biased in viewpoint, whose major policies as regards politics and class conflicts are determined solely by the owner; the editorial council in such a paper, of course, is not entirely free.[13]

---

[11] Sept. 28, 1930, p. 14.

[12] The editorial council of the Milwaukee *Journal* is composed of the five editorial writers.

The editorial council of the Chicago *Tribune* is composed of the editor-in-chief, three editorial writers, and two political correspondents.

The editorial council of the New York *Times* is composed of the publisher, the editor-in-chief, the managing editor, the business manager, and thirteen editorial writers and business and editorial executives.

[13] As to whether or not an editorial writer is ever compelled to express opinions that he does not hold, no generalization will be accurate. The matter can be sufficiently understood, however, from a careful reading of Chapter XIV.

The importance of the council also varies in different newspapers. The editorial council in some newspapers supervises closely the writing of all serious editorials; in other papers, however, it meets only to determine the policy of the newspaper as regards the most important questions.

In some newspapers the meetings of the council are informal rather than formal, depending in large measure on the personality of the publishers and the character of the ownership and control of the newspaper. Editorials about trivial or noncontroversial matters are not usually discussed in conference, but are written by an individual editorial writer or other member of the staff and are submitted to the chief editorial writer. In general, however, the editorial policy of a newspaper is too complex for one man to supervise. The editorial council necessarily has a great responsibility. The editorial council of the Chicago *Tribune*, for example, meets six days a week in sessions that last three hours.

The following description of the editorial quarters of the New York *Times* furnishes a picture of the setting in which editorials are written for the larger metropolitan newspapers:

The Editorial Department on the tenth floor occupies quarters designed to suggest nothing so much as the studious atmosphere and surroundings of university cloisters. . . . Here, ranged stall after stall, are some 20,000 reference books and current periodicals close packed on its shelves—a central reservoir from which important information on any of a thousand subjects may be drawn at a moment's notice. Around this, in oak and glass-partitioned offices, are the individual quarters of the Editor-in-Chief and his associate editorial writers, equipped with further reference books and special sources of information. . . .

At the far end of the department is the Conference Room, a large Caen stone and stucco-lined chamber, with slightly vaulted ceiling and black-and-white tiled floor. It is a quiet chamber as befits the thoughtful conference and deliberation that takes place around a long council table in its centre. . . . Here at midday, is held the council of the editorial staff, attended as well by the Publisher with his executive assistants. Here the day's news is discussed and analyzed and the topics of leading interest or importance selected for assignment by the Editor-in-Chief to the various editorial writers. And it is one of the proudest boasts of the *Times* that never at any time has any man on its editorial staff been requested

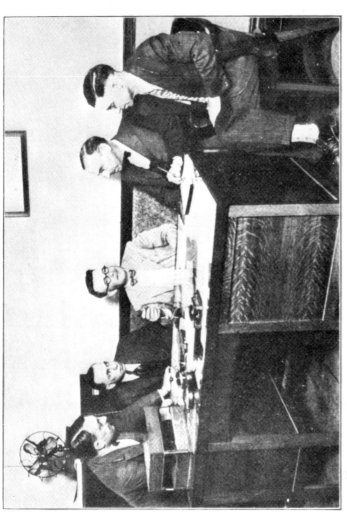

THE MILWAUKEE JOURNAL EDITORIAL STAFF HAS AN INFORMAL DISCUSSION OF CURRENT EVENTS EVERY MORNING. *Reading from left to right:* F. Perry Olds, Fred W. Luening, J. D. Ferguson, D. W. Swiggett, Will C. Conrad

to write on any subject an opinion that was not in conformity with his own views and beliefs.[14]

How the Council Works.—The editorial council of—let us say—an afternoon newspaper usually functions in the following manner. The editorial writers, after having read the morning newspapers and perhaps the proofs of some early stories scheduled to appear in their own newspaper, begin the day's work in a conference. They discuss the news dispatches and decide which subjects shall be selected for editorial comment. Further, they discuss thoroughly each of the subjects and arrive at a conclusion as to what ought to be said about the event or the question. Proceeding upon the assumption that "many heads are better than one," the council usually finds that the views of each editorial writer are modified to some extent by the discussions in the conference. Finally, each of the editorial writers is assigned a subject for an editorial, the selection usually being determined by the special knowledge known to be possessed by each of them, or the special knowledge exhibited by each of them during the discussion. An editorial writer who does not agree with the conclusions of his associates is not assigned to write an editorial that expresses views with which he does not agree. He writes the editorial assigned to him, however, in his own style and in conformity with the opinion of the council. After he has completed the editorial assigned to him, he submits it to the chief editorial writer, who either approves it in its entirety or makes changes which he thinks ought to be made; these changes, however, have for their purpose the alteration of expression rather than the revision of opinion.[15]

Study and Investigation.—An editorial writer on a large newspaper usually prepares only one or two editorials a day.

[14] *The Making of a Great Newspaper* (a publication of the New York *Times*), p. 12.
[15] It is not to be understood that the editorial policy of the ordinary newspaper is always determined day by day. On matters about which the newspaper has a definitive policy there is little discussion by individual writers, for one particular writer usually writes as he pleases within the bounds of the definitive policy. New policies, however, are discussed in council, and sometimes considered through several subsequent meetings. Old policies, too, are sometimes modified as time goes on or as conditions change.

The time required for the actual writing is seldom more than an hour or two. The editorial writer spends most of his time during the day in study. Sometimes his study takes the form of research in the files of clippings in the newspaper's library; sometimes it involves consultation of government reports and records that are available either in the newspaper's library or in the public library; sometimes it requires the reading of history, of current books about public questions, and of many foreign and American newspapers and periodicals; sometimes it requires consultation with public officials and civic and business leaders at their offices and homes, or in hotels and restaurants; sometimes it requires the commandeering of reporters' services in investigating specific conditions. Always it is a search for facts that will throw light upon a subject, whether the facts are to be used in editorials or as a background for deciding future editorial policy.

A criticism sometimes heard of editorial writers is that they spend too much time reading editorials in newspapers—that is, the opinions of other editorial writers—and insufficient time in reading reports and books. Obviously the editorial writer must keep abreast of events and of the trend of opinion as reflected in the newspapers; otherwise his editorials will lack the all-important newsy flavor; but his chief task is the interpretation of social, economic, and political phenomena, and he ought not to rely entirely on secondary sources, such as newspapers, for his data. Knowledge of all kinds is being literally dumped into the world. Not all of this knowledge, however—at least, not all of it that is important—is dumped into the world through the newspaper flume. It pours in at many places not readily accessible to the casual reader. It is put into books, periodicals, pamphlets, and research reports, and must be dug out by those who desire to be trustworthy interpreters of modern life.

An editorial writer, however, need not try to be master of all knowledge. If, in this complex age, he elects that province, he is quite likely to have only a smattering of several kinds of knowledge. It is sufficient that he master one or two fields. Realizing this limitation, the large newspapers therefore have tried to acquire a staff of editorial writers who are specialists. One editorial writer, for example, may know a great deal about finance or social economics or taxation; another may understand constitutional law or local politics or foreign politics; another may have devoted considerable study to the housing problem or to city planning. Some newspapers also publish editorials that are prepared by the reporters who have special knowledge of certain phases of public affairs, as, for example, the city hall reporter, the market editor, the dramatic critic, or the veteran police reporter who has studied the psychopathic treatment of criminals or the condition of state reformatory institutions. These men frequently are better informed than the editorial writer who is isolated in his office. Sometimes editorials are even contributed by outsiders who have expert knowledge of a specific subject; and newspapers sometimes recruit their staff of editorial writers not only from the ranks of working newspapermen, but from the legal and teaching professions. Of the three editorial writers on the Chicago *Tribune,* for example, one is a former lawyer, one a former college professor, and one a former political correspondent.

The Factor of Timeliness.—Not only must the editorial writer possess a fund of special knowledge, but he must be prepared to present conclusions to his readers on short notice. Interpretative editorials are not written as the consequence of the writer's mood, but as the consequence of an event. Nearly every editorial is hung on a "news-peg." An event precipitates a question, and the newspaper is compelled to comment on it. Some newspapers try to comment on events as soon after they happen as possible; others comment two or three days after an event has been reported. The newspaper which elects to make immediate comment proceeds on the assumption that the editorial page, like the first page, ought to be newsy; but in any case there is a compulsion to comment immediately. As a consequence, the editorial writer has a more difficult task than the historian, who can delay making an interpretation until more facts are available. For example, let a man eminent in public life—the Secretary of State, let us say—terminate his career by death or resignation, and the editorial writer must quickly organize for review in his mind all of the important policies and public acts for which the Secretary of State was mainly responsible; he must evaluate them and pass judgment on the official's career or term of office. This requirement not only tests the editorial writer's historical sense, but demands that he be constantly making judgments which are to be stored away for future use; that is to say, he must constantly sit in judgment on all important events whether or not he expresses editorial judgment at the time he formulated it.[16]

Editorial Analysis.—*It has been said of editorial writing that it involves ten per cent of writing and ninety per cent of analysis.* In a wide sense the statement is accurate. For although it may seem to the uninitiated that the technique of editorial writing is simply one of presentation of thought— "that common illusion of young men, that facility in composition indicates the existence of thought," as Godkin has put it— there is, in fact, much more behind a good editorial than mere facility of expression and logical organization. Sir James M. Barrie, himself once a leader writer, has suggested the following definition of an editorial:

> 2 pipes equal 1 hour,
> 2 hours equal 1 idea,
> 1 idea equals 3 paragraphs,
> 3 paragraphs equal 1 editorial.

Effective editorials, it is true, are in great measure the result of skillful and apt expression, but even in greater measure they are the product of intelligent analysis. It is with the process of analysis that most of the subsequent chapters are concerned.

---

[16] Since the subjects that the editorial writer discusses are, to a great extent, imposed upon him by events, there arises not only the question of infallibility but the question of intellectual honesty. For a philosophic discussion of this aspect of editorial writing, see "Confessions of an Editorial Writer" in the *New Republic*, April 28, 1926.

CHAPTER II

EDITORIALS OF DEFINITION

The only purpose of some editorials is to help the reader to understand what he reads in the news columns. For example, the reader sees the term, "Bank for International Settlements," but he may not have any clear idea as to the real purpose or nature of the organization. He reads about "Fascism" or "Syndicalism" or "Kuomintang," but he may not know with any definiteness what the terms mean. He reads about events in a Central European country frequently without understanding what kind of country he is reading about, although it is the unstable countries of Central Europe that hold the germs of a future world war. He reads about a particular conflict between capital and labor and infers, perhaps, that the conflict began spontaneously, whereas the sources of the trouble are in the past.

Before the reader can think clearly about any event or situation, he must understand thoroughly what it is he is trying to think about. Because news reporters often overestimate the fund of specific and technical knowledge possessed by their readers,[1] editorial writers prepare editorials that are calculated to help the reader to an understanding of the event or situation. This is done in several ways.

1. **Providing a Geographical Setting.**—The simplest type of clarifying editorial is one which merely places an event in its geographical or physical setting. A few events reported by the press have meaning in illocality; for example, it is possible

---

[1] Even editorial writers sometimes overestimate the reader's fund of information, as is shown by the following letter received by the Chicago *Tribune*: "Maywood, Ill., Aug. 11.—Now comes your editorial, 'The Advance in the Rediscount Rate,' about which much has already been said in your columns. Would it be asking too much for a concise explanation for the layman through your columns of just what rediscount means, and what effect it has upon the money circulation of a government?"

for a newspaper reader in any country to understand the conditions that cause an epidemic of contagious disease, since the conditions are within the experience-world of nearly all individuals. But very few events or questions can be thought about except that they have reference to a specific physical setting; especially is it true of political phenomena that their meaning cannot be derived without reference to space and place. For example, when one reads about political events in some of the Balkan countries, the events will have for him a false meaning if he pictures the governments, peoples, and the economic conditions of those countries as being exactly like the American government, the American people, or American economic conditions. The event has a clear meaning only when the reader knows that the Balkan peoples, for the most part, are clannish fighters whose system of jurisprudence does not entirely outlaw blood feud and whose mountains divide them into strong ethnocentric groups.

The following editorial was written to provide the reader with geographical data concerning a series of events which concerned the future peace in the Adriatic region:

KING OF ALBANIA

Just as we were beginning to think that the institution of monarchy was on the wane, a new crowned head has appeared. It is King Zogu of Albania whose coronation was reported yesterday.

Zogu, however, is not the despotic ruler of vast domains. Albania, which is just opposite the heel of the Italian boot, is smaller in area than the states of Vermont and Connecticut. It is a mountainous country deepcut by streams that flow out to the Adriatic. It contains no railroads and only 300 miles of highway.

Zogu is King of Albania, but he is hardly King of the Albanians. The 832,000 subjects of Zogu were formerly subjects of the Turkish Sultan. Sixty-seven per cent of them are Mohammedan, and they are uniformly illiterate. Because of the broken character of

the topography of the country and the separation of the people into isolated groups,
organized life centers in the tribe. The tribes
are imbued with fanatical local prejudices,
and the "nation" is one huge vendetta. A
few Albanians live in towns, but 87 per cent
live in the country, leading a primitive sort
of agricultural life. Albania has no fabri-
cating industries except for the domestic
manufacture of a coarse woolen cloth. The
other industries are approximately those of
the pastoral stage—the production of wool,
skins, corn, olive oil, and tobacco. Ownership of the land is by a few wealthy mag-
nates. Albania is in the flea belt.

Zogu is King by treachery. The Slavic
element (anti-Italian) helped him to power,
but he sold out to Mussolini. While Zogu was
president he borrowed money from Italy and
used much of it for the construction of military roads; Italian officers are now engaged
in training his armies. Italians regard the
Adriatic as *mare nostrum,* and the Albanian
coast is only 45 miles from Italy—less than
half of the distance from Florida to Cuba.
Zogu is King of Albania; Albania is an
Italian "protectorate." What will Yugo-
Slavia have to say about this?

No discussion of the Philippine independence question is
possible unless we consider the geographical setting of the
islands. We must know, for example, that the islands are one
group in a chain that runs from Japan to Australia, taking in
Japan's Formosa and the Dutch East Indies. From the north-
ernmost of the Philippines to the Japanese island of Formosa
is a distance of sixty-five miles, and from the southernmost
point in the Philippines to Borneo (British and Dutch de-
pendencies) and the Dutch East Indies is a distance of only
twenty miles. Any constitutional change in the Philippines
would have repercussions throughout the Far East affecting
immediate British, Japanese, and Dutch interests and perhaps
conditions in India and Korea. Just as important, too, in any
discussion of the Philippines are the factors of economic and

human geography. Readers who desire to have sound opinions on the Philippine question must consider the relation of the natural resources of the Philippines to American tariff favors and to the possibility of economic penetration of the Philippines by the Japanese, as well as the following factors of human geography: the status of the Mohammedan tribes and the tropical lethargy of the majority of the people.[2]

The editorial writer ought not to neglect to study economic and political geography. The data that they provide are indispensable to an understanding of the problems of world politics. The location and amount of mineral deposits in the Far East and the Ruhr Valley, the natural boundaries of Italy, the artificial boundaries of Poland, the abundance of water in the Sudan, the coast line of Jugo-Slavia; these are only a few of the facts of geography that help to explain the chief problems of world politics such as tariff disputes, imperialism, armaments, and alliances. The explanation of human and group behavior in all its aspects depends in some measure on a knowledge of geography; for the phenomena of geography— climate, peoples, land, minerals, capital, waters, harbors, etc.— are contributing elements in the culture pattern of a people. We cannot adequately describe or predict the behavior of a people without reference to the people's physical environment, a fact which historians, sociologists, and political scientists have come to appreciate fully.[3]

2. **Providing an Historical Setting.**—For the clarification of many questions, the historical background is helpful. We sometimes cannot understand the meaning of a conflict unless we know its roots; we cannot understand the meaning of a specific article in the Constitution unless we know the circumstances under which it was adopted; we cannot thoroughly

---

[2] Some light is thrown on the Philippine problem by the following books: Nicholas Roosevelt, *The Philippines: a Treasure and a Problem;* W. C. Forbes, *The Philippine Islands* (2 vols.) ; Storey, Morefield, and Michauco, *Conquest of the Philippines by the United States.*

[3] The student would do well to read Isaiah Bowman, *The New World* (4th ed.) ; Isaac Lippincott, *Economic Resources and Industries of the World;* L. D. Stamp, *The World, a General Geography;* H. B. George, *The Relation of Geography and History;* J. Fairgreve, *Geography and World Power* (5th ed.) ; F. J. Turner, *The Frontier in American History.*

understand the significance of a great revolutionary movement unless we compare it with a similar movement in history. Editorials frequently try to provide such historical settings. The following editorial from the Louisville *Courier-Journal* is an example of one specific type:

THE CONFLICT IN MEXICO

The conflict between the State and the Church in Mexico, now in an acute stage, is little understood in this country. Its beginning dates back almost to the conquest by Cortez in the early part of the Sixteenth Century. The Church soon exercised an authority in Mexico superior to that of the State. Ten per cent of the products of the land and various other benefits went to the Church and it became immensely wealthy.

It grew so powerful that a Viceroy was excommunicated by the Archbishop of Mexico and compelled to flee. The growth of the Church was such that by 1644 the town council of Mexico City petitioned the Spanish King to stop the foundation of religious houses which, it was claimed, owned half the property in the country.

When Joseph Bonaparte was placed on the Spanish throne, Morelos, a Mexican priest, who was later executed, called a Congress which drafted a Constitution, declaring that "it does not profess or recognize any other religion than the Catholic, and that it shall never permit or tolerate public or secret practice of another." "The Roman Catholic religion," said the first Mexican Constitution, "is the only one to be professed in the country."

In 1812 a Constitution was promulgated attempting to deprive both the King and the Church of much of their power and many of their prerogatives. Ferdinand of Spain, after agreeing to accept this Constitution, subsequently rejected it, backed by the Church and the army. It was restored in 1820 by an uprising in Spain, when the Mexican ecclesiastics brought forward Iturbide to lead a movement for Mexican independence. Independence was attained in 1821, when Iturbide specified as one of the bases of the new State the maintenance of the Roman Catholic religion, with the privileges of the clergy. The first article of the plan for the new State forbade all religions except the Roman Catholic.

After Emperor Iturbide's defeat in a revolution and execution in 1824, a new Constitution was adopted, said to have been modelled on that of the United States, but providing that "the religion of the Mexican nation is and shall perpetually be the Roman Catholic. The nation protects it by wise and just laws and forbids the exercise of any other." Under this Constitution a law was enacted providing that "every Mexican has the obligation to profess the religion of his fatherland."

The privileges of the clergy, such as exemption from the jurisdiction of the civil courts and their control of educational and monastic institutions, were retained in the Constitutions of 1826 and 1843. By the middle of the century, according to one historian, the Catholic hierarchy controlled "two-thirds of the productive wealth of the country, dominated economic life and monopolized the great opinion-forming agencies, religion, education and charity."

It was in 1854 that the Government, supported by the Church, was overthrown by a revolution and Benito Juarez appeared on the scene as Minister of Finance in the cabinet of the new President. Juarez was a real statesman—William H. Seward called him the greatest statesman with whom he had ever come in contact. Juarez soon secured the enactment of a law subjecting both the clergy and the army to trial by the civil courts.

In 1857 a new Constitution was adopted, abolishing ecclesiastical and military special privileges. This Constitution was hotly resisted by the Church, which ordered the people to refuse to take the oath to support it. Calles today is attempting to enforce some of the provisions of that Constitution, re-incorporated in the Constitution of 1917.

Juarez issued a series of laws aiming to separate Church and State, going so far as to expel the Papal Nuncio and other ecclesiastics for disobedience. He was succeeded by Maximilian as Emperor, backed by the Church, but resumed the presidency when his forces captured and shot Maximilian in 1867.

Various amendments to the Constitution of 1857 for the separation of Church and State were adopted and for their enforcement a code of laws was issued. Porfirio Diaz allowed the Constitution and the laws to lapse. Then in 1917, under the Carranza Government, the Constitution of 1857 was superseded by the Constitution of 1917, which is the organic law of Mexico today. This Constitution is even stronger than the previous one for separation of Church and State.

The "Law of Calles," signed by the President on the 14th of last June, provides penalties for the violation of the provisions of the Constitution, and went into effect on the last of this month.

It is thus the issue of the present conflict has been joined.

The provisions of the Constitution which the Mexican Government is now attempting to enforce forbid religious denominations to own real estate, church buildings or any other buildings; to possess invested funds or other productive property; to maintain convents or nunneries; to conduct primary schools; to administer charitable institutions; to solicit funds for their support outside of church buildings; to hold religious ceremonies outside of church buildings; to clothe their ministers in a way indicative of their calling. Among many other restrictions ministers are forbidden to criticise publicly the fundamental law of the land, while all ministers must be Mexican by birth.

Since July 31 Calles has been trying to

enforce these laws, and the Roman Church has been unyieldingly resisting them. The Hierarchy promptly ordered all the priests from the churches. The churches are still open, under Government control, but there are no masses or other services conducted by the priests. In addition, the Catholics are seeking to bring pressure to bear on the Government by enforcing an economic boycott, refusing to buy anything but the barest necessaries and forswearing all luxuries and amusements. The priests who agreed to abide by these laws of the Government have been excommunicated.

Whatever the merits or demerits of the issue, whatever the extremes on either side, here is a plain conflict between the Church and the State, with both parties to it manifesting an uncompromising spirit.

The Government regards the conflict as one to abolish the temporal power of the Catholic Church in Mexico; the Catholic Church regards it as a conflict to abolish religion in Mexico.

It is a struggle between the Government and the Catholic Church because the Protestants have accepted the Government's regulations. Moreover, there are very few Protestants in the country, between 12,000,000 and 13,000,000 of Mexico's 14,000,000 inhabitants being reported as Catholics.

In the foregoing editorial the recital of history merely serves to bring the question up to date. The editorial is helpful to the reader because it traces the roots of the conflict. But the historical data recited are not absolutely indispensable to a definition of this question; the reader can reason soundly about the conflict between Church and State in Mexico without possessing knowledge of the history of the conflict.

Some events, however, do not yield a true meaning unless they are studied in their historical setting, unless they are considered with reference to time. An example was the decision of the United States Supreme Court in 1895 which held invalid the income tax law passed by Congress in 1894. The Supreme Court held—and with logic—that the law violated that section of the Constitution which forbade the levying of direct taxes unless they were levied "in proportion to the census or enumeration hereinbefore directed to be taken." [4] This provision in the Constitution has now been amended, and a graduated income tax is levied; but in 1895 it was apparent that, although the provision was out of date, it legally stood in the way of a federal income tax law and ought to be amended. The New York *World* made this plain in an editorial which gave to the constitutional provision its historical setting:

> The section of the Constitution declaring that direct taxes shall not be laid down "unless in proportion to the census or enumeration" was one of the compromises adopted [by the framers of the Constitution] to quiet the jealousies and fears of the original States. It was one of the guarantees retained by the States in surrendering their power to levy imposts.
>
> But it is as foreign to its purpose and application to the conditions of our times as is the anachronistic and cumbersome machinery of the Electoral College, of which custom has made practically a dead letter. If the Constitution were to be revised today, the convention would no more think of enacting that income, from whatever source, shall not, if necessary, be taxed wherever earned and enjoyed, than of providing that internal revenue taxes on spirits and tobacco shall be apportioned according to population, instead of collected wherever those articles are manufactured.
>
> There were free States and slave States

[4] "Representatives and direct taxes shall be apportioned among the several states which may be included within this Union, according to their respective numbers, which shall be determined by adding to the whole number of free persons, including those bound to service for a term of years, and excluding Indians not taxed, three-fifths of all other persons. The actual enumeration shall be made within three years after the first meeting of the Congress of the United States, and within every subsequent term of ten years, in such manner as they shall by law direct."—Art. I, sec. 2.

to be united. The question of representation was very grave and even dangerous to the project of union. The slave States claimed representation in proportion to their total population. The free States contended that representation should be given only in proportion to the free population. . . .

Finally a compromise was reached under which the slave States were to have representation on the basis of their free population plus three-fifths of their slaves. But Story tells us "in order to reconcile the non-slaveholding States to this agreement it was agreed that *direct* taxation should be apportioned in the same manner as Representatives."

Thus the provision was merely a part of the compromise on slavery. All the conditions that led to it have utterly passed away. We no longer have slave States, and only three times in our history has there been any levy of direct taxes in the sense in which the words are used in the Constitution. . . .

Nothing could be more foreign to the purposes of the Constitution-makers than the use just made of this clause by the attorneys of great corporations to compel unequal and unjust taxation. They aimed only at making the slave States pay direct taxes in full proportion to the representation allowed to them.

The framers of the Constitution could not foresee our conditions. They knew nothing of multi-millionaires or great corporations. They could not anticipate a time when a single family would own more houses in New York than then existed in any of our cities. They could not foresee that a time would come when nearly all the burdens of taxation would fall upon the poor and the moderately well-to-do, while the rich paid nothing on their wealth towards the support of the Government. Certainly they did not put any clause into the Constitution with intent to protect invested wealth against the payment of its fair share. Yet that is precisely the use now to be made of the direct-tax clause under the ruling of the Supreme Court.

The following controversial editorial likewise has for its purpose the definition and clarification of American foreign policy in relation to time; it exhibits how the meaning of Washington's advice has been distorted by present-day isolationists.

WHAT WASHINGTON REALLY SAID

Senator Herman Thomas's address on Washington's birthday, warning against "entangling alliances," reveals a misunderstanding of history that is deplorable in one who has so much influence in national affairs. Such untrue historical statements as Senator Thomas made, because they come from him, are accepted popularly in place of what is or ought to be in the school textbooks.

Washington, of course, never warned his countrymen against "entangling alliances." That was Jefferson's phrase. What Washington actually said was this: "The great rule of conduct for us in regard to foreign nations is, in extending our commercial relations, to have with them as little *political* connection as possible."

But even this statement had a meaning in its time that Washington never intended it to have for all time. For, further in his address he says: "With me a predominant motive has been *to endeavor to gain time to our country to settle and mature its yet recent institutions,* and to progress without interruption to that degree of strength and consistency which is necessary to give it, humanly speaking, the command of its own fortunes."

Washington's words can be understood only if they are given their proper setting. They were spoken during the Napoleonic wars in which all Europe was engaged, and at a time when political parties in America divided on the question of sympathy with France or with Great Britain more than they divided on domestic issues. In this country the two parties were called Federalist and Anti-Federalist, but better names at that particular time would have been Pro-British and Pro-French, or perhaps more accurately, Neutralists and Francophiles.

In 1778 we had made a treaty of alliance with Louis XVI and it was decisive in securing our independence from Great Britain. When, following the French Revolution, the Directory and afterward Napoleon engaged in war with Great Britain, Washington's cabinet was divided as to whether or not the United States was obliged to side with France. Hamilton held that we ought to be neutral; Jefferson held that we should aid France.

Legally and morally, Jefferson was in the right, but, in the judgment of Washington and Hamilton, who desired the country "to mature its yet recent institutions," self-interest out-weighed legal and moral obligation. Every country in Europe was *forced* to side with one or the other powers, and America was saved only by the fact of her distance from Europe. Yet we did not finally escape. In 1794, in order to avoid England's wrath, we were forced to sign the humiliating Jay treaty, and in 1798 we were forced to fight a desperate naval war with France.

Washington's Farewell Address was, in a sense, a partisan message. It was an appeal to the people to stand by the Federalist doctrine of neutrality. It was not made, of course, with partisan intent, but to the Pro-French party it meant nothing else. The Jeffersonian party, so long as it was out of office, continued its Pro-French attitude; and Jefferson never avowed neutrality—despite our humiliation by the French Republic in the "X.Y.Z." mission—until he was forced by the Federalists in the House of Representatives either to adhere to that policy or to see Aaron Burr chosen President in his stead. After Jefferson's election, however, he followed Washington's policy "to steer clear of *permanent* alliances with any portion of the foreign world."

Helpful to the reader, also, is the editorial that draws an *historical parallel.*[5] The following editorials are examples:

(1)

FACTORS IN THE CHINESE SITUATION

To the Western reader of the news from China during the past decade who was unfamiliar with Chinese history, the chaos that existed was sufficiently explained by the Revolution itself, the Civil War between North and South, the existence of the Tuchuns (military leaders) and their armies and the interference of foreign powers.

As a matter of fact, all these are accompaniments of that chaos, not primary causes. The causes are of deeper significance and are of a more spiritual nature. In analyzing them the student will discover that China's evolution has been similar to that of Europe, but that China has been compelled in three decades to face situations and solve problems that have required as many centuries for Europe to solve.

The remarkable movement in western Europe known as the Renaissance was what its name indicates, a rebirth. It was a rebirth of old, long-forgotten ways of looking at life, the way of pagan Greece and Rome.

To the Greek and Roman, life on this earth was the one thing worth while. Death meant the passage to a dark, cold, cheerless existence. Hence the desire to get as much as possible out of life. . . . Man and his works, art, literature, philosophy, science, were the things worthy of man's attention.

The pagan era was succeeded by the Christian era with its doctrines of the fall of man and his evil nature. Christianity, as taught in the Middle Ages, predicted the emptiness of the earthly life and the joys of the other world, of heaven, the abode of

---

[5] See Chapter VIII for a discussion of the historical parallel editorial when used in controversy.

those who had despised the body and had conquered its cravings.

When the Renaissance, the rebirth, took place, men naturally turned with avidity to the literature dealing with man and his works, that is, to the literature of Greece and Rome, which now became the content of the New Learning.

The humanities were arrayed against the divinities. The pursuit of the New Learning often played havoc with men's thoughts and conduct. Opinions on nearly all subjects were unsettled, particularly on the subject which had hitherto dominated the entire life of man, religion. Moral restraints were loosened and license in conduct often held sway.

But the New Learning was one of the greatest gains to humanity. It freed the human spirit from the trammels of a thousand years and started man on his evolution to his present state of culture.

The China of today has been invaded by a New Learning—Western culture. The essential element of Western culture is science. Science is based on a refusal to accept anything upon authority. It has no reverence for tradition. Investigation to get the facts and to be guided by them regardless of preconceived ideas is its chief characteristic. One can readily see what havoc the introduction of such learning would make in Chinese life. For nearly three thousand years the whole of Chinese civilization was founded upon authority, the authority of the ancestors. To such an extent was this true that ancestor-worship had become the very core of Chinese culture. The views of the ancestors as given in the classical literature became the sole material of education. The perfect reproduction of those views without a single variation was the aim of learning. The scholar who could accomplish this best was sure of high reward, of influential position in the mandarinate. . . .

It can be readily understood, therefore, why during almost the entire nineteenth century

. . . the Chinese regarded Western education with indifference when not with disdain. . . . [After the defeat of China by Japan in 1895, however] practically the whole of the old learning was discarded and the Chinese feverishly undertook the rapid assimilation not only of science but of most of the elements of Western culture.

But to do so was to shake the very foundations of Chinese civilization. The spiritual life of the Chinese people, their traditions, their beliefs, their ideals, were embodied in the classics. The classics taught that the whole social system is founded on the family, in which the entire control is in the hands of the father. Western civilization exalts the individual. In China the individual counts for little. Even outside the family the individual has rights only as a member of a guild or some other kind of fraternity. To exalt the individual was to aim a blow at the whole social system. To reject ancestor-worship was to loosen the moral bonds which were founded upon it without replacing them by the control of the individual conscience as in the West, for that control was the product of centuries of development in the West. . . .[6]

(2)

FORGED DOCUMENTS

Somebody has suggested that the whole trouble about Mr. Hearst's Mexican documents, printed to prove that the Mexican government was paying money to United States Senators and others or at least to agents who were supposed to be paying it to the Senators, comes from an error in the printing rooms— that the documents were intended to run in the comic pages and got into the news sections by mistake.

That is a flippancy not entirely unwarranted as a way of putting true value on the docu-

[6] Stephen P. Duggan in *Political Science Quarterly*, Vol. XLIV (September, 1929), pp. 379-383.

ments. But it is quite possible that the American people ought to educate itself a little in the matter of forged political documents, since the rather generally accepted explanation of the Mexican government in this case is that the documents are forgeries.

Forged papers as a part of either official "diplomacy" or of the schemes of unofficial cliques interested in fomenting trouble have not been common enough on this side of the Atlantic, happily, to produce a hearty skepticism when documents that are preposterous on their face bob up. They have been common enough in the Old World, and we may be in for some of the same experience.

The distorting of a telegram by Bismarck, making the Franco-Prussian war inevitable, is a familiar fact of history. The so-called Zinoviev letter to British communists, used so effectively in the last British general election, remains in a foggy state as to its genuineness or falseness, but it never has been proved to be genuine and the British government long ago lost interest in trying to prove it.

The forged documents in the Dreyfus case threatened the existence of the French republic, and had the world upset before their real nature was shown. Dr. Masaryk, then a member of the Austrian parliament, now president of Czecho-Slovakia, played a main part in exposing as forgeries a set of documents prepared under the auspices of an Austro-Hungarian ambassador, several years before the World War, the forgeries being intended to further several devious Hapsburg purposes in the Balkans. In fact, these forgeries were the basis of charges against Serbia almost identical with those made by Austria-Hungary in 1914 in starting the war.

Time and again forged documents which caused political crises have been proven, sometimes after they had accomplished all their mischief, to be the work of agents provocateurs.

It is easy for a government that is embar-

> rassed by publication of documents to call
> them forgeries. But also there is the fact
> that documents calculated to embarrass gov-
> ernments often have been forgeries. In a
> time of calm between nations they can usually
> be fairly judged. In time of great strain they
> have many a time had tragic consequences.[7]

3. Identifying and Classifying Forces.—Editorials that
identify and classify the parties to a conflict are of great assistance to the reader. Some editorials of this type reveal the
newspaper's sympathy with one of the parties and, in that
degree, are controversial editorials; but frequently editorials
are neutral. The following editorial, which was written for
the Foreign Policy Association *News Bulletin* by Agnes Stewart
Waddell, is an example of a clear identification and classification of the forces that were involved in the unsuccessful
revolution in Mexico in 1928:

Mexico Resorts to Force

> Once more Mexico gives evidence that it is
> far from being a political democracy. The
> revolutionary movement which began on
> March 3 comes as a great disappointment to
> those who had hoped with ex-President Calles
> that Mexico had finally arrived at a point
> where a transition could be made "from a
> one-man rule to a more permanent and stable
> rule of institutions and laws."
> The immediate occasion for the revolution
> was the intensification of the election cam-
> paign which should culminate on the third
> Sunday of next November, when extraordi-
> nary presidential elections will be held. . . .
> The situation is very similar to that in
> October, 1927, when the presidential candi-
> dates, Arnulfo Gomez and Francisco Serrano,
> realizing that their opponent, Obregon, was
> certain of being elected, tried revolution as
> the only means by which they could obtain
> power. Since 1927, however, certain changes

[7] Des Moines *Register.*

have occurred which render the present situation more serious. In subsequent trial of Toral, moral responsibility for the act was fixed on a Roman Catholic nun. This and the subsequent measure requiring all priests to register their addresses on penalty of being considered implicated in the recent reprisals against the government, have greatly increased the seriousness of the Catholic question. Valenzuela [a revolutionary leader] has not missed the opportunity of bidding for Roman Catholic support, and his nickname "Captain General of the Cristeros" shows the extent to which he has become identified with that element.

The *labor group* is also disaffected. The CROM, the most powerful labor organization in Mexico, which supported the Calles Government during the 1927 crisis, withdrew its support of Provisional President Portes Gil last December and ordered all its members who held government offices to resign. This was a protest against the labor legislation which Portes Gil was pushing and to which they were strongly opposed.

But the revolt is not merely the result of conflicting principles. *Personal ambition* which has with few exceptions been at the root of all Mexican unrest is again the driving force. And, as usual, the sources of discontent prevailing among certain elements have eagerly been seized by the rebel generals to vindicate their revolt. Just as in December, 1923, de la Huerta justified his rebellion by alleging that Obregon was "imposing" Calles on the country, the leaders of the present movement allege "the secret rule of Plutarco Elias Calles," and state that it is their aim to terminate that rule and restore religious freedom.

4. **Resolving the Issues.**—Some editorials enlighten the reader because they resolve the issues in a pending conflict or controversy. The chief purpose of such editorials is to provide the reader with adequate standards of judgment. Not infre-

quently this type of editorial contains historical background and achieves the double purpose of identifying and classifying the forces involved in a conflict as well as resolving the issues. The editorial on page 31, entitled "Mexico Resorts to Force," is an example.

The following editorials have for their purpose the explanation of the issues in a conflict or a controversy:

(1)

LAUNCHING BIRTH CONTROL ISSUE

The birth control issue that has been kicked around and has been kicking around for a good while is going to become a live issue in legislative halls. The New York League of Women Voters, by a vote of 200 to 4, will ask the coming legislature to enact a law making it legal for physicians to give birth control information to married couples. The question has been on the indorsed list of the league for a long while; now the league members say it is time to start a campaign.

The matter will be hotly debated, no doubt about that. There will be those to say that it is morally wrong to do anything to limit the size of families. There will be others to point out that it is right from the standpoint of economics and health to keep families within the bounds in which parents can support them properly. The theory is that three children, let us say, properly clothed and nourished and educated, are worth more to the state than six undernourished, underprivileged youngsters. Then there will be a third class in the argument—those who have nothing to say as to the right or wrong of the thing but who contend that since birth control in one way or another is bound to be practiced, it is better to make competent medical information available. They look only to the practical side.

The rest of the country will watch the New

York state contest with a good deal of interest.[8]

(2)

NAVAL MATHEMATICS

When Prime Minister MacDonald announced at Geneva that all but three of the twenty points under discussion in the naval negotiations between England and the United States had been settled, it might have looked as if the job were nearly done. Yet all depends upon what those three points are. That they are knotty enough to keep both governments hard at work at them has been made abundantly plain since Mr. MacDonald spoke. Two of the points lie on the surface of the whole affair. They have been clearly laid down by President Hoover as his indispensable conditions. These are that there be absolute parity between the British Navy and our own, and that there also be a reduction in naval armaments. Now, as events have shown, it seems easy to get either of these two points separately, but when the attempt is made to obtain them both at once there is danger of one destroying the other.

Ever since the Geneva Conference of 1927, the British Government has declared its purpose never to build against the United States, and freely to concede the desirability of having the two navies on a parity. After England has decided how many and what classes of war vessels she requires, she is perfectly willing that the United States should have an equal naval strength. So far so good. But for this country to gain an equality with British cruisers, it would be necessary for it to build several thousand tons more of them than are contemplated in our naval program. Where, then, would reduction come in? The British are willing to place their minimum strength at sea considerably lower than they did two years ago. In other words, they are

---

[8] Milwaukee *Journal.*

ready to meet Mr. Hoover's desire for a reduction. But even after they have made theirs, they will still have a cruiser strength so much larger than ours that we should have to expand our navy, instead of reducing it, in order to be on a parity with them.

This is the mathematical dilemma with which President Hoover and his advisers are now struggling. It might seem that the contradiction between parity and reduction is too absolute to be overcome by any kind of yardstick or slide-rule. But perhaps the relativity that is upsetting astronomy and geometry will help to solve this problem in naval mathematics.[9]

(3)

WHAT IS THE FACT?

Has the House Ways and Means Committee voted a gift of about $180,000,000 to the corporations of the country at the direct expense of consumers?

Democratic members of the committee contend that the application of a 2 per cent reduction in the federal tax on corporation income for the year 1927 amounts to just that.

They say that the corporations have already collected their 1927 taxes from the consumers, and that to cut those taxes 2 per cent simply turns about $180,000,000 back into corporation treasuries.

Republican members of the committee argue that since the first payment of taxes on 1927 corporation incomes won't be due until March 1, 1928, the corporations have not yet started to collect from consumers to pay these taxes, and won't start until the first of the year.

The validity of either of these arguments is purely a question of fact.

It's well established that corporations compute their taxes as part of the cost of production, and build up tax reserves to meet the payments when they are due.

[9] New York *Times.*

Do they build up these reserves during the year the income is earned or during the year the taxes on it are to be paid?

If funds to pay taxes are set aside during the year the income is earned, then the Democrats are clearly right. By making a 2 per cent cut in the federal tax on 1927 corporation incomes the Ways and Means Committee has simply declared a $180,000,000 bonus for corporation stockholders.

If the corporations haven't yet started to build up funds to pay taxes on their 1927 incomes, then there's no compelling reason why the cut should not be made effective next March.

What's needed to settle the argument between the Democratic and Republican members of the House Ways and Means Committee is a set of facts.

If the committee has the facts it ought to produce them. If it hasn't, it ought to waste no time in getting them.[10]

Sometimes editorials that resolve the issues are in the nature of "debunking" explanations. The following editorial, which appeared in the Milwaukee *Journal* during the presidential canvass of 1928, is an example:

IMMIGRATION LAW BUNK

"I am heartily in favor of removing from the immigration law the harsh provision which separates families," says Gov. Smith in his acceptance address. "We shall amend the immigration laws to relieve unnecessary hardships upon families," says Mr. Hoover in his. What do they mean?

When the immigration law went into effect back in 1924, there were in this country thousands of immigrants who had left wives and children in the old country. They meant to bring them over as soon as the needed money was available. Then came restriction. Quota

---

[10] Cleveland *Press.*

numbers were required for these families and for some countries quota numbers were insufficient to meet demands, even though 50 per cent of the total was set aside expressly for reuniting families. This preference cleared the situation for most nationalities. But a number of family heads, particularly from South Europe, have now been without family life for four years. Both Mr. Hoover and Gov. Smith express concern for them. But need they?

The immigration act admits free of quota wives and unmarried children under 18 of American citizens. In less than another year every immigrant who arrived before the law of 1924 will have been here long enough to qualify for citizenship. Thus, before a new president has been in office six months, the situation will have been cleared for those interested enough in this country to seek citizenship. Why should we worry so much about the rest? If these do not wish citizenship, there is no good reason why they should not go back to their families abroad.

To be sure, there are certain minor changes needed in the law which controls the immigration of families. Hereafter, split families should not be received at all. The age of unmarried children admitted free of quota might also be raised to 21. But these things are too minor to have place in the condensed statements of presidential candidates. The only possible reason for the inclusion in them of immigration "hardships" is politics. Both Hoover and Smith are playing to the "foreign vote" in this matter, and both deserve no credit for it.

Resolving the issues in a controversy or conflict for the enlightenment of the reader is also accomplished by means of graphical representation, but this method is frequently an oversimplification of the issues. The cartoon on page 303 illustrates the method.

5. **Defining Movements and Organizations.**—The purpose and the nature of important organizations, institutions,

mass movements, concepts, policies, judicial processes, and instruments are frequently misunderstood or not understood at all by readers. The reader's misunderstanding usually results from his being exposed to false propaganda, but his failure to understand is the result of his unenlightenment. In some instances, the thing misunderstood is not really complex, but simple and easily explained.

The following editorial, which appeared in the New York *Times,* was timely when it was published because of a disturbance of the peace by some members of the Industrial Workers of the World. Unfortunately for the purposes of our discussion of the interpretative editorial, it denounces the mass movement it is describing, yet it is an excellent example of an editorial of definition in that it differentiates Syndicalism, trade unionism, and Socialism.

SYNDICALISM

"Syndicalism" is a name first used in France, then borrowed in England, for the kind of labor agitation here practised by the Industrial Workers of the World. It has no connection necessarily with trades unionism or with Socialism and, though there are trades unionists and Socialists who have in some degree worked with the Syndicalists abroad, the leaders of both schools are opposed to it. The basic doctrine of the Industrial Workers, as of the Syndicalists, is the destruction of the profits of capital, in order that the workingmen may take over all industry for themselves. The method of effecting this destruction tried by the Syndicalists in France was the general strike. In the same spirit and for the same end, the sympathizers with the Syndicalists in England undertook through the coal strike to cripple all the industries of the country. In the United States the Industrial Workers announce their intention to bring about strikes wherever and whenever they can, not for the betterment of conditions, but for the injury of capital. . . .

The dream of the radical Industrial Workers is one that may well be attractive to the more ignorant of the workers. It rests on a plausible fallacy. It assumes, because profits on production cannot be had without labor, that labor creates all production and is entitled to all the profits resulting. The assumption, in the light of the history of industry, is monstrous, but it does not necessarily seem so to the man in the mine or at the spindle. It is, indeed, conceivable that workers in co-operation, using their savings as capital and providing direction and planning by representatives chosen from their own number, might secure all the profits from their production and that these might be remunerative. As a matter of fact, productive co-operation has almost without exception proved unprofitable on any considerable scale. But any co-operative organization and administration of industry is but vaguely regarded by the Syndicalists and the Industrial Workers. All their energies are directed to the destruction of capital by the gradual forcible seizure of all profits, or, rather, by the practical abolition of profits.

One of the features of this agitation is the hostility shown to the preservation of order by the police and the military. In France the agitators have tried to get the soldiers to pledge themselves not to obey orders in case of violence in strikes. The same thing was undertaken in England, and the noted leader, Tom Mann, and his printers were fined for such efforts. In this country, wherever they have dared to do so, the Industrial Workers have incited forcible resistance to all agencies for the preservation of order. This, of course, strikes at the roots of society and is a savage attack on the rights of the feebler and poorer sections of every community. It is a bald assertion that might makes right, with the fatal consequence that those having the greatest need of protection will suffer most. When, however, the small property owners get this fact clearly in their minds, short work will be made of the agitators. The apostles of brute anarchy present a picturesque spectacle in the general disturbance of ideas now prevalent, but in reality they are not very dangerous. Probably they serve a good purpose in showing the real tendencies of the theories they are engaged in spreading.

When the general subject was under discussion in the House of Commons, Mr. Hewins, the English economist, made a cogent speech in which he demonstrated that Syndicalism was not logically a form of Socialism, or of trades unionism, but was peculiarly savage, intensified, and destructive individualism and selfishness. That unquestionably is what it is, and we have faith enough in the essential principles of justice and altruism which have slowly but surely evolved from the experience of the race since it emerged from barbarism, to believe that this latest effort at reaction to the rule of force will not prevail.

The following editorial is an explanation of the purpose of an institution, the League of Nations. Although not written in the conventional editorial manner, because it was prepared as an explanation for high school students, the editorial illustrates how an editorial writer's analysis pierces through the less significant details to locate the central purpose of the organization described:

. . . Modern diplomacy began during the feudal period when princes sent messengers to each other to act as their personal representatives in planning war and marriages and alliances and other delicate affairs.

With the union of the small states into the great modern states of Europe the system was maintained. As trading among nations developed and as states grew more powerful, the dealings of states with one another required that the messengers be stationed permanently at foreign courts to represent the interests of their prince, that is, of their nation.

Because the permanent messengers, or ambassadors, originally represented a royal sovereign they were treated royally in the foreign capital to which they were assigned. Thus there grew up a diplomatic ceremonial or etiquette.

As international dealings became more complex it was found that the ambassadors could not attend to every separate case, so treaties were made in order to lay down general rules of conduct and to establish definitive agreements between various nations.

Some of the treaties, of course, were secret, and the ambassadors set themselves up as much cleverer and much more influential men than they really were. So, by the year 1800, the diplomatic system represented a specialized profession which engaged in plotting and counter-plotting, whispering, lying, concealment, and intrigue. It produced a veritable network of inflammable tissue which was more likely to cause a war than to prevent one.

At various times since 1800, European nations found their mutual dealings so important and so complex that negotiation could not be accomplished by ambassadors alone. This was especially true at the close of a big war in which several nations had participated.

Then the nations would send representatives to meet in a "conference" or a "congress," and they would get together around a table to settle their disputes and claims as equitably as was consistent with their individual interests and ambitions.

That, in brief, was the system which prevailed up to 1919. Nations, in other words, settled their difficulties (1) by diplomatic correspondence; (2) by diplomatic conversation between the representatives of two countries; and (3) by occasional "conferences" which met only after a big war or once every seven or eight years.

Is it to be wondered, then, that in between conferences, national hatred smoldered and national distrust grew in the various nations? Is it to be wondered that nations were afraid to trust one another when treaties were secret and conspiracies were envisioned in the every move of another nation?

Something, indeed, needed to be done to remedy the evils growing out of the hardened old diplomatic system. That was recognized at the close of the World War, and the peace conference set up new international machinery and provided a new basis for conducting international relations.

The Covenant of the League of Nations provides (1) that all treaties made by member-states of the League are to be registered and published; (2) that regular meetings of diplomatic representatives of the member-states are to be held at a regular meeting place—Geneva; and (3) that international differences are to be settled by conciliation, arbitration, or adjudication.

The League of Nations has three divisions: (1) An Assembly, which meets once a year to discuss international relations; (2) a Council, which meets at least three times a year to conciliate differences; and (3) a Secretariat, or full-time international civil service, which coördinates the various committees and commissions of the League and is always on the job in the interest of preserving peace.

The World Court has a permanent panel of judges which is available for the judicial settlement of questions of international law.

Thus has diplomacy changed at the command of democracy.

Examples of editorials that define policies, instruments, concepts, and organizations could be multiplied indefinitely, and a newspaper that contained many of them would approximate a textbook. The psychology of readers, however, places a limitation on the number of such editorials that can be published, for the reader demands that most editorials have a basis in the latest news. Yet it is true that some newspapers would have more educational value if they published more editorials of definition.

THE NATURE OF DEFINITION

The foregoing examples of editorials of definition have been cited for the purpose of showing that one of the functions of the editorial is to provide the reader with more adequate standards of judgment than is furnished by the episodic news story. Little effort was made to explain the process used by the editorial writer in formulating definitions. We shall notice now the process in a little more detail.

To define a thing is to classify it in its relation to other things. We state it in terms of the class to which it belongs, differentiating it from other things in the same class. A definition has two parts. The first part, technically called *genus,* identifies the thing defined as belonging to an inclusive class; the second part, technically called the *differentia,* identifies the thing in the respects of which it is different from the other members of the class, or *genus.* For example, "chimpanzee" is defined as "an anthropoid ape smaller and less ferocious than the gorilla." The *genus* in this definition (for the purposes of this discussion, though not for the purposes of the zoölogist) is "anthropoid ape," and the *differentia* is "smaller and less ferocious than the gorilla." When one examines several different things and observes that they have *common* characteristics, he is warranted in inferring that they belong to one inclusive class (*genus*). This is the process of classification. When he proceeds further to note their *different* characteristics, he is warranted in formulating a definition the first part of which is the *genus* and the second part the *differentia.*

Formulating definitions in our thinking, and analyzing definitions that are presented to us, is not always an easy performance. The following facts about definition ought to be kept in mind: (*a*) Definition involves implication; and (*b*) the purpose that one has in mind often determines whether or not the definition is accurate.

Definition Involves Implication.—The formulation of a definition is an inductive process. It is the making of a generalization. This process, like all the rest of our thinking, consists precisely in *noting the relationship of things—their* common characteristics and their differentiating characteristics. If we observe the relationship of things accurately, our thinking is sound; if we observe the relationship of things inaccurately, our thinking is unsound. For example, if we are to do sound thinking about mass movements such as Syndicalism, Socialism, etc., we must understand their philosophy and tactics sufficiently to differentiate between them. Thousands of Americans have no clear concept as to the difference between Socialism, Syndicalism, Communism, and Anarchism, and many persons think they are the same mass movement. It was for the purpose of clarifying popular ideas about Syndicalism that the New York *Times* published the editorial that is reprinted on page 38.[11]

Purpose in Definition.—Definition, if it is to be useful in our thinking, must be adapted to *our specific purpose.* We define a thing according to the use it is intended for: a horse, to the zoölogist, is only a member of the equine family, but to the farmer it is an animal used for purposes of transportation and cultivation. Likewise, the terms "urban people" and "rural people," for the purposes of the Census Bureau, are only convenient terms for differentiating between persons who live in towns of more than 2,500 population and those who live in lesser divisions; but for politicians who have in mind specific political issues, the terms are used in a different sense, as is explained in the following editorial from the New York *Times,* published on the eve of the 1928 presidential election:

Urban and Urban-Minded

The political fortunes of Alfred E. Smith, a product of the sidewalks of New York, are frequently examined in the light of the urban versus the rural traditions. Now that a majority of the population of the United

---

[11] For an explanation of the various mass movements, see Bertrand Russell, *Proposed Roads to Freedom;* John Spargo, *Syndicalism, Industrial Unionism and Socialism;* Selig Perlman, *A Theory of the Labor Movement;* R. N. Postgate, *The Bolshevik Theory;* L. S. Reed, *The Labor Philosophy of Samuel Gompers;* A. D. Lewis, *Syndicalism and the General Strike;* D. J. Saposs, *The Labor Movement in Post-War France;* S. H. M. Chang, *The Marxian Theory of the State.*

States is urban, by the findings of the United States Census of 1920, people have hastened to ask whether the time has not come when the American people will accept as readily a man who has risen from the city streets as from the farm or the towpath. In such a study there is usually overlooked the distinction between the technical census use of "urban" and the ordinary meaning we attach to the word. For the purpose of the Census Bureau, "urban" is all incorporated places with a population of 2,500 or over. But for practical purposes, such as a presidential election, it is obvious that the large village and the small town are not always or perhaps often "urban."

Substituting the urban psychology for the technical census term, it is not true that the urban population of the United States in 1920 was 51.4 of the whole population. A village of 5,000, a town of 25,000 in the midst of an agricultural community, may be, and usually is, rural-minded. . . .

Such conclusions are justified by common usage. In Ohio, for instance, it has been said that Mr. Hoover's strength is urban and the late Senator Willis's strength was rural. But this was correct only in the non-technical sense. Chillicothe with 15,000 people and Marion with 28,000 people are urban for the census takers but rural as regards Mr. Hoover. We do not think of Canton, Ohio, as urban, yet it had 87,000 people in 1920. We may question whether Des Moines, with a population of 126,000 in 1920, can be called urban for political purposes. Los Angeles, of metropolitan size, shelters a very large population that is rural in the concrete sense of not being many years removed from the farm. And at the apex in New York City there are hundreds of thousands of people who are urban physically but not urban-minded. The official urban preponderance in the United States Census will have to be much more than 51.4 per cent. before we can speak of a truly urban majority of the American people.

Likewise, in our thinking about the League of Nations, the purpose we have in mind determines what kind of definition we shall make.   Actually the League of Nations is a piece of international machinery designed as an improvement on the prewar diplomatic machinery; it is not a superstate or a supergovernment.   Yet it was possible, prior to Germany's entrance in 1926, to define the League of Nations as an instrument designed and controlled by the victorious powers for the purpose of preserving the treaties of settlement.

The importance of observing the relationship of things will become more apparent to the reader as he examines the chapters that follow.

CHAPTER III

EDITORIALS OF EXPLANATION

The type of editorial discussed in the previous chapter is usually published because the subject matter is timely. The newspaper has just reported a diplomatic crisis involving a little-known country, Albania, or the beginning of a revolution in Mexico, or a Syndicalist riot somewhere in Europe or America. The editorial writer therefore responds to the unuttered queries of his readers: "What kind of country is Albania?" "What are they quarreling about in Mexico?" or "What is Syndicalism—is it the same as Socialism?"

A second type of editorial is the one whose purpose is to explain an event so as to reveal the concealed motive or the non-apparent policy that has motivated it. This type of editorial tries to answer the questions, "Why is this?" and "What does this mean?" Such an editorial, however, does not attempt to explain cause in the formal sense in which we think of the inherent cause of an event, but rather it explains the motive and policy "behind" an event.

In discussing this type of editorial, this chapter attempts only to *describe* in a realistic way how events are actually analyzed by the editorial writer or the editorial council. In the next chapter the process of analysis is *explained*, rather than described, in terms of an act of thought.

The Process of Analysis.—The process of preparing an editorial which answers the question "Why is this?" is about as follows. An editorial writer (the time is 1927) brings to the attention of the council a dispatch which reports, let us say, the passage of a resolution in the annual convention of the American Federation of Labor favoring voluntary restriction by the Mexican Government of Mexican emigration to the United States over the opposition of many members who desired to petition Congress to extend to Mexican immigrants

47

the quota restrictions applying to European immigrants. This news dispatch presents a paradox: why is the American Federation of Labor, which so aggressively demanded and influenced the passage of drastic immigration laws in 1923 and 1924, now (in 1927) so eager to compete in the labor market with immigrants from Mexico? What, in other words, is the Ethiopian in this woodpile? All of the editorial writers in the council perceive the necessity for an editorial explanation; they realize that their readers will be perplexed by the resolution. Discussion ensues. Eventually the council concludes that it has arrived at the true explanation, and one of the editorial writers—probably the one who contributed the most significant ideas in the discussion—is assigned to write the editorial.[1]

What was the explanation? By what analytical process did the editorial council arrive at an explanation of this paradox?

The process of explaining a concealed motive or a nonapparent policy is simply a process of *arranging a set of data into a pattern of thought and then testing the validity of this hypothesis by inquiring as to its real probabilities.* It means the construction of a tentative hypothesis and then, perhaps, the rejection of the hypothesis, the construction of another hypothesis, and then another, until finally a hypothesis has been suggested which seems to be consistent with the probabilities.

With reference to the American Federation of Labor resolution, for example, one editorial writer in the council constructed an explanation based on the assumption that the members of the Federation, being for the most part skilled craftsmen, perceived no danger to themselves from an influx of unskilled labor from Mexico, and that consequently they played to the grandstand with a *beau geste.* This was a plausible explanation, for it had considerable basis in fact and took account of the realities of American mass psychology as it is sometimes played with by the leaders of organized labor. This explanation was abandoned, however, after one of the colleagues of the author of the explanation pointed out that the American

---

[1] In many newspaper offices, of course, this matter would not be discussed in council; an individual editorial writer would prepare the editorial without consulting his colleagues and would submit it to the editor-in-chief.

Federation of Labor was at that time engaged in recruiting membership from the ranks of unskilled labor and was waging a fight in the interest of labor generally for many other objectives than mere increases in wages.

What was probably the real explanation was suggested by a third editorial writer who had been paying close attention to labor union activities in years past. He observed that the American Federation of Labor today is intensely interested in promoting a class-consciousness, or at least a solidarity among workingmen for their protection from unfair treatment such as unfair judicial decisions and competition with child and convict labor, and for the procurement of more leisure, more educational advantages, and more social welfare legislation. To give this data more significance, the editorial writer recalled for his colleagues the organization, in 1918, by the late President Samuel Gompers, of the Pan-American Federation of Labor, the visits to Mexico of Mr. Gompers, and the postwar tutelage given to Mexican labor unions by the American Federation of Labor. To the editorial writer who pursued this line of thought, the explanation stood out clearly, the hidden motive appeared, the Ethiopian in the woodpile turned out to be the desire for labor "solidarity" on the American continent—a goal which American and Mexican labor organizations were co-operating to achieve. The resolution, indeed, was a gesture, but a gesture to Mexican labor, not to the American public. On this hypothesis the editorial writer constructed an editorial as follows:

Toward Labor "Solidarity"

The A. F. of L. convention yesterday passed a resolution favoring voluntary restriction by the Mexican government of Mexican emigrants to the United States. In order to pass the resolution, it was necessary for high officials of the Federation to put pressure on those delegates who desired to petition Congress to extend the European quota restrictions to Mexican immigrants.

Is this a practical joke—this action which, in the strenuous business of getting a living,

is equivalent to the North Side Gangsters
Hootch Distributors, Inc. inviting the South
Side Gangsters Hootch Distributors, Inc.
to "come over and sell your booze in our
territory and we shan't molest you"? On
its face, the resolution is paradoxical, but to
those who have followed the evolution of the
labor movement in America it does not appear
to be such a piece of irony.

Under Samuel Gompers' leadership the
A. F. of L., following the war, set out on a
program to preserve its wartime gains. An
increase in the wage scale was not the sole
objective. Gompers and his associates looked
toward labor "solidarity" as a goal. They
perceived that if the wage level and the workingman's standard of living were to be permanently maintained in the face of future
business depressions, the labor movement must
offer something more tangible than merely
higher wages for a brief period.

All of the factors that have entered into
the formulation of the broad program of the
A. F. of L. cannot be told here, but the goal
of labor "solidarity"—call it "class consciousness," if you wish—is among the paramount
objectives. Shortly before his death Gompers
made a trip to Mexico City, and the Mexican
labor movement has been under A. F. of L.
tutelage ever since. This fact—not the fact
that the A. F. of L. is a craft organization
caring nothing for the welfare of unskilled
labor in America—is the explanation of the
resolution of yesterday. The resolution was
a fraternal gesture to Mexican labor; a pronouncement of the common interests of workingmen on the American continent, a bid for
labor "solidarity." [2]

More Complex Analysis.—The explanation of a perplexing event or situation requires not only an insight into public

---

[2] See *American Federationist*, Vol. XXXIV, pp. 1305-1306; also Samuel
Gompers, *Seventy Years of Life and Labor*, Vol. II. At its 1928 convention the American Federation of Labor reversed its policy by the
adoption of resolutions which urged that Latin-American immigrants be

affairs, but a habit of examining all the circumstances that surround the event or the situation. The meaning is not always on the surface and may even be concealed in the pages of history. It was, for example, a matter of much comment in 1927 that so few editorial writers explained the true significance of the Geneva naval conference. *Editor and Publisher* took the editorial writers to task in the following language:

> The question is asked by a magazine writer, "Are editorials worth reading?" The answer is, "Yes, when they are worth reading."
> Some months ago we examined the editorials that had appeared in a scattered list of newspapers, picked at random, based on the astounding news from Geneva that the conference called at the suggestion of the President of the United States, looking to reduced naval armaments, had resulted in dismal failure. We had our own opinions, gleaned from news columns, concerning the cause of this startling set-back in the plan for gradual disarmament for which the whole world yearns. We search these editorials for light.
> With but two exceptions these editorials were words, mere words. The reader, after perusal of them, was no wiser. They were not worth reading, because those who wrote them had not been able to connect up the significant facts.[3]

In order to explain how an editorial council would seek to discover the real significance in this problem of national defense, it is necessary that we have in mind the circumstances of the conference. In 1922, the five large naval powers—Great Britain, the United States, Japan, France, and Italy—signed a treaty at Washington which fixed the ratio for battleships among the powers as follows: Great Britain 5; the United States 5; Japan 3; France and Italy 1.67. No agreement, however, was made as to a ratio of cruisers. By 1927, the United States having constructed only two new cruisers, it became apparent to the American Government that England had far out-

---

held to a minimum and that a more careful watch be kept on the borders to prevent the smuggling of aliens. Apparently the Mexican Federation of Labor had not been able, after the passage of the 1927 resolution, to persuade the Mexican Government to place a voluntary restriction on emigration. The 1928 resolutions are printed in newspapers of Nov. 27, 1928.

[3] Jan. 14, 1928, p. 28.

distanced this country in cruiser power, and that the United States would have to adopt one of three courses: (*a*) abandon its desire to attain parity with Great Britain; (*b*) inaugurate a cruiser-building program aimed at attaining parity; or (*c*) try to induce Great Britain to reduce the number of her cruisers. The economical Coolidge administration decided upon the last-mentioned policy. Mr. Coolidge invited the powers who were signatory to the Washington treaty to meet at Geneva to discuss a reduction in cruisers, and Great Britain and Japan accepted the invitation.

Early in the conference there was a misunderstanding as to whether or not the United States and Great Britain were to have the same ratio in cruisers, but Great Britain eventually made it clear that she did not object to parity. Later, however, an *impasse* developed as to whether reduction in cruisers should be by global tonnage or by category. Great Britain adhered to the formula of reduction by category; that is, she preferred that each nation be permitted an equal number of large cruisers (cruisers of 7,500 to 10,000 tons with 8-inch guns) and an equal number of small cruisers (cruisers of 6,000 tons or less with 6-inch guns). The United States, on the other hand, desired parity by global tonnage; that is, that each nation be permitted an equal tonnage of all classes of ships, and that each nation be permitted to decide for itself whether it would use its tonnage for large or small cruisers. The United States maintained that inasmuch as she had few naval bases, small cruisers were of little use to her, and it was necessary, therefore, for her to be allotted a considerable number of large cruisers. Great Britain, however, maintained that she required small cruisers to protect her world-wide commerce in time of war, otherwise she would be starved into submission; and moreover, since large cruisers were "aggressive" ships, she would need to have as many large cruisers as the United States plus a large number of smaller cruisers—more small cruisers than the United States had need for.

The acceptance of Great Britain's formula would not have permitted any reduction in cruisers by either power. The cruiser strength of each country—if the United States con-

structed as many small cruisers as Great Britain needed, and
if Great Britain constructed as many large cruisers as the
United States needed—would have been in excess of 500,000
tons. This was more tonnage than the United States possessed at the time, and the United States desired a reduction to
approximately 300,000 tons, or at most to 400,000 tons.
Obviously no *reduction* could be achieved unless Great Britain
would abandon her formula; obviously *parity* was not possible
unless the United States would abandon her stand. The crux
of the situation was that Great Britain was afraid to let the
United States have more "aggressive" cruisers than herself,
and the United States was afraid to permit Great Britain to
have more "commerce destroyers" than the United States
thought necessary.

While the delegates at the conference were engaged in these
fruitless debates, the editorial writers in America were trying
to make what explanations were necessary. Most of the explanations were superficial. Some of the editorials explained
the difference between 6- and 8-inch guns, and talked about
British naval bases in the Caribbean; that is to say, they explained the obvious. Some tried to penetrate below the surface of the discussions to discover a way out of the *impasse*.
Some explanation of naval technology was, no doubt, necessary;
but what really perplexed newspaper readers in the United
States was the question, "Why should there be this naval
rivalry between Great Britain and the United States? Do we
expect to fight Great Britain for world markets? Are we
merely jealous for reasons of prestige?" Those, after all,
were the essential questions. How would an editorial council
go about answering them?

The process of analysis, where it was done, was about as
follows. The editorial council examined first the more obvious
factors. The editorial writers hoped that by a process of
elimination of conjectures—that is, *by the testing of the validity
of each plausible pattern of explanation*—they would reach
finally a true explanation. The first factor to be examined
was the character of the delegates. Was the rivalry due entirely
to the fact that the delegations from both countries were com-

posed chiefly of naval experts? That is, was the dispute chiefly a matter of national and professional prestige, rather than a real national danger? To some extent, yes, but not entirely, it was decided. For had not President Coolidge and Secretary Kellogg provided the American delegates in advance with instructions which included the formula for parity and for large cruisers? And had not the British delegation at one time returned to London to confer with the Cabinet, which had supported the delegates' position? The professional character of the delegates, of course, partially explained the *impasse,* but that was not the real reason for the naval rivalry. The editorial council was certain about this factor, and eliminated it as not being the essential explanation.

The council next passed to a second explanation offered by one of their number. "War between the two countries is indeed thinkable," suggested one of the editorial writers. "The two nations are great commercial rivals. The United States has taken away much of Great Britain's South American trade, is selling more to Canada than is Great Britain herself, is making a bid for the markets in the Orient, is exercising a financial hegemony that was formerly Great Britain's, is England's creditor for the war debts, and is bidding for much of Great Britain's carrier trade. America's success is not only injuring Great Britain's economic position, but is threatening her traditional prestige. The Tory Government is a bunch of die-hards. The present American Government is just as conscious of this conflict of national interests, and it desires to provide an adequate navy looking toward a possible commercial war which will decide which nation is to be supreme for another generation." [4]

This argument, it was objected, was not an adequate explanation. "It is true that there is a conflict of economic interests, and the question of national prestige is involved," asserted one editorial writer, "and it is indeed possible that a commercial— a modern Punic—war could ensue. But hasn't it been made plain since 1918 that war, as an instrument for promoting

---

[4] For a detailed discussion of Anglo-American commercial rivalry, see Ludwell Denny, *America Conquers Britain* (1930).

international trade, does not, in the final accounting, pay for itself, especially a war between the leading powers of the world?[5] Any basis for assessing the possibility of an Anglo-American war, in my opinion, must be one that has more validity than this one. The American people and the American Government are not at this time willing to build a navy for anything but national defense, and the British electorate has the same attitude."

"Why, then," asked another editorial writer, "does the United States demand naval parity with Great Britain? If it is not entirely a question of national and professional prestige, if it is not entirely a question of a possible commercial war, why does the United States Government so desire a large navy?"

"I think I have it," another editorial writer spoke up. The speaker was a man who had sought for the explanation by examining the historical relations between the two countries. Having read diplomatic history with reference to sea law and to previous American quarrels with Great Britain, his insight into the question had led him to an explanation. He proceeded to elaborate it for his colleagues.

"Every one of our wars and near-wars with European countries," he said, "has been the consequence of a European war in which the blockading belligerents have disregarded our rights as a neutral. We had a naval war with France in 1798 because she interfered with our shipping and treated us shamefully in other respects; we fought Germany in 1917 on the same issues. One of our wars and another near-war were with Great Britain because of her interference with our shipping during a continental war in which she was engaged. In 1812 we declared war on Great Britain,[6] and in 1915 and 1916 we were on the verge of going to war with her because of her blockade of

---

[5] E. R. A. Seligman, "World Peace and Economic Stability," *Proceedings of the Academy of Political Science,* Vol. XIII, pp. 197-203, and P. T. Moon, *Imperialism and World Politics,* pp. 526-558.

[6] Interference with our shipping provided a reason for our declaring war against Great Britain in 1812, but recent historical research has exposed other reasons, such as the desire of western Americans to annex Canada and Florida and to end the menace of British-subsidized Indian attacks on the western frontier. The latter reasons were probably more compelling than the interference with our shipping. See J. W. Pratt, *Expansionists of 1812.*

German ports and her interference with our shipping. I recall in that connection the hundreds of protests from cotton planters, meat packers, and others which deluged our State Department; the economic distress of the South and certain sections of the West; the embargo on our importation of dyestuffs and machine knitting needles from Germany, which distressed the silk and textile industries; and even interference with our mails.[7] I remember the relatively small size of the American navy and the decision made by Congress and the President in 1916 to provide the United States with a navy even larger than Great Britain's.[8]

---

[7] Diplomatic correspondence recently published contains evidence that Great Britain, although prohibiting American firms from importing machine knitting needles, herself imported them from Germany. The American Ambassador in London was instructed to state that this policy savored of "discrimination favoring British at the expense of American commerce under the guise of a war measure."—*Foreign Relations of the United States, 1926* Supplement, pp. 571-580.

[8] In the minds of some Congressmen in 1916, the spectacle of Japan's aggressive policy in China was an important factor in deciding their vote for the increase in our navy, and shortly after the Battle of Jutland a few Congressmen were afraid of a possible future conflict with Germany; but, on the whole, Great Britain was the power against whom the navy was to be built. Some light is thrown on the character of opinion at the time by Arthur Bullard, "Our Relations with Great Britain," *Atlantic Monthly*, Vol. CXVIII (October, 1916), pp. 451-461; Archibald Hurd, "The United States and Sea Power: A Challenge," *Fortnightly Review*, Vol. CXI (February, 1919), pp. 175-189; and Hector Bywater, *Sea Power in the Pacific*, pp. 72-77.

Since this section was written, a portion of the posthumous memoirs of Robert Lansing, Secretary of State, 1915-1919, has been published. "I have wondered sometimes," wrote Mr. Lansing, "what would have been the result if Count von Bernstorff's advice had prevailed with his government and if submarine warfare had been abandoned. Would not the United States have been forced to continue her unheeded protests to Great Britain for the many flagrant violations of international law by the British navy? Would not the American people have become more and more irritated at the British disregard of their rights and have demanded naval convoys or armaments for American ships engaged in legitimate trade with neutral countries bordering on the North Sea? Could a clash with the British navy have been avoided? And would a clash have resulted in war? An American to-day, reviewing the two years preceding the declaration of war by Congress in April, 1917, may feel a chill of fear as he sees how the mere change of policy at Berlin in regard to submarine warfare—a change that nearly took place—might have reversed the whole course of events, and how that change did not take place because those then in control of the German Government turned a deaf ear to the wise counsel of the German Ambassador at Washington. The Allied Powers may thank German stupidity and stubbornness for saving the situation. Submarine warfare may have been a blessing in disguise."—"The Difficulties of Neutrality," *Saturday Evening Post*, April 18, 1931, p. 105.

And only recently the memoirs of British and American diplomats and officials have revealed how near we were to war with Great Britain and how determined we were to protect our neutral rights and our economic welfare.

"Reviewing all these facts, it seems plain to me that in a possible future continental war in which Great Britain would be engaged and in which, as a great naval power, she would pursue her historic policy of blockade, the circumstances would in all probability produce strained relations between herself and the United States. The strained relations, while they might not culminate in war—as they did not quite in 1915 and 1916 because of Germany's destruction of American ships and because of the Allies' borrowings in the United States—would bring us perilously near to war. And the United States, it now appears, is resolved to preserve her rights on the sea during future European wars. She has apparently resolved to support her diplomatic protests with an adequate navy, even though she never resorts to war. She may even desire a navy large enough to convoy her merchant vessels across the seas; for it is a conspicuous fact in military history that weak neutrals can avoid participation in a general war only by submitting to the trespasses of the belligerents." [9]

This explanation revealed to the other editorial writers that the last speaker had a clearer comprehension of the problem of sea power than any of them possessed, and accordingly they agreed that he should prepare the editorial. This writer, moreover, having revealed himself as a student of the problem, hence-

[9] The foregoing discussion takes into account only those factors which were important at the time of the abortive naval conference; it makes no attempt to explain the developments that have followed the adjournment at Geneva. Nor does it consider the question of an agreement concerning "freedom of the seas" or an agreement regarding the attitude of the United States in the event of a "public" war or an attempt by the League of Nations to enforce Article XVI of the Covenant. These questions were indeed in the minds of the delegates at the Geneva conference, but it is not necessary to consider them in order to explain the policy of the American delegates. These questions would need to be considered, however, in the light of events subsequent to the summer of 1926. The only factors considered here are those which are necessary for the illustration of how an editorial writer analyzes a particular type of editorial. Much light is thrown on the problem by J. M. Kenworthy and George Young, *Freedom of the Seas,* and P. B. Potter, *Freedom of the Seas in History, Law, and Politics,* Part III.

forth prepared all the editorials dealing with naval policy without consulting his colleagues to any great extent. The editorial council, having discovered an "expert" to deal with this field of the news, seldom discussed the matter in future conferences.

Biased Explanations.—Sometimes newspapers that have definite policies as regards certain broad questions provide their readers with biased explanations of events which bear upon the question. In some instances of this kind, a newspaper may become so suspicious of those who oppose its viewpoint that it perceives bad motive in every move of the opposing camp and becomes, as a consequence, easily susceptible to untrue suggestion. Although the newspaper is a responsible institution, it is subject to this kind of human weakness just as persons are.

Biased explanations are sometimes due to prejudice and sometimes to ignorance; usually, however, they are the result of a combination of prejudice and ignorance. Some of the explanations of a Russian proposal at a disarmament conference in December, 1927, provide a typical example of a biased explanation that proceeds from ignorance as well as prejudice. The proposal of M. Litvinov, the Russian delegate to the League of Nations Preparatory Disarmament Commission at Geneva, took away the breath of the diplomats as well as of the editorial writers. His plan provided for the total disarmament of nations—not a mere reduction in armament.

Russia's motive in presenting the amazing proposal was difficult for editors to interpret. The variety of explanations was almost as numerous as the number of possible explanations that occurred to the various editorial writers. But there was hardly an editorial writer who sincerely assessed the motives of the Russians; nearly every explanation reflected a prejudice against the Communists.

A newspaper in Washington, D. C., for example, asserted that the proposal had for its purpose the effecting of a bloc, with Russia and Germany as the nucleus of a combination of powers to oppose the nations of western Europe. To a paper in Fargo, North Dakota, the Russian proposal appeared to be a bid for recognition of the Soviet régime by the United States

Government. A New York newspaper said that the real purpose of the proposal was to "silence the little cliques of Communist intellectuals scattered around the world who do not like to see Soviet Russia sitting at the same table with the capitalist states." Behind the Russian proposal, said a Hartford, Connecticut, paper, was the scheme to relieve Russia "of the expense of maintaining one of the largest armies in the world, and to set free millions of dollars for revolutionary propaganda all over Asia." The Russian plan, in the opinion of a Louisville paper, was "but a grand gesture," and Russia "would like nothing better than to see other nations completely disarmed" so that she would "be left free to 'bore from within' all over the world."

Some of these explanations contain a bit of truth—especially the last two—but the main explanation is simpler than any of the foregoing and is based on an accurate comprehension of the motives of the Russian Government and the real position of Soviet Russia in the European system; it is, besides, a more sincere explanation. The Russian proposal, it is true, was a grand gesture which Russia knew in advance would not be accepted, but its purpose was simply to expose the "hypocrisies" of the capitalistic states who were "only pretending to disarm" and to show the world that Russia is not a military "menace." It was a proposal that caused the common people all over the world to gasp in astonishment, but afterward, on reflection, to doubt the necessity for expensive armaments. It was meant to be a great object lesson to men of peace everywhere—nothing more. Newspapers that explained the proposal in any other way were not only ignorant of the governing factors in Soviet Russian foreign policies, but were giving expression to their conscious or unconscious bias.[10]

Example: Russian "Dumping."—A similar biased assessment of Soviet Russia's motives was made by several American news-

---

[10] It is true, of course, that Soviet Russia is the one nation whose foreign policy is forwarded better by the propaganda than by the military weapon, but this fact is so obvious that M. Litvinov could not have expected capitalistic states to agree to complete disarmament. See Louis Fischer, *The Soviets in World Affairs,* Vol. II, Chap. XXVII; W. H. Chamberlin, *Soviet Russia,* p. 232; and Salvador de Madariaga, *Disarmament,* p. 60.

papers in 1930 as the result of the shipment of Russian pulpwood and manganese to the United States and the "dumping"
of Russian wheat in Europe. Since the world was experiencing
a period of economic depression, it was natural that this "dumping" should cause some editorial writers to believe that the
Russian Government was acting from destructive motives. One
New England paper expressed the following opinion:

> They [the Russians] are engaged in a war
> as terrible in many ways as any that uses
> guns, cannons, bombs, and poison gas. They
> are engaged in trying to destroy American
> industry by means of their ability to undersell
> the American producer because they pay no
> wages to workers. That this is done as much
> to shake the faith of the American laboring
> man in his government as it is to put Russian-
> made goods on the American markets, no
> one who has studied the situation will deny.

Any one who understands the principles of international trade
and who was familiar with economic conditions in Russia in
1930 ought to have known that Russia had no way of obtaining
necessary foreign capital except by exporting goods. The
price that she received for her exported goods was of little
consequence to her, for the credit she established by selling
abroad was absolutely essential to the success of the Five-Year
Plan. Russia merely exported those products of which she
had a surplus in order to establish credits in foreign countries
with which to purchase producers' goods and services (i.e.,
machinery, technical advice, etc.). If, by dumping, Russia was
able to embarrass capitalistic nations, she was perhaps glad, but
that motive was entirely incidental in 1930. Had foreign
nations extended long-term credit to the Russians, much of the
so-called dumping would have been unnecessary; and if commodity prices had not fallen much lower in 1930 than the
Russians had anticipated in their Five-Year Plan, they would
have consumed at home large quantities of certain exported
products. In the future it is quite possible that the Soviet
Government may be able to attack capitalism by dumping, but

for the decade after 1930 the sole motive behind dumping is to acquire the trade balance which is so necessary to Russian industrial success at home.

Orr in Chicago Tribune

ASSESSING A MOTIVE

Explaining National Policies.—Nothing that is done by modern journalists can hold more danger for civilization than the irresponsible assessment of the foreign policy of another nation than their own. In America, where there is a surer feeling of national security, the press is less inclined to point an accusatory finger at foreign governments than is the continental European press, and it is not always looking for bogeys in foreign chancelleries; but there is nevertheless too much suspicion. "Nations," writes the biographer of Colonel House,[11] "are even more suspicious of one another than individuals, and such suspicion, as in individuals, is nine times out of ten unfounded."

"In most investigations of British foreign policy," writes Viscount Grey, "the true reason is not to be found in far-sighted views or large conceptions or great schemes. A Minister beset with the administrative work of a great office must often be astounded to read of the carefully laid plans, the deep, unrevealed motives that critics or admirers attribute to him. . . . If all secrets were known it would probably be found that British Foreign Ministers have been guided by what seemed to them to be the immediate interest of this country without making elaborate calculations for the future." [12]

Any assessment of national policy must rest on realities. Some events may be spectacular and thus seem of great import, but the statesmen who set them off are seldom pioneers blazing new trails or altruists possessed of Messianic illusions. The American policy in China, for example, is based on our national interests and only incidentally has the appearance of altruism. Journalists ought to perceive these realities, but sometimes their imagination supplies factors which have no basis in reality. At the conclusion of Prime Minister MacDonald's visit to President Hoover, in 1929, a prominent Washington correspondent interpreted the conversations to mean that Great Britain and the United States had agreed to pool their navies to enforce peace throughout the world. This explanation was given wide currency, and the American Secretary of State had to deny the truth of the interpretation. The French Foreign Office placed this interpretation on the conversations and did not relinquish it until the London naval conference had got under way several months later, despite the efforts of American diplomats to explain the real nature of the conversations. The explanation had no foundation in fact, for it is an axiom of American

---

[11] Charles Seymour, *The Intimate Papers of Colonel House*, Vol. IV, p. 29.
[12] *Twenty-five Years*, Vol. I, p. 6.

foreign policy that the American people will not approve of any commitment which so much as resembles an alliance.

Although biased explanations usually ensue from prejudice and ignorance, they are frequently the result of attaching too much significance to a trivial or a collateral detail. Suspicious newspapers, therefore, frequently seek for an Ethiopian in the woodpile, although none is lurking there. This attitude was adopted by some British newspapers in 1914 in connection with the repeal by the American Congress of the Panama Canal tolls provision exempting American coastwise shipping, contrary to the Hay-Pauncefote Treaty; the journalists' suspicion was reported by Ambassador Page to the President, as follows:

I'm sometimes driven almost to despair of the newspapers, even of those that we think of as the most careful. For instance, here comes this great triumph of the repeal of the offensive Panama tolls discrimination, which, so far as I know, is an unparalleled achievement—to make a big legislative body reverse itself. [Yet] That perfectly meaningless, asinine amendment receives a degree of attention in the Washington dispatches to the London papers that is discouraging. They pretend that it somehow weakens the repeal and that it shows (somehow, God knows how) that the President's power is weakening. It seems to be the very strongest evidence of the President's personal power. . . . The enemies of the President and the professional enemies of Great Britain all ranged themselves bravely—and fell. Yet they call it a grudging victory. . . .

Queer lot, these fellows [newspaper men]. Yet they do not see the victory; they are impressed; they are grateful; they do admire you—all in their slow, dumb way, but they stick at that amendment. Why was it put there if it means nothing? They constantly do precisely such tricks in Parliament; but when somebody else does such a trick, they suspect some nigger in the woodpile.[13]

Assessing a Personal Motive.—The foregoing examples of unfair assessment of motive apply to the policy of governments rather than to the motives of individuals. It is in connection with the assessment of personal motive in public life that insincerity and ignorance most often reveal themselves. The untutored layman, whose sense of justice is keener than his

---

[13] *Life and Letters of Walter Hines Page,* Vol. III, pp. 61-62.

understanding of the complex milieu in which he lives, is quick
to attribute false motive to wealthy men and to men in public
life. In the "Letters to the Editor" column appear frequent
attacks on the motives of public men. The following example
is typical:

> These college professors who are urging
> the United States to enter the World Court
> are nothing but paid propagandists. If they
> are not receiving money for their articles and
> speeches advising us to become entangled with
> John Bull, then they are either knaves, fools,
> or traitors.
>
> I venture to say that if you will check the
> income of Prof. W. H. Cox, you will find
> some of the same British smell on it that you
> found on the pay that your paper receives for
> printing editorials.
>
> Men like Senator Morris are sooner or
> later going to be the salvation of this country
> by kicking traitors, grafters, and fools out of
> positions where they can sell or influence the
> public of this country.—JUNIUS.

This sort of attack is to be expected from unthinking laymen,
and it was typical of earlier journalists, but it has no excuse
in this day when it comes from the editors of respectable newspapers. We find, however, that some editorial writers, in spite
of their learning, are nevertheless human. For example, in
1929, following the oil scandal disclosures, when Mr. John D.
Rockefeller, Jr. was trying to force Colonel Robert W. Stewart
from the chairmanship of the Standard Oil Company of
Indiana as an object lesson in business ethics, a Milwaukee
newspaper charged that the real reason for Mr. Rockefeller's
demand for Colonel Stewart's resignation "is that Stewart was
not loyal to Standard Oil, but showed signs of siding with
J. P. Morgan and Sir Henri Deterding against the Rockefellers
in the battle for oil."

It has frequently been said that able business men who are
desirous of serving the government of their country, state, or
city are loath to accept public office or appointment because of
the unmerited personal attacks that are sometimes directed at

their motives. This is sometimes true, for it frequently happens that public officials have performed acts and have formulated policies with the purest of motives, only to have their motives impugned by unfriendly editors. In an earlier day we witnessed a great deal of this kind of crimination. For example, Alexander Hamilton's policy of having the national Government assume the debts of the individual states was said by Republican editors to have for its object the enrichment of the rich speculators in state securities at the expense of the ex-soldiers and, indeed, the policy did result in an orgy of speculation to the advantage of the rich, but its real object was to put the national Government on a sound fiscal basis and to establish its credit. Had this policy not been put into effect, a long period of anarchy would probably have resulted during the Napoleonic wars.

When Mr. Philip Snowden, the Labor Chancellor of the British Exchequer, went to a reparations conference at The Hague in 1929 and threatened to break up the conference unless Great Britain were granted an increase in her proportion of the reparation payments, some editors said that he was a pacifist turned jingo, appealing to the base nationalistic interest of the British electorate so that he and his party associates could hold on to their offices. But such an assessment of Mr. Snowden's motives fails to take into consideration his whole career as a pacifist and the pacifist-liberal attitude of his Government on every other international matter at that time up for settlement, such as the Labor party's policy as regards Egypt and India, the League of Nations, obligatory arbitration, and naval armaments. The real explanation of Mr. Snowden's attitude at The Hague is to be found in his temperament and his conviction that England was entitled to a just share of reparations.

Nor could anything have been more unfair, or as untrue as the motives attributed to President Cleveland when, toward the end of his second administration, he sent a sharp message to Congress concerning the Venezuelan boundary dispute with Great Britain. Some Republican editors, during this crucial period in our foreign relations, declared that the President's defiance of Great Britain was only a trick to bring popular support to his unhappy administration; and some Populist editors declared that the President's action was meant to upset the stock market in the interest of Wall Street speculators. The simple truth was that President Cleveland sincerely believed— and later events proved him correct—that a bold stand would not result in war but, on the contrary, would force a softening of the British attitude.[14]

Assessment of personal motives, like the assessment of national policy, must have a basis in reality: the explanation must be consistent with human nature and with the realities of the situation. An example of how some editorial writers disregarded the data of common sense was illustrated in 1927 when they accused President Coolidge of insincerity in issuing his "I do not choose to run for President in 1928" statement. Some editorial writers pointed out that this statement was a political trick to obtain for Mr. Coolidge a renomination without his having to contest for it. This view, however, is not consistent with what we would expect of Mr. Coolidge as a politician: it is quite doubtful that he would risk his reputation for straightforwardness when he could have had the nomination by merely asking for it.[15]

Exposing Bad Motive.—It is not to be understood, however, that all men in business and public life are blameless and that editorial writers should hesitate to reveal trickery and sham in high places. The public welfare demands fearless denunciation of the mountebanks and predatory business men of whom there is an abundance. Intelligent editorial writers— those who understand human nature, who know the associations and affiliations of public men, who understand the forces that give direction to community and national life, who, in short, have insight into realities—are usually able to reveal sham and dishonesty without having to criminate men of unselfish purpose. It is to such editorial writers that we look to enlighten the public when exploiters and demagogues attempt obfuscation of public questions and concealment of their own motives.

---

[14] See F. L. Paxson, *Recent History of the United States,* pp. 210-211, and R. McElroy, *Grover Cleveland,* Vol. II, Chap. VI.
[15] See F. R. Kent, *Political Behavior,* Chap. II.

The method to be employed in exposure of this kind is well illustrated by an instance in which editorial writers exposed the inconsistent votes of certain rural Congressmen on the tariff bill of 1930. In 1929 President Hoover summoned a special session of Congress to provide farm relief by means of a tariff revision in favor of the farmers. The House of Representatives, however, instead of revising the tariff in the interests of farmers, threw a sop to the farmers in the form of some duties on farm products, but increased the duties of several manufactured articles that farmers must buy. Some of the Congressmen elected by agricultural constituencies voted for the bill because the Old Guard Republicans had threatened them with loss of committee assignments in the regular session which was to follow the special session. If these Congressmen had been sincere representatives of their constituents, they would have voted against the bill regardless of the threats to their personal prestige in that political sheepfold, the House of Representatives. They chose, however, to vote for the bill, calculating that either the Senate would rewrite the bill in the interests of agriculture or that the President would veto it, thus avoiding at the last the wrath of their constituents. This practice, however, tends to undermine representative government. When a Congressman subordinates the interests of his constituents to his own personal interests, the House of Representatives becomes no more representative than was the British House of Commons prior to 1867. The practice makes for government by special interests instead of government by public opinion. Unless the people come to understand this weakness of the House of Representatives, nothing can prevent our government from drifting toward oligarchy. Unless a Representative is willing to vote as his constituents expect him to vote, he ought to be retired regardless of whether or not his constituents escape injury as a result of the action of the Senate or the national Executive. But such misrepresentatives will go scot-free if editors do not expose them.

Doubtful Explanations.—The editorial writer who has a background of knowledge can be reasonably sure of most of his conclusions. But there are frequent instances in which he cannot evaluate accurately all the variable factors in a situation and, in consequence, cannot honestly interpret motives and policies. In such instances only two courses are open to him. He can either present his conclusions in a biased manner, drawing a conclusion where no valid conclusion can be drawn, or he can frankly present his conclusions as guesses and without attesting in an authoritative manner to their validity. When the editorial explanation of an event is accompanied by a statement or an inference that it is not presumed to be authoritative, it serves to enlighten the reader but at the same time does not commit the editorial writer to a particular viewpoint.

Such editorial treatment was accorded in several instances to the diplomatic exchanges between the United States and Great Britain in May, 1926. The British Government sent a note to our State Department suggesting that Secretary of the Treasury Mellon revise certain figures relating to the inter-Allied debts which he had embodied in a letter sent to President Hibben of Princeton University.[16] The figures cited by Secretary Mellon purported to show that Great Britain, under the terms of the inter-Allied debt settlement, stood to collect more money from France, Belgium, and Germany than she would be required to pay to the United States. The British note was an unprecedented practice in diplomacy and was equivalent to asking the United States to discipline one of its cabinet members. In consequence, the American State Department replied immediately and bluntly that the United States regarded Secretary Mellon's correspondence with President Hibben as a "purely domestic discussion," and that the United States Government "does not desire to engage in any formal diplomatic exchanges on the subject." Thus the United States picked up the brickbat and hurled it back at Great Britain.

In explaining why Great Britain had indulged in such an unusual diplomatic practice, editorial writers were perplexed. Several explanations were plausible. One was that the British note was meant solely for "domestic consumption"; that is to say, it was an attempt of the Conservative Government to de-

---

[16] A part of this correspondence is reprinted in J. M. Mathews, *American Foreign Relations,* pp. 9-10.

ceive the British electorate by blaming the United States for the enormous tax budget which the Cabinet had just presented in the House of Commons. This was a plausible explanation because the distressing economic situation in Great Britain as compared with the prosperous situation in the United States would lead many British voters to blame the United States for the high taxes rather than the British Government; this trick, moreover, is a favorite device of unfortunate politicians. A second explanation was that the note was a gesture meant to assuage France. This was also plausible because the French press was engaged at the time in attacking Great Britain's relentless policy of collecting her war debt from France and had cited as proof of alleged British harshness the figures used by Secretary Mellon. A third explanation was that the members of the British Cabinet—the Tory die-hards in particular—had "lost their heads" and were irked at the United States for refusing to pull Great Britain's chestnuts out of the fire in connection with the massacre in February of Europeans and Americans by Chinese soldiers at Nanking. This, too, was a plausible explanation, for the United States had refused to join with Great Britain and other European powers in an identic note to the Chinese Nationalist Government demanding unfair guarantees and reparation. Any one of these explanations being plausible, it was not possible to ascribe the British Government's action to a specific motive. Some editorial writers therefore listed all three of the explanations without vouching for the validity of any one of them. These explanations served to enlighten readers, yet they did not commit the editorial writers to a specific opinion.

Explaining the Effect of an Event.—The explanations discussed in the foregoing sections answered the reader's question, "What does this mean?" and their purpose was to enlighten the reader with regard to a paradoxical, mysterious, or elusive situation for which there was no obvious explanation. A different species of interpretative editorial is one which tries to answer the question, *"What will happen next?"* Frequently there is reported an event of great importance which gives rise to such questions as, "How will this incident affect the price of securities?" "How will this affect the political fortunes of President Hoover?" "How will this affect the foreign relations of the United States?" The answers to such questions are discovered only after a review of the historical, sociological, economic, or political data underlying the situation. Editorial analysis of this kind assumes a special knowledge upon the part of the editorial writer of certain economic or sociological phenomena and principles, or of the conditions in a particular foreign country or in a particular section of the United States.

There are various kinds of editorials that predict the effect of an event. A few of them are listed below:

1. President Ebert, the first president of the German Republic and a Socialist, dies before completing his six-year term (1925). What will the effect be? In the ensuing election, will the Socialists again triumph, or has the rising sentiment for monarchy reached the point at which it can overthrow the Republic and the liberal constitution? Will the patriotic feeling engendered by the French occupation of the Ruhr react upon the present republican régime which has been relatively helpless against the Franco-Belgian aggression? Does Ebert's death mean the death of the German Republic?

2. President-elect Obregon, the strong man of Mexico, is assassinated (1928). Does his death mean the end of governmental stability in Mexico? Will the United States finally have to intervene in order to protect the property of American citizens? Will Mexico be left to the mercy of selfish military leaders and bandits? Will the clerical group now come into power and arrest the educational and agrarian reforms? Will the labor group succeed to power and establish a Communist régime? Will President Calles have to remain as an extralegal dictator until conditions shall warrant another attempt to set up self-government?

3. The United States, first among the nations of the world, signs an "equal" tariff treaty with the Chinese Nationalist Government just at the moment when governmental stability in China seems to have been attained (1928). What will this mean to the future of self-government in China? What will it mean to American trade with China? What will it mean to Japan and England—in short, to peace in the Pacific? Does it mean that recognition will follow by other powers and that Japanese soldiers will eventually get out of Manchuria?

4. Congress passes the Sherman Anti-Trust Act which forbids unreasonable combinations in restraint of interstate commerce (1890). Will this act stagnate business? Will it apply to monopoly

in manufacturing as well as to transportation? Will it prevent an interstate railway from purchasing the stock of its competitor? Will it forbid every combination in restraint of trade, or only those combinations which are unreasonable in their final effect? Will the act apply to labor unions that boycott the purchase of certain interstate goods? Will it prevent certain associations of manufacturers from circulating price lists among themselves?

5. The United States Supreme Court hands down a decision which repeals the income tax provision in the so-called Wilson Tariff Bill (1895). Will this make for more or for less prosperity? Will it increase the national discontent and stimulate the growth of Socialist parties? Will it help the Democrats' chances in the next presidential election? Will it mean finally the adoption of a constitutional amendment authorizing Congress to levy a direct tax?

6. The Federal Reserve Board raises the rediscount rate (1920). Will this restrict credit to the extent that the present building boom will decline? Will it hinder the financing and marketing of crops? Will it affect the price level? Will it reduce the value of invoices of stock? Will it restrict speculation in stocks? Will it stimulate the bond market, and, if so, will not this be a good time for the City Council to sell the park improvement bonds authorized by the voters last month?

The editorial writer who prepares editorials of this type must have a special knowledge of the conditions in a particular country or section and an adequate understanding of certain economic, political, and sociological phenomena.

The discussion of editorials that involve causal relation is continued in Chapter V, in which controversial as well as interpretative editorials are examined.

CHAPTER IV

HOW WE THINK

In the previous chapter the attempt was made to present a realistic explanation of how an editorial writer analyzes an event or a situation in order to give it meaning. The chapter described the editorial writer's technique of analysis as it actually proceeds and without reference to the technique employed by the scientific investigator. An examination of both techniques, however, reveals that they are the same: the thinking process of the scientist engaged in solving a problem is almost precisely like that of the editorial writer who analyzes an event or a condition. All thinkers, for that matter, proceed in the same manner, for the thinking process consists—we repeat—*merely in arranging a set of data into a tentative pattern of thought (hypothesis), and then testing the soundness of the pattern by inquiring into the real probabilities of the explanation.*[1]

The Four Steps in Thinking.—Although nearly all of us are capable of thinking straight, it is nevertheless helpful if we analyze the act of thought. John Dewey, who wrote in 1910, *How We Think,* has placed himself in the debt of all of us who desire to do straight thinking. By analyzing several typical acts of thought, Dewey showed that there are five steps in the process. This explanation of how we think is examined in this and subsequent chapters, although we have modified Dewey's explanation by omitting his first step. In our discussion we shall deal with the act of thought as if it consisted of four separate steps.[2]

---

[1] *Supra,* pp. 48 ff.
[2] The first step described by Dewey is termed "the recognition of a problem." A discussion of this step is omitted from our discussion, and we begin our examination as if the first step were "the clarification (definition) of a problem."

The four steps are as follows:

1. The clarification of the problem by identifying or defining it.
2. The rise of suggestions for the solution of the problem and their elaboration into a tentative pattern of explanation. [Induction.]
3. The testing of the tentative conjecture or hypothesis to discover whether or not it is consistent with all the known facts. [Deduction.]
4. [Assuming that the tentative solution has been rejected]— The elaboration of further suggestions into other hypotheses until finally an hypothesis has been constructed which seems to be sound.

Illustration.—The stages of a simple act of thought are illustrated concretely by Dewey, as follows:

Projecting nearly horizontally from the upper deck of the ferryboat on which I daily cross the river, is a long white pole, bearing a gilded ball at its top. It suggested a flagpole when I first saw it; its color, shape, and gilded ball agreed with this idea, and these reasons seemed to justify me in this belief. But soon difficulties presented themselves. The pole was nearly horizontal, an unusual position for a flagpole; in the next place, there was no pulley, ring, or cord by which to attach a flag; finally, there were elsewhere two vertical staffs from which flags were occasionally flown. It seemed probable that the pole was not there for flag-flying.

I then tried to imagine all possible purposes of such a pole, and to consider for which of these it was best suited: (a) Possibly it was an ornament. But as all ferryboats and even the tugboats carried a like pole, this hypothesis was rejected. (b) Possibly it was the terminal of a wireless telegraph. But the same considerations made this improbable. Besides, the more natural place for such a terminal would be the highest part of the boat, on top of the pilot house. (c) Its purpose might be to point out the direction in which the boat was moving.

In support of this conclusion, I discovered that the pole was lower than the pilot house, so that the steersman could easily see it. Moreover, the tip was enough higher than the base, so that, from the pilot's position, it must appear to project far out in front of the boat. Moreover, the pilot being near the front of the boat, he would need some such guide as to its direction. Tugboats would also need poles for such a purpose. This hypothesis was so much more probable than the others that I accepted it. I formed the conclusion that the pole was set up for the purpose of showing the pilot the direction in which the boat pointed, to enable him to steer correctly.[3]

The simple act of thought described in the foregoing paragraphs is as complete as is any act of thought. Except for the fact that the natural scientist can usually submit his hypotheses to laboratory verification, the stages in his thought process and in the thought process of the ferryboat passenger are precisely the same. The first paragraph illustrates the first step in an act of thought, namely, the clarification of the problem; the other paragraphs illustrate the second, third, and fourth steps.

Reasoning: A Shuttle-like Process.[4]—For purposes of analysis we have broken up an act of thought into its "steps," calling the second step (the elaboration of particular suggestions into an hypothesis) induction, and the third step (the testing of the hypothesis by applying it to a known particular) deduction. These steps, in actual thinking, are not as independent of each other as our analysis suggests. Thinking, as a matter of fact, is a shuttle-like movement from induction to deduction and back again. The mind moves, as Professor McClure has explained,

from a problem to some tentative explanatory conception and from that conception back to the initial facts to see if the proposed solution has any explanatory value. It is a kind of "cut and try" procedure. First, you cut to get things in shape, and then you try to see if they fit. Inductive discovery is the cutting; deductive proof is the fitting. In any concrete case of thinking the two processes are continuous. They can be separated only for analysis and description.[5]

Example: the Problem of Sanctions.—The cut-and-try nature of reflection, which was illustrated in the reasoning of the ferryboat passenger, is best exhibited in a complex problem,

---

[3] *How We Think* (D. C. Heath & Co., New York, 1909), pp. 69-70; reprinted by permission. Dewey quotes a class paper submitted by one of his students.

[4] In the discussion that follows we shall consider only the last three steps in an act of thought; the first step—the clarification of a problem— was anticipated in the chapter concerning "Editorials of Definition."

[5] M. T. McClure, *An Introduction to the Logic of Reflection*, pp. 215-219, *passim;* reprinted by permission of Henry Holt & Co.

and especially in a problem of public policy which is conditioned by the realities of national self-interest. The problem of how to provide security against international war is such a problem. Since international conflicts will always arise, the problem of preserving peace is chiefly one of substituting judicial settlement for the traditional ordeal by force. This involves, first, the establishment of an accepted international tribunal which will designate as "aggressor" that nation which refuses to abide by the rule of submitting a dispute to judicial settlement or to abide by the settlement after it has been made; and, second, the application of some coercive measure against the violator of the rule.[6]

That much is simple enough; but what kind of coercive measure—"sanction," it is called—shall be applied?[7] In answer, several suggestions come to mind, namely, military sanctions, economic sanctions, and the sanction of public opinion. Some minds jump at the suggestion of military sanctions. Why not, they inquire, establish a League of Nations which, in the event of a breach of the international peace, will designate the aggressor state and will require all other member states of the League to join in enforcing peace on the aggressor nation?

This suggestion has much to recommend it. It was put forward in the United States during the World War by the League to Enforce Peace and was indorsed by President Wilson; it is the central scheme vaguely envisaged by Article X of the League of Nations Covenant.[8] Yet, the member states do not agree at the present time as to how this sanction should be applied; nor do they agree even that it ought to be applied. A few members favor the creation of an international police force,

---

[6] See Articles XII, XIII, and XV of the League of Nations Covenant. The value of conciliation is ignored in this discussion, and the term *judicial settlement* is not used in its technical sense.

[7] An excellent discussion of this problem, though not an up-to-date one, is contained in D. Mitrany, *The Problem of Sanctions* (London, 1925), and J. M. Spaight, *Pseudo-Security* (London, 1928). See also, Salvador de Madariaga, *Disarmament* (London and New York, 1929).

[8] "The Members of the League undertake to respect and preserve as against external aggression the territorial integrity and existing political independence of all Members of the League. In case of any such aggression or in case of any threat or danger of such aggression the Council shall advise upon the means by which this obligation shall be fulfilled." See also Article XI.

and a few favor the creation of a League of Nations air force, but some others are not willing to contribute their armaments to any such military and naval force. The United States has even refused to join the League of Nations because of the possibility that Article X would permit of the application of military sanctions; for the people of the United States, like most other peoples, are reluctant to "fight on foreign soil in a foreign cause," especially if such intervention is calculated to preserve the "iniquitous" provisions of the Treaty of Versailles. Nor is Great Britain, in the present circumstances, willing to have her navy used to enforce peace upon an aggressor nation. So far from willingness to rely on military sanctions are several member-states that this solution of the peace problem is recognized at the present time as being unavailable as a blanket solution.

A second suggestion is the application of economic sanctions. The League of Nations Covenant provides for this sanction in Article XVI,[9] but it does not meet all the objections of the United States; nor does it meet objections of several other nations inasmuch as the precise character of economic sanctions has never been defined. It is quite possible that economic sanctions capriciously applied would do more harm to some of the nations applying them than to the culprit nation. The character of economic sanctions which have been either suggested or provided for include the refusal to trade and communicate with the aggressor, the rendering of financial assistance to the nation attacked, and the establishment of a "pacific" blockade against the aggressor. The blockade sanction, since it would be contrary to international law in so far as states not members of the League are concerned, would be a peculiarly difficult one to apply. Great Britain, for example, would be called upon

---

[9] "Should any Member of the League resort to war in disregard of its covenants under Articles XII, XIII, or XV, it shall *ipso facto* be deemed to have committed an act of war against all other Members of the League, which hereby undertake immediately to subject it to the severance of all trade or financial relations, the prohibition of all intercourse between persons residing in their territory, persons residing in the territory of the Covenant-breaking State, and the prevention of all financial, commercial, or personal intercourse between persons residing in the territory of the Covenant-breaking State and persons residing in any other State, whether a Member of the League or not."

to use her great navy for blockade purposes, but she would have no assurance that the United States would not disregard the blockade as she would be entitled to do under international law. British statesmen do not believe that they could afford to risk a war with the United States in order to enforce this sanction, and, as a consequence, it is being urged that the United States, a nonmember of the League, ought now to declare as a matter of policy that it would not trade with a Covenant-breaking state. But the United States at the present writing (1931) has not been willing to make this declaration, although resolutions embodying such a declaration have been before the Senate Committee on Foreign Relations since February, 1929. The United States does not wish to make such a definite commitment for such indefinite circumstances. Recalling the present inability of historians positively to assess "war guilt" in connection with the World War, the United States is by no means certain that the League's designation of the aggressor would not be a political rather than a just designation. Thus a vicious circle of distrust exists which makes the application of the provisions of Article XVI so uncertain that the nations of the world continue to rely on self-help as their best means of "security."

The third sanction is that of public opinion, and the United States is the chief nation which advocates it. Unable to agree to either military or economic sanctions, the United States has advanced this sanction in the form of the Kellogg-Briand treaty to "outlaw" war.[10] Although this treaty provides no penalty for violation of the rule laid down in the treaty (that is, that nations shall not resort to arms), yet the implication is that the public opinion of the world is sufficient deterrent to an aggressor. The nations, of course, do not believe that public opinion in itself is adequate to deter an aggressor nation, as is evidenced by their failure to reduce appreciably their armaments. But this sanction is the only one to which the United States at the present time is willing to agree. Thus far

---

[10] See J. T. Shotwell, *War as an Instrument of National Policy and Its Renunciation in the Pact of Paris*. For a criticism of the Pact, see Salvador de Madariaga, *Disarmament*.

the United States has not even been willing to declare that it will refuse to furnish munitions to a belligerent nation.[11]

The foregoing discussion of the problem of sanctions, which exhibits the cut-and-try nature of reflection, is typical of those problems which involve public policy. It shows that thinking consists chiefly in elaborating suggestions and then pursuing the consequence of the suggestions. In this problem, the final stage, of course, has not been completed. It is an unsolved problem.

Example: Unemployment Insurance.—The cut-and-try nature of thinking is also illustrated in another unsolved problem— that of unemployment. Until 1931, Americans had attacked the problem of periodic unemployment by the method of providing temporary charitable relief until business conditions themselves had remedied the condition. In 1931, however, when upwards of seven million workers were out of employment, we considered unemployment insurance as a possible remedy. But Americans could not agree as to whether insurance plans should be inaugurated voluntarily by employers or whether the state should make unemployment insurance compulsory for employers, just as it had earlier made workmen's accident compensation compulsory. Those who advocated the compulsory plan were met with the assertions that it was "socialistic" and that it would result in a "dole" system. Those who advocated the voluntary plan were met with two assertions: (a) that the small number of such plans then in existence showed that most employers would not undertake an insurance plan if not compelled to do so; and (b) that those employers who, in the absence of state compulsion voluntarily inaugurated the plan, would have higher production costs than their competitors who refused to inaugurate the plan. While this debate was in progress in state legislatures and the national Congress, millions of men and their families were in want.

It is beyond the scope of this book to suggest a definitive solution of the problem, but the student might well explore the

---

[11] As provided for in the Capper, Porter, and Burton resolutions placed before Congress in 1928 and 1929. For a discussion of these resolutions, see Foreign Policy Association, *Information Service*, Vol. VI, No. 9, "The United States and the League of Nations."

situation in all its aspects, inquiring as to what is meant by the "dole" (has it been misrepresented?) ; as to what has been the experience of European countries with compulsory unemployment insurance ; as to what voluntary plans have succeeded and why; as to whether legislation, if any, should be enacted by the national Government or by the separate state legislatures, etc.[12]

The Nature of Generalization.—Generalization is the name we apply to a general truth derived by the process of induction. A scientific "law," for example, is a generalization from particular data. The particulars are observed as to characteristic *resemblances,* and a general truth is induced as to their resemblance in respect of some point or points. A generalization, in other words, is a statement as to the *relation* of the particulars of a class in respect of some characteristic. The hypothesis of organic evolution—that all forms of animal life have descended from a common ancestry—is one of the most sweeping generalizations ever made. It is based on an observation of the *resemblance* of the various species of animal life. The proof of the generalization is furnished by the phenomena of embryology, comparative anatomy, paleontology, and blood tests. In comparative anatomy, for example, it is observed that animals have *homologous* structures: "the foreleg of a lizard, the wing of a bird and of a bat, the burrowing shovel of a mole, the flipper of a whale, the foreleg of a horse, and the human hand" are homologous in structure. Observing these phenomena, the natural scientist infers a generalization,

[12] The following references will be helpful: P. H. Douglas and Aaron Director, *The Problem of Unemployment;* A. B. Forsberg (ed.), *Selected Articles on Unemployment Insurance;* Lewisohn, Commons, Draper, and Lescohier, *Can Business Prevent Unemployment?;* "Germany's New Unemployment Insurance," *American Labor Legislation Review,* Vol. XIX (March, 1929), pp. 97-105; "Unemployment Insurance in Foreign Countries," *Labor Review Monthly,* Vol. XXVII (December, 1928), pp. 62-72; H. B. Butler, *Unemployment Insurance in the United States* and *Unemployment Problems in 1931; International Labour Office Annual Review* (1930) ; Mary B. Gilson, *Unemployment Insurance in Great Britain,* Vol. II; Harold Callender's series of articles in the New York *Times* (Sunday, Section 9) on unemployment insurance systems in various countries, Oct. 4, Oct. 11, Oct. 18, Oct. 25, Nov. 1, 1931. A vast ephemeral literature in this subject was produced in 1930 and 1931, and many books and reports were published which are too numerous to mention.

namely, that these homologous structures are modifications of a single primitive type—that is to say, that all animals have a common ancestor.

To the scientist, the theory of organic evolution is a working hypothesis that is acceptable because the only other possible theory of the relation of the various forms of life—the "special creation" theory—is plainly not true; when tested, it is found to be inconsistent with the known facts. Other scientific generalizations, such as Newton's laws of motion and Joule's laws of heat, admit of empirical verification. In the field of human phenomena, however, generalization is seldom verifiable. When, for example, the editorial writer generalizes as to principles and policies and conduct, the best that he can do is to adduce a great many particulars which are alike in respect of some point of the principle, the policy, or the mode of conduct under discussion, and trust to logic to prove his hypothesis. If he argues that slavery is always an evil and is never justifiable, he can adduce so many particulars from the past experience of the race that his generalization will be accepted; but when he asserts the proposition that capital punishment is a deterrent to murders, his opponents can cite just as many particulars to substantiate a contrary theory.[13]

The Causes of Unsound Thinking.—The thinking process of some persons frequently ends with the second step. That is to say, they derive a generalization and accept it without testing its validity. Their failure to complete the thinking process may be due to several causes. In the first place, they may be so *unfamiliar with the subject matter that only a few suggestions come to their minds,* and, as a consequence, they are unable to elaborate any hypothesis but an inadequate one. An uninformed editorial writer, for example, who would jump to the conclusion that the American Federation of Labor, in 1927, did not object to the admission of Mexican laborers because most Mexican laborers are unskilled would be furnishing his readers with an inadequate explanation;[14] likewise, the

---

[13] The only alternative to solving a problem by logic is social experimentation. See pp. 236-237.

[14] *Supra,* pp. 47 *ff.*

editorial writers who explained the Anglo-American disagreement at the 1927 naval conference as being due solely to the presence of admirals and propagandists lacked adequate knowledge of diplomatic history and consequently were not capable of elaborating a complete explanation.[15]   Unless we have knowledge (experience) to furnish us with suggestions, we can elaborate only a few hypotheses, and may, in consequence, come to accept one that is invalid.

In the second place, hasty generalization may be due to the fact that *the thinker is too lazy intellectually* to pursue a thought to more than a superficial depth; or it may be due to the fact that he is a visionary who evolves a theory from ready data because he lacks the intellectual vigor to harmonize theory and fact, as illustrated in the case of the "outlawry of war" school of peace-workers, led by Senator Borah, who are eager to believe that public opinion is an adequate sanction for the prevention of war and that there is no necessity for an organization of the international community.

A third cause of false generalization is *intellectual dishonesty.* This is frequently evidenced in the thinking that is done about certain major social evils and their causes. How to reduce the postwar crime wave, for example, is a problem that is challenging editorial thought, and some newspapers are attributing prohibition as the sole cause, just as prohibitionists formerly attributed alcoholic liquor as the sole cause. Problems of this character do not admit of simple analysis. The editorial writer who names prohibition as the sole cause of recent lawlessness has obviously not completed his analytical process. His observation (study) has presented the suggestion that prohibition is the sole cause of postwar lawlessness, and he has accepted the hypothesis without testing its consistency with other facts. But he is not an honest thinker if he regards this explanation as final. If he is to derive a valid conclusion, he must seek for other suggestions, must elaborate new hypotheses, and must test them all for consistency with fact. It is in this process that the third step in the thinking process—deduction—is valuable.

---

[15] *Supra,* pp. 51-57.

Testing an Hypothesis.—What is the deductive method by which the thinker tests his conjecture or hypothesis? Only a brief explanation will be given here because a subsequent chapter deals exclusively with the methods of deduction. Essentially, the testing of hypotheses consists in the pursuit of an "if . . . then" train of thought. That is to say, it consists in reasoning out the consequences that are involved in the conjecture or the hypothesis that our mind is entertaining. It is the reasoning out of these consequences, moreover, *by the aid of our memory and our imagination.* Referring to Professor Dewey's problem of the ferryboat pole with the gilded ball,[16] we observe the operation of this "if . . . then" method of testing conjecture. *"If* the pole is an ornament, *then* why do tugboats have them, too?" *"If* the pole is used as the terminal of a wireless telegraph, *then* why do tugboats have them, too, and why, *then,* isn't the pole on the highest part of the boat?" *"If* the pole is used by the pilot to point out the direction of the boat, *then* . . . well, I see . . . that is exactly what the pole is used for; isn't it lower than the pilot house so that the pilot can see it, etc.?"

It is thus, by using our memory and our imagination, that we are able to evaluate suggestions. Our *past experience* tells us that such and such an object has a certain purpose or a certain relation, that such and such a thing belongs in a certain class, and that such and such a mode of conduct has certain consequences.

Editorial writers, in discussing events and policies, think in precisely this manner. A political phenomenon, let us say, demands an explanation. Immediately, if the editorial writer has had *experience* as a political writer or observer, one or more explanations (hypotheses) present themselves. The editorial writer's success in testing these explanations is dependent on his knowledge of politics *previously acquired.* Say, for instance, that in February, 1898, immediately after the sinking of the *Maine,* a war with Spain is threatened and certain Republican Senators, hitherto known to be jingoes in their attitude toward Spanish rule in Cuba, rush into print with

---

[16] *Supra,* pp. 73-74.

statements counseling peace. Why do they do it? Have they, in all sincerity, changed their bellicose attitude to one of pacificism? This explanation is almost instantly discarded by the editorial writer, for he knows from his contacts with professional politicians that nine times out of ten they are motivated either by partisan or by personal interest rather than by sincere conviction. It may be, he reflects, self-interest, that is, the championing of a policy because it is favored by one's constituents. But *if* it is self-interest, *then* why do they not keep up their character as jingoes? Would they not be bigger popular heroes if they demanded freedom for Cuba? But probably it is partisan interest which motivates them. If it is a partisan interest, then . . . Yes, it is partisan interest . . . I see now . . . the administration wants to avoid a war and these partisan Senators *are merely upholding the policy of the administration:* a political party must have solidarity. But what is the proof of this conjecture? The test is simple—for the editorial writer who has knowledge of practical politics. He *remembers,* perhaps, how such matters were handled between the White House and Congress when he was a Washington correspondent, and he now *imagines* a White House breakfast to which these Senators had just been invited and requested to fall into line with the administration's policy; if not a White House breakfast, then some other subtle pressure by the President's personal representatives in Congress. The experienced political writer knows the signs that he sees; he understands the meaning of certain actions. His reasoning is simply common sense; his so-called insight is merely the result of his past experiences projected on the field of his imagination.[17]

Experience Gained from Reading.—The editorial writer cannot interpret all events, nor can he expound important questions if he relies solely on his concrete personal observations made during his past experience: he must also have experiences gained from reading history and other subjects. Sup-

---

[17] For a more comprehensive discussion of the "if . . . then" process, see E. A. Burtt, *Principles and Problems of Right Thinking* (Harper & Bros., New York, 1928), Chap. IV, and Columbia Associates in Philosophy, *An Introduction to Reflective Thinking* (Houghton Mifflin Co., Boston, 1923), Chap. V. See also Chap. IX, *infra.*

pose, for example, that an editorial writer, at the beginning of the business depression in 1929, had desired to explain the nature of the business cycle (i.e., the periodical fluctuations of boom and depression) : he must know economic history and the principles of economics. The question of what causes periods of business prosperity and depression has long vexed economists. Professor Jevons several years ago evolved the theory that sun-spots affect the size of crops and consequently cause business cycles. An "if . . . then" test of the consequences of this theory shows that it is not true: "*If* sun-spots cause business cycles, *then* why do not business cycles occur every ten years, as sun-spots do?" Unless the editorial writer *knew* that sun-spots occurred approximately every ten years and that business cycles did not occur with such regularity, he could not test Professor Jevons's theory.

Nor could the editorial writer test the Marxian theory of business cycles if he did not know something about economics. That theory is as follows: during a period of prosperity more goods are produced than the public can consume, and, as a consequence, a business depression ensues and continues until production and consumption again become balanced. This theory is likely to be accepted—in fact, it is widely accepted—unless one understands the nature of exchange. It is not true, however. It is not possible for a community to have so little purchasing power that it cannot buy all the goods produced; for the goods produced are the purchasing power that is exchanged for the goods produced. That is to say, "prosperity" is a status of balanced production; it endures as long as each producer of a commodity can exchange his goods for another's goods. The goods produced by one producer constitute the 'demand" for the goods of other producers. Unless the editorial writer, in 1929, understood this principle of economics, he could not have reasoned out the consequences of the hypothesis: he could not have thought, "*If* business cycles are caused by overproduction, *then* how is it that production of goods can exceed purchasing power?"

Experience gained from reading is a necessary part of the editorial writer's equipment. If one wishes to understand the truth of this statement, let him read in the files of the *Nation* the editorials of E. L. Godkin, who was steeped in a knowledge of history, jurisprudence, and "political economy," and compare them with the editorials of Godkin's contemporaries. Godkin's knowledge gave him such an insight into the current questions of his day that one who now reads his editorials marvels at his understanding.

On the other hand, a knowledge gained from reading, unless it be vitally affected by one's concrete association with realities, results in an academic and doctrinaire attitude toward public questions.[18] The fault of relying entirely on books and of hugging closely a pet theory cannot be laid to Godkin, who was no doctrinaire in the sense that Greeley was; but one who has studied Godkin's reasoning at the end of his career in the nineties cannot suppress the feeling that Godkin viewed some of the newer problems of democracy and industrialism with an academic and aristocratic detachment. When one reads the columns of the New York *World* during the same period and contrasts its editorial viewpoint with that of Godkin's *Nation* and *Evening Post,* he cannot but wonder at Godkin's lack of sympathy for the common man and his disillusionment as regards the theory of democracy, an attitude which reflected a detachment from the real concerns of life. Godkin, of course was no long-haired theorist or visionary, but the universities and pulpits today have a goodly number. Journalism, of course, has need for more scholars, but it is obvious, too, that the editorial chair is no place for a doctrinaire.

---

[18] A few college professors and editors, in their attitude toward public questions, are somewhat akin to the schoolboy whom Dr. Edwin E. Slosson described: "In one of our largest high schools where a reference librarian is employed to provide books needed for theme writing, a boy lounged up to the desk and remarked, 'Gimme the books for today's theme.' 'What is the topic?' asked the librarian. 'What I Saw on the Way to School This Morning,' replied the boy."—Address before the American Association for Adult Education, at Cleveland, Ohio, May 26, 1927.

CHAPTER V

CAUSAL AND FUNCTIONAL RELATIONS

The Relation of Things.—When we think, we merely relate one thing to another. Right thinking consists in relating one thing rightly to another, that is, in inferring a right relation of the terms used in our thinking. Suppose we are thinking about "war" and in that connection we entertain the idea, "diplomat." What is the relation of "war" and "diplomat"? Do diplomats *cause* war? Many naïve men have said so; and if one happens to have just been reading S. B. Fay's *The Origins of the World War,* his mind may be so filled with facts about diplomats and their relation to war that he may assume a close relation of the two terms. If, however, he had previously read Anton Mohr's *The Oil War,* or Francis Delaisi's *Oil: Its Influence on World Politics,* his mind will have entertained the idea of "commercial rivalry" in relation to "war," and, as a consequence, when he comes to read the diplomatic history of the origins of the World War he is not so impressed with the relation of "war" and "diplomat" as to assume as a universal proposition that wars are always caused by diplomats. On the contrary, he may come to believe—especially if he has just been reading the minutes of a particular meeting of the League of Nations Council—that diplomats sometimes prevent war.

The relation of the terms "war" and "diplomat," whatever that relation is, is expressed by a verb. When we come to examine, in Chapter IX, the nature of propositions, we shall perceive the importance of expressing the relation of terms correctly. Sometimes the relation inferred of two terms is one of *inclusion,* as in the categorical proposition, "All horses are quadrupeds," the copula *are* expressing the inclusion of horses in a class—quadrupeds. Sometimes the relation inferred is a *causal* relation, as "Haste makes (causes) waste" and "Germs cause disease."

This chapter is chiefly concerned with an examination of the last kind of inference—that which involves a causal relation; it also examines another type of relation not yet mentioned, namely, *functional* relation. The other types of relation are considered in subsequent chapters.

Hasty Generalization.—Causal relation is not always easy to perceive and verify. We frequently mistake a mere association of things for a causal relation. A factor is not causal merely because it is associated with an effect. For a factor to be causal, it must meet two requirements: (*a*) it must be antecedent to the effect; and (*b*) it must be an indispensable antecedent. We seldom forget to consider the first requirement—antecedence. Indeed, we are more likely to assume that mere antecedence means cause. Most of our superstitions, for example, arise out of this confusion of antecedence with true cause. A man who observes a black cat cross his path and who immediately afterward suffers a misfortune makes the inference that the cat is the cause of his ill luck. This fallacy, which has been named *post hoc, ergo propter hoc* ("after that, therefore because of that"), occurs frequently in public discussion. Some economists assert that the so-called law of economics that, in the course of a business depression, wages must follow the decline of prices and interest rates before there can be recovery from the depression is such a fallacy. The "historical" school of economists—i.e., those who try to predict the course of business cycles by observing the movements of prices, wages, and interest rates in past depressions—point to the fact that always recovery has occurred *after* a decline in prices, wages, and interest rates. But, say some other economists, this is no proof that wages must *necessarily* come down before recovery can take place: it is quite possible that recovery would occur without employers reducing wages. There is no positive answer to this debate because in all past depressions employers have reduced wages.[1]

---

[1] For a statement of these two contrary views with specific reference to the last business depression, see the articles by T. J. Wertenbaker and Leo Wolman in *Current History*, Vol. XXXV (October, 1931), pp. 16-24.

More often, however, we overlook the second requirement: we infer that some factor is the cause of a phenomenon without taking the trouble to inquire as to whether or not it is an indispensable cause. We must not only inquire as to whether an antecedent factor was *present* in every instance in which the phenomenon occurred, but we must inquire as to whether it was ever *absent* when the phenomenon occurred. It may happen that a specific factor is invariably present when a phenomenon occurs, but unless we know that the phenomenon does *not* occur in the absence of this factor, we cannot be sure that it is a cause of the phenomenon.

Mill's Methods.—Specific methods for verifying inductive hypotheses which involve causal relations were first devised by John Stuart Mill (following Herschel). These methods are five in number, but essentially they involve only two principles. Mill states them as follows:

> The simplest and most obvious modes of singling out from among the circumstances which precede or follow a phenomenon, those with which it is really connected by an invariable law, are two in number. One is, by comparing together different instances in which the phenomenon occurs. The other is by comparing instances in which the phenomenon does occur, with instances in other respects similar in which it does not. These two methods may be respectively denominated the Method of Agreement and the Method of Difference.[2]

Mill might also have called them the principles of "presence" and "absence." We shall examine four of these five methods separately.

1. *Method of Agreement.*—If two or more instances of the phenomenon under investigation have only one circumstance in common, the circumstance in which alone all the instances agree is the cause (or effect) of the given phenomenon.[3]

This method may be represented symbolically as follows: If a set of circumstances a,b,c,d,e produce the effect K, and the set of circumstances a,l,m,n,o also produce the effect K, then

---

[2] *A System of Logic,* Book III, Chap. VIII.
[3] *Ibid.*

we can assume that the *common* factor *a* is the cause of the effect *K*.

How the method may be used in the field of social phenomena is illustrated by Professor Clarke, as follows:

Suppose, for example, that we wish to know the cause of agitation all over the world on the part of peoples who are demanding either political independence or the transfer of the region in which they live from the rule of one nation to that of another. Between 1920 and 1928 such agitations, amounting at times to revolutions, occurred in the Riff, India, Egypt, Syria, Haiti, Nicaragua, and the Philippine Islands; in parts of Poland, Lithuania, and Italy; and in some of the ports of China which were held by European nations, to cite at random the first cases which come to mind. We have now to inquire what circumstances, if any, all of these cases have in *common*. Plainly the movements could not have been the result of racial temperament; they were found among white, black, and yellow peoples. They could not have been the result of poverty; some of the regions concerned were enjoying unprecedented prosperity. They could not have been the effect of economic discrimination; in several of these localities the people were treated as full citizens of the land to which they were supposed to owe allegiance. In this manner the elimination will continue. Finally this point will be examined and it will be discovered to have been common to all the groups concerned, namely, *resentment at being subject to a government which was not chosen by the governed.* We may therefore make the induction that the simple desire for self-determination was the basic, though, of course, not the only cause of the unrest under consideration.[4]

2. *The Method of Difference.*—If an instance in which the phenomenon under investigation occurs, and an instance in which it does not occur, have every circumstance in common save one, that one occurring only in the former; [then] the circumstance in which alone the two instances differ is the effect or the cause, or an indispensable part of the cause, of the phenomenon.[5]

This method may be represented symbolically as follows: If a set of circumstances *a,b,c,d,e* are followed by the effect *K,* and a set of circumstances *a,b,c,d* are not followed by the effect *K,* then the circumstance *e* is the cause of the effect *K* or is causally related to it.

---

[4] E. L. Clarke, *The Art of Straight Thinking* (D. Appleton & Co., New York, 1929), pp. 166-167. Italics not in original.
[5] Mill, *op. cit.*

As an example, when Pasteur was trying to verify his hypothesis that the appearance of bacteria in a liquid was caused by some substance in the air, he filled a series of vessels with a sterilized liquid and arranged that the air could enter some of the vessels but not the others. Observing, then, that bacteria appeared in only those vessels in which air could enter, he had proof of his hypothesis that organisms carried by the air produced the bacteria. Thus the several instances had every factor in common save one, and that one, occurring in the former, was the cause of the phenomenon.

The difficulty in applying the Method of Difference to social problems is the difficulty of conditioning the investigation so that the two instances have *every circumstance in common save one*. For example, the Governor of Maryland, in 1929, declared that prohibition was the cause of lawlessness in certain American cities. He pointed to Chicago, in which the criminal situation was terrifying, and to Baltimore, in which the criminal situation was being "successfully handled." Chicago, he said, "is in Illinois which has a state prohibition act, but Baltimore is in Maryland which has never incorporated the Volstead Act into state law." This statement of causal relation undoubtedly has much truth, but it is an unreliable generalization because it does not consider any of the other possible causes of crime in Chicago as compared with Baltimore. If one is to make scientific application of the Method of Difference, he must make sure that the two instances examined have every circumstance in common *save one*.[6]

---

[6] Prohibition doubtless is the major cause of crime in Chicago, for the enormous profits accruing from the illegal liquor traffic provide criminals with vast funds for bribery, intimidation, and the employment of able attorneys. But it is probable that if prohibition were not in effect, the crime situation in Chicago would still be worse than it was prior to the inauguration of prohibition. According to the Chicago Employers' Association, business rackets cost Chicago $136,000,000 in 1929; enormous sums have been stolen from the public funds and from individual taxpayers by the assessing officials and by employes in some of the other governing bodies; the gambling racket is enormously profitable; and the inadequate administration of criminal justice and the inadequate criminal code of the State of Illinois are largely to blame for the city's inability to punish and prevent crime. In this connection, see the letter of the Crime Investigating Committee of the Chicago Church Federation to the Association of Commerce, published in the Chicago *Tribune*, July 9, 1930.

Although neither the Method of Agreement nor the Method of Difference alone is always reliable in social investigation, a combination of the two methods is more likely to locate the true causal relation.

3. *The Joint Method of Agreement and Difference.*—If two or more instances in which the phenomenon occurs have only one circumstance in common, while two or more instances in which it does not occur have nothing in common save the absence of that circumstance, the circumstance in which alone the two sets of instances differ is the effect, or the cause, or an indispensable part of the cause, of the phenomenon.[7]

This method may be represented symbolically as follows:

If the circumstances
a,b,c,d produce the effect K;
and a,b,x,y produce the effect K;
and a,b,l,m produce the effect K;
then both a and b are probably causally related to K.

But if
a,e,i,o do not produce the effect K;
and a,u,v,w do not produce the effect K;
and a,x,y,z do not produce the effect K;
then b is probably causally related to K, but not a.

A simple illustration of the method is Darwin's experiment upon the cross-fertilization of flowers.

Darwin placed a net about one hundred flower heads to protect them from bees. At the same time he exposed another hundred flowers to the bees. Here we have the two groups between which comparison is to be made. He obtained the following results: the protected flowers failed to yield a single seed, while the others produced 68 grains' weight of seed, which he estimated as numbering 2,720 seeds.[8]

The Joint Method is essentially a case study method. The investigator collects information regarding a certain question from various instances, noting both the resemblances and the

7 Mill, *op. cit.*
8 R. W. Sellars, *The Essentials of Logic* (Houghton Mifflin Co., Boston, 1917), p. 224.

differences of the cases. For example, an investigator wishes
to discover the cause of a typhoid fever epidemic in a college
community. He studies conditions, first, in each fraternity and
boarding house in which there was a reported illness to see if
any food factor is *common* to all of them; and second, he studies
other fraternity and boarding houses—that is, those in which
no case of illness was reported—to discover whether the *absence*
of any of the food factors found in the former houses will give
him a clew as to the cause of the epidemic. For example, first,
he discovers that all the "ill" houses obtained water and milk
from the same source, namely, the city water supply and
Warren's Dairy, but obtained meat and green vegetables from
different sources. He constructs a table as follows:

METHOD OF AGREEMENT

House	Water	Vegetables	Meat	Milk
Betas	City water	Jordan's	Johnson's	Warren's
Kappas	City water	Miller's	Schultz's	Warren's
A. O. Pi's	City water	Jordan's	Baker's	Warren's
Rundell's	City water	Thomas's	Green's	Warren's

He infers that *either* the city water supply or the milk supply
(i.e., Warren's Dairy) could be the source of the epidemic.
But to make sure which it is, if either, he investigates some of
the fraternity and boarding houses in which no cases of illness
were reported. He constructs a table as follows:

METHOD OF DIFFERENCE

House	Water	Milk	Vegetables	Meat
S. A. E.'s	City water	Jones's	Miller's	Green's
Dekes	City water	Jones's	Hill's	Schultz's
Delts	City water	Jones's	Jordan's	Baker's
Morris's	City water	Jones's	Thomas's	Schultz's

Since both the "ill" and the "well" groups had the same
source of water supply, the inference suggested in the first
table that either the water or the milk supply is responsible will
have to be revised; for the "well" houses had the same source

of water supply as the "ill" houses. Obviously, water cannot be the cause of the epidemic. The milk supply, however, is the only factor that is *common* to all the "ill" houses and is *absent* from all the "well" houses; therefore, it is probably the causal factor.

The Joint Method was used by a writer for the *Saturday Evening Post* who analyzed the statistics regarding bank failures [9] in the United States. The following is an adaptation of his argument.

A total of 5,600 banks failed during the past nine years. Of the various causes which have been assigned, two can be eliminated as not being characteristic. These are defalcation of officers, and crop failures. Very few banks have failed because of the criminal act of officers. Crop failures cannot cause a bank to fail unless there are several successive crop failures in the locality, and it is an exceptional community which has a succession of crop failures.

Two other probable causes of bank failures are too many small banks, and land booms. It is the first of these two factors which has led to the suggestion that branch banks should supplant the independent banks in small communities: the advocates of branch banking point out that of the 5,600 banks which failed in the last nine years more than 60 per cent had a capital of $25,000 or less and were located in towns of 1,000 population or less. The advocates of branch banking jump to a hasty generalization, however, when they assume that bank failures are chiefly caused by the existence of too many small banks; for in sections in which bank failures have been epidemic, thousands of small banks, which were conservatively managed, have survived. A small independent bank *can* be as safe as a large one. Although Iowa had 528 bank failures in nine years, Connecticut had only two; although Florida and Georgia had 499 failures, Vermont and New Hampshire had only one. If we are to account for bank failures, we must look elsewhere for the causal factor instead of merely in the size of banks and communities.

The chief factor that has caused bank failures is the land

---

[9] "Preventable Bank Failures," Aug. 16, 1930, p. 6*ff.*

boom.   Wherever there have been many bank failures, there we find a land boom that has exploded.   The failure of a bank does not always follow immediately after a land boom has ended, but

McCutcheon in Chicago Tribune

CAUSE ESTABLISHED BY OBSERVING THE PRESENCE AND ABSENCE OF
A COMMON FACTOR

usually sometime afterward.   Two-thirds of the bank failures of the last nine years were in eleven states in which there had been land booms.   More than a thousand bank failures were in Florida, Iowa, and Georgia.   Against these localities which had land booms, place New England and New Jersey, which, with $2,500,000,000 more in deposits, had only eighteen bank failures in nine years.

Neither the Method of Difference nor the Joint Method, however, is sufficient for locating a causal factor when the conditions are such that one cannot say with assurance that certain factors are totally absent. We noticed this situation in discussing the Method of Difference in our reference to the relation of crime and prohibition in Baltimore and Chicago. Mill, however, devised another method which is sometimes to be employed under such conditions. He called it the Method of Concomitant Variations.

4. *Method of Concomitant Variations.*—Whatever phenomenon varies in any manner, whenever another phenomenon varies in some particular manner, is either a cause or an effect of that phenomenon, or is connected with it through some fact of causation.[10]

This method is frequently applied to commonplace problems when two factors vary in a constant relationship. For example, it is obvious that the position of the moon is a causal factor in the ebb and flow of tides; and everybody has observed that the number of cases of certain pulmonary diseases, such as pneumonia, varies with the seasons.

How the physical scientist makes use of the method is illustrated by Pasteur's test of his hypothesis that dust particles in the air are carriers of germs. Pasteur filled twenty bulbs with a putrescible liquid, removed the air, and sealed the bulbs hermetically. He carried them to a place near the city streets, and opened them. Microörganisms appeared in all of them. Then he filled and sealed sixty other bulbs from which the air had been removed. He carried twenty into the open country, twenty to Jura (850 meters above sea level), and twenty to Montavert (2,000 meters above sea level). At each place he opened them, allowing the air to rush in, and quickly sealed them. On examination he found that in the twenty bulbs carried into the open country there were eight which contained microörganisms, in the second twenty there were five, and in

[10] Mill, *op. cit.*

the third twenty there was only one. Arranged in tabular form, the results were:

Montavert	1 bulb
Jura	5 bulbs
Open country	8 bulbs
Near city streets	20 bulbs

Thus there was found a concomitant variation—a reciprocal relationship—between the appearance of microörganisms and the density of the air: where the dust particles were densest, more germs were found.

The Nature of Explanation.—In following the foregoing discussion of Pasteur's experiments, the reader may have noted that Pasteur was engaged not merely in discovering the cause of bacteria, but the explanation of bacteria. Scientific investigation is often concerned with the discovery of universal explanations of phenomena rather than merely the cause of their behavior. Although Mill spoke of the Method of Concomitant Variations as one which is applied when causal relation is to be determined, the method has a much broader application. The universal scientific "laws," such as Pasteur's explanation of the origin of bacteria and Joule's kinetic theory of heat, are broad, organic explanations of the relations of phenomena.

In undertaking any thorough investigation, the social investigator does not deal with simple and fixed relations, but with *variables*. He discovers that the relation between two or more factors in his problem is a *reciprocal* relationship. He cannot say that one of the factors has a definite meaning independent of the other, so he observes their reciprocal relationship. How this method is used to explain social phenomena is illustrated by the "explanation" of business cycles that was current prior to 1930.

Illustration: Business Cycles.—Although their inferences cannot be stated in as neat a formula as were Pasteur's, economists have discovered a reciprocal relationship—a concomitant variation—between bank credit and business cycles. It cannot be said that bank credit *causes* the unhealthy business expansion which results in business cycles, but it can be said that bank credit *permits* the condition to develop; there would probably be no business cycles if it were not for the operation of bank credit. In this sense, bank credit can be said to be one of the chief "explanations" of business cycles.[11]

Application of Mill's Methods.—Quite often the editorial writer can employ one or more of Mill's methods to ascertain the relationship of factors in a problem. Generally, however, the methods have application only within a larger inductive setting. The mind that uses them, as Professor Sellers warns, "must be active in conjecture, interpretation, and analysis."' The complex problems that vex society do not admit of simple analysis, for the factors are several, and frequently they are elusive. Moreover, a simple analysis of a problem into its several factors is not a final analysis; nor is a mere correlation of variable factors a true explanation of cause. It is not usually sufficient merely to obtain a correlation; one must know rather definitely—perhaps quantitatively—what is the *real degree* of mutual relationship of the factors, what is the *weight* of each factor in its relation to other factors. For example, in the following illustrated editorial from the New York *Daily News* there is presented a concomitant variation of two factors—prohibition and increase in murders. What is the logical force in the correlation of prohibition and increase in murders? What real degree of mutual relationship does the curve exhibit? What is the weight of prohibition as a causal factor? Can we accept the correlation without examining it in a larger inductive setting? Are there other factors? If so, what is the relative weight of these other factors?

---

[11] The explanation of business cycles contained in L. E. Rufener, *Principles of Economics,* Chap. XXIX, is descriptive of the depressions of 1907 and 1921. It shows how an expansion of bank credit causes a depression, but on the surface it does not seem to explain the business depression that began in 1929. A close examination of all the causal factors in that depression, however, will reveal that most of them are equivalent to bank credit as a causal factor, as, for example, installment selling, the movement of gold, the decline in the price of silver, the construction of suburban homes on borrowed capital, the inflation in the stock market, etc. All these factors affected the purchasing power of consumers. The following references are helpful in explaining business cycles: W. C. Mitchell, *Business Cycles;* A. B. Adams, *Economics of Business Cycles;* and H. W. Sprague, *Bank Credit and Business Cycles.*

Presented here is a graphic chart which reflects the rise of the tide of murder in the two largest cities of the United States: New York and Chicago.

Police records in the two cities furnished the figures from which the chart is made. The period covered is the fifteen year stretch from 1914 to 1928 inclusive.

Yearly murder totals for each city are given at the foot of the chart. Chicago's total in the upper row, New York's in the lower. The curves represent murders per 100,000 of population. This explains why the chart shows Chicago to be about twice as tough as New York. Chicago's murders have not been much more numerous, but our population is about twice as large as Chicago.

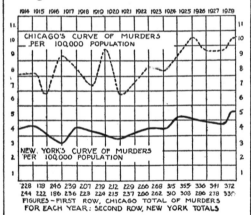

FIGURES – FIRST ROW, CHICAGO TOTAL OF MURDERS
FOR EACH YEAR: SECOND ROW, NEW YORK TOTALS

These murder waves are worth some analysis.

In 1920 New York and Chicago reached almost their record lows for the fifteen year period. Chicago's figure dropped to 6.94 per 100,000, New York's to 3.81.

It was in 1920, you will remember, that the eighteenth amendment and the Volstead act went into effect after a period of wartime prohibition, and many people settled down to the belief that liquor was gone for good.

What happened next? Bootleggers, beer runners and whisky racketeers began to see that there was money for them in federal prohibition. Maybe that had nothing to do with murders in great cities. But what other cause can you logically assign to the fact that in 1921 Chicago's murder index rose to 7.41 per 100,000 and New York to 4.17? The rise continued in both cities in 1923. Murder paused on the new high level in '23. It has been doing well in both New York and Chicago since that time.

The last four years have been record murder years in New York.

Chicago chalked up a fifteen year murder record in 1926, and almost hit it again in '28, while the years between were surpassed only by the freak peak of 1919.

There must be a reason for this increase of murder in the cities since 1920.

Only two important changes of government have affected the entire nation in the fifteen years covered by the chart. One was prohibition; the other, universal woman suffrage. We haven't heard of any murders that could be charged up to the fact that women have the vote—though a writer did complain in a recent Voice of the People column that her husband had stopped speaking to her because she voted for a few Democrats on Nov. 5.

There is known to be much money for some people in the illegal liquor traffic. There will always be men willing to shoot to kill where money is the prize. The logical as well as the easiest conclusion is that prohibition has more than any other one thing to do with the steady increase of murders in the cities.

Functional Relation.—When we seek for a complete explanation of certain phenomena by measuring the *degree* of relationship of the factors, we speak of the relation thus determined as a functional relation. Perhaps the reader has encountered the term in his course in college algebra: "If two variables are so related that when a value of one is given, a corresponding value of the other is determined, the second variable is called a *function* of the first." [12] This relation may be represented graphically on lines of reference called "co-ordinate axes," and the degree of relationship of the two variables is called the "coefficient of correlation." A perfect correlation, for example, is expressed by the coefficient $+1.0$; a high degree of correlation is expressed by $+0.7$ to $+0.9$; and a low degree of correlation by less than $+0.3$.

The Editor and Scientific Method.—Editorial writers, of course, do not make much use of such statistical methods, but the method is discussed here in order to emphasize the necessity for accurate data and to inform the prospective editorial writer about the interpretation of those mathematical symbols which he will frequently encounter in the research reports which come to the editorial desk.[13] Some of these reports have no meaning whatever if the symbols are not understood by the reader.

If the editorial writer, moreover, has an understanding of scientific method as it is used in social investigation, he will tend to be more cautious in making and accepting his own generalizations which he derives by the "arm-chair" method. In social thinking, scientific method is not merely a method, but a discipline. It emphasizes the necessity of patience and objectivity and it guards against wishful thinking. Editorial writers sometimes propose or advocate remedies for social ills after having given little thought to the specific problem. The problem of crime is an instance. If the true causes of current lawlessness are to be found, we must apply a scientific technique. By a scientific technique, however, is meant only the usual thought process—but the usual thought process acting on reliable data. The following technique, for example, represents only the four steps of an act of thought, yet they are steps which are accurately guided:

---

[12] H. L. Rietz and A. R. Crathorne, *College Algebra*, p. 32.

[13] The following books furnish a comprehensive explanation of statistical method, including the principles of "coefficient of correlation" and "probable error": W. I. King, *The Elements of Statistical Method*, Chap. XVII; G. C. Whipple, *Vital Statistics*, Chaps. XII and XIII; L. L. Thurstone, *The Fundamentals of Statistics*.

1. A felt social need which requires analysis, satisfaction, or cure. [In this instance, a remedy for crime.]

2. The phrasing of the need or perhaps a small part of it in the form, "What is the effect of *a* upon *b*?" [Say, of *prohibition* upon *lawlessness.*]

3. The definition, preferably in quantitative form, of the variables *a* and *b*.

4. The adoption of a unit of measurement for each variable.

5. The experimental arrangement by which paired observations may be obtained for *a* and *b*. [That is to say, numerous cases in which there is correlation.]

6. The statistical analysis of these observations to determine objectively the degree of the relation between *a* and *b*.

7. The interpretation which consists in reading causality into the observed concomitance of the two variables.

8. The formulation of more problems which arise from doubts in the interpretation and from which the cycle repeats itself. [That is, the testing in the same manner of other suggested causal factors, such as *defective legal machinery,* etc.] [14]

The Nature of a Problem.—Social problems, looked at from the point of view of how they are to be solved, may be thought of as being in three categories. First, are those which can be solved by right thinking without recourse to elaborate scientific method. Second, are those which can be solved only by experts who apply elaborate scientific method. Third, are those which, because they rest on philosophical foundations, can be solved only by social experimentation. The third type of problem is discussed in Chapter XI. The first type—that which can be solved merely by right thinking—is discussed on more than half the pages of this book. The second type—that which requires application of elaborate scientific method—has already been discussed in this chapter.

The Need for Experts.—It is for the solution of this second type of problem that experts are required. This type of problem requires quantitative measurement and statistical interpretation, and the editorial writer who attacks such a problem must seek the assistance of scientific experts. The editorial council room is not an adequate laboratory, and it does not

---

[14] Adapted from L. L. Thurstone; cited by C. E. Merriam, *New Aspects of Politics,* p. 126.

contain a staff of trained field workers and statisticians. The editorial writer therefore ought to have recourse to the various reports of investigations made by a staff of experts.

So evident is the need for experts in the solution of certain social problems—especially those involving economic factors —that some publicists have suggested that a newspaper ought not to attempt to enforce its solution of a problem on the public. Mr. Lippmann, for example, has suggested that public opinions ought to be organized for the press instead of by the press.[15] This suggestion must not be accepted too readily, however. In the first place, certain problems in the first and third categories mentioned in the previous section cannot be solved by experts any better than by editors. In the second place, the leadership of the press is necessary to obtain the public acceptance of any solution suggested by experts. The public will not enact expert solution of problems unless there is an organization of its will by such agencies as the press, the clergy, group organizations, etc. Recent history exhibits scores of instances of this failure to obtain public assent to experts' suggestions. A few of the examples are the reports of President Harding's Coal Commission in 1922, Great Britain's Royal Coal Commission in 1925, the numerous reports of the Tariff Commission, the Federal Trade Commission, the Interstate Commerce Commission (as regards railroad consolidation), the Federal Council of Churches, the so-called Wickersham Commission, the various crime commissions, universities, and similar bodies.

Problems Arise Because of Change.—A problem is the result of change. Some one factor undergoes a change and this compels a readjustment of certain dependent factors. Thus there was no parking problem before the automobile, but the change in traffic conditions ensuing from the invention and use of the automobile has compelled the widening of streets, the enlargement of the police force, and the construction of elevated boulevards. These changes, in turn, have increased taxes, have diminished the ability of police to combat crime, and have induced more people to live in suburbs. The political situation

---

[15] *Public Opinion*, p. 32.

in Manchuria, following the Russo-Japanese War of 1905, was relatively stable for several years, but Japan's economic development of Manchuria encouraged the migration of millions of Chinese and Koreans. This new condition, arising contemporaneously with Chinese nationalism, has upset the old adjustment of interests. Each factor in a situation is a dependent variable, and a change in one factor alters its relationship with another dependent variable.[16]

It is this matter of change that makes editorial analysis an interesting work. It likewise demands that the editorial writer be heroic. The editorial writer must understand that the future of society is still to be made and that it can only be made by a realistic attack on present problems. He must be heroic enough to admit to himself that the solution of present problems must be followed by the subsequent solution of the newer problems which will arise after the present ones have been solved. He ought not to put any faith in a foreordained progress, nor ought he to give way to disillusion. Godkin spent a whole career trying to aid in the solution of the problems of democracy by applying the theories of nineteenth century "liberalism," but toward the end of the century, when he peered beneath the surface of these theories, he viewed the future of democracy almost with despair. Those who are society's counsellors and leaders can only be heroic: the very nature of a problem demands this attitude.

---

[16] See Walter Lippmann, *The Phantom Public*, pp. 88-90.

CHAPTER VI

EDITORIALS INVOLVING CAUSAL RELATIONS

Editorial thought, as it is presented to the reader in an editorial, does not necessarily reveal all the steps in thinking that were taken by the editorial writer in his analysis. All that matters in the editorial itself is that the argument be convincing. It goes without saying, of course, that the editorial writer should argue only what he believes, but he is under no compulsion to describe his whole technique of thinking for the reader. After arriving at an opinion which he sincerely believes, he formulates his argument in a literary form that is calculated to cause his reader to accept his opinion.

Arguments that involve causal relation are of two kinds: (*a*) argument from cause to effect; and (*b*) argument from effect to cause.[1]

ARGUMENT FROM CAUSE TO EFFECT

Argument from cause to effect consists in taking a known cause and inferring from it a determinate effect. The purpose of such argument is to show that a circumstance or combination of circumstances (cause), *by reason of its very nature,* is capable of producing a certain effect, which is in dispute. Thus, in a criminal trial the prosecutor tries to prove that the defendant committed the murder because he had sufficient motive. "Henry Wilson had a motive to desire the death of Warren Wheeler. He was in love with Wheeler's wife, and she was in love with him. Wheeler carried $125,000 in life insurance of which his wife was designated beneficiary. Wilson was in financial distress because of his gambling debts, and he faced social disgrace." Inherent in these circumstances (motives) there is sufficient cause to produce the effect which is

---

[1] There are also, of course, arguments from one effect to another effect of the same cause and "arguments from sign"; they are touched on briefly in the following sections.

in dispute, namely, "Who killed Warren Wheeler?" Hence the labels that are sometimes applied to this type of argument— "argument from antecedent probability" and "argument *a priori.*"

Kinds of A Priori Argument.—Arguments from cause to effect may argue from the present to the future, from the past to the future, from the past to the present, or from the past to a less remote past. In any instance, however, the argument is that the circumstances are, *by their nature,* such as to produce the disputed effect. Thus, an editorial writer, having in mind the labor vote, argues that "under state ownership and operation of public utilities the state-made rates will tend to be lower for the small consumer and higher for the large consumer: it is in the nature of politics that this effect will result." Another editorial argues that "now that the salary of state legislators has been increased from $500 to $2,400 a term, the membership of the legislature will be improved in character: it is in the nature of things that better men will be attracted to office by such a salary." Another editorial argues that "better municipal government will be a collateral effect of municipal ownership and operation of public utilities: in the nature of the situation, the voters, who will be consumers and users of service, will watch their bills closer and the men who make the bills, that is, the politicians." Another editorial argues that adoption of the city-manager plan of government would naturally result in an inadequate distribution of taxes:

> The distribution of taxes would be directly affected by the proposal. The people have always jealously guarded their right to elect by ballot an assessor of their choice. Do they now wish to surrender that right and leave his selection to a manager who, *by reason of his association and environment as a high salaried man,* might find it difficult to understand the viewpoint of the small tax-payer?

Most editorials that argue from cause to effect, however, are more elaborate than these simple arguments, as, for example, the following editorial on the nature of the World Court:

If we expect that the World Court judges
will be entirely impartial in their decisions,
we are only fooling ourselves.

It is not common sense to expect that
decisions upon concrete cases involving directly or indirectly the policies and interests
of the nationals who compose the Court will
not be colored and influenced by a perception
of the importance of those policies and interests to the nations represented.

Nor are all of the present judges of the
Court entirely free from a political viewpoint. The last three gentleman appointed
—Hughes, Fromageot, and Sir Cecil Hirst—
have had diplomatic careers. A judge sat-
urated in the diplomacy and policies of a
nation cannot seriously be expected to fulfill
the impartial and independent functions theo-
retically assumed to be performed by the
tribunal.

Likewise it is argued that chain and branch banks, by reason of
the nature of their relation to their customers, will not serve
the local community as well as home-owned unit banks:

. . . In the matter of receiving deposits
he [the branch banker] will be exactly like
the unit banker, but in the matter of loans
his technique must be entirely different. He
may, but probably does not, know intimately
a prospective debtor. He may be satisfied
that his character and antecedents and con-
nections are such that his loan is good without collateral, but this will not satisfy his
superior officers in the central city who do
not know the debtor. His loans must necessarily be made primarily on the basis of
collateral, and the collateral in small local enterprises is almost automatically excluded on
account of the cost and time involved for an
investigation sufficient to satisfy the central
officer.

He will be an important factor in the community and he will be treated with great
respect and deference, but he will never be-

> long to the inner circles of the business life because he is an outsider who represents foreigners, and contrasted with the head of the unit bank which preceded him, he is an employe and not an owner. He will be well informed on investments which his particular institution happens to be offering to the public, but not being a part of the community, he will not be particularly well informed as to the real needs of his clients. If an investor wants a bond of a particular interest rate, maturity, and so on, he can supply it to him quite as quickly as the grocer would give a customer a pound of sugar, but when another prospect comes whose social and family and temperamental peculiarities require that he be given guidance, he may and probably will sell the bond, but he will not render the service that the banker now does.

Sometimes argument is *from a hypothetical circumstance* (*cause*) *to a future effect,* although for the purposes of argument we treat the cause as a known cause. For example, the Chicago *Tribune,* in February, 1898, argued that a war with Spain would stimulate rather than depress business in the United States:

> . . . One of the earliest effects [of a war with Spain] would be to improve the times by stimulating business, which has been in a state of chronic depression for more than four years past. . . .
>
> Large numbers of men would be employed upon our fortifications and in rushing our new ships to completion. There would be a demand for labor in all directions which would set to work thousands who have been unemployed, and the demand for labor would make an increased demand for food supplies. This would help the farmers, who would get more money for their products, would make more transportation business for the railroads, and would call for increased facilities and more laborers in all their various de-

> partments.   As a consequence of all this,
> stocks and bonds would be advanced instead
> of depreciated in value.
>
> The end of all this, when the first scare
> is over, would be a general business "boom,"
> and if the war should be protracted the
> boom would grow all the greater.   Indus-
> tries would thrive, agricultural and manu-
> factured products would find a ready market,
> commercial activity be promoted, towns and
> cities increase in population, money would
> be brought into circulation, and there would
> be such an era of general business activity
> as the country has not seen for a generation.

Argument from cause to effect is sometimes *from the past to the less remote past or the present*. The following example is an attempt by Democratic orators to account for the business depression that occurred during the second term of President Cleveland. According to this argument, the previous Republican administration (past) should be blamed for the then present conditions, not the Democrats who were just then in power.

When the Democracy came into power in 1893 it inherited from its Republican predecessor a tax system and currency, a system of which the McKinley and Sherman laws were the culminating atrocities.

It came into power amidst a panic which followed upon their enactment with strikes, lockouts, riots, civil commotions, while scenes of peaceful industry in Pennsylvania had become military camps.

Besides its manifest features the McKinley law had thrown away fifty millions of revenue derived from sugar under a special plea of a free breakfast table, and substituted bounties to sugar planters, thus increasing expenditure, thus burning the candle at both ends, and making the people pay at last for their alleged free breakfast.

From this joint operation of the McKinley law and the Sherman law, an adverse balance of trade was forced against us in 1893; a surplus of $100,000,000 in the treasury was converted into a deficit of $70,000,000 in 1894; and engraved bonds prepared by a Republican Secretary to borrow money to support the Government were ill omens of preorganized ruin that awaited the coming Democracy and depleted treasury.[2]

The foregoing argument may not appear at first glance to be *a priori*. It seems to argue from a known cause to a known effect rather than from a known cause to an effect that is in question. It makes no difference in this instance, however, that the effect (a business depression) is a reality: the dispute is as to who is to blame for the effect, and the Democrat proves that the causes cited were *capable of producing* the effect regardless of the policy of the Democratic administration which is in power.

Tests of A Priori Argument.—In some of the arguments quoted above, the reader has doubtless noticed their inconclusiveness. Only by empirical verification can we determine whether or not a cause can produce a particular effect. However, there are two logical tests which we can always apply to such argument.

1. *Is the alleged cause sufficient to produce the effect?* When a physician gives a patient an opiate to induce sleep, he knows that the desired effect will follow. His *past experience* tells him that the nature of opium is such that, if taken in a sufficient dose, it will induce sleep. In the same way we can argue from our observation and experience (gained either by contact with life or by reading) that certain circumstances, by their nature, are capable of producing a specific effect. But the circumstances must *of themselves* be able to produce the effect. It is not a sufficient argument to say that they will tend to produce the disputed effect (unless, of course, we are arguing only about tendencies). An analysis of the argument quoted above—that better municipal government will result from municipal ownership and operation of public utilities—will show that it is doubtless true to a considerable extent, but public control of the utilities which citizens use will *not of itself* produce better government, even though it does cause voters, who are users, to keep a steadier eye on their local government.

---

[2] Cited by O'Neill, Laycock, and Scales, *Argumentation and Debating,* p. 141.

Inadequate, also, was the argument of certain alarmist editors who, in 1930, envisaged a Communist revolutionary plot in the "dumping" by Russia of pulpwood, manganese, and coal in the United States. The argument of these editors was that the Russian Government, by such a device, hoped to ruin American industries, throw workers out of employment, and then spread Communist propaganda among them. As a matter of fact, the amount of goods "dumped" by Russia was so insignificant as to make little difference in American industry; the United States does not produce nearly as much pulpwood and manganese as it uses. The Russian Government, moreover, had no other motive than to establish credits in this country which it could use to buy producers' goods for use in Russia; the more goods that Russia exports to the United States the more goods she will buy here, and the more goods she buys here the more men will be employed in the United States. Of the same type of alarmist argument was that of certain American labor leaders who declared, in 1930, that European borrowing in the United States would stimulate foreign industry in competition with American industry and thus injure the American standard of living. European borrowing in the United States, until 1930, was chiefly by European governmental units, not by European industries; until the manufacturing industries of Europe begin to borrow in the United States to a greater extent than they now do, there is no cause to worry about their borrowing hurting the so-called American standard of living.

2. *May not other causes intervene to prevent the alleged cause from producing the effect in question?* Even though a set of circumstances is of itself capable of producing a certain effect, it is possible that other circumstances may have intervened which will make inoperative the known cause. "The cause may be always present, and even its exact nature may be known, and yet the complex circumstances attending it may be of such a character that one alone, or two or more combining, may neutralize the operation of the cause." [3]

---

[3] J. G. Hibben, *Logic, Deductive and Inductive*, p. 6.   Quoted by W. T. Foster, *Argumentation and Debate.*

One of the most profound arguments from cause to effect that was ever presented fell to the ground because of the inability of its author to perceive and to foresee that other causes than those considered would intervene to prevent the known cause from producing the effect he predicted. Karl Marx, observing the industrial conditions of the Victorian era and applying the Ricardian theories of economics and the Hegelian dialectic, constructed the thesis that capital would gradually become concentrated in the hands of a few owners, with the result that the exploited workers would take possession of industry and conduct it in the name of the State. In all probability, Marx's prediction would have eventuated had the capitalism which he described—that which was existent between 1817 and 1847—continued without change. But Marx overlooked several factors which—although some of them were inherent in the circumstances at the time of his Communist Manifesto—have turned capitalism in a new direction. These factors have been enumerated by Professor Commons as follows: (1) The diversification of the ownership (though not the control) of capital—the result of the passage of laws which have made easy the incorporation of joint stock companies. (2) The stabilization, through the common law, of the "good" customs of capitalism. (3) Labor legislation. (4) The development of trade unionism. (5) State regulation of capitalism.[4]

The following editorial from the Atlanta *Constitution* was written on January 17, 1919, the day that the thirty-sixth state ratified the Eighteenth Amendment to the Constitution. It illustrates how a thinker is likely to miscalculate the inherent nature of the factors in *a priori* argument. The argument in the editorial, in effect, is this: that inherent in the conditions which made prohibition moderately successful in the states there is sufficient cause to make prohibition even more successful in the nation; and, in addition, there will be the restraint on the hitherto wet states which have been transporting liquors to

---

[4] For an extended discussion, see John R. Commons, "Marx Today: Capitalism and Socialism," *Atlantic Monthly*, November, 1925. See also *infra*, pp. 133-137.

the dry states. The predicted effect had not come to pass by 1931.

> More than two-thirds of the state legislatures have ratified the proposed prohibition amendment to the national constitution, and one year after the proclamation of the amendment the United States will be committed to the policy of nation-wide prohibition.
>
> After the courts have passed upon the validity of the amendment opposition to it will subside and the United States will become a "dry" and sober republic.
>
> [For] Nation-wide prohibition does not entail an experiment in the principle, because it already has been tried and proved in the states which of their own initiative adopted it.
>
> The chief difficulty the prohibition states have had in enforcing their prohibition laws grew out of the fact that the wet states deluged their sister dry states.
>
> [And now] With the power of the United States government back of the enforcement of the law, and with no wet states to debauch the dry ones, there can be no doubt what the outcome will be: It will be Prohibition!

Several newspapers were unduly alarmed in May, 1929, over the decision of the United States Supreme Court in the widely heralded O'Fallon railroad valuation case. The Transportation Act of 1920 provided that rates should be fixed by the Interstate Commerce Commission so that the railroads would earn a fair return on their property value, and the St. Louis and O'Fallon Railroad, in a suit which eventually went to the Supreme Court, contended that the Interstate Commerce Commission, in valuing railroad property for purposes of rate making, should take into account the factor of "reproduction" value as well as the factors of historical cost and prudent investment. The Supreme Court upheld the railroad's contention. Some newspapers, considering only the factor of reproduction, greeted the court's decision with the prediction that twenty-one billion dollars would be added to the value of the railroads, and that, as a consequence, the railroads could charge extortionate rates; a few newspapers went so far as to declare that the ultimate effect of the decision would be government ownership of railroads. The following editorial is representative of this type of *a priori* argument, predicting increased rates:

> Under yesterday's decision of the United States Supreme Court, twenty-one billion dollars are added to the valuation of the railroads under the "reproduction new" theory. This means that railroad rates will be adjusted in such a way as to bring a return on this huge additional valuation which has now been projected on to the American railroad inventory. It must be remembered that for every $1 levied in additional freight rates that $5 is transmitted to the ultimate consumer in the cost of living. The huge significance of yesterday's decision, therefore, becomes apparent.
>
> By laying down the rule that the railroads are entitled to a valuation on what it would cost to rebuild the railroads at the present time rather than a valuation which represents the actual amount invested, it is estimated that twenty-one billions of new value have been pumped into the railroad valuation structure of the country. With billions of dollars being artificially projected on the railroad structure of the country, with millions of dollars being added in new tariff schedules, with billions of dollars being added to the utility structure by the holding company financing scheme and the "reproduction new" theory, prices are bound to soar in order to bring a return on this huge valuation now being reared by American business and finance. How long will the American people be able to stand the kiting prices necessary to make this return?

In constructing this cause and effect argument, the newspaper failed to take into account the operation of another factor

which would prevent the exploitation of shippers—and, ultimately, of consumers—by the railroads: it does not necessarily
follow that rates will be increased in proportion to the increase
in valuation, or that rates will be increased at all; for the
Transportation Act of 1920 requires that the rates shall be
reasonable in themselves.   That is to say, there are other factors
involved which, by their nature, would prevent the effect predicted.   This view is reflected in an editorial in the Chicago
Journal of Commerce, as follows:

> The victory won by the railroads in the
> O'Fallon case will give the railroads a de-
> cidedly higher valuation than the interstate
> commerce commission approves and will
> therefore tend to relieve the railroads of
> some of the onerous rate restrictions now
> imposed by the commission.   However, the
> victory does not signify a general increase
> in freight rates.   The conception of a general
> increase, and particularly of a general in-
> crease proportioned to the increase in valu-
> ation, has been assiduously implanted in the
> public mind.   That conception is invalid.
> There will be no general increase.
>   It has been declared that if valuations
> are fixed on a basis of reproduction cost,
> the railroads of the country will be valued
> at forty billion dollars.   But the Supreme
> Court does not say now, any more than it
> has said in other decisions in analogous cases
> for several decades, that reproduction cost
> must be the sole basis of valuation.
>   . . . Reproduction cost, then, is only one
> of the factors to be considered.   The Supreme
> Court insists that the Interstate Commerce
> Commission shall not blithely ignore that fac-
> tor, as it appears to have done. . . .
>   Since reproduction cost will be only one
> of the factors in the valuation, the railroads
> do not expect a valuation of forty billion
> dollars.   And they will not ask for a new
> rate structure on the basis of a forty-billion
> valuation.   If they did ask for it, they would
> not get it.   Even if formally assured by the

Commerce Commission that they were entitled to it, they would not get it. The Commerce Commission has said that the railroads are entitled to a 5¾ per cent return on the low valuations which the Commission has fixed. But the Commerce Commission has established such rates as to prevent the railroads as a whole from earning the 5¾ per cent return which the Commission itself has said is fair. So there is no ground for expecting that the Commission will grant a fair return on a forty-billion valuation.

Reproduction cost is to be only one of the factors in valuation. And valuation is only one of the factors in rates. The law requires that all rates established shall be reasonable. Therefore, no matter what the valuation, rates cannot be raised so high as to crush shippers. Indeed, such a result would tremendously injure the railroads, partly by decreasing traffic, and partly by stimulating a demand for new federal legislation to curb railroad rates. So the lurid pictures that have been painted, depicting the extortionate charges to be exacted by the railroads if they won the O'Fallon case, are unfounded in fact.

What, then, will be the benefits derived by the railroads from the new valuation? First, the less unprosperous railroads will be saved most of the sums they must now pay to the Commerce Commission under the recapture clause. A number of the railroads are earning more than 6 per cent on their present valuation, and therefore must surrender one-half of all their income in excess of the amount which the Commerce Commission has declared is 6 per cent. Hardly any of the railroads will earn more than 6 per cent on a new and reasonable valuation; and consequently there will be very few payments under the recapture clause. Second, as the railroads under the new valuation would be shown to be earning a decidedly smaller percentage return than has been shown under the old valuation, there will be a greater moral power behind the rail-

> roads' requests for increased rates and their
> resistance to lowered rates. In cases in which
> the Commerce Commission shall not believe
> that rate increases would impose an unrea-
> sonable burden upon the shipper, the low
> percentages of the railroads' return will con-
> stitute a persuasive psychological argument in
> favor of the increase.[5]

Only the well-informed editorial writer can guard against making mistakes in *a priori* argument. The layman can make predictions which appear to be obviously true, but in many fields of activity there are conditions which check the operation of the obvious cause so as to nullify naïve prediction. For example, it was assumed for many years that increasing the fares charged by street railway companies would permit the companies to increase earnings, but it has now been discovered that the public patronage of street railways decreases after the fare has been raised to a certain level.

The editorial writer who makes predictions ought to have a thorough knowledge of all of the factors in the situation, particularly when the situation deals with foreign peoples or with conditions in sections of the United States that are remote from the editorial writer. Americans have many misapprehensions regarding the character of people in other sections of the country, and especially regarding European and Oriental peoples. For example, thousands of Americans, including some newspaper editors, have given credence to the prediction regarding a "Yellow Peril." In recent years the "Yellow Peril" has assumed a new form: Americans have listened credulously to a prediction that the Russian Soviet Government would organize China on a communistic basis and use the man power and physical resources of China to conquer Western civilization. Such *a priori* argument fails to consider the operation of

---

[5] May 22, 1929.

At the present writing, it is not possible to say what will be the effect of the O'Fallon decision. The opinion of the court is hazy, the Interstate Commerce Commission is uncertain, and the railroads do not appear to expect any general rate increases. A good interpretation of the court's decision is contained in an article, "Undetermined Issues in Railroad Valuation under the O'Fallon Decision," by W. L. Ransom, in the *Political Science Quarterly,* Vol. XLIV, pp. 321*ff.*

factors other than racial egotism and the tactics of the Russian Communists.

3. *Is there a complete connection between the cause and the effect?* Some arguments involving causal relations are quite far-fetched. A chain of causes is constructed which has one

Orr in Chicago Tribune

A CHAIN OF CAUSES

or more weak links. These weak links are only suppositions, not proofs, and the argument cannot progress past them. For example, in 1898, when the country faced two major problems —the danger of a war with Spain and agitation by Western and Southern farmers for a double standard of currency—the

Chicago *Tribune* argued that a war with Spain would automatically put an end to the agitation for free coinage of silver. With silver dollars then worth only 44 cents, the agitators— who were chiefly debtors—wanted the silver dollar arbitrarily made equal to a gold dollar through the fiat of Congress. War prosperity, the *Tribune* argued, would make many of these debtors into creditors, and they would naturally insist on being paid in gold. This chain of argument that the war would make prosperity, that prosperity would make creditors out of many debtors, and that the newly made creditors would desert the ranks of the free-coinage-of-silver agitators, had one weak link. It was the first link in the chain: it was not necessarily true that the war—a probable short war—would produce prosperity.

ARGUMENT FROM EFFECT TO CAUSE

Argument from effect to cause is from a known fact (effect) back to a supposed, disputed fact (cause). We say that such and such a condition is "due to" a specific cause. We argue that the cause operates or has operated because the known fact is the effect of it. For example: "There is ice on the pool this morning; evidently the temperature last night was 32 degrees Fahrenheit or lower." The fact of the ice *can be accounted for* only by the lower temperature. This type of argument is sometimes called *a posteriori* ("from what comes after") because we argue *"from* what comes after" *to* what previously existed or has previously occurred.

Illustrating this type of argument in both a positive and a negative way is Dorothy L. Sayers' explanation of why the detective story did not appear until recent times:

It may be as Mr. E. M. Wong has suggested . . . that throughout this early period a "faulty law of evidence was to blame, for detectives cannot flourish until the public has an idea of what constitutes proof, and while a common criminal procedure is arrest, torture, confession, and death." One may go further and say that, though crime stories might, and did, flourish, the detective-story proper *could not do so* until a public sympathy had veered around to the side of law and order. It will be noticed that on the whole, the tendency of early crime-literature is to admire the cunning and astuteness of the criminal (Jacob, Esau, Reynard the Fox, Ballads of Robin Hood, etc.). *This must be so* while the law is arbitrary, oppressive, and brutally administered.[6]

Argument from Sign.—Much *a posteriori* argument is nothing more than "argument from sign," a type of argument which some rhetoricians differentiate entirely from *a posteriori* argument. Argument from sign is the inference of a present fact (effect) from its association with another fact in the past. It is inference that is based merely on *association*. Thus, when the barometer is low we say it is a "sign" of rain; and when the locomotive engineer observes the green signal he infers that the track is clear. The inference in these cases rests upon the association of phenomena in the past: when the barometer was low it always rained; when the green signal appeared before the engineer the track was always clear. Neither the barometer nor the green signal are causes of an effect; they are merely indicators, and the inference in each case rests upon an implied generalization. In these two cases the inferences are sound, but when such inferences are made in the fields of economics, politics, and morals—fields in which there are so many elusive factors to interpret—they are not always sound.

This type of argument often parades as proof. In some instances in economics, politics, and morals, when it is argued that a particular condition is due to a specific cause, the only proof adduced that the known effect proceeded from the alleged cause is an association of phenomena prior to the effect.

Tests of A Posteriori Argument.—Some of the tests for *a posteriori* argument have already been indicated. They are rather obvious because the clew to detection of error is the fact of *accompaniment:* is the alleged cause a real cause, or does the inference arise merely from association of phenomena in the past?

1. *Is the alleged cause sufficient as a real cause?* The following argument, written before the adoption of national prohibition, asserted that prohibition in Kansas had caused a great increase in school enrollment:

---

[6] *The Omnibus of Crime*, p. 11. Italics not in original.

> Prohibition is the best friend of educa-
> tion. . . . During the last nine years [since
> 1901] the enrollment of the State University
> has risen from 1,150 to 2,063; the Normal
> from 1,630 to 2,860, and the Agricultural
> College from 870 to 2,192. Besides that,
> 9,000 young men and women are attending
> denominational institutions and 4,548 attend-
> ing business colleges. The value of school
> property has advanced from $10,000,000 to
> $16,000,000.

Prohibition alone could not have produced this effect. This argument has no more logical force than Mr. Brisbane's assertion that "the Czar abolished vodka for a while, gave the Russian people a chance to think, and they abolished him." The prohibition of vodka, of course, did not release any remarkable train of ratiocination among the Russian masses, nor did the "thinking" of the Russian masses have much to do with the abolishment of the Czar.

How are we to know whether or not an alleged cause is a real cause. Are there any ready standards by which we can evaluate them, or any ready clew that we can use? The only way that one can know whether or not an alleged cause is a real cause is to *know* that it is a real cause. That is to say, our *knowledge* tells us. If we have a fund of information about the subject under discussion, we may know what is the real cause. If the alleged cause is contrary to what we know about human nature or the realities of politics, for example, then we will probably reason that the alleged cause is *inconsistent with* known facts about human nature or about politics, or whatever subject is under discussion.

For example, the following editorial explanation of the result of an election is not consistent with what we know about human nature. In 1892, the Chicago *Tribune,* then a Republican organ, assigned as one of the chief reasons for the defeat of the Republicans in the presidential election the fact that "many native born citizens"—clerks, professional men, shopkeepers, etc.—voted for Cleveland because they wanted to stop the influx of immigrants by voting for Democratic policies which, they believed, were calculated to bring down wages. "The only way to arrest this enormous inflow from Europe," the *Tribune* declared, "was to break the magnet which drew them hither—high protection wages—so they voted for free trade." Is it consistent with human nature that men will deliberately vote against a policy which they believe will bring them high wages?

2. *Is there no other cause which could have produced the effect?* Sometimes an *a posteriori* argument asserts that a known effect is due to a specific cause, but overlooks the potentiality of other causes. The fact that a particular brand of breakfast food is the most popular in Milwaukee may be due to the fact that it is the brand most advertised in Milwaukee newspapers—as one newspaper claims—but such an explanation takes no account of the intrinsic quality of the breakfast food. Although illiteracy was more prevalent in Southern than in Northern states in 1896, it was not necessarily the cause—as the New York *Evening Post* alleged—of Southern states voting for the policy of free coinage of silver advocated by the Democrats; such an explanation takes no account of the unhealed Civil War wounds.

Again, it is argued by an official of an electric power company that the higher wages and shorter hours which American workmen have enjoyed since 1900 have been due to the effective application of electric power in industry. The only proof that the effect proceeded from the alleged cause is the *accompaniment in time* of the changed conditions of workers and the effective application of electric power in industry. The effect was doubtless due, in large measure, to the effective application of power, but there were other factors as well, namely, better factory management, the application of scientific inventions and discoveries, more effective utilization of materials and natural resources, and the increased bargaining power of labor organizations.

A typical example of *a posteriori* argument that is unsound because it fails to consider all the causes is the argument in which a political party takes all the credit for the current prosperity. The following editorial appeared in the Philadelphia

Press, a Republican organ, during the congressional elections
of 1914:

> Between the years of 1900 and 1910 was
> the last decade of Republican control of the
> affairs of government. During that period
> the manufacturing capital of the country in-
> creased from nine billions of dollars to over
> eighteen billions; the value of manufactured
> products from thirteen billions to twenty-one
> billions; the value of the materials used in
> manufacture from six and a half billions to
> twelve billions.
>
> During the Republican decade the number
> of employees engaged in manufacture in-
> creased from five millions to seven and a half
> millions; the wages and salaries paid to em-
> ployees of manufacture from two and a half
> billions of dollars to four and a half billions.
> The number of savings bank depositors went
> up from six millions to nine millions; the
> amount of their deposits from two and a third
> billions of dollars to four billions. Our ex-
> port trade increased two hundred and fifty
> millions of dollars in value. The value of
> our farm property was doubled.
>
> That is what the Republican administration
> did for the United States. What has Demo-
> cratic administration done?
>
> By the first of this year Democratic poli-
> cies were in action and their methods under-
> stood by the business world. The new tariff
> law was in operation, and new laws to regu-
> late trade announced. The period from the
> first of January to the first of July, when
> the European war had no effect upon our
> own conditions is, therefore, a fair period to
> take as a test of the state of the country
> under Democratic rule.
>
> During that period of six months the com-
> mercial failures in the nation increased in
> amount over seventy per cent, and banking
> failures sixty per cent. Railroad earnings
> fell off nearly ten per cent in gross amount,
> and the number of idle freight cars, a sure

barometer of trade, increased over two hundred per cent. The balance in the general fund of the Treasury decreased twelve per cent. The gold shipped from the country increased one hundred and forty per cent. The period used for this comparison is the first six months of 1912, a time when the country was under Republican rule, and before the Presidential election of that year had unsettled the future.

These are the facts in the case. They measure the difference to the country between the domination of the two parties. They tell the story of the change that came with Democratic victory. Which party does the country prefer to have as manager of its affairs? That is the question of this year. How can there be any answer save the return of the Republican party to power and a consequent return to the good times of the decade when it ruled with wise and constructive hand?

Unsound and ridiculous as is the foregoing editorial, it nevertheless represents the kind of argument that has kept the Republican party in power almost continuously since 1896. For the American people have associated American prosperity with Republican policy. Our industrial prosperity since 1896 has been due only slightly to the policies of the Republican party, but in larger measure to other factors such as the abundance of our natural resources, the American genius for invention and organization, and the existence of a great domestic market which has no tariff barriers. The Democratic party, however, deserves in great measure its ill reputation. Until the appearance of Bryan in 1896 the Democratic party had included large numbers of business men. But Bryan's remedy for the economic distress of the time—a double standard of currency with free coinage of silver—alienated business men in general. His policy threatened to destroy the credit structure of the country. Bryan was again the candidate for President in 1900 and in 1908, and his name was associated with unsound currency policy. That fact, together with the party's advocacy of free trade and the fact that the South dominated the party, gave the Democratic party an ill reputation which has continually adhered to it. These factors and others have kept the Republican party in power almost continuously since 1896, and the period of its ascendancy has coincided with an era of economic prosperity. Yet it is true only in small degree that the party's policies have been the cause of prosperity, although Mr. Hoover, in 1928, implied in his speech of acceptance that all of the material prosperity of the country, as evidenced by the many radios, automobiles, etc., was due to Republican policy instead of to the enterprise, energy, and character of the people.

It is party tactics for a major political party to "view with alarm" the record of its rival and to "point with pride" to its own record, charging up to its rival whatever is ill and taking credit to itself for whatever is good. Republican speakers in 1896 were so eager to assess Democratic blame for the panic of 1893 that some of them eventually, in a hazy way, blamed the Democratic tariff of 1894 for the panic of 1893.[7] The British elections of 1880 ousted Disraeli's Conservative Government and returned the Liberals to power with a gain of more than two hundred seats in the House of Commons. Liberals attributed their victory to the unpopularity of Disraeli's policy of imperialism, but there is reason to believe that six years of poor harvests had more effect on the result.

"Dawn-seeing."—The tendency of the human mind to accept inadequate causal explanations has helped to make of the United States a happy hunting ground for reformers. Fanatics are constantly exploiting the good side of human nature by preaching that the elimination of a single evil will lead to a wholesale solution of the world's difficulties. Professor Shorey has called this mental weakness "dawn-seeing." It consists in assigning one evil as the sole cause of moral, political, or economic distress, and preaching that the elimination of this one evil will lead to a millennium of happiness. Some public men—professors, international bankers, politicians, and editors—were saying, in 1921, that the miserable condition of European countries—as evidenced in unbalanced budgets, unstable govern-

---

[7] F. L. Paxson, *Recent History of the United States*, p. 206.

ments, national hatreds, growing armaments, etc.—was due to the failure of the United States to cancel the war debts. Some moralists, in 1918, were crying such slogans as, "Liquor is the germ of evil in the human heart"; "Drunkenness is at the bottom of the misery of our working population, not the industrial surroundings"; "The saloon produces 80 per cent of our criminals"; "The saloon is responsible for most of the 60,000 girls who go astray into immoral lives every year." Civilization is too complex for public leaders—especially editorial writers—to indulge in "dawn-seeing."

CHAPTER VII

ARGUMENT FROM EXAMPLE: GENERALIZATION

Editorial argument, dealing as it does with public questions, usually concerns a principle or a policy. The editorial writer argues, with reference to a particular situation, that a specific principle should be adhered to or that a specific policy ought to be pursued; or he opposes a specific principle or policy. He maintains that the principle he is advocating is true or sound, or that the policy he is advocating is wise or expedient, or untrue, unsound, unwise, inexpedient.

Argument about principles and policies (as distinct from argument about cause and effect) is usually *argument from example*. This method of argument is either "argument by generalization" or "argument from analogy." If, in arguing about a specific case, the editorial writer tries to prove some general principle that is applicable to the case, we call that method "argument by generalization"; as, for example, when the editorial writer, in arguing about whether or not his city government should buy and operate the street car lines, tries to prove that government ownership of public utilities is sound *in principle*. If, however, in arguing about the same case, he merely tries to show that his city government ought to buy and operate the street car lines because government ownership has been successful in Detroit, we call that method "argument from analogy." In the one instance the editorial writer argues from a set of particulars (examples) to a general truth; in the other case he argues from one particular to another particular, sometimes implying a general truth.

The present chapter discusses the first method, and the following chapter discusses the second method.

The Nature of Generalization.—Generalization, as we said in the previous chapter, consists in observing a set of facts, noting their relationship with respect to some point, and inferring a general truth regarding them. The inference of a general truth from a set of particulars, we called induction. Bishop Whately has described the process as follows: "We consider one or more known individual objects or instances of a certain class as fair specimens, *in respect of some point or other,* of that class; and consequently draw an inference from them respecting either the whole class or other less known individuals of it." [1]

Now, in argument, when we are maintaining the truth of some general proposition, all that we do is to cite some particulars as specimens and point out their relationship (resemblance) with respect to some point or other of the class. That is to say, when we argue the wisdom of a specific policy or the soundness of a specific principle, we cite certain *examples* as proof of the soundness of the principle or the wisdom of the policy. If we cite a sufficient number of particulars as specimens, and if the specimens chosen are fair specimens with respect to the point of relationship, our argument is probably sound.

When the British Parliament, for instance, was debating the wisdom of the Stamp Tax, the tax on tea, and the other revenue and enforcement measures against which the American colonists were complaining, Edmund Burke, an opponent of the measures, argued that His Majesty's Government could not expect as much obedience from the American colonists as from his subjects who resided in the British Isles. Burke enunciated the principle that *"in large bodies [of subjects], the circulation of power must be less vigorous at the extremities."* He argued by generalization, adducing two forcible examples to prove the general truth.

In large bodies [he argued] the circulation of power must be less vigorous at the extremities. Nature has said it. The Turk cannot govern Egypt, and Arabia, and Curdistan, as he governs Thrace; nor has he the same dominion in Crimea and Algiers, which he has at Brusa and Smyrna. Despotism itself is obliged to truck and huckster. The Sultan gets such obedience as he can. He governs with loose rein, that he may govern at all; and the

---

[1] Richard Whately, *Elements of Rhetoric*, p. 52. Italics not in original.

whole of the force and vigor of his authority in his centre is derived from a prudent relaxation in all his borders. Spain, in her provinces, is, perhaps, not so well obeyed as you in yours. She complies too, she submits, she watches times. This is the immutable condition, the eternal law, of extensive and detached empire.[2]

The following editorial illustrates how argument by generalization is used to prove that *government control of the price of surplus agricultural products is not a sound policy,* or, as the editorial itself expresses the truth, "It is not possible to alter the orthodox laws of production and trade."

> Farm politicians who are eager to guarantee the farmer a high price for his surplus products in the world market through the assessment of an equalization fee would do well to study the history of similar attempts by various governments.
>
> A few years ago the Brazilian Government undertook to regulate the sale of coffee in world markets by receiving and shipping only so much as the foreign markets could consume at a high price. The price of coffee, accordingly, has risen. But the vast stores of surplus coffee, for which the plantation owner was paid in part by the Government, have increased year by year because there has been no attempt to regulate production. The great surplus of unsold coffee is increasing every year, and the Brazilian Government is straining its borrowing capacity to the utmost to recompense the growers.
>
> What will finally happen to the stores, to the price of coffee, and to the Government's credit nobody can predict. But one fact is certain. The withholding of coffee from the foreign market and the high price that this policy has produced has stimulated the growing of coffee in other countries, just as the attempt by the British Government to control the export of rubber from its colonies has stimulated the growing of rubber in Brazil

---

[2] *Burke's Speeches and Letters on American Affairs* (Everyman's Library), p. 96.

> and Liberia, and the efforts of Cuba to regu-
> late the supply of sugar has stimulated the
> growing of sugar in Hawaii, the Philippines,
> and the United States.
> Government control of agricultural and raw
> products has not succeeded anywhere it has
> been tried. *It is not possible to alter the
> orthodox laws of production and trade.*

Tests of Argument by Generalization.—Although subsequent sections discuss at fuller length the nature of false generalization, we note at this point two tests of an argument by generalization.

1. *Are a sufficient number of specimens of a class cited to warrant an inference regarding the whole class?* Nearly all induction is imperfect. The only perfect induction is that which proceeds from the enumeration of all the specimens of a class; but this is seldom necessary even in investigation in the physical sciences. Since, in the social sciences, it is not entirely possible to develop universal laws, as it is in the physical sciences, the best that can be accomplished is an approximation of sound hypotheses which are sufficiently true as working principles.

Some of the editorial argument that we read is unsound because the generalizations have been derived from an insufficient number of specimens in a class in respect of the point in dispute. The opponents of public ownership, for example, frequently cited, prior to 1930, the unfortunate example of municipal ownership of street railways in Seattle to prove that municipal ownership does not generally succeed. Obviously, this single example is not sufficient to prove the generalization. Much of the argument about prohibition was, prior to the adoption of the Eighteenth Amendment, and now is, hasty generalization based on an insufficient number of specimens examined. The following argument, published in 1912, is a typical illustration of hasty generalization:

> *Dry states are superior economically to
> wet states.* Missouri, which is wet, has a
> total population of 3,300,000, but its assessed

property is only $1,650,000,000. Kansas, which is a dry state, has a population of only 1,600,000, but its assessed property is $2,750,-000,000.[3]

Orr in Chicago Tribune

ARGUMENT FROM EXAMPLE: GENERALIZATION

2. *Are the specimens chosen fair specimens in respect of the point at issue?* False generalization sometimes ensues from an unfair comparison of the specimens chosen. For example,

---

[3] In this argument certain relations were observed. The two states were compared as to population, property value, and the presence and absence of prohibition laws. On this basis a generalization was constructed. Can argument by generalization also be causal argument? See discussion about Marx's philosophy, pp. 133-137.

the advocates of public ownership of street railways sometimes point to the success of municipal ownership in Monroe, Louisiana, on a mere 5-cent fare as an example to prove their thesis. Yet, on close examination, one notes peculiar attributes of the specimen chosen to prove the universal rule. Monroe, Louisiana, in 1920, had a population of only 12,675; the city operated only ten miles of track; there was no problem of expanding population and, consequently, no large extensions of trackage to be financed; the distances traveled were short, and consequently the issuance of transfers was not expensive.

Nor, on the other side of the question, could a contrary universal principle be established if Seattle were used as a typical specimen, even though a large number of identical specimens were cited. For Seattle is not a typical specimen: the city railway property was unloaded on the city government by its private owners at a price which was twice its actual value, and, as a consequence, the fixed interest charges on this unreal capitalization represent a higher charge than a typical specimen would have to bear.[4]

THE NATURE OF "EXPLANATION"

The foregoing discussion of argument from example by generalization is descriptive of how an editorial writer argues about a principle or a policy. We should not assume, however, that the simple tests which were listed provide an adequate technique for thinking about complex generalizations. Some generalizations involve so many factors and require such accurate interpretation of the relations of the factors that we usually speak of them as "explanations." Darwin's theory of organic evolution and Joule's laws of heat, for example, are "explanations"; so is Karl Marx's theory of Communism. Such a generalization involves the interpretation of causal factors as well as the interpretation of mere resemblances and differences. It is a series of inferences based upon the observation of particulars, with finally one general truth emerging as an "explanation." An "explanation" has the comprehensiveness and

---

[4] C. D. Thompson, *Public Ownership*, pp. 236-243.

the definitiveness of a "law"; it *relates* all of the phenomena in such a way as to enable us to *understand* the phenomena, to *know why* the behavior of molecules and stars and social classes is what it is. Two illustrations of this process, one of a very simple generalization and the other of a more complex generalization, are recited below.

Illustration: Public Utility Economics.—An electric street railway company requested permission of the state public utilities commission to increase its fares on the ground that its present earnings were insufficient to permit it to make certain track extensions which were badly needed on the outskirts of the city. The City Attorney objected to the increase. "Why don't you *borrow* the money for extension?" he inquired.

"We can't," replied the company's attorney. "The cost of obtaining capital is prohibitive because of our low earnings. It is a principle of utility economics that *the cost of obtaining capital varies with the earnings of the utility.*"

The attorney for the street railway then proceeded to prove the truth of the principle by generalization. He first cited figures to show a *relationship* between the extensions made by the various public utilities in the United States and the amount of capital they had added (presumably borrowed) between the years 1921 and 1927. He cited these instances:

The electric light and power companies, which increased their generating capacity by 91 per cent, added 112 per cent to their capital; the telephone companies, which increased the number of telephones by 37 per cent, added 58 per cent to their capitalization; the gas companies, which increased their gas mains by 27 per cent, added 81 per cent to their capitalization; the class 1 steam railroads, on the other hand, which increased their tracks only 4 per cent, added only 15 per cent to their fixed capital, and nearly all of this amount went to pay for cars and locomotives instead of trackage; the electric railroads, which *decreased* their trackage by 7 per cent, added to their fixed capital only one-half of 1 per cent.

Arranged in tabular form, the figures undoubtedly revealed a close relationship between the extensions and the amount of added capital:

Type of Utility	Per Cent of Extensions	Per Cent of Added Capital
Light and power companies	91	112
Telephone companies	37	58
Gas companies	27	81
Steam railroads, class 1	4	15
Electric railroads	−7	½

"This relation between extension of service and increase of capital is really a relation between extension of service and *the ability of the utilities to attract capital*," the attorney went on to explain. He then proceeded to show a relation between the earnings of utilities and their extensions of service. He cited these relationships:

Type of Utility	Per Cent of Extension of Service	Per Cent of Earnings
Light and power companies	91	7.2
Telephone companies	37	7.0
Gas companies	27	5.5
Steam railroads, class 1	4	4.9
Electric railroads	−7	4.1

"Thus, it is evident," the street railroad attorney concluded, "that those utilities which had low earnings—the same utilities which failed to extend their services—were not able to borrow capital with which to make extensions. When they talked to investment bankers about issuing bonds, they were always told that the bonds would have to bear a high interest rate and that they would have to be sold at a discount from par.

"Thus, you see the plight the electric railroads are in. At the present time we should have to pay a prohibitive rate of interest on borrowed capital. Unless we are permitted to increase our earnings, we cannot make any extensions, for *the cost of obtaining capital varies with the earnings of the utility*."

Illustration: Marxian Philosophy.—It was by observing the relationship of particulars that Karl Marx was able to construct his closely reasoned philosophy of Socialism, namely, that the present capitalistic organization of society contains the seeds of its own destruction and that it will, in the nature of things, be transformed into a different type of social organization. Marx, perceiving the State as an institution through which particular interests were conserving their privileges, envisaged a transformation of the State into an institution through which, in the future, all men in all classes would realize freedom. This transformation was inevitable, thought Marx, because gradually wealth would be concentrated in the hands of a few, and the proletariat, in the nature of things, would dispossess the few and establish a class dictatorship. He derived this theory by relating his observations of industrial society in the first half of the nineteenth century to the theories of Hegel and Ricardo.

Hegel, who had lectured at the University of Berlin only a few years prior to Marx's study there, had constructed the theory that history is an unfolding of man's progress toward freedom. In examining the epochs which history recorded, Hegel perceived certain resemblances: he observed that history seemed to proceed teleologically by a process of thesis, antithesis, and synthesis; that is to say that every historical situation which developed was afterward changed by a conflict ("contradiction"), and that out of the conflict arose a new situation which was an harmonious adjustment—a synthesis. The prime mover in history, said Hegel, is Absolute Idea; because of this force, man will realize freedom in the State. This evolution of human freedom is preordained. Hegel gave his theory a rhapsodical interpretation when he inferred that the freedom of man was being realized in the Prussian State—the State in which he was then living.[5]

---

[5] The following quotation summarizes in an incomplete way Hegel's dialectical "explanation": "The Orientals have not attained the knowledge that Spirit—Man *as such*—is free; and because they do not know this, they are not free. They only know that *one* is free. . . . The consciousness of Freedom first rose among the Greeks, and therefore they were free; but they, and the Romans likewise, knew only that *some* are free, —not man as such. . . . The Greeks, therefore, had slaves; and their whole life and the maintenance of their splendid liberty, was implicated with the institution of slavery. . . . The German nations, under the influence of Christianity, were the first to attain the consciousness, that man, as man, is free."—*Lectures on the Philosophy of History* (Sibree translation), pp. 18-19.

After Marx left Germany, in 1843, he resided in France and England (in the latter country from 1849 until his death in 1883), where he had opportunity to observe the effects of the Industrial Revolution. Examining the phenomena in the industrial situation, he noted a resemblance to the Hegelian theory of history. He perceived, for example, that in England the semicommunistic (feudal) organization of society by which the farm laborers had shared the "common" land had been destroyed by the private enclosures; and, further, that the farm laborers had been forced to go to the towns to earn a living in the recently established factories. Observing the miserable conditions under which these wage slaves worked, and noting the fact that their wages were not above the level of subsistence, Marx perceived the motivation for a change through conflict—antithesis. He "observed" that the prime mover in history is "mode of production." As the mode of production has changed, social classes have changed. Thus when the mode of production was *slavery* we had one type of social organization, but when the mode of production was *serfdom* we had a different type of social organization. And now that the mode of production is *wage-slavery* we have a new type of social organization—a small class which owns the tools of production (capitalists) exploits a larger class (proletarians).

Next, by applying Ricardo's theories of rent and wages to the existing situation, Marx believed he was sound in predicting that the proletariat would constantly increase and the entrepreneurs would gradually acquire possession of the world's wealth until a time would be reached at which the proletariat, in the nature of things, would dispossess the few and set up a Communist state in which, eventually, there would be no social classes and no class struggle—synthesis!

Ricardo's theory of rent,[6] then currently accepted by economists, was, in brief, that land rent is determined by the labor cost of producing on the least productive land. The wages of

---

[6] For an explanation of Ricardo's theories, see J. K. Ingram, *A History of Political Economy* (rev. ed.), pp. 126*ff*. The best statement of Marx's historical materialism is in S. H. M. Chang, *The Marxian Theory of the State*, Chap. II. Although Marx lived in England after 1849, he had developed his theory of history before coming to England.

the laborer, Ricardo reasoned, could not generally rise above the current level of subsistence of the laborer. Therefore, since wages were inalterably fixed by "iron law" at the level of the laborer's subsistence, any increase in the rent of land would go to the owner exclusively. The same situation, Marx observed, existed in industry—the capitalists were gradually accumulating all of the wealth which ensued from the laborer's productivity. Thus, by relating the Ricardian and Hegelian theories to his own observations of the current industrial system, Marx evolved a theory which, in the light of the then current conditions, he had adequate reason to believe was sound.[7]

What was especially novel in Marx's generalization—and what, incidentally, provided Socialism with a tactic as well as with a philosophy—was Marx's relating of economic and social phenomena to political phenomena: the necessity for the proletariat to seize control of the State as well as control of the tools and materials of production and distribution.[8]

This brief exposition of the process of Marx's reasoning is illustrative of all creative thinking. The creative thinker is one who so understands the phenomena he observes that he is able to perceive the relationship (resemblances) inherent in the particulars, and thus to organize his data according to a central principle.

The foregoing explanation of Marxism, as the reader has doubtless observed, is too complex to be discussed under the head of argument from example, which is merely a rhetorical method. It is more complex than the principles discussed early in this chapter. Marx's theory involves many factors—some of them causal—and it represents the taking of many observations by its author. It deserves to be called an "explanation,"

---

[7] The factors which Marx failed to foresee are discussed on page 111. The student who wishes to understand Marx's economic theories, especially his theory of "surplus value," should read *Capital*.

[8] A point about Marx's theory which is often misunderstood is that the seizure of the control of the State by the proletarian class and the establishment of a proletarian dictatorship was to be only a temporary arrangement. According to Marx, the State would gradually "wither away": eventually a new régime would ensue in which there would be no class distinctions at all, and hence no need for a special apparatus, such as the State, for the domination of other classes by the capitalists. See Nicolai Lenin (V. I. Ulianov), *The State and Revolution*, pp. 94-96.

just as Darwin's hypothesis of evolution and Joule's laws regarding heat are "explanations." An "explanation," as natural scientists use the term, is a broad generalization based upon the taking of many observations and the interpretation of many factors, some of them causal. Marxism is, first, a broad explanation of the organization of capitalistic society and, second, a scientific prediction about the future organization of society.

Oversimplification.—The creative thinker, in organizing data according to a central principle, should beware of oversimplification. Many attempts at social theory are found, on examination, to be oversimplifications. That is to say, they fail to organize *all* the data according to the central principle and leave part of it unaccounted for. In history and sociology, for example, we have the explanations of Hegel and Sombart, which do not explain all the data of history or of society. Some writers, in their eagerness to reduce all the data of a situation to their thesis, deliberately misinterpret a portion of their data in order to make it fit their theory; Taine's *History of the French Revolution* is an excellent example of the misinterpretation of data to make it accord with a central organizing principle. The editorial writer who examines broad theories must be cautious about accepting them; the world is full of "isms," which, on close examination, reveal themselves to be unsatisfactory explanations.

Many such theories, however, although not entirely sound, are useful in orientating one's thinking. Marxism, for example, does not square with all the data of human experience, yet it is a very useful explanation of a social situation. Again, there is obviously no such *system* as "capitalism," [9] yet the situation

---

[9] Professor F. W. Maitland, with a twinkle in his eye, has pointed out that in England there never was any such system as "feudalism":
"Any talk of a feudal system is a comparatively new thing: I should say that we do not hear of a feudal system until long after feudalism has ceased to exist. . . . Coke in his voluminous works has summed up for us the law of the later Middle Ages, but in all his books, unless I am mistaken, there is no word about the feudal system. . . . For a 'feudal system' we must turn from Coke to a contemporary of his, that learned and laborious antiquary, Sir Henry Spelman (1562-1641). . . . Now were an examiner to ask who introduced the feudal system into England? one very good answer, if properly explained, would be Henry Spelman, and if there followed the question, what was the feudal system? a good answer to that would be, an early essay in comparative juris-

which we call capitalism needs some synthetic explanation such as Marx has given it if we are to be able to remedy its inherent evils.

Our Experience-World.—Professor C. A. Beard, in his *An Economic Interpretation of the Constitution of the United States,* explains the conflict which centered about the framing and ratification of the Constitution on the theory that it was a conflict between the commercial and propertied classes, on the one hand, and the small agrarian and propertyless classes, on the other hand. Some other eminent historians, although taking this class conflict into consideration, give much emphasis to the conflict between the large and the small states and the conflict between centralization and state's rights. The advantage in accepting the latter theory is that it accounts for *all* the data of the situation; the disadvantage in accepting it is that it probably gives less weight to the economic factors than they deserve. Historians differ in the emphasis they give to these theories; the truth, however, lies in the data of the situation, if they can be discovered: without a complete set of data one would not know precisely how much weight to give to each of the types of conflict. Yet, a group of college students calling themselves "Young Communists"—sophomores, juniors, and seniors—denounced a historian at their university as "narrow-minded" because he did not accept Professor Beard's thesis *in toto.* These students were practically unacquainted with the historical data of the period, yet they had convictions about the interpretation of the data. They *wanted* to believe the economic interpretation, and the lack of data was no obstacle to their belief.

---

prudence. Spelman reading continental books saw that English law, for all its insularity, was a member of a great European family, a family between all the members of which there are strong likenesses. This was for Englishmen a grand and striking discovery; much that had seemed quite arbitrary in their old laws, now seemed explicable. They learned of feudal law as of a medieval *jus gentium,* a system common to all the nations of the West. The new learning was propagated among English lawyers by Sir Martin Wright; it was popularized and made orthodox by Blackstone in his easy and attractive manner. If my examiner went on with his questions and asked me, when did the feudal system attain its most perfect development? I should answer, about the middle of the last century [the eighteenth]."—*The Constitutional History of England,* pp. 141-142.

The soundness of our generalizations is limited by the quantity and the quality of our data; that is to say, by the scope of our *experience-world*. The ordinary child probably makes the generalization that "all adult persons are kind," for the data of his experience-world bear out such an hypothesis until he has met a sufficient number of unkind persons to cause him to doubt it. There are, however, a few Oliver Twists in the world who, early in life, make the generalization that "all adult persons are unkind." In both cases the generalizations are derived from the child's experience-world, and to the child who makes them they are true. The experience-world of every thinker is derived in part from his personal experiences and observations and in part from his reading.

Because so many voters have a small experience-world, they frequently proceed to make false generalizations. Their reasoning may be sound in so far as it is based on their meager data, but, lacking complete data, they accept the *simplest* explanation—that is, they accept that explanation which can be accounted for by the limited data of their experience-world. For example,

> . . . farmer-peasant logic and reasoning are sound within the field of phenomena of their direct experience and knowledge, and often are defective, faulty, and biased in the field of the phenomena outside of their direct experience and on subjects generally little known by them. The same is true about any city group with the difference that the sphere of the direct and indirect experience of each of these groups is different. . . . They [farmers] often use vitalistic interpretations of economic and social forces. Farmers live personal lives. Their families and commodity organizations are essentially personal. As a result, their customary method of interpreting economic and social forces is essentially vitalistic and personal. They often blame the market-man for low prices. If the cream test is low, they oftentimes blame the butter-maker rather than themselves or their cows. The ruling political party is held responsible for the price level.[10]

Farmers in our Western states have nearly always rallied to the standard of the politician with a panacea or the politician

---

[10] P. A. Sorokin and C. C. Zimmerman, *Principles of Rural-Urban Sociology* (Henry Holt & Co., New York, 1929), pp. 296-300; reprinted by permission.

who explained the current economic evils with a neat formula and with reference to a far-off place such as Wall Street. Many city people are almost as naïve about some other matters and are easily persuaded to believe in some imagined "conspiracy" organized against their interests, as, for example, the bugaboo of the "Whiskey Trust" ten years after the enactment of the national prohibition laws. Most of these "systems" which haunt the naïve mind have some basis in fact, and some of them represent at least a half reality; but the readiness of the naïve individual to accept the existence of some "conspiracy" or some political set-up inimical to his interests is due, like his eagerness to accept some simple philosophic system, to the narrowness of his experience-world. Because he cannot comprehend all the factors in a complex situation, he accepts a simple explanation which can be accounted for with reference to his limited experience-world. There are probably thousands of Americans who believe that newspapers generally accept money for adopting certain editorial policies and that the votes of most Congressmen on legislative measures are determined by bribes.

The Meaning of "Insight."—Speaking of Greeley, who was something of a doctrinaire, Charles A. Dana once said:

He was a man of immense ability, of instincts of extraordinary correctness in many respects, and of the power of expression, of telling what he knew in a delightfully picturesque, humorous way, which not merely instructed the hearer and reader, but gave him a sense of delight from the mere art that he applied in the telling. He had no great advantages of education. He had picked up his education as he went along reading in the winter evenings by the firelight, and never wasting a chance of learning something. But he lacked one of the most precious faculties, which it is another great object of the college education to cultivate and bring out, and that is what we call the critical faculty, the judgment which when a proposition is stated to you or a fact is reported, looks at it calmly and says, "That is true" or else "That is false"—the judgment, the instinct, the developed and cultivated instinct which knows the truth when it is presented and detects error when it comes masquerading before you. This great man of whom I am speaking, this great and brilliant journalist, one of the greatest we have produced, was deficient in that faculty.[11]

[11] *The Profession of Journalism.* Cited by Allan Nevins in *Journalism Quarterly*, June, 1928, p. 4.

This indispensable faculty which Greeley lacked and to which Dana did not try to attach a name we shall speak of here as "insight." Insight, as was suggested on pages 82-83, is the product of our memory and our imagination. It is the faculty of referring a novel problem to our experience-world for a suggested explanation or for a critical test. Or rather, from the point of view of creative thinking, it is the faculty of focusing our imagination on a problem and making the inductive leap by aid of our experience-world.

Illustration: What is a Lobbyist?—The faculty of insight is difficult to describe, but an illustration of how it operates may help to make its meaning clearer. In 1930, a Senate committee brought to light the fact that the national Capital was densely populated with "lobbyists"; that many corporations, trade associations, churches, and labor unions maintained a corps of special representatives at Washington for the purpose, in some instances, of supplying information to Congressmen in connection with certain legislative measures, and, in other instances, for the purpose of inducing Congressmen to support or oppose certain measures in which the corporations, associations, and institutions were interested; and that some of these lobbyists were drawing large salaries and were spending large sums of money for entertainment and publicity. This situation, except as to its magnitude, was nothing new to the public mind. At various other times the public had become aware of the activities of lobbyists, and several remedies had been proposed for abolishing them. But by 1930 it had dawned on the public mind that it was not really possible to eliminate lobbyists. Several editorial writers, however, denounced the activities of lobbyists, and some of them went so far as to refer to the lobby as constituting a "dangerous invisible government." But one editorial writer, at least, examined the lobbyist in the light of reality to see what actual function he performed.

This editorial writer recalled some of his personal contacts with lobbyists in Washington. Some lobbyists, he remembered, were mere propagandists trying to exploit government in the selfish interests of their commercial clients, and some were pretending to be serving clients though actually bluffing about their "influence." There were others, however, who performed a real function of representation: they represented the interests of their clients as legitimately as the elected Congressmen represented their constituents in specific geographical areas. Suddenly the real explanation of the lobbyist came to the editorial writer. His mind leaped to the generalization: the legitimate lobbyists are *functional* representatives, just as the Congressmen are *territorial* representatives; they represent interests and groups in the state as the Congressmen represent territorial areas.

From this point the editorial writer's mind proceeded to elaborate his "inspired" generalization, and gradually a complete explanation was unfolded. Why shouldn't corporations, trade associations, labor unions, and institutions be represented in Washington? Why isn't functional representation just as indispensable as territorial representation? And isn't mere territorial representation in modern times an inadequate form of representation? Isn't functional representation, after all, an older form of representation than territorial representation: when Anglo-Saxon representative government had its beginnings in the summoning of the nobility and clergy to Winchester and Westminster to consult as to the supplying of royal revenue, did not those who were summoned really represent property and institution rather than geographical area? Does territorial representation, in the last analysis, represent a *unit of opinion and self-interest,* or just a section of the map? Isn't functional representation precisely what Fascist Italy asserts to have brought about with its representatives of fifteen "syndicates" composing the Chamber of Deputies? If—since functional representation in our own eighteenth century pattern of government is extralegal—lobbyists were forbidden at Washington, would we not have to make some constitutional provision for the representation of interests? Could Congress, in this complex era of civilization, get along without the expert advice of functional representatives? Hasn't the necessity for functional representation in the past been largely obviated because functional interest has happened to coincide with sectional interest? In the very beginning of our national Government, were not lobbyists *elected* to Congress in the persons of those Federalist members who owned government securities and voted for the treasury to redeem them at par? Who were the slaveholders elected to Congress but antebellum lobbyists? Who but elected lobbyists were those business men who composed the millionaires' club, the Senate, in the days before Senators were elected by direct suffrage? Who but elected lobbyists of the beet sugar interests today are Senator Smoot of Utah and Senator Waterman and Representative Timberlake of Colorado? And who but elected lobbyists of Pennsylvania manufacturing interests are Senators Grundy and Reed of Pennsylvania? Isn't government, after all, something real rather than academic—the governments which existed under Edward I and George III and the governments of the industrial age? Isn't it an impossible task absolutely to make economic and social realities fit an academic pattern? Should not the vicious practices of lobbyists be prevented, but their necessary activities be recognized as an essential, though an extralegal, part of government? [12]

How "Working Principles" Mature.—This illustration of so-called insight emphasizes the fact that the experience-world of the editorial writer must be derived from acute observation. Insight—in so far as it functions in the analysis of public affairs—is a quality which is derived either from actual participation in public affairs or from acute observation of them. Insight implies a first-hand, close-up understanding of human phenomena. This quality in a thinker, when it is accompanied by a fund of information, constitutes what is sometimes called "seasoned knowledge" and "maturity of judgment"; and it exhibits itself as "common sense." In the mind of an editorial writer, it takes the form of a set of "working principles" by

---

[12] The discussion in this section is not meant to be a defense of the methods employed by special interests to obtain legislation favorable to themselves. If certain Congressmen, by means of "log-rolling," obtain favors for special interests, that is no reason why lobbyists should not be given a hearing by committees and by individual Congressmen. But the fact that certain special interests are more articulate than the mass of taxpayers sometimes results in an unequal distribution of favors at the expense of the general citizenship. For example, Premier Tardieu of France, in 1930, complained that the French Parliament added to the budget $160,000,000 of expenditures for various schemes, many of which the Cabinet opposed as not being in the general interest.

means of which he leaps to tentative conclusions and then tests them critically. Applied in concrete instances, these "working principles" tell him that "the governments of national states do not usually act from purely altruistic motives," that "a third political party in the United States cannot, for a long time at least, gain control of the Government," that "taxes once voted in time of peace never are lowered," that "the essence of politics is compromise and expediency," that "in modifying the structure of government we must beware of giving too much discretion to bureaucrats," that "appellate judges in their decisions reflect their individual social philosophy," that "the proletarian is not necessarily more virtuous, because of his poverty, than is the bourgeois." Such a set of "working principles" (or a different set), although subject to frequent revision by the editorial writer, helps him to "know the truth when it is presented" and to "detect error when it comes masquerading before you." It keeps his judgments within the bounds of reality, prevents him from putting too much credence in doctrinaire theories, and provides him finally—whether or not his "working principles" be sound—with a viewpoint.[13]

Insight and Inspiration.—Although we usually think of insight in connection with critical analysis, and of inspiration in connection with creative thinking, the two mental processes are alike in one respect: memory plays an important rôle in both. So-called flashes of insight, like flashes of inspiration, are at bottom rather flashes of memory. Our concrete experiences and our generalizations are deposited somewhere in the back of our mind, and, when suddenly set off, come with an uprush to our immediate consciousness. Professor Burges Johnson reports a conversation with the poet Vachel Lindsay, which illustrates the rôle that memory plays in inspiration. The poet, he said, had lived for years in a town where more than half of the population was Negroes.

This had led him to speculate about them, as his mind grew more mature, and to develop some philosophy of his own as to the tragedy of their present situation, the savagery of their background,

---

[13] For a further discussion of viewpoint and "first principles," see *infra,* Chapter XIV.

and the hope that might lie in their future. He came to feel that perhaps their one great contribution to mankind might be a spiritual gift. All of this thinking had eventually slipped into the background of his mind.

One day as he was travelling in a Pullman a sudden flashing glimpse of that old speculation came to him, but now it was like a telegram in code. Perhaps the rhythm of the car wheels had gotten into his head; perhaps the porter came through the car. At any rate he found himself saying:

> "Then I saw the Congo creeping through the black,
> Winding through the forest with a golden track."

Where it came from he did not know. "Call it ouija board stuff if you like," said he to me.

"Anyhow," said the poet, "I was content with my poem. It summed up in condensed fashion all my philosophising about the negro. But if I put that couplet into type it would mean nothing whatever to those whose thoughts had not travelled the whole distance with mine. I must settle down to the plodding task of interpreting my vision. Sheer craftsmanship would then determine whether or not I could make others see what I had seen or feel what I had felt." [14]

It would be erroneous to identify insight very closely with inspiration, but the foregoing description of inspiration reveals what is common to both processes of reflection—the rôle of memory. In whatever terms insight may be explained—and the foregoing section is indeed an imperfect explanation—it is evident that insight derives from the quality of the thinker's personal experiences, from the character of his reading, from his habit of disciplined reflection, and from some quality of imagination that is difficult to define. With reference to some public questions—practical politics, say—insight is more effectively exercised by a newspaper man who has had wide and intimate contacts with reality; with reference to other public questions—a matter of international law, for instance—it is more effectively exercised by a scholar whose knowledge is technical and specific.

---

[14] *Free-Lance Writer's Handbook,* pp. 223-224; copyright, 1926, by The Writer Publishing Company; reprinted by permission. The student should compare this "recall" explanation of insight with the explanation in Chapter X.

CHAPTER VIII

ARGUMENT FROM EXAMPLE: ANALOGY

Argument from analogy, like argument by generalization, is based on the resemblance of particulars. But, unlike argument by generalization, argument from analogy does not infer a general truth from a set of particulars: it merely infers that what is true of one particular is also true of another particular.[1] We compare two cases and find them essentially the same. Case A—the case in dispute—is regarded as essentially the same as the other case, AA, and, therefore, what is true of AA we can *logically infer* from A. For example: "Since the postal service (Case AA) is operated successfully by the government, so can the telegraph service (Case A) be successfully operated by the government." We do not regard the two cases as precisely alike, but *essentially* alike. We recognize that there are certain differences, otherwise the two cases would be only one case with a single class-name; but we say that the differences are negligible as compared with the resemblances.

As Minto has defined it, analogy is an argument in which the "ground of inference is the resemblance between two individual objects or kinds of objects in a certain number of points; and the inference is that they resemble one another in some point, known to belong to the one, but not known to belong to the other."[2] That is to say, the postal service and the telegraph service are alike in certain respects—both transmit communications, both are monopolies, etc.; the postal service, however, is different from the telegraph service in the respect of government operation. Now, can we argue soundly that, for the purposes of government operation, the two utilities are *essentially* alike? Is there such a preponderating resemblance between the two services in some points as to justify a *further*

---

[1] See p. 126.
[2] W. A. Minto, *Logic: Deductive and Inductive*, p. 368.

146

comparison in respect of the point that is known to belong to the one but not known to belong to the other? Is the planet Mars, which is like the Earth in respect of the source of its light, its succession of day and night, and its control by the law of gravitation, also like the Earth in the respect that it is inhabited? Does the known resemblance extend *further* than we know—to an unknown particular?

It is this inductive leap—this inference from a known particular to an unknown particular—that constitutes proof by analogy. It is an effective type of argument because of its simplicity, but its logical force rests upon the real resemblance of the two particulars. In a subsequent section we shall discuss some effective tests of analogy.

Kinds of Analogies.—We can differentiate three kinds of analogies according to the things compared:

1. An analogy which compares two things.

2. An analogy which infers that what is true of a particular in one sphere of life or in one field of activity is true of a particular in another sphere of life or another field of activity.

3. An analogy which compares a present situation with an historical situation and infers that the two situations are essentially the same—that is, an historical parallel.

1. *Comparison of Things.*—Analogies which are comparisons of things (i.e., institutions, public bodies, taxes, labor, and as many other things as there are class-names to identify them) do not usually possess much logical force; for the argument merely asserts a resemblance in the *relations* which the things compared bear to some other thing. This relationship may be expressed as follows: $a:x::b:x$. If we argue, for example, that it would be sound public policy to establish a tariff commission to fix tariff rates because it has been sound policy to establish the Interstate Commerce Commission to fix railroad rates, we are comparing the two bodies in respect of their relationship to Congress. For, in each instance, the body is exercising a power which Congress delegates to it; and the argument would run as follows: "Congress delegates power to the Interstate Commerce Commission to fix railroad rates; it

would be just as sound public policy for Congress to delegate power to a tariff commission to fix tariff rates."

What robs such an argument of logical force is the fact that

Gundersen in Madison (Wis.) Capital Times

ARGUMENT FROM EXAMPLE: ANALOGY

it is essentially *generalization from a single example.* Although the definition of argument from analogy is "an argument which proceeds from particular to particular," most analogies *imply* a general truth. In the foregoing argument, for example, there is implied the generalization, "It is always sound policy for Congress to delegate rate-fixing powers." This generalization is not necessarily sound, even though the example of the Interstate Commerce Commission be a sound example. It does not necessarily follow that it would be sound policy for Congress to delegate the power of fixing income tax rates, tariff rates, or postal rates.

A simple example of the kind of analogy which compares two institutions as particulars is the argument by Mr. Oliver Baldwin, a Laborite member of the House of Commons. Mr. Baldwin is supporting the socialist theory of government: he compares the State and the family and infers that the State has the same relation to the individual that the family has.

> Would a large family tolerate the cornering of food, money, and clothes, for instance, by one member? Would they say nothing if the wages they brought home were used to buy pearls for the eldest sister while the rest went without food? Would they acquiesce to an arrangement whereby one of the brothers should have a whole room to himself while the other brothers slept two in a single bed, three in a double one, and one on the floor? Would they agree to revere with an especial reverence one of the brothers because he were named Marmaduke and happened to look more of an imbecile than the others? Yet the people are content in England to look with admiration and reverence on those that are called duke or earl or lord.[3]

This argument, although it has a degree of logical force, is not conclusive; yet it probably has as much logical force as any other argument from analogy which compares two institutions. Mr. Baldwin's comparison of the State and the family is only one of the many analogies which have been made in discussions about the nature of the State. The Scholastics, for example, likened the body of mankind to an organism, and, citing St.

---

[3] Signed article published in Hearst morning papers of June 4, 1929.

Paul's figure of "one body, many members," [4] argued the resemblance between the body in Christ and the body politic.
The sun and moon, the body and soul, were likewise cited as
proof of the relation of the spiritual power to the temporal
power.[5] The same kind of argument and almost the same
concepts underlie the modern organismic theory of the State,
particularly the theory of the present Italian Fascist State.
The State is conceived by the Fascist philosophers as a biologic
organ composed of cells (individual citizens). If there is to be
"liberty" in the State, say the Fascists, both the cells and the
organism must fulfill their appointed functions; that is to say,
the individual must subordinate himself to the will of the State.
If we grant the truth of this analogy, there is adequate justification for Fascist suppression of speech, press, and assembly.[6]

Analogies of this type are not conclusive arguments because
they only prove that two things are alike in the *relation* they
bear to other things. We do not prove that the objects themselves are alike: we only prove a *resemblance of relations:* the
analogy extends no further. Yet this type of argument is
sometimes effective because it *reënforces* other argument.

Sometimes, however, analogy of this kind comes near to
being proof. Several volumes of contemporary social theory
to which much weight is attached have their basis of proof in
analogy; as, for example, Freud's theory regarding atavism, as
contained in his *Totem and Taboo,* and Everett Dean Martin's
explanation of crowd behavior, in *The Behavior of Crowds.*

Sometimes, however, analogy is stretched too far, as in
Fourierism, a nineteenth century utopian Socialism, the validity
of which rested on an analogy between the current economic
order and the phenomena of phrenology, a pseudo-science.
Likewise, the argument is stretched too far in some editorial

---

[4] "For as we have many members in one body, and all members have
not the same office; so we, being many, are one body in Christ, and
every one members one of another."—Romans xii: 4, 5.

[5] See W. A. Dunning, *A History of Political Theories: Ancient and
Medieval,* Chap. VII.

[6] See H. W. Schneider, *Making the Fascist State,* pp. 101-113. See
also F. W. Coker, "Organismic Theories of the State," Columbia University Studies (Vol. XXXVIII, No. 2), pp. 124-139; and W. Y. Elliott,
The Pragmatic Revolt in Politics, Chaps. X and XI.

arguments, as, for example, the following effort to draw an analogy between the effect produced on American wages by a low tariff and the effect produced by convict labor.

> The workingmen have for many years declared their undying hostility to the competition of convict labor, and say they will be forced to take lower wages if the few thousands of convicts in the United States are permitted to compete with them.
>
> If the Democrats were known to be in favor of convict labor, the Democratic workingmen would rise up and howl and vote against the candidate of their party.
>
> If the Democrats should declare next week [in the party platform] that the convicts in Joliet should be allowed to make shoes, cigars, barrels, and farm wagons to the greatest possible extent because consumers would get those articles at lower prices and be benefitted thereby, the city would give a nearly solid Republican vote. But if the Democrats should say that foreign-made goods should be admitted duty free because they are so cheap and because the consumer would be benefitted, the workingmen would throw up their hats.
>
> They do not seem to be able to see that *there is little difference,* so far as they are concerned, between competing goods made by convicts and competing goods whose cheapness is due to the fact that the men who make them get low wages. *The only difference* is that they would come from the penitentiaries in small quantities and from England by the shipload.

2. *Comparisons in Different Spheres.*—A second type of analogy is one which compares a particular in one sphere of life or in one field of activity with a particular in another sphere or field and infers that what is true of the known particular is also true of the particular that is in dispute. This kind of analogy sometimes has great logical force. The following editorial, for example, carries a considerable amount of conviction;

it argues *a fortiori*[7] that the ethics which operate in the field of international finance will also operate in the field of international politics so far as the interests of American citizens and of the American nation are concerned.

> Sir Hugo Hirst of the General Electric Company of England will not abandon his program to swindle American stockholders. A new issue of stock will be offered exclusively for British consumption, and the American shares, which comprise a majority of the stock, will decrease in value. . . .
>
> What private capital in Great Britain has done to American interests has been legitimately taken as an illustration of what British diplomacy is prepared to do to the United States if we should join the World Court.
>
> Morality in international finance is more highly developed than in international politics. British capital has violated a fundamental code of conduct, a primitive financial obligation, the destruction of which prevents further business between nations as it would between individuals. Having demonstrated its ability, unlawfully, to confiscate American property, what assurance have we that Britain would have any higher standards in her diplomatic dealings with us if we should trustingly enter the World Court?

This argument, which has great logical force, does not, however, constitute proof; for no argument by analogy constitutes proof. It has the logical strength of a generalization from a single instance. The inference concerning the World Court, moreover, has no logical force here, for that question constitutes a separate argument. In order for it to have logical

---

[7] The argument *a fortiori* reasons that "if a certain thing is true in a given case, much more will it be true in a supposed case where the conditions are more favorable" (J. F. Genung, *The Working Principles of Rhetoric*, p. 613) ; as, for example, "Wherefore, if God so clothe the grass of the field, which today is, and tomorrow is cast into the oven, shall He not much more clothe you, O ye of little faith?" and, "If tariff barriers are causes of international conflict among the Powers, they are even more dangerous when erected by the small, isolated states of eastern Europe, whose neighbors are so many."

force, the editorial writer would have to construct a separate argument which included the major premise that "Entrance of the United States into the World Court puts the United States in a position where she can be cheated by Great Britain." Whether or not this major premise is true is an argument which would have to be developed separately; in this instance the editorial writer simply assumes that it is true and is understood by the reader.

Few analogies of this type have as much logical force as the foregoing example seems to have. It is not often possible to infer, with any logic, that what is true of a particular in one sphere of life or in one field of activity is true of a particular in another sphere or another field. The following editorial, however, seems to have considerable logical force:

> When someone in the family is ill, the neighbors are not called in to decide whether he has scarlet fever or a cold, whether he needs hot lemonade or cold compresses. The best medical aid which can be procured by the family is summoned to the bedside. The medical man, after hearing the history of the case and making a diagnosis, prescribes the necessary treatment.
>
> In like manner, when someone is accused of a grave crime, a legal mind should weigh the evidence, and a board of psychiatrists, alienists, and lawyers, after studying a convicted man's record, should decide what kind of sentence would be most beneficial to him and to society.

3. *Historical Parallel.*—A third kind of analogy is the historical parallel. It reasons from a known particular in the past to a disputed particular in the present or the future. It argues that the present or the future will be like the past. The following editorial from the *New Republic* is an example:

> The situation regarding hydroelectric power in the United States today is in many ways analogous to that regarding railroads

during the middle decades of the last century.

At that time the railroad map of the country was drawn and the important trunk lines were laid down once and for all. This was accomplished by unrestricted private enterprise; roads were built wherever the promoters thought they would be most profitable, and the country has been suffering ever since from the bad job they made of it. Too many lines were built in some places, too few in others—mistakes which cannot now be rectified without an expenditure so tremendous that it is out of the question. The next decade will see the completion of a similar process in regard to power. Already, the network of giant power transmission lines has been thrown across the country, and once more, there has been but little attention to the ultimate needs of the population or indeed to anything except how to make the largest possible profits in the shortest time. It is not merely a question whether the state or federal government can develop power as economically as can private operators in the same territory. In the long run the best interest of the people as a whole may be served by giving public service in certain regions before it can be made to pay for itself, or by locating lines, not where they are needed today but where they will be needed 10 or 20 years hence.

The managers of electric companies have a duty to their stockholders which is paramount; the government has a duty to the people of the whole community.

The following example is adapted from two editorials in the Chicago *Tribune:*

The Republican party, although seemingly without serious elements of disintegration in it, is permitting itself to become that same instrument of oppression which the Federalist party became before it died. In enforcing the Volstead act it treats the democracy precisely as the Federalists endeavored to do in administering the alien and sedition laws. There is the same draconic disregard of principles and individuals.

The defense of liberties in the history of the republic has gone at various times from one party to another. Jefferson, a Democrat, inspired and directed the fight against the autocracy of the Federalists endeavoring in the time of Adams to suppress opinion, destroy free speech, put down opposition, and restrict popular democracy with the sedition act, an act which destroyed them.

Lincoln, a Republican, organized the government which put down the slave owning aristocracy which had made it treason to refuse to help a federal officer in pursuit of a fugitive slave and unlawful to petition congress for the abolition of slavery.

The country is now in the period of its third great autocratic attempt upon the liberties and rights of individuals and upon the essential principles of American government.

It is not likely that this will be in permanent accord with the purposes and demands of the American people. The period necessary for their recovery and for their retaking of their ancient rights may be unknown, but the probability is that they will make it short. The Republican-Democrats of Jefferson's time were wrong on economic theories, but they were right in popular liberties. The public is hard to lead on economic theories, and a party which remains as fundamentally wrong on moral and constitutional questions as the Republican party is today can hardly hope to remain in power.

There is the warning to the party to seek means of reconverting itself into a party of principles and probity as well as one of economic soundness.

The writer who argues by means of historical parallels should be careful in three respects: (*a*) he should be certain of his historical facts; (*b*) he should be cautious about assuming that "history repeats itself"; and (c) he should not take for granted that his reader is familiar with the historical data to which he is referring.

The following editorial is an example of an historical parallel which is based on untrue facts:

> The liquor traffic has never obeyed the law and it never will. The first organized rebellion against the laws and authority of this nation was made by the anarchist saloon in the Pennsylvania Whiskey Rebellion which cost the Washington administration an army of 15,000 men and the largest single expenditure of the infant government to suppress.
>
> The nation was not twenty years old when the liquor traffic rose in rebellion against the law, and it has been in rebellion ever since. It has never obeyed the law and it never will.

The so-called Whiskey Rebellion in 1794 was not an effort of the "saloon" to avert control of the "liquor traffic." The farmers on the Western frontier distilled and sold whisky because it was not possible to transport bulky grain to market over the impassable roads, though a keg of whisky could be carried on horseback. Their rebellion was merely a protest against one of the first direct taxes levied by the new Federal Government. More than anything else it was a class rebellion, and no moral element was involved. No parallel with present conditions can be based on any such interpretation as the foregoing editorial presents.[8]

It is true, in a sense, that "history repeats itself," but "it is a sense that cannot be defined, and in such a sense that definite inferences drawn from the principle are more likely to be false than true." One who studies history closely undoubtedly extends the range and depth of his experience-world and thus obtains a clearer insight into public questions; but history, of course, does not prove anything, for history, no matter how much synthesis is given to it, is only the record of *unique*

---

[8] For an explanation of the class struggle of which the Whiskey Rebellion was only one incident, see C. A. and M. R. Beard, *The Rise of American Civilization*, Vol. I, Chap. VIII.

events.[9] An historical parallel is merely a generalization from a single example, as the following case shows:

One of the points frequently made in a discussion of the problem of Philippine independence is that withdrawal of the United States would be followed by an economic penetration by the Japanese. Some opponents of independence for the Filipinos even argue that economic penetration by the Japanese would inevitably be followed by military invasion, and they point to the invasion of Mexico by the United States following the economic penetration of that country by Americans in the forties. This, of course, is argument from analogy, but there is implied in the argument the generalization, "Economic penetration of a country by a neighboring country is inevitably followed by military conquest." The only proof of the generalization that is given in the argument is the single example of the Mexican War. Editorials involving historical parallel serve to reënforce argument, and sometimes they are even true parallels, but ordinarily the historical parallel has for its purpose illustration rather than proof: it clarifies what one has already proved and thus helps to clinch an argument.

When an editorial writer cites the data of history for the purpose of proving or suggesting a parallel, he ought to be careful to set forth enough of the data to provide his reader with an understanding of the specific historical situation. To do this thoroughly may sometimes require more space than the subject warrants, but unless a true picture is provided, the argument, in so far as many readers are concerned, is wasted. The editorial writer ought not to assume that his readers will understand all of the casual historical references that he makes in the course of an editorial. Editorial writers of fifty years ago were fond of drawing parallels from Greek and Roman history, and today the editorials in the Italian newspapers contain many parallels from classical history; but the readers addressed fifty years ago were more familiar with classical references than are readers today outside of Italy. Modern

---

[9] For a criticism of the methods of the school of "historical" (or "institutional") economics, which ventures predictions as to periodic price levels, etc., see the chapter by F. H. Knight in *The Trend of Economics* (R. G. Tugwell, ed.), pp. 264-266.

readers are no longer educated in the classics, and almost any argument containing a classical reference is, from the reader's standpoint, likely to be an argument from an unknown particular to an unknown particular.

False Analogy.—In order to test argument from analogy, we can make two inquiries: (a) are there a sufficient number of points of resemblance between the particulars? and (b) granted that there are many points of resemblance, is an essential point of difference overlooked which is sufficient to destroy the force of the analogy?

1. *Few Points of Resemblance.*—Frequently arguments from analogy are advanced which, although accepted by the naïve mind, really have too few points of resemblance for the analogy to have probative force. The naïve mind is inclined to accept such analogies because it has little knowledge of the details. Such an argument we call far-fetched, but to some minds it is not at all far-fetched. The arguments of the Scholastics, referred to in a previous section, seem to us today to be extremely far-fetched, yet at the time they were made they were almost universally accepted because the age was sensitive to dualism.[10] The following excerpt from the majority opinion in the District of Columbia Minimum Wage Case, decided by the Supreme Court in 1923, illustrates the oversimplification of the points of resemblance in particulars. Mr. Justice Sutherland, in condemning the principle of a minimum wage for women, said:

In principle, there can be no difference between the case of selling labor and the case of selling goods. If one goes to the butcher, the baker or grocer to buy food, he is morally entitled to obtain the worth of his money but he is not entitled to more. If what he gets is worth what he pays he is not justified in demanding more simply because he needs more; and the shopkeeper, having dealt fairly and honestly in that transaction, is not concerned in any peculiar sense with the question of the customer's necessities. Should a statute undertake to vest in a commission power to determine the quantity of food necessary for individual

---

[10] Perhaps the simplest form of analogy that we meet every day is the symbolic representation of nations and ideas in the newspaper cartoons. Oftentimes these pictorial representations are oversimplifications.

support and require the shopkeeper, if he sell to the individual at all, to furnish that quantity at not more than a fixed maximum, it would undoubtedly fall before the constitutional test. . . . A statute requiring an employer to pay in money, to pay at prescribed and regular intervals, to pay the value of the services rendered, even to pay with fair relation to the extent of the benefit obtained from the service, would be understandable. But a statute which prescribes payment without regard to any of these things and solely with relation to circumstances apart from the contract of employment, the business affected by it and the work done under it, is so clearly the product of a naked, arbitrary exercise of power that it cannot be allowed to stand under the Constitution of the United States.[11]

Is this a true analogy? Does the employer bear the same relation to his employee that the shopkeeper does to his customer? Is the relation between the employer and the employee as casual as that between the shopkeeper and his customer? If the employee's only means of support is the wages paid by her employer, is she not entitled to a living wage? Is the end of industry only profits—is industry an institution so detached from society that it has no obligations to the women who are so indispensable to society? Moreover, assuming that the increase in wages is partly passed along to the customer, are not the people obliged to furnish a living wage to all those members of society who are engaged in productive labor?

2. *The Essential Point of Difference.*—The surest clew to a false analogy is the detection of the essential point of difference. In any comparison there are points of resemblance and points of difference, so the soundness of the analogy must rest upon the relative importance of the points of likeness and difference. Whenever some point of difference is so essential that it outweighs the points of resemblance, the analogy, for the purposes of logical proof, is destroyed. The following editorial is an example of an analogy which disregards the essential point of difference:

> The recent flood of articles by physicians condemning their brothers in the profession for fee-splitting with surgeons and specialists

---

[11] Adkins *et al. v.* Children's Hospital, 261 U. S. 525.

to whom they send patients has met with
no logical refutation.

This particular practice of the profession
has been deplored as being unethical in the
holy profession of medicine. Yet in all
other trades and professions it is not condemned.

Why should medicine, after all, be governed by an entirely different set of ethics
than the other professions? A business man
isn't condemned for accepting a commission
for sending a customer to a certain company.
A commission and a split fee are essentially
the same.

The following editorial, which is a refutation of an argument
from analogy, points out the essential point of difference in an
argument by analogy:

Senator James Spurlock has introduced in
the legislature a revenue measure which will
place a tax on the sale of cigarettes.

The only reason offered for the introduction of the bill is that it offers an easy
method of raising revenue. That is the excuse always offered for sales tax bills.

The sales tax is always dangerous because
of the insidious appeal which it offers that
it is placing the tax only on the consumer.
It is a tax which in any form is a burden,
and every extension of the sales tax principle means an added danger to all consumers that the next article on which it will
be imposed is one of which they are users.
There are many people who are opposed to
cigarettes and do not smoke them. It is
believed they will all agree the cigarette
smoker should be taxed for his luxury. The
friends of the bill do not seem to foresee
that a few years hence a similar tax will
be proposed on tea.

Senator Spurlock defends his bill by comparing it to the gasoline tax, which, also,
is a sales tax. If a tax on gasoline, which
is used in business as well as pleasure, why

not a tax on cigarettes, which are a luxury? he asks.

Senator Spurlock overlooks one difference —and it is the essential difference—between the three-cents-a-gallon gasoline tax now levied in this state and his proposed tax on the consumption of cigarettes.

It is this. The proceeds of the gasoline tax are used solely for road building and maintenance purposes. The people most benefitted are those who use the roads. The people of this state are not the only travellers on our highways; the thousands of tourists who come here and use our roads help to pay for them by paying the gasoline tax. In effect, the gasoline tax when used only for road building and maintenance purposes is *a toll paid by those who use the highways.* The cigarette tax in no way comes within this class. It is a sales tax *pure and simple* devised for the sole purpose of raising *revenues to meet general state expenditures.*[12]

Analogy in Creative Thinking.—Although the discussion in this chapter has shown that analogy is only an incomplete kind of proof, it nevertheless has a value for the creative thinker. It *suggests* hypotheses which the thinker verifies by other ways of thinking. For example:

The first suggestion which led Harvey to discover the circulation of the blood came through analogy. He learned from his master that the valves in many veins lie open as long as the blood flows through them toward the heart, no longer. He thought of the many analogous mechanical contrivances, such as animal traps and tide-water gates, which have similar valves adapted to definite ends. This suggested the question what similar end might be served by the valves in the veins. But this suggestion was for Harvey merely a starting point; he proceeded to test the analogy by careful experimentation. He tied arteries and veins and observed the effects of the flow of the blood. For nineteen years he kept up this observation and study, until he had traced to his

---

[12] Adapted from Madison *Wisconsin State Journal.*

own satisfaction the entire course of the blood through the human body. Thus he verified a theory suggested by analogy.[13]

Likewise, sociologists, by studying the symbiotic relation of insects, animals, and plants, have derived a more complete understanding of that human symbiosis which we call society.

ILLUSTRATIVE ANALOGY

The type of analogy we have been discussing is sometimes called *literal* analogy because it is argument which presumably has probative force. Some analogies, however, do not parade as proof, but have for their purpose the strengthening of an argument by way of illustration. They are usually rich in imagery and are consequently called *figurative* analogies. A figurative analogy, taken in this sense, is only one of the four "figures of association." Rhetoricians list these figures as follows: (*a*) simile; (*b*) figurative analogy; (*c*) metaphor; and (*d*) allegory. Although a discussion of these figures of association properly belongs in the chapter on "Editorial Style," we examine them here because of their similarity to literal analogy.

Simile.—Simile is an expressed (or implied) likeness of objects which are of different classes. The word is derived from the Latin adjective *similis* which means "like." The simile is employed more in exposition and description than in argumentation. The figure is so familiar that it is not necessary to cite an illustration here.

Figurative Analogy.—Like simile, figurative analogy expresses a likeness; but where simile expresses a likeness between two objects of a different class, figurative analogy expresses a likeness between the *relation* of two objects.[14] Simile expresses a ratio $(a:b)$; figurative analogy expresses a proportion $(a:x::b:x$; or $a:x::b:y)$. Figurative analogy is precisely like the literal analogy we have been discussing, except that it does not presume to have logical strength, only illustrative

---

[13] Adapted from J. G. Hibben, *Logic, Deductive and Inductive*, Chapter XIII. Quoted by W. T. Foster, *Argumentation and Debating.*
[14] See pp. 146-147.

force. It is elucidative, not logical. It is merely an elaborated simile. It usually describes an unfamiliar concept or condition in terms of a familiar one. Ordinarily it consists in making a statement of a concept or of a condition of affairs, following with the statement of another concept or condition of affairs which it asserts to be analogous, the latter statement being presumed to be familiar to the reader. The second statement, which is frequently ridiculous or grotesque, is usually introduced by a phrase—"as if" or "it is much the same as."

(1)

Great Britain declares that we ought to reduce our tariff; which is just as if the chickens next door demanded that we leave our garden gate open.

(2)

It is rather absurd, when you come to think of it, that when a President of the United States makes a so-called Good Will trip to our neighboring states to the south [referring to President Hoover's trip to South and Central America in 1929], he should travel amid all the trappings of war on our hugest dreadnaught. Of course, he can say that it doesn't mean anything, but it's something as if, when your neighbor drops in for a friendly evening at bridge he should draw his six-shooter and lay it ready to hand before he deals.

Usually the best analogy is a plain or homely one—an analogy which cites a plain or a familiar parallel; analogies taken from the classics are no longer understood by the ordinary reader. Some examples of effective figurative analogies used in editorials are the following:

(1)

The Northwest is about as warmly attached to the Republican party as is the Irish Free State to the United Kingdom.

(2)

What the astute psychologist reading the great masterpieces of literature chiefly notices is the frequency with which their authors descend to the obviously banal. It is like contemplating a rose garden cluttered with Jimpson weeds or drinking champagne mixed with sarsaparilla.—H. L. MENCKEN.

(3)

A fundamentalist clergyman whose son is entering the ministry announces that he is watching him closely to make sure that no modernistic ideas enter his brain.

That conscientious father might get an idea from the Flathead Indians. They fasten a board against the baby's head when it is born, keep it there, and make sure that the head stays flat.—BRISBANE.

(4)

A university is like a watch. You may strip it of chain and charm, and still it runs. It may have a battered case, and keep good time. But its works must be perfect. A bookless dumbbell in a castle is insignificant, a philosopher and a book in an attic may change history's course. Given zeal for knowledge, and high leadership, the buildings of a university are of secondary importance. The teaching personnel are the works of the watch.

(5)

. . . Yet how can a jury form any opinions on so technical a question as mental disease? Even if it had the benefit of sound evidence it would be as helpless as if it tried to diagnose some physical diseases. But it does not even have this. In the present case, as in most cases that are tried this way, the best it can do is to make up its mind between two sets of alienists, both of them obviously biased in favor of their retaining fees. Thus it is in much the same position as it would occupy if it were asked to hear a chiropractor swear the deceased suffered from a curvature of the spine, a chiropodist swear that he suffered from bunions, and then decide whether he died from the effects of a railroad accident.—New York *World*.

(6)

A news event, to the layman, is like an explosive noise he hears outside. He rushes out to learn what it was, what caused it, and what the effects are. He makes observations of the place where the noise seemed to come from and he makes inquiries of eye-witnesses and of others whose arrival preceded his own. The trained newspaper reporter comes along some time afterward to make observations and inquiries. His explanation in the newspaper the next day will probably be much more accurate than the explanation gathered by the layman who was almost on the spot. The reason is that the newspaper reporter is trained to make observations and inquiries. His "reportorial sense"—his sense of the probabilities and his evidential judgment—is much better than that of the layman. This fact is true of news reporting whether the news reported be an automobile accident or a disarmament conference. The lay critics of the press have no conception of the great accuracy of the American press considered in the light of the difficulties that news reporting involves. Imagine some professors of history reporting spot news of the London disarmament conference!

Metaphor.—Metaphor expresses a likeness between objects, not by comparing them or by comparing their relations, but by *identifying* an object of one class with an object of another class. The word *metaphor* is derived from two Greek words which mean "to transfer"; metaphor, accordingly, is a figure in which the meaning inherent in one object or concept or situation is transferred to another. Because metaphor identifies one object with another instead of comparing two objects, it is a stronger figure of association than either simile or figurative analogy. For example, the metaphorical phrase,

That great trading corporation, the British Empire

is more forcible than the simile,

The British Empire is like a great trading corporation.

The metaphor expresses closer association and, being a briefer statement, consequently has more force.

Some metaphors which were at one time striking have survived as stock expressions. Thus there is a tendency for the writer to adopt a worn expression and unconsciously elaborate it so that it has the effect of what is called a "mixed metaphor." Shakespeare committed this fault in his line, "to take arms against a sea of troubles." Gouverneur Morris mixed a metaphor in an impassioned speech in 1801 when, in referring to the Constitution which he thought was imperiled by the Republicans' proposal to repeal the Federalist judiciary act, he said: "Cast not away this anchor of our safety. *I have seen its progress.* I know the difficulties through which it was obtained, etc."

Allegory.—Allegory is a figure of association which is fundamentally a metaphor but one which is extended by narrative. Allegory has all the concreteness of metaphor; in addition, it has justification in psychology because of the tendency of the human mind to dramatize abstract ideas. The most effective allegories in literature have had a moral purpose, as, for example, *Pilgrim's Progress;* but modern controversy has contributed many allegories that have no relation to morals.[15]

---

[15] For a discussion of the argumentative strength of allegory during medieval times, see Henry Osborn Taylor, *The Medieval Mind*, Vol. II, Chaps. XXVIII and XXIX. Men in those days sought for reality, not in the tangible phenomenon, but in what the phenomenon might be conceived to symbolize. "Therefore, in the higher political controversies, even as in other interests of the human spirit, argument through allegory was accepted as legitimate, if not convincing; and a proper sequence of thought was deemed to lie from one symbolical meaning to another, with even a deeper validity than from one palpable fact to that which followed from it."—p. 309.

The following editorial from the Conservative London *Daily Express* illustrates the use of simple allegory in argument. Written in 1926 during an unusual period of post-war unemployment in Great Britain, it was a rebuke to local poor relief agencies which were disbursing public poor relief funds with an overgenerous hand:

> There was once a woman who was presented with a cheque-book. It was long before the days of business and political women, lady barristers, editresses, and the like; and perhaps her husband neglected to explain the principles of banking. Whatever be the cause, she drew cheque after cheque without concerning herself as to the state of her account, until at last one of them came back marked with the letters R. D. Her husband impounded the cheque-book and gave her a lesson in finance.
>
> West Ham Board of Guardians were like the lady with the cheque-book. The Minister of Health, more paternally, perhaps, than conjugally, has taken away the cheque-book they proved themselves incapable of using, and has installed some one else to pay their bills. No other course is possible with a spendthrift who refuses to live on his income.

It is quite easy to invent narrative for the purposes of argument, but it is difficult to embody the essential truth in narrative. The editorial writer, therefore, ought never to permit his eagerness for convincing his readers to exceed his zeal for telling the truth. Below are two allegories employed by writers who were discussing the Anglo-American naval controversy. The first of the allegories illustrates an essential truth; the second is an oversimplification of a complex controversy. The first allegory is from an article by Señor Salvador de Madariaga, former chief of the Disarmament Section of the League of Nations. He is explaining that the politicians and statesmen who are responsible for the calling and holding of disarmament conferences are motivated principally by a desire to reduce the tax budgets of their countries rather than by a desire to reduce the possibilities of future wars.[16]

(1)

In the old days when Florence led the world there were five bankers in the city well known for their friendly rivalry. They were all solid and sound men, fearful of God, loving their good wives and enjoying their still better mistresses. Of these, Signor Jonathani and Signor Giovanni Toro had so many that neither the curious town nor the fortunate bankers themselves knew the exact number thereof; Signor Nipponi, Signor Gallo, and Signor Savoia had a lesser, though still comfortable number.

But winds cannot always blow fair, and a foul weather having set in on the seas of business, the five rivals and friends bethought themselves of the necessity of reducing their costly establishment.

So Signor Jonathani, the wealthiest of the group and therefore its leader, called a conference of the five, and it was decided, not without difficulty, for the five men were healthy and loved their flesh and the ladies were fair and brought them much pleasure and prestige—it was decided, I say, that Signor Jonathani and Signor Giovanni Toro should limit the number of their fair friends to five apiece; Signor Nipponi to three; while Signori Gallo and Savoia should be reduced to one each with occasional visits to one other, which visits they would carefully keep equal in number; and in order that their credit— I mean their financial prestige—should not suffer thereby, the five friendly rivals agreed to make it quite clear to the curious city that their sacrifices were made in defence to the sanctity of marriage.[17]

---

[16] *Atlantic Monthly,* Vol. CXLIII, pp. 527-529; reprinted by permission.

[17] Observe that the nations personified here are given their appropriate Italian names: the United States, "Jonathani"; Great Britain, "Giovanni Toro"; and so on.

(2)

Once upon a time there were two neighboring families who went under the well known names of Smith and Jones. They had been young folks together, and were distantly related. They had had a few family feuds, but they got along well together on the whole, and had prospered.

When automobiles came in, each family had its automobile. When it became stylish to have two automobiles, the Smiths were not far behind the Joneses. When it became stylish to have three automobiles the Joneses were not far behind the Smiths. One day the Smiths took a notion into their heads that they should have more automobiles than the Joneses. They bought a car for each of the children, and one for each of their servants.

The Joneses said that this was the height of extravagance and foolishness, but what could they do? The two families had been equally leaders in the community for years, and the Joneses could not afford to fall behind. So they, too, ordered cars for all their servants.

This pretty little allegory of everyday life has its parallel in international nonsense. Call the Smiths England and call the Joneses America, use the word cruiser in place of automobile, and you have the whole story of the disarmament conference impasse and deadlock.

Reduced to simplest terms, it becomes an absurdity.

CHAPTER IX

HOW THE MIND FALLS INTO ERROR

We frequently hear people say, "He can't think"; or (the intelligentsia say) "The man in the street can't think." A more accurate assertion would be, "He *doesn't* think"; or "The man in the street *doesn't think about anything except his private concerns.*" As a matter of fact, most persons can and do think. The ordinary man does a great deal of thinking, but his conclusions are usually private decisions; he does little thinking about public affairs.[1] If he were stimulated, he could do a great deal of thinking of a public and social kind, but his fund of information about public and social questions is too limited for him to think about them profoundly and often. It is a lack of information, after all, which is the chief limitation on the ordinary person's ability to think. Yet, there are other causes— though less significant—of erroneous thinking. It is the purpose of this chapter to analyze these other causes.

Causes of Unsound Thinking.—In varying degrees the human mind is endowed with the ability to perceive the *relation* in things. Some minds are alert and "open," and they consequently perceive relation; other minds are dull and "narrow," and they "can't think." It is this dullness of mind—explained by the psychologists perhaps in terms of "attention"—and this narrowness of mind—explained by the psychologists in terms of egotistic "wishes" and "desires"—which are the causes of erroneous thinking that we shall examine here. For they—as well as lack of information—lie at the foundation of erroneous thinking.

In the first place, we fail to perceive the relation of things— causes, effects, parts, wholes, etc.—because of our inattention to the *distinguishing characteristics* of things. "The foundation of all reasoning is the recognition of a *similitude;* reasoning

---

[1] See J. H. Robinson, *The Mind in the Making*, pp. 1-9.

may be roughly defined as the transition from a known fact to a second unknown fact, by means of a resemblance. . . . There is no act of reasoning in the world which does not contain . . . the affirmation of a resemblance; but this affirmation takes different forms and is called by different names: comparison, classification, recognition, etc." [2]

Our failure to identify and recognize the essential characteristics of things is the result of our lack of concentration on the matter that lies before us. Alexander Hamilton once said of himself: "Men give me some credit for genius. All the genius I have lies in this: When I have a subject in hand I study it profoundly."

In the second place, we fail to perceive the relation of things because *we do not want to see them.* That is to say, our egotistic wishes and desires hide from us the true meaning of data. Our preconceived notions and prejudices are difficult to put aside, and our emotions invade our thought chambers. In subsequent chapters we shall again refer to the rôle of desires in editorial thinking and writing, as it affects both the writer of editorials and the reader.

The Syllogism.—In order to understand how inattention and egotistic desires interfere with straight thinking, we shall have to examine some of the content of logic, and in particular that part of logic which treats of *deductive* thinking. Deduction, as we have said before, is not really thinking, but one of the processes in thinking—the verifying process. For example, we say, "If this case is diphtheria, the symptoms *a, b, c,* and *d* should be present; these symptoms are present; therefore, this case is diphtheria."

The logicians have worked out the technique of this process of verification of an hypothesis to a fine point. They have invented a mechanism of deduction which they call the syllogism. The syllogism is defined as "an argument in which three propositions are so related that one of them (the conclusion) follows from the other two." [3] Thus, the following is a syllogism:

---

[2] Alfred Binet, *The Psychology of Reasoning* (3d ed.), pp. 86-87.
[3] R. W. Sellars, *The Essentials of Logic,* p. 107.

Major premise: All sterling silver is expensive.
Minor premise: This piece of silver is sterling.
Conclusion: This piece of silver is expensive.

A syllogism does not "prove" anything in the sense that it is a series of steps by which the mind proceeds from one proposition through a second proposition to a third proposition (the conclusion). The mind merely *states* two propositions (called the major premise and the minor premise), and the conclusion is necessarily implied from the statement of the two propositions. The conclusion necessarily follows because of the logical *relation* of the premises. For a conclusion to be valid, all that is necessary is that the propositions be stated in a logical relation: the validity of the conclusion is self-evident provided that the logical relation of the premises has been stated. The syllogism merely *exhibits* conveniently the data of an act of reasoning already performed.

How the Syllogism Tests Reasoning.—The value of formulating our reasoning in the syllogistic form arises from the nature of the major premise, which is usually a general truth. Every conclusion that we reason out is referred for testing to this major premise. If our reasoning does not contain a major premise, or imply one, our reasoning is not logical.[4] For example, a justice of the United States Supreme Court, in a decision involving a minimum wage law said, "If, in the interest of the public welfare, the police power may be invoked to justify the fixing of a minimum wage, it may, when the public welfare is thought to require it, be invoked to justify a maximum wage." This kind of reasoning is termed *non-sequitur* because "it does not follow" that if the law is invoked to fix a minimum wage, it could also be invoked to fix a maximum wage. The conclusion does not follow because the conclusion is not referred to a general truth. Such reasoning cannot be stated syllogistically because it neither contains nor implies a major premise. The thinker who tries to arrange

---

[4] When a syllogism does not contain a major premise, yet obviously implies one, we call the syllogism *enthymeme.* An example is cited on page 204.

What some logicians call "immediate inference" is not syllogistic reasoning, but simply a restatement of a proposition in different words.

his reasoning in syllogistic form and discovers that it contains no major premise knows that his propositions are not logically related—that his conclusion, in consequence, is not true.

More important, though, than exhibiting that a line of reasoning contains no major premise is the function of the syllogism in revealing that the major premise is probably untrue. For example, let us examine a statement in André Siegfried's *America Comes of Age:*

The great newspapers, as every one knows, live entirely by their advertising. Logically, therefore, they are bound to fall sooner or later under the influence of high finance and big business, which pays for publicity.[5]

When we attempt to arrange this argument in syllogistic form, we observe that the major premise is implied, namely, "The revenue that the great newspapers receive determines their editorial policy." Arranging the argument, then, in syllogistic form, we have the following propositions:

The revenue that the great newspapers receive determines their editorial policy.
High finance and big business furnish all the revenue of the great newspapers.
High finance and big business determine the editorial policy of the great newspapers.

As a result of arranging our thoughts in this manner, the major premise of the argument, which was not even stated by M. Siegfried because he took for granted that it was true, stands out in relief. The longer we examine this premise the more we begin to cast about for evidence of its truth. We perhaps make inquiries of newspaper men and advertisers whom we meet, and, as we read criticisms of the press in books and in the critical reviews, any evidence that we note which tends to prove or disprove the generalization is registered on our intelligence. Thus, if we are open-minded, we resist being "taken in" by a statement which we do not empirically know to be true, and wait until we have obtained convincing evidence.[6]

---

[5] P. 243.
[6] Siegfried's conclusion is examined further at pp. 179-182.

This is what was meant when we said in a previous chapter that deduction is a process of testing a tentative hypothesis by inquiring as to its consistency with the known facts. The fact that we refer our conclusion to a general truth either causes us to perceive the inconsistency of our conclusion with the general truth or to doubt the general truth itself and thus to doubt our conclusion. The thinker ought to habituate himself to this method of reasoning. He does not usually have to write down his reasoning in syllogistic form, but he should mentally trace his reasoning in syllogistic form just as if he had written it down. As a matter of fact, this is what a thinker does anyway, though he is not conscious of doing it. What he should do is to *be conscious of the method.* If he does this, he will see not unrelated phenomena but broad principles; he will come to be more critical of the numerous suggestions he encounters and may even come to revise some of the principles he has tentatively held. This is what is sometimes meant when we speak of "thinking through" a problem.

Types of Fallacies.—An error in deductive reasoning is called by the logicians a *fallacy.* A fallacy arises from the fact that the three propositions of the syllogism are, in some manner, not logically related. Fallacies may be due to two causes, namely: (1) an illogically stated relation between the premises; or (2) an ambiguity in the statement of the propositions.

Logicians are in the habit of saying that fallacies are either *formal* or *material.* By formal fallacies are meant those which violate the rules of the syllogistic mechanism. By material fallacies are meant those which result from misapprehension of the meaning of a proposition (usually of a term) or a false assumption regarding the argument. That is to say, a material fallacy has to do with the *substance* of the argument, a formal fallacy with the *form* of the argument. Actually there is no difference between formal and material fallacies, but it is convenient for us to examine them as if there were a difference.

Rules of the Syllogism.—The key to an understanding of the syllogism is the rule that the syllogism is made up of three terms. Although it is made up of three propositions of two terms each, it does not contain six terms, but three terms, for the same terms are used twice.   Thus, in the following syllogism—

$$M \text{ is } P$$
$$S \text{ is } M$$
$$S \text{ is } P$$

—there are only three terms.   It is these *common* terms which relate the three propositions logically, which bind them in logical relation.   The term that is common in the premises—*M*—is called the *middle* term.   The subject term of the conclusion—*S*—is called the *minor* term, and the predicate term of the conclusion—*P*—is called the *major* term.[7]

Obviously there is no logical relation of the premises in the following reasoning:

All sterling silver is expensive.
This piece of silver is plated.

for, instead of three terms, there are four.

In the following syllogism, however, there is logical relation, for the syllogism contains only three terms:

All sterling silver is expensive.
This piece of silver is sterling.
This piece of silver is expensive.

One might think that it is easy to perceive that a syllogism contains four terms instead of three, and that the mind, consequently, is not likely to fall into error.   But it is extremely difficult sometimes to perceive that a syllogism contains four terms when it *seems* to contain only three.   Nearly all fallacies are of this kind and, though they have different names, they are, in the last analysis, fallacies of four terms.

Before we discuss the reasons for four-term fallacies, we shall list four rules of the syllogism.   There are at least a dozen formal fallacies which are due to the violation of some rule of the syllogism.   Some of these are:

---

[7] The reader will notice that the symbols are initial letters: S = subject term; P = predicate term; M = middle term.

1. In every syllogism there should be three, and not more than three, terms, and these terms must be used throughout in the same sense (Fallacy of Four Terms).

2. The middle term must be distributed at least once in the premises (Undistributed Middle).[8]

3. No term ought to be distributed in the conclusion that was not distributed in the premises (Illicit Major).

4. No conclusion can be drawn for two particular propositions (Undistributed Middle or Illicit Major).

THE FALLACY OF FOUR TERMS

Why do we fail to observe that some syllogisms contain four terms? Why do there sometimes *appear* to be three terms when actually there are four? There is one of two reasons: (1) there is an *unwarranted assumption,* or (2) there is an *ambiguity* of terms in the syllogism. These two factors account for all fallacies.

1. Unwarranted Assumption.—We examine first a four-term fallacy that is the result of an unwarranted assumption. This type of fallacy consists in *assuming something which we have no right to assume.* Professor Burtt has an excellent example of such a current fallacy which relates to a public question: "George Washington told us to avoid entangling alliances; we certainly ought not, then, to join the League of Nations."[9] When we try to formulate this reasoning in a syllogism we perceive that the mechanism has four, instead of three, terms:

Entangling alliances are things George Washington told us to avoid.
The League of Nations is an entangling alliance.
Therefore, the League of Nations is something we ought not to join.

Obviously, a logical relation of the terms has not been stated; for, although the middle and minor terms conform to the rule, the *predicate term in the conclusion is not the same as the*

---

[8] For an interesting discussion of the inadequacy of this rule, see B. B. Bogoslovsky, *The Technique of Controversy* (London, 1928).

[9] E. A. Burtt, *Principles and Problems of Right Thinking,* pp. 227-228.

predicate term in the major premise.   Represented symbolically, the reasoning is:

$$M \text{ is } P$$
$$S \text{ is } M$$
$$S \text{ is } X$$

The only logical conclusion that can be deduced from the premises is: "The League of Nations is something George Washington told us to avoid." This, of course, is an absurdity, since George Washington never heard of the League of Nations. It is only by constructing an additional major premise that we can state a relation that logically justifies the original conclusion. That premise is: "We ought to do nothing that George Washington told us to avoid." Then, by constructing two different syllogisms, we can reason as follows:

(1)

We ought to do nothing that George Washington told us to avoid doing.
Joining entangling alliances is something George Washington told us to avoid.
Joining entangling alliances is something we ought not to do.

(2)

Joining entangling alliances is something we ought not to do.
The League of Nations is an entangling alliance.
The League of Nations is something we ought not to join.

Thus, by assuming an additional premise ("We ought to do nothing that George Washington told us to avoid"), and by reasoning from it, we have reached our original conclusion, "The League of Nations is something we ought not to join." But we could not logically have reached this conclusion had we not assumed the general truth, "We ought to do nothing that George Washington told us to avoid." But this general truth is an assumption *we are not warranted in making;* for, when one begins to ask himself whether or not we ought to do nothing that George Washington, in 1797, told us to avoid doing, he perceives that logic has no place in his reasoning.

There is no logical reason that could possibly justify the premise that we who live in the twentieth century ought to do nothing that George Washington told us to avoid doing. Of course, by our own independent reasoning we might arrive at the conclusion that we ought not to do such and such a thing, and this thing may turn out to be the same thing that George Washington, in 1797, warned his countrymen against; but there is no logic in the conclusion that we ought to avoid a thing that George Washington said we ought to avoid. Were it not for our use of the syllogistic mechanism in testing our conclusion, however, we might not have perceived the invalidity of our conclusion.

Why do so many persons fail to perceive this unwarranted assumption in the syllogism? The reasons are two: either they are so *inattentive* that they fail to perceive that an unwarranted assumption is implied, or they are so *prejudiced* that they fail to perceive it. In many cases, our slovenly thinking is due to our prejudices rather than to our inattention. For example, most of those who are isolationists as regards foreign commitments of the United States are already prejudiced against the League of Nations, and the line of false reasoning which we have just examined is a mere *rationalization* of their prejudices. Such reasoning is readily accepted as logical by some isolationists because they wish so much to believe it is logical that they do not "think through" the assumption on which it depends for validity.[10]

2. Ambiguity.—The four-term fallacy which we have just been discussing resulted from the intrusion into the argument of an unwarranted assumption, but a four-term fallacy may also result from the ambiguous use of a term. When one term is used with two different meanings, it is the same as if a fourth term had been added. Four-term fallacies that result from the ambiguous use of one term—say, the middle term—may be represented symbolically as follows:

---

[10] Even in mathematics, four-term fallacies occur which are due to unwarranted assumption. "It has been found by a large amount of experience," says Professor Moulton, in his *Introduction to Astronomy*, "that errors more frequently enter through unexpressed hypotheses than in any other way." (Rev. ed., p. 534.)

$$M^1 \text{ is } P$$
$$S \text{ is } M^2$$
$$S \text{ is } P$$

Such fallacies are sometimes difficult to perceive because the ambiguity is often one of *quality* rather than quantity. We use a term—*advertisers,* for example—in two different senses but without making this apparent in the argument. We may fail to distinguish between the kinds of advertisers, or we may think of advertisers in one way in one term, and in a different way in another term. Thus, our term which *appears* to be M is in reality two different terms—M^1 and M^2.

Frequently this ambiguity in the use of a term is a failure to distinguish between the whole and its parts. For example, an *individual* advertiser in a newspaper may act in one way, but the *whole body* of advertisers may act in an entirely different way. This ambiguity is illustrated in M. Siegfried's argument, which is quoted here in full:

> The great newspapers, as every one knows, live entirely by their advertising. Logically, therefore, they are bound to fall sooner or later under the influence of high finance and big business, which pays for publicity. Whenever an editorial contradicts their views, the captains of industry can easily exercise a little pressure. "Your editorials are not up to our standards," they write; and the editor, realizing what he is up against, gives in. Otherwise the paper goes to the wall. The national interests thus possess an effective means of moulding the public to their own ends by withholding what they think it should not know and presenting each subject from the desired angle. A rigid code is soon built up from which there is no escape, though people are soon unaware of its existence.[11]

It is difficult to tell from the context exactly what M. Siegfried means. He speaks of "captains of industry" and "national interests" coercing editors in order to mold the "public to their own ends," and he asserts that refusal on the part of the editors means that "the paper goes to the wall." It is evident, however, that the idea in his mind is that the newspapers are property-minded and that they are wedded to the dogma of "business

---

[11] *Op. cit.,* p. 243.

first"; also, that this circumstance is due to coercion by advertisers. That many of the "great" newspapers are property-minded and that they accept the dogma of "business first" is obvious to the thoughtful reader of newspapers, but that this is due entirely or primarily to coercion by advertisers is not necessarily a valid inference. To precisely what factors the property-mindedness of newspapers is due is explained at length in Chapter XIV.

From M. Siegfried, however, we derive the picture of an occult conspiracy (of which "the people" are "unaware") among the bankers and "captains of industry" to coerce editors with reference to their discussion of questions of public policy. He gives us a picture of a great *whole*—a capitalistic body which he calls the "national interests"—composed of several individual *members* who are alike in respect of the fact that they want to dictate in a malign way what shall be published in editorial and news columns, and that *this body (the "national interests") is identical with the body of newspaper advertisers.* This notion assumes that the individual advertisers compose an integral group in the same sense that a farmer's coöperative, the Christian Science Church, or the Third International is an integral group, and that this body of advertisers brings pressure to bear on editors.

In objective reality there is no such body of advertisers. There is, indeed, a body of advertisers (an aggregate of individuals), and they are all capitalists; even the newspapers themselves belong to the body of advertisers and are capitalists. But what some of the *members* of this body of advertisers do or attempt to do as individuals is not necessarily true of the whole body or of the whole "membership." A few individual advertisers may try to dictate editorial policy to the great newspapers, but they are almost without exception unsuccessful. In the first place, the great newspaper itself is possessed of as much financial independence and economic power as is the ordinary advertiser, and is able to resist economic pressure. It usually does resist pressure because its financial success depends on "reader-confidence." In the second place, the individual members of the body of advertisers are not alike in the respect that they all—*collectively*—desire a certain piece of news published or suppressed.[12]   One of the members—say, a department store—may desire to have a particular piece of news suppressed, but the other advertisers have no individual or collective interest in this suppression.   The great newspaper has sufficient financial independence to refuse dictation by a single advertiser or by any single sub-group of advertisers; all of the department stores of New York City, for example, which together make up the largest sub-group of advertisers in New York, use only 16 per cent of the total advertising space in New York newspapers. The relation of the newspaper and the advertiser is essentially the relation of seller and buyer.   The advertiser who desires to sell his goods *must* buy space in the newspaper.   If he does not buy it, he himself suffers.   Moreover, what the advertiser buys from the newspaper is space, not the newspaper's editorial influence.   To assume that those individual businesses which buy space from the newspapers are identical with the "national interests" who desire to mold "the public to their own ends," and to infer as a consequence that the great newspapers permit these advertisers to determine their editorial policies, is to confuse the whole and its parts.[13]

It is this consideration of the whole and its parts that M. Siegfried overlooks, and it reveals his argument as a four-term fallacy.   He unconsciously *substitutes* one meaning of his term for another meaning of the same term, and thus has an argument that contains four terms.   Such formal fallacies, when considered as material fallacies, are called fallacies of *specific accident*[14] because their invalidity is due to false quality, or accident, rather than to false quantity.[15]

---

[12] There is an important exception to this statement; it is discussed in Chapter XIV.

[13] This discussion takes no notice of the "free publicity evil" or of the more vicious economic coercion of newspapers by banker-creditors. Our discussion concerns only the relation of the advertiser and the newspaper with reference to questions of public policy.

[14] *Infra,* p. 195.

[15] A careful examination of M. Siegfried's statement reveals that it rests on a more inclusive generalization, namely, "All businesses try to please their customers."   This is the thought that M. Siegfried doubtless had in his mind, for it is a relation of things which the most naïve mind has perceived.   But here, too, the fallacy is due to an ambiguity of terms

We do not, however, wish the reader to accept this refutation of M. Siegfried's reasoning as absolute. His conclusion contains a considerable amount of truth. American newspapers, as a matter of fact, are property-minded, and their editorial policies are sometimes based on the dogma of "business first." Their editorial policies, moreover, have some relation to advertising. Just what this relation really is is discussed in Chapter XIV under the head of "Editorial Policy." We have examined M. Siegfried's conclusion, however, because it is only a half-truth. It, rather than an obvious fallacy, was selected to illustrate a four-term fallacy due to ambiguity because most controversies, after all, involve half-truths. The error in most of our thinking results from our failure to perceive the *real* relations in things. To perceive a certain relation in things and then to infer without further examination that this is the *real* relation is to do slovenly thinking. Straight thinking demands that we look profoundly into things to perceive *all* the relations. Quite often the real relation in things is a subtle one which is not readily perceived.[16]

MATERIAL FALLACIES: UNWARRANTED ASSUMPTION

In the preceding section we said that virtually all of the material fallacies, in the final analysis, are formal fallacies and, in particular, fallacies of four terms. We shall discuss the material fallacies separately, however—even repeating in some instances what has already been said about them as formal fallacies—because the main purpose is to show how they occur in editorials that discuss public problems.

Of the material fallacies, there are two kinds: (1) fallacies of unwarranted assumption; and (2) fallacies of equivocation, or ambiguity.

—a substitution of the whole and the part; for the great newspaper, although a business, is not like the ordinary kind of business. The newspaper, as a business, has two kinds of customers—advertisers and readers—and it is compelled to please the readers as well as the advertisers, that is, to furnish them with fact. This relation of newspaper and reader, moreover, is not precisely like the relation of newspaper and advertiser: one is the usual relation of seller and buyer, the other is a relation which comprehends moral responsibility.

16 In this connection, see pp. 330-332.

Fallacies of unwarranted assumption are those which result from the injection into an argument, either through error or design, of an unwarranted assumption. Such arguments *appear* to be valid, but really are fallacious because the propositions are not logically related. The unwarranted assumption sometimes escapes detection because of the reader's inattention or his prejudice in favor of the conclusion. An unwarranted assumption is injected into an argument either in the conclusion, as in the case of the fallacy of "irrelevant conclusion," or in the premises. There are five fallacies of this type: (1) irrelevant conclusion; (2) irrational evidence; (3) begging the question; (4) complex question; and (5) *non-sequitur.*

1. **Irrelevant Conclusion.**—When a person proves something different from the point at issue, the fallacy is termed "irrelevant conclusion," or "ignoring the question." The fallacy frequently occurs in refutation in which the writer, either from design or misapprehension, refutes a point that is different from the issue in dispute. In such an instance the proof is valid, but it is beside the point; it is irrelevant to the issue in dispute; as, for example, when a prosecutor, appealing to the passions of a jury, proves that an atrocious crime has been committed instead of trying to prove that the defendant at the bar committed the crime in question. It is a common trick in argument to set up a "straw man" and demolish him.

Sometimes, however, the person who is arguing merely mistakes the point at issue. Mr. William Jennings Bryan, for example, proved to thousands of persons that some of the alleged *causes* of evolution are not valid, but what he asserted he was proving (but failed to prove) was the falsity of the hypothesis of evolution. He inadvertently set up a straw man —he called it "Darwinism"—and demolished it completely. Scientists had already discredited some of the *causes* cited by Darwin and others to prove the hypothesis of evolution, but they have never challenged the evidences of evolution. Scientists unanimously agree that the hypothesis of evolution is true in so far as any scientific law is true, but they do not agree. as to the causes of evolution; it is quite possible for evolution to be true, even though we do not know what caused the process.

2. Irrational Evidence.—A subdivision of the fallacy of irrelevant conclusion which many logicians classify as a separate fallacy is the fallacy of irrational evidence. It is possible that a reader's ignorance or inattention will cause him to accept this fallacy, but more often it is emotion or prejudice which affects his reasoning. This fallacy has several forms of which we shall examine four. They are: (*a*) *argumentum ad hominem*, (*b*) *argumentum ad vericundiam*, (*c*) *argumentum ad populum*, and (*d*) *argumentum ad ignorantiam*.

(*a*) *Argumentum ad hominem* consists in directing the argument against the *character of one's opponent* instead of against the proposition in dispute. Newspapers sometimes fall into this error when they oppose a proposal that is in the public interest on the ground that the sponsors of the proposal are of bad or untrustworthy character or have ulterior motives. For example, an equitable franchise contract arranged between a city government and a street car company is opposed by a newspaper on the ground that the "interests" are agreeable to it, but without an examination into the merits of the contract. The mere suspicion that the street car company, which in the past has cheated car riders, is now agreeable to an equitable contract does not constitute a valid argument that the contract now under consideration is unfair to the car riders. The fairness of the contract ought to be determined solely by an examination of the contract; if its provisions are fair and its guarantees adequate, it ought not to be opposed.

This type of argument, which is justifiable in some circumstances because of the past record of the man or the body that is sponsoring a proposal in the public interest, is never justified when it is used as a mere subterfuge to escape answering a valid argument. An example of this type of argument is that which has been directed at the various proposals of Judge Ben B. Lindsey, the Denver juvenile court judge, who has frequently pointed out some of the inequities in our economic system and who has recently proposed what he believes would be an improvement in the marriage relation. Reactionary forces in American society have heaped abuse upon Judge Lindsey, and sometimes they have not examined his arguments.

One such castigation of Judge Lindsey's character is typical of *argumentum ad hominem;* it appeared in a propaganda magazine published under the auspices of a national political party and supported by the financial contributions of certain big business men. It argues against liberalism by attacking the character of a liberal.

> Judge Ben Lindsay [*sic*] of Denver, has been the darling of the self-styled "liberals," and a favorite on the chatauqua circuit. His latest pronouncement shows how easily a "liberal" blossoms into radicalism. He is writing articles for two sensational magazines in which he advocates "trial marriage," that people should be permitted to live together in the marriage relationship without marriage, and change partners at will so long as there are no children. He also has been lecturing in a Denver church on the subject. The Supreme Court of Colorado had deprived him of his judicial office through a decision affirming that his election was procured through palpable election frauds.[17]

Human nature is peculiarly susceptible to *argumentum ad hominem.* The tendency of the mind is to personify issues and to shirk thinking, and a frequent result is the emotionalizing of public questions which ought to be settled simply on their logical merits. The naïve mind, moreover, knows little about technical questions—for example, street car franchises—but is acquainted with personalities and has grown suspicious of utility corporations.

Newspaper men, especially, should be warned against the confusing of personalities and of issues. In the first place, the tendency of the professional newspaper worker, who observes the sordid side of humanity, is to become cynical with regard to public men and public bodies. In the second place, the news-

[17] Perhaps no better example of *argumentum ad hominem* in public discussion has been furnished in recent times than the retort of certain Southern and Western Democrats in the spring of 1931 with reference to certain proposals made by John J. Raskob, chairman of the party's National Committee. Mr. Raskob's proposal regarding prohibition was apparently sincere, but it did not receive an examination in some quarters because Mr. Raskob was a Catholic and a big business man.

paper itself should guard its own reputation so as not to become the victim of *argumentum ad hominem.* It should so direct its policy that it does not make readers suspicious of its own motives, for the public will hesitate to follow a leader with respect to a sound policy if, in the past, the leader has been connected with unsound policies. The public will desert a newspaper it has learned to distrust just as numerous voters, in the first quarter of the present century, deserted the Democratic party after Bryan's advocacy of the free coinage of silver. An example of this tendency of the public is furnished by the case of the Chicago *Tribune.* This newspaper, which in recent years has conducted a courageous campaign against the demagogues and grafters who were in political control of the state government of Illinois and the government of Chicago, has had difficulty in convincing some voters of its own sincerity. For several years the *Tribune* itself was in politics to the degree that some of its owners held public office and affiliated with local factions within the Republican party. As a consequence, the politicians whom the *Tribune* recently opposed were successful to a high degree in making martyrs of themselves by asserting, *ad hominem,* that the *Tribune* only desired political power for itself.

(*b*) *Argumentum ad vericundiam* is an appeal to the reverence that the reader has for a great name instead of an appeal to the intellect of the reader with reference to the question in dispute. The Scholastics, for example, based their arguments in large part on the mere authority of Aristotle. *"Ipse dixit,"* they said—and that proved almost any question that was in dispute. A recent instance of *argumentum ad vericundiam* which was applied with success was the use made of Washington's Farewell Address in opposition to the proposal that the United States should join the League of Nations. Even in connection with the question of public ownership, the appeal has been used editorially. The following is an example:

> If the continuing encroachments of this government on business are to continue, then what are we drifting toward? The nationalization of American industry?

> Are we to stand in a few years as Russia stands today, or are we to go along the path of private industry and initiative *as Abraham Lincoln said we should?*

What George Washington said about "entangling alliances" is of no consequence to Americans of the twentieth century, but it certainly is of no less consequence than what Abraham Lincoln, the country lawyer, said about private industry in 1860. It is the latter type of *argumentum ad vericundiam* that is so insidious—the type which cites as authority in a specific field some person who has prestige in an entirely different field. What Ford and Edison and Mellon think about the subtle questions underlying foreign affairs ought to have much less probative force than what an under-secretary of state or a professor of political science thinks; yet the naïve mind reveres a person in one field of human activity and transfers that reverence to another field that is totally different. An understanding of the prestige that such men as Coolidge and Mellon possess is one of the keys to a comprehension of the subtle processes of public opinion.

References to the opinions of authorities, however, is an excellent method of reënforcing one's argument. To quote Montesquieu, for example, on the necessity for an independent judicial branch of government to check the legislative branch lends strength to one's argument, provided that the argument already possesses a high degree of logical force.

(*c*) *Argumentum ad populum* is a name given to an argument which is plainly an appeal to the prejudices and emotions, instead of the intellects, of an audience. This fallacy is discussed at length in Chapter XIII.

(*d*) *Argumentum ad ignorantiam* is an attempt to shift the burden of proof by the assertion that "unless you can disprove what I say is true, then it must be true." This fallacy is not usually encountered in editorial writing. It is not so much an argument or a part of an argument as it is a method of meeting an attack. For example, a state official who had been a member of the Ku Klux Klan was accused of having been a member; he denied the charge, but when proof of his membership was brought forward he ignored it on the theory that if he refrained from controversy and merely contented himself with a simple denial the voters would not believe the charge. The psychology underlying this method was that he "refrained" from engaging in politics on a "low level."

This method of ignoring a charge on the assumption that it will not be universally believed has also a second advantage in some circumstances: it places the soft pedal on publicity. Sometimes the best strategy is to ignore a charge that is made by an obscure person or newspaper. To answer it is simply to give to it more substance and more publicity than it deserves. An explanation of how this method is applied in practical politics is explained in an interesting manner by Frank R. Kent in his *Political Behavior* in a chapter entitled, "Never Handle a Hot Poker on the Front Porch."

3. **Begging the Question.**—Probably the most common of the fallacies of unwarranted assumption is begging the question, or, technically, *petitio principii*. This fallacy consists in covertly assuming the truth of some principle that is the precise equivalent of the principle to be proved. The fallacy has two forms, which may be differentiated under the following heads: (*a*) assuming an unproved premise, and (*b*) reasoning in a circle.

(*a*) *Assuming an Unproved Premise.*—The first form of this fallacy consists in assuming a broad principle which is inclusive of the one in dispute and deducing from it the very one which is in dispute.[18] A ludicrous example of begging the question is contained in Boccaccio:

A servant who was roasting a stork for his master was prevailed upon by his sweetheart to cut off a leg for her to eat. When the bird came upon the table, the master desired to know what had become of the other leg. The man answered that storks had never more than one leg. The master, very angry, but determined to strike his servant dumb before he punished him, took him next day into the fields where they saw storks, standing each on one leg, as storks do. The servant turned triumphantly to his master; on

---

[18] This fallacy is something like the fallacy of simple accident (i.e., the application of an abstract principle without reference to qualifying conditions), which is discussed on p. 201.

which the latter shouted and the birds put down their other leg and flew away. "Ah, sir," said the servant, "you did not shout to the stork at dinner yesterday; if you had done so, he would have shown his other leg too." [19]

The servant had humorously assumed a broad principle which included the very proposition he sought to establish, namely, that *all* storks—live and roasted storks—will put down the other leg when they are shouted at. The servant's argument is not more fallacious, however, than is some of the serious argument about public affairs which begs the question; for the fallacy in every instance consists in *taking for granted what one's opponent would not admit if its significance were really understood.* The servant's argument is hardly more fallacious than was the serious argument of many lawyers, business men, and judges during the last quarter century against the enactment of laws to regulate the working hours of women and children on the ground that "all legislation is bad which interferes with the right of a person to make a free contract." This type of argument takes for granted the very proposition that is in dispute.

An historic example of begging the question is the reasoning by which the United States Supreme Court has arrogated to itself the right to declare statutes unconstitutional. The doctrine of judicial supremacy, which was fixed in our working constitution by Chief Justice Marshall in Marbury *v.* Madison in 1803,[20] has historically had *political* justification because of our federal form of government; but the principle is not authorized by the Constitution and has no *logical* justification unless by logic we mean that force of logic which is inherent in circumstances. Justice Marshall arrived at his conclusion by begging the question. Since his reasoning is quite extended, it is more convenient here for us to examine a subsequent decision which embodies the same argument. In Adkins *et al. v.* the Children's Hospital of the District of Columbia, Mr. Justice Sutherland said:

---

[19] Quoted by H. B. Smith, in *How the Mind Falls into Error,* p. 65 (Harper & Brothers, publishers); reprinted by permission.
[20] Cranch, *Supreme Court Reports,* Vol. I, p. 135.

If, by clear and indubitable demonstration, a statute be opposed to the Constitution, we have no choice but to say so. The Constitution, by its own terms, is the supreme law of the land, emanating from the people, the repository of ultimate sovereignty under our form of government. A Congressional statute, on the other hand, is an act of agency of this sovereign authority (the Constitution), and, if it conflicts with the Constitution, must fall, for that which is not supreme must yield to that which is. To hold it invalid (if it be invalid) is a plain exercise of the judicial power—that power vested in courts to enable them to administer justice according to law. From the authority to ascertain and determine the law in a given case there necessarily results, in case of conflict, the duty to declare and enforce the rule of the supreme law and reject that of an inferior act of legislation, which, transcending the Constitution, is of no effect, and binding on no one.[21]

Now the conclusion does not follow from the premises because *the conclusion is the very proposition which the jurist selected as a major premise.* For, if an act of Congress is the act of an agency of the sovereign authority (the Constitution), so is an act of the Supreme Court, which is also an agency of this supreme authority. To assert that "that which is not supreme (Congress) must yield to that which is" (the Constitution) is an acceptable proposition, but to infer, as Justice Sutherland did, that the Supreme Court is supreme over Congress is to prove that which was assumed as a premise.

Because much of our erroneous thinking about fundamental problems is a begging of the question, another illustration is given. A most insidious form of the fallacy is apparent in the argument of that school of "liberals" which asserts that the cure for the evils of democracy is more democracy. Mr. Walter Lippmann discusses their argument, as follows:

It was assumed that the popular will was wise and good if only you could get at it. They proposed extensions to the suffrage, and as much voting as possible by means of the initiative, referendum, and recall, direct election of Senators, direct primaries, an elected judiciary, and the like. They begged the question, for it has never been proved that there exists the kind of public opinion which they presupposed. Since the Bryan campaign of 1896 this school of thought has made great conquests in most of the states,

---

[21] 261 U. S. 525.

and has profoundly influenced the federal government. The eligible vote has trebled since 1896; the direct action of the voter has been enormously extended. Yet that same period has seen a decline in the percentage of the popular vote cast at presidential elections from 80.75 per cent in 1896 to 52.36 per cent in 1920. Apparently there is a fallacy in the first assumption of this school that "the whole people" desires to participate actively in government. Nor is there any evidence to show that the persons who do participate are in any real sense directing the course of affairs. The party machines have survived every attack. And why should they not? If the voter cannot grasp the details of the problems of the day because he has not the time, the interest or the knowledge, he will not have a better public opinion because he is asked to express his opinion more often. He will simply be more bewildered, more bored and more ready to follow along.[22]

(b) *Reasoning in a Circle.*—The second form of begging the question is called "reasoning in a circle." It consists in taking two propositions and using them each in turn to prove the other, as, for example, the classic argument: "We can be sure that there is a God, for the Bible declares it; and we know that the Bible is true because it is of divine origin." Another example of reasoning in a circle is the argument that the value of a public utility for rate-making purposes should be arrived at as the value of any other going concern is arrived at, namely, by capitalizing its net earnings on the basis of a fair return. Obviously this is unsound reasoning, for the net earnings of a regulated public utility are determined in the first place by the rate of return which the state permits it to charge the public. Reasoning in a circle appears in long arguments, especially in those of political speakers; it is seldom apparent, however, in editorials.

4. **Complex Question.**—A fourth type of fallacy of unwarranted assumption is that of the complex question, which consists in posing to an opponent a question which he cannot answer categorically without admitting the truth of the assumption; as, for example: "Have you left off beating your wife?" Such a question was asked in a newspaper advertisement of Alfred E. Smith, the Democratic candidate for president in

---

[22] *The Phantom Public,* pp. 35-37 (The Macmillan Company, publishers, 1925) ; reprinted by permission.

1928, when he spoke in Omaha. The advertisement challenged Mr. Smith to answer whether or not he thought prohibition was "good for the country." Under the circumstances, this was a complex question inasmuch as Mr. Smith stood for control of liquor by state and local governments, but opposed national control under the Volstead Act. Mr. Smith's answer was that the country to date had had no opportunity to determine whether prohibition was desirable inasmuch as the prohibition law had not been well enough enforced to show what would actually happen under prohibition.

5. **Non-sequitur.**—Some logicians recognize a fallacy called *non-sequitur,* which is simply a fallacy of four terms in which the premises are so illogically related that no valid conclusion can be deduced from them.[23] The following syllogism illustrates *non-sequitur:* "All Republicans favor a protective tariff. President Hoover is a Prohibitionist. Therefore, President Hoover favors a protective tariff." Such a syllogism is so obviously invalid that the most naïve mind can detect the fallacy, but in the course of an extended argument it sometimes happens that arguments of this type gain acceptance. An example of *non-sequitur* was given on page 172.

An example of *non-sequitur* was given on page 172.

MATERIAL FALLACIES: EQUIVOCATION

Deduction sometimes is unsound notwithstanding the logical relation of the premises. The fallacy then is the result of an equivocation, or ambiguity, in the terms of the propositions— essentially a fallacy of definition.

This ambiguity is sometimes quantitative and sometimes qualitative.

Fallacies Involving Quantity.—Frequently there is a confusion of the relation of the whole and its parts. Sometimes, in the course of an argument, one affirms something of a part which is true only of the whole, or one affirms something of the whole which is true only of one or more of the parts considered separately. When this substitution of meaning occurs in an argument, there is obviously an ambiguity which makes the argument invalid.

---

[23] *Supra,* p. 172.

Fallacies that confuse the whole and its parts in this manner are traditionally known as *division* and *composition,* although, in so far as the form of the argument is concerned, they are merely four-term fallacies. In the last analysis, they are inductive fallacies in that they are generalizations derived from too few specimens of a class.

Division.—The fallacy of division is committed when one assumes, usually inadvertently, that what is true of the whole is also true of the parts taken separately. This is the result of using a term collectively in the major premise and distributively in the minor premise, as when one attributes some characteristic to a member of a group which is true only of the group as a whole. For example, one cannot infer that since the Pi fraternity has a low standard of scholarship, John Jones, a member of the fraternity, has a low scholastic record; or that since the Catholic Church condemns birth control, William Williams, a Catholic, does not practice it. This type of fallacy, of course, is rather easily detected.

Composition.—Of more frequent occurrence than the fallacy of division is the fallacy of composition, which is the reverse of the former. This fallacy is committed when one assumes something of the whole which is true only of one or more of the parts considered separately. It occurs most frequently in arguments about groups or collections of persons. For example, it was argued, prior to 1920, that since state-wide prohibition was so effective in nearly all of the states, national prohibition would be just as (or even more) effective. Likewise, much of the talk about "Latin-America's" opposition to the policies of the United States assumes that the individual Latin-American states are firmly "united" in their opposition to United States policies; to a certain degree this unity does exist, but on the whole the individual Latin-American states are more jealous of each other than they are of the United States, and the predicted "unity" never amounts to much in international affairs. The same fallacy is observed in the following excerpt from an editorial which speaks of "Europe" wanting to get the United States into the League in order to exploit American wealth:

> . . . The effort to get the United States into the League is not motivated by a desire to obtain the advice of the United States in adjusting international quarrels, as is commonly presumed by the League and Court advocates in this country. Europe has plenty of intelligence and does not have to come to the United States for more. Europe does want American wealth. It had it once and lost it, but it has never outgrown the notion that America is, by right of discovery, the colony of Europe to be exploited by European interests. Europe cannot recapture America by conquest, but it dreams of recapturing it by subterfuge.

There is sometimes an element of analogy in arguments of this type. For example, the French Nationalists were arguing, prior to the adoption of the Dawes plan, that the ability of the German nation to pay reparation to the Entente Allies could be calculated on the same basis that the ability of the individual German to pay his creditors is calculated.[24] This fallacy has been exposed by economists, as follows:

> It is reasoned that an individual's ability to pay is measured by the excess of his income over expenditures; for example, if a man's income is $10,000 per year and his expenditures $8,000, he can pay a debt of $2,000. Why is not a nation's ability to pay to be measured in the same way?
> The answer is that a nation's excess of production over consumption does not consist of money which can be turned over to a foreign nation. When before the war Germany's annual production exceeded her consumption by 2 billion dollars, this did not mean that Germany had 2 billions in cash stowed away somewhere. It meant rather that there was created in Germany each year 2 billion dollars' worth of new factories, equipment, railroads, etc.—capital goods which could be thenceforth used in expanding the industrial output of Germany. New German factories, railroads, canals, highways, improved lands, and enriched soil cannot be turned over to foreign lands in payment of reparations. In fact, a relatively small proportion of any nation's ordinary savings is available as a means of making foreign payments.

---

[24] See André Tardieu, *The Truth About the Treaty.*

One cannot therefore assume that a nation's ability to pay is measured by the excess of production over consumption.[25]

Fallacies Involving Quality, or Accident.—There are three fallacies of equivocation which are due to a confusion in the qualitative meaning of terms. These are: specific accident (ambiguous middle), simple accident, and converse accident. These fallacies are different from those of division and composition in that they are not concerned with numerical aggregates and their units, but with *logical wholes* and their *attributes*. Except for the second and third of these fallacies—simple accident and converse accident—we shall not try to differentiate them very clearly from the fallacies which involve quantity; for the distinction is important only to the logician.

Specific Accident.—Under the head of formal fallacies, we have already discussed the fallacy of specific accident, or ambiguous middle. Siegfried's argument in which he failed to distinguish between advertisers as individuals and advertisers as the members of a coercive interest-group was an example. The fallacy of specific accident is the result of a substitution— usually an inadvertent one—of meaning in the terms, the substitution being due to the failure of the thinker to distinguish as to the *kinds* of members within a class. This fallacy, in the last analysis, is the result of an inability to classify things, that is, an inability to perceive the essential *quality* in things which makes them alike in one respect but which differentiates them in another respect.[26] The following letter from a lawyer to an editor is representative of this type of fallacy:

I'd like to see you discuss the question I ask below. I think your position is right, but I don't find it easy to satisfy my mind that it is consistent. Give us a little political education if you can.

Here's the question. You are campaigning for publicity of Senate votes taken in executive session. Are you also in favor of publicity of votes of individual electors in popular elections? Do you wish to alter the present law that "upon receiving his ballot, the voter must retire alone to a booth, etc."? If you believe in the

---

[25] J. F. Bass and H. G. Moulton, *America and the Balance Sheet of Europe,* pp. 184-185.
[26] *Supra,* pp. 43 *ff.*

secret vote (the "Australian" ballot) why doesn't the same reasoning lead to contentment with the existing Senate practice?

If this argument were put in syllogistic form, it would be about as follows:

> All those who vote should be protected by secrecy.
> Senators are those who vote.
> Senators should be protected by secrecy.

This is clearly a four-term fallacy, for the ambiguity in the middle term makes of it actually two different middle terms. The middle term—the one which relates the three propositions logically—is "those who vote." The ambiguity in the term is one of quality: the term does not distinguish between the *kinds* of voters or the difference in *function* of Senators and ordinary electors. The elector who votes at the polls is responsible only to himself—he is sovereign; the Senator, being the chosen representative of the sovereign voter, is responsible to the voter, and the way he votes in the Senate ought to be made known to the voter who elects him.

Examples of the Fallacy.—How the fallacy occurs in thinking about public problems such as government ownership of public utilities, the incidence of taxation, and the tariff is illustrated in the following examples:

It is argued that public ownership of power sites and power plants will result in a great reduction in the price of electrical energy to the residential consumer. Undoubtedly some reduction would follow because it is possible for a government to obtain capital at a cheaper price; also it would eliminate an excessive profit to private manufacturers of power wherever an excessive profit is being made. But the argument, as it is usually stated, neglects to differentiate the various cost factors involved in supplying electricity to the residential consumer. The cost of supplying electric energy to the residential consumer is not in its "generation" alone. The cost includes also "transmission" to the substation, "distribution" through individual meters to the residential consumer, and "general expense." This cost per kilowatt hour is apportioned about as follows:[27]

---

[27] These are representative figures of several privately and publicly operated systems in the Middle West, obtained by Professor Edward

Cost Factors

	Cents
Generation (by steam plant)............	.8
Transmission (including lost energy)....	1.16
Distribution (including fixed charges on distribution system, metering and billing)	2.38
General expense	.93
Total cost	5.27

The cost of generating electric energy by a steam plant, as the table shows, is only 15 per cent of the total cost. The saving that could be made by generation by a hydroelectric plant and from government financing is not sufficient to make much difference. Whether or not it is possible to effect a saving in transmission (including loss of energy), distribution (including fixed charges on the distribution system and cost of metering and billing), and general expense is a question which has nothing to do with *generation* of power by a government.[28]

The discussion of questions which demand a technical knowledge cannot be settled without the assistance of experts, but politicians frequently express opinions on these questions. Whenever there are errors and deceptions, therefore, it is the duty of newspapers to point them out. The questions of public ownership, taxation, water transportation, and the tariff especially demand "debunking" by expert analysts. An example of

Bennett, of the University of Wisconsin, from state regulatory bodies and from other sources.

[28] It should not be inferred that this discussion disposes of the argument for public ownership of power resources. The cost of electric energy to residential and industrial consumers is only one of the factors involved in the question.

Nor ought the student to make hasty conclusions as to the whole problem of private *versus* public ownership of electric utilities. A distinguished engineer has made studies from which he has derived the conclusion that the cost of distribution ought not to exceed 1.5 cents a kilowatt-hour, and it is evident from the prices of holding company securities that large profits have accrued either from the charging of excessive rates or from the watering of stock. In view of the conflicting statistics, it has been suggested that the government can set up publicly owned and operated plants at Muscle Shoals and other places to be used as standards for comparison with privately owned utilities. We are told that to refrain from such experiment is to permit propaganda, not experience, to furnish the facts.

how a newspaper corrected an invalid conclusion is the New York *World's* refutation of an argument made by the Republican candidate for Vice-President in 1928. In arguing the necessity for a tariff, the candidate told an audience of farmers that more than two-thirds of American imports are "products which can be grown on our own farms." His use of terms was ambiguous, for the imported products which he asserted could "be grown on our own farms" were not all farm products. The *World* refuted the argument as follows:

> In his speech in Rhode Island the other day Senator Curtis declared that on the tariff issue "the Democrats hope to fool the American people and secure their support." And thereupon Mr. Curtis undertook to do a little fooling of the people on his own account. He told his audience that we import over $3,000,000,000 worth of farm products every year, "of which over $2,000,000,000 are products which can be grown on our own farms."
>
> To arrive at such a figure for agricultural imports Mr. Curtis has simply added up the totals for the first six major groups of commodities as they are classified by the department of commerce. These six groups show a total value for 1927 of $3,254,000,000. While the titles of these groups—animals and animal products, vegetable food products, inedible vegetable products, and so on—might indicate that they are farm products, as a matter of fact they include much more. The animal products group includes, for example, such things as fish, furs, ivory, sponges and ostrich feathers. Under vegetable products are included bananas, cocoa, coffee, tea, spices, rubber. The six groups include even wood, paper and cotton goods made of American cotton.

The failure of voters to think soundly about the distribution of taxes is frequently due to their failure to differentiate the classes of tax-paying property. The following is an example: In a certain state, the state and local revenues are derived almost entirely from taxes on real and personal property; individuals who own no general property pay almost no taxes direct to the state, and corporations pay taxes only on the property they own.   With a view, therefore, to equalizing the tax burden, a legislator introduced a bill to provide for the levying of a tax on the income of individuals and corporations.   The bill provided also that taxes paid on general property could be deducted from the tax due on income.   This bill was opposed by one newspaper on the ground that it was not fair to the thousands of city dwellers who paid a tax on real property *indirectly* in that the owner of the property that they rented simply passed along his property tax to the tenant in the form of rental charges.   This argument was true, of course, but it ignored the fact that a large part of the state's wealth was escaping taxation—that corporations were paying almost no taxes except those which they paid indirectly in rental charges or directly on their general property.   The inference of the newspaper's argument, however, was that the *whole* wealth of the state was already being taxed by means of the levy on general property.   The argument was as follows:

> The income tax bill now before the senate is just another effort of the farmer to shift the tax burden to the city man.
> The bill provides for a tax on individual income, but taxes paid on real estate or personal property may be deducted from any tax due on income.
> The sponsors of the bill assert that it will be equitable for the reason that it will equalize the tax burden which now rests entirely on general property.   The bill, they say, will prevent tax dodging by those persons who own no real property.
> It will do nothing of the kind.   It will merely double the burden of the city dweller who lives in a rented house or apartment, and will leave the farmer's burden where it now is.   To levy an income tax on individuals and to permit a deduction because of taxes paid on general property would merely exempt the owners of real estate from the income tax

> while at the same time it would double the
> tax now paid by the tenant, which amounts
> to about 2½ per cent of his income.

This argument is not erroneous in so far as it purports to prove that the tenant would be doubly taxed, but it is erroneous if it implies that a tax on general property is a tax on the *aggregate* of wealth. For the argument ignores the fact that the proposed bill would levy a tax on the earnings of corporations as well as on individuals. Under the system in which general property bears the whole burden, the earnings of the ordinary corporation are escaping taxation almost entirely. The issue then resolves to the question of whether the corporations shall pay taxes even though the city tenant pays double, whether the corporations shall pay taxes and the farmer pay on both his property and his income (i.e., eliminating the provision for a rebate on the general property tax), or whether general property shall continue to bear the whole burden and the corporations shall escape taxation on their earnings.

It is not the purpose of this discussion to lay down principles regarding taxation, but to show that the problem of taxation turns upon a logical differentiation of the whole and its parts, that is to say, the *kinds* of property that must bear the burden. If taxes ought to be levied on wealth in all its forms and wherever it is found, then the foregoing editorial is fallacious. Tax systems differ throughout the forty-eight states and throughout the world. They are not always determined by either logic or justice, but by the relative force that the various kinds of taxpayers can exert on the Government. At the present time the propertied citizens have more influence in the Government than the unpropertied citizens, but gradually the unpropertied citizens are obtaining more influence with the result that the propertied classes are beginning to assert that a discrimination is being made against them in the matter of taxation (e.g., the graduated income tax, death tax, etc.).[29]   The protest, however, is heard in Europe more than in the United States.

---

[29] Some light is thrown upon the question of income tax by two studies made by the National Industrial Conference Board, viz., *The Fiscal Problem in Illinois* and *The Tax Problem in Wisconsin*.

Simple Accident.—Ambiguity in argument sometimes results from the application of an abstract principle to a concrete case without allowing for qualifying conditions or unusual circumstances. In syllogistic arrangement, it amounts to an ambiguity in terms. This fallacy is usually called the fallacy of "simple accident." It is an insidious type of argument because the abstract principle from which the conclusion is deduced is, for many purposes, true; but it is not always and forever true without qualifications.[30] The following syllogism, for example, is illustrative:

> Every man has the right to inculcate his opinions.
> A judge is a man who possesses all of the rights that other men possess.
> A judge has the right to inculcate his opinions (under all circumstances).

The phrase, "under all circumstances," is tacked on to the conclusion for emphasis, but this type of argument, which is seldom formulated in syllogistic form, does not contain a qualifying phrase, and the reader, swept on in the swift current of the argument, neglects to make the distinction of the judge as a man and the judge in his capacity of magistrate.

This fallacy is apparent in the dogma of the "fundamentalists" who secured the enactment of laws forbidding the teaching of evolution in state-supported schools. The dogma was brought out in its clearest application in the argument made by the late William Jennings Bryan at the Dayton, Tennessee, trial. Mr. Bryan argued from the major premise that a majority of voters has the right to decide what shall be taught in their schools. If Mr. Bryan's premise is accepted, then his conclusion is inescapably valid. But his premise is not true. His argument consists in applying a general principle to an individual case, *the principle holding true in politics but not necessarily holding true in other fields.* Students of the history of political thought understand how the dogma of majority rule came to find acceptance in politics and religion. It originated as a spiritual doctrine out of the feeling of mutual respect that

---

[30] Strictly, the fallacy of simple accident is an inductive fallacy.

men have for one another; it is a corollary of the principle that men are equal in the sight of God. And now it means to the "fundamentalists" that "all men are equally good biologists before the ballot box of Tennessee." That is to say, all opinions are equal. This premise manifestly is not true; and if it should be followed to a logical conclusion, it would result in a tyranny by mediocrity.[31]

The fallacy of simple accident, which is frequently committed by the idealists and the narrow-minded, sometimes is apparent in argument that concerns governmental policy. Statesmen and politicians, who are more amenable to the demands of expediency than are reformers and professors, frequently find themselves in conflict with doctrinaires over the application of a principle. For example, some of the Latin-American states represented at the Pan-American Congress in 1928 argued that the general principle should be laid down that no state should ever intervene in the domestic affairs of another state. Certain groups of anti-imperialists in the United States, in whose minds was fresh the recent intervention of the United States in Nicaragua and Haiti, supported this view. Obviously the principle is a sound one, for it lies at the foundation of international ethics. But its universal application is not consistent with the psychological and economic realities that determine—at least for the present—whether there shall be order and stability in the Caribbean region and whether European states shall be prevented from dominating some of the nations of the western hemisphere.[32]

The fallacies committed by the doctrinaire are discussed at length in a subsequent chapter, and it is only necessary here to point out that there is as much narrow-mindedness in the views of some of those who claim to be realists as there is in the views of the idealists. For example, a newspaper that is something of an imperialist in its policy attempted to argue *against* the

---

[31] A profound and most interesting discussion of the dogma of majority rule is contained in Mr. Walter Lippmann's *Men of Destiny,* Chap. V, from which the above discussion was adapted.

[32] For a statement of the present status in international law of the practice of intervention, see A. S. Hershey, *The Essentials of International Law and Organization* (rev. ed.), pp. 236-245.

application of a general principle regarding intervention in Latin-American states in a manner which marked the argument as sophistry. This newspaper said:

> A rule for intervention cannot be laid down. It is no more always right than it is always wrong. Human ills can be attributed to it. Some of the great human benefits have been derived from it. France and Spain intervened in the domestic affairs of Great Britain when they took the side of the British colonies. It was done for purposes of their own, but the result was the guaranty of the republic of the United States. Great Britain intervened when Greece was fighting Turkey for its freedom. France intervened to help Italy out from under Austria. The United States stepped in when Great Britain and France were in a critical period of the war with Germany.[33]

Converse Accident.—The type of unsound argument which generalizes an abstract principle from a concrete case is called the fallacy of "converse accident." Strictly, it is an inductive fallacy, for it consists in generalizing that whatever is true under certain circumstances is always and forever true. One who argues, for example, that a college education is not worth while because Thomas A. Edison, Henry Ford, and Alfred E. Smith lacked it, is committing this fallacy. Likewise, the clergyman in Wichita, Kansas, who defended the fashion of girls wearing no stockings, on the ground that the Virgin Mary and other women in Christ's day wore no hose, committed the fallacy of converse accident.

Since the purpose of this chapter is to show how invalid deduction is often due to inattention and prejudice, we shall say no more for the present about the fallacies of accident; for most of the so-called fallacies of accident are not really due to invalid reasoning so much as to a lack of a true sense of "values," a subject which is examined in Chapter XI.

---

[33] Do you think that the arguments cited here refute the thesis of the anti-imperialists? Could better arguments be presented? See C. G. Fenwick, *International Law*, Chap. X.

FORM OF EDITORIAL ARGUMENT

It is hardly necessary to observe that the argument presented in an editorial is not arranged in syllogistic form. Nor is it often that any kind of argument is so arranged. Sometimes, however, editorial arguments consist of a general premise, a particular premise, and a conclusion, as in the following editorial from the Philadelphia *Public Ledger:*

> A good bill must be clear in its terms, reasonable in its provisions or restrictions, simple in its application and not too far ahead of public opinion. The local option bill now before the State Legislature meets all of the essential conditions. By requiring the petitioners to represent 25 per cent of the vote cast at the last general election it guards against the expense and disturbance that a handful of extremists might cause; by specifying a special election on the granting of licenses it takes the liquor question out of party politics; by putting three years between elections it gives ample time to judge of results, and precludes many abuses that thrive in places where the liquor question is fought annually. Moreover, it represents the solemnly plighted word of Governor Brumbaugh to the people of the Commonwealth, which the Legislature must co-operate with him to redeem.

Enthymeme.—More often, however, editorial arguments take the form of enthymeme, that is, an argument in which one premise is unexpressed. Ordinarily it is the major premise that is lacking, as in the following editorial from the Baltimore *Post,* in which the unexpressed major premise is, "A criminal law which costs more to enforce than all other criminal laws should be repealed."

> The federal Government during the next fiscal year will spend approximately 50 million dollars in its attempt to enforce prohibition.

It will spend only 14 million dollars for foreign relations and the protection of American interests abroad.

It will spend only 42 million dollars for "general law enforcement."

It will spend only 28 million dollars for the promotion and regulation of commerce and industry.

It will spend only 40 million dollars for the promotion and regulation of agriculture.

It will spend only $5,750,000 for the promotion of labor interests.

It will spend only 19 million dollars for the promotion of public health.

It will spend only $12,500,000 for the promotion of public education.

It will spend only 21 million dollars for science and research.

And the present appropriations for prohibition enforcement, according to dry leaders, are wholly inadequate.

It is a good rule when reading an argument that is in the form of enthymeme always to ask one's self, "Now what is the major premise of this argument?" Practice in referring a conclusion to a general truth will result in the analysis of many false assumptions which otherwise one would be inclined to accept.

Chain Argument.—Sometimes argument is arranged in the form of a chain, as in the following editorial from the Kansas City *Star,* which is a form of catechism:

Whom are the boulevards of Kansas City built for?

The people of Kansas City.

Have the people been able to use them more extensively than ever of late?

Yes, through the advent of the jitneys, which carry thousands of people over the boulevards every day.

But do not the jitneys help wear out the boulevards?

Yes, just as the use of a book in the public library helps wear out the book. If the books in the public library were not handed out to be read, there would be no need for new ones. If all vehicles were kept off the boulevards they would last much longer. But it is generally assumed that library books and public boulevards are to be made of the most service possible, even if it does wear them out.

Is it the jitney drivers who help wear out the boulevards?

No, it is the people who are able to ride over the boulevards in large numbers for the small sum of five cents who produce the wear.

If the city administration should drive the jitneys off the boulevards who would be the chief sufferers?

The people who own the boulevards, and whose only opportunity to get their money's worth from them comes from ability to ride in the jitneys.

Ordinarily, editorial argument is not formal. In the first place, most argumentative editorials merely discuss a single phase of some large problem. In the second place, it is not at all necessary that argument be presented by a formal method: the human mind does not require it. As a matter of fact, there are informal ways of presenting argument that are more understandable to the reader than is the formal method.

CHAPTER X

THE CREATIVE AND CRITICAL FACULTIES

In a previous chapter we said of insight that it is the faculty of focusing our memory and our imagination on a set of data and making a judgment by the aid of our experience-world. That explanation required a certain degree of amplification, but we postponed making it until we had examined some other considerations which would add to the clarity of our explanation.

"Learning" and "Sagacity."—One may examine insight from two sides. From one point of view, insight can be considered as a critical faculty; from another point of view, it can be considered as a creative faculty. William James had in mind both of these faculties when he talked about the faculties of "learning" (recall) and "sagacity." [1] By "learning" James meant that critical faculty which—as Dana expressed it—enables one to say, when a suggestion is presented, "That is true" or "That is false." It is our memory coming to aid in *recalling* the consequences or implications of an hypothesis.

By "sagacity" James meant that creative faculty which enables one to single out of a mass of data the relevant factor —to *abstract* from a concrete datum its *"essential* attributes." In other words, sagacity is the ability to look at data in the right way, the significant way. For example, one may think of this piece of paper as a white substance, as a rectangular substance, or as a combustible substance; but what the paper *really* is is a substance we write on or print on. When we conceive a mass of data in the right way, and at the same time in a novel way, we are performing an act of creative thought. Creative thinking is the conceiving of data in a way it has never been conceived before and in the significant way. For example,

---

[1] James explains reasoning in terms of the syllogism in an ingenuous way. See his *Principles of Psychology*, Vol. II, Chap. XXII. For an illuminating application of the process, see Everett Dean Martin, *Psychology*, pp. 120-123.

scientists who were seeking for an explanation of the cause of organic evolution looked at the same data that Darwin examined but it was Darwin who first seized upon the *significant* factor of modification in plants and animals and produced the explanation of "natural selection." Marx, looking at a mass of old data in a new way, made a *new combination* of the data and was able to announce the "discovery" of a new social law. Likewise, Dr. Sigmund Freud, by his *way of looking at things,* originated theories that have revolutionized the science of psychology.[2] "Sagacity," thus (to use the terms employed in Chapters III and IV), is the ability to summon to the mind fruitful suggestions.

Suggestion Through Analogy.—Why do so few people perform creative thinking? Why are so few persons able to abstract the essential attribute of concrete data, yet able to perceive the truth after some more sagacious person has discovered it? There are several reasons, but the chief one is this: a concrete datum often has so many attributes that one does not extract the essential one unless he is aided by an associated idea. Darwin probably would not have thought of "natural selection" (that is, the modification of plants and animals by environment) if he had not thought first of how animals are modified by stock breeders.[3] William James relates an interesting incident in explanation of why so many persons do not think creatively:

I am sitting in a railroad car, waiting for the train to start. It is winter, and the stove fills the car with pungent smoke. The brakeman enters, and my neighbor asks him to "stop that stove smoking." He replies that it will stop entirely as soon as the car

---

[2] Freud, however, on one occasion prior to his concentration on the symbolic content of dreams and reverie, exhibited a painful lack of originality. "Freud had just missed a spectacular rise to fame when he failed to recognize the anæsthetic possibilities of cocaine in surgery. He published a review of the literature on cocoa; and a young Vienna colleague, Køller, struck by some of the data which Freud had assembled, announced the discovery in 1884 which immortalized his name in medical history. Freud pondered for many years on why the idea should have eluded him, and perhaps his desertion of the laboratory was due to his sense of partial failure."—Harold D. Lasswell, *Psychopathology and Politics*, p. 19.

[3] See Martin, *op. cit.,* p. 121.

begins to move. "Why so?" asks the passenger. "It *always* does," replies the brakeman. It is evident from this "always" that the connection between the car moving and smoke stopping was a purely empirical one in the brakeman's mind, bred of habit. But, if the passenger had been an acute reasoner, he, with no experience of what the stove always did, might have anticipated the brakeman's reply, and spared his own question. Had he singled out of all the numerous points involved in a stove's not smoking the one special point of *smoke pouring freely out of the stove-pipe's mouth,* he would, probably, owing to the few associations of that idea, have been immediately reminded of the law that a fluid passes more rapidly out of a pipe's mouth if another fluid be at the same time streaming over that mouth; and then the rapid draught of air over the stove-pipe's mouth, which is one of the points involved in the car's motion, would immediately have occurred to him.[4]

Thus imagination comes to the aid of the creative thinker. One who visualizes a situation—as in the instance described by James—or one whose imagination is rich in suggestive analogy —as in the case of Darwin—is usually a "sagacious" thinker. And if one adds to his sagacity learning—that is, a large experience-world—he is said to possess insight.

The Importance of "Learning."—Although the capacity to do creative thinking is merely the capacity to conceive data in a novel way, fruitful social thinking requires, in addition, the capacity to test novel hypotheses. One must not only have "sagacity," but "learning" as well; he must not only be able to conceive data in a novel way, but he must be able to know whether or not he has conceived the data in the *right* way. Some thinkers, endowed with the faculty of "sagacity," are able to create brilliant new conceptions which are sound in part, but, in final analysis, are inconsistent with reality. When these thinkers, in the face of criticism, adhere to their theories, we speak of them as "theorists" and "doctrinaires."

The failure of those thinkers to admit the inconsistency of their theory with the known facts is due to either of two causes: (*a*) they do not know what are the real facts, or (*b*) they are so pleased with the beautiful theory that they refuse to admit the real facts. In the first category the cause is plain ignorance;

---

[4] *The Principles of Psychology* (Henry Holt & Co., New York), Vol. II, pp. 342-343; reprinted by permission. Italics not in original.

in the second category it is wishful-thinking. We shall discuss each of these factors in turn.

Kinds of Ignorance.—A thinker's ignorance, in the sense in which the word is used here, is sometimes an ignorance of technical facts, sometimes a lack of "inside" information, and sometimes an ignorance of human nature as the result of detachment from real life.

1. *Ignorance of Technical Facts.*—Oftentimes the experience-world of the thinker does not make him aware of the real facts. This is especially true of thinking that involves technical factors. For example, some politicians have urged the public ownership of hydroelectric power sites on the ground that the generation of electrical energy by a hydroelectric plant is necessarily cheaper than by a steam plant. There are doubtless valid reasons why the public should own or should be able to recapture hydroelectric power sites, but the cheapness of hydroelectric generation is not one of them; as a matter of technical fact, generation by steam is usually cheaper. Why this is true is explained in a subsequent section.

2. *Lack of "Inside" Information.*—It is not only a lack of technical knowledge which causes a thinker to accept an impractical theory, but a lack of "inside" or "close-up" knowledge. It is often easier for the "outsider," who has no "inside" knowledge of finance, business, and government, to accept a neat formula that fits his limited experience-world than it is for him to understand and accept the real explanation. A sort of "law of parsimony" seems to determine the theories accepted by the lay thinker. Whenever the mind grapples with a perplexing problem, it is not content until it discovers an explanation. An explanation, therefore, is always found which fits the individual's experience-world. Any other explanation is beyond his comprehension. Our primitive ancestors, unable to account for certain natural phenomena, explained them in supernatural terms. The explanations were satisfying for the time—so long as men lived in the ancient and the medieval world—but they were not real explanations and therefore do not suffice for us who inhabit the realistic modern world. In regard to some problems today we are just as prone as were our ancestors to

accept unreal explanations because they fit our experience-world. Many of the "conspiracies" and "plots" that we hear about in connection with world politics, national politics, and "Wall Street" are readily believed by thousands of people because the political event or the economic situation is one which cannot be explained in terms with which the naïve individual is familiar, and the naïve thinker, as a consequence, accepts a romantic explanation—an explanation for which a pattern has been constructed in his *imagined* experience-world by the motion pictures or the novels of Mr. E. Phillips Oppenheim.

This human frailty is sometimes exploited by politicians and propagandists. An excellent example of the practice was the abortive effort of the Secretary of Agriculture, during the 1930 Congressional elections campaign, to shift the blame for falling wheat prices on to the Russian Soviet Government. Wheat had fallen to its lowest price in twenty-four years as a result of certain elusive economic factors of which the chief ones were supply and demand. Fearing that the Republican administration would be unfairly blamed for the low price of wheat, the Secretary of Agriculture announced that a trading operation of the Russian Government on the Chicago Board of Trade, on September 9—a comparatively small trading operation—had contributed to the depressed prices. Officials of the grain exchange immediately exposed the falsity of the accusation. This effort of an official of the Government to mislead the public, although proceeding from an insincere motive, was undertaken with the full knowledge of the psychological principle that the naïve mind tends to accept that explanation of a question which is the simplest explanation because the real explanation is not comprehended by his experience-world; Russia, since November, 1917, has been a land of mystery, and we have believed many strange things of the "incomprehensible" Bolsheviks.[5]

---

[5] Another example of this principle was produced in 1930 when Mr. James W. Gerard published a list of fifty-nine American business men who, he declared, were the "real rulers" of the United States, the inference being that "big business" controls public affairs. Just how close is the relation between so-called "big business" and government is a fact that only historians of a later day can determine; but there is much evidence of the fact that individual business men, aside from contributing campaign funds and receiving certain tariff favors, have little influence

The Rôle of the Image in Thinking.—"It is the essence of ordinary thought," says John Dewey, "to grasp the external scene and hold it as reality." [6]   Thus the mind that visualizes two scenes, one of nature's water pouring freely over a falls and the other of coal being laboriously extracted from the earth, is apt to conclude that generation of electrical energy by the hydro-electric method is necessarily cheaper than by the steam plant, even though the opposite is usually true.   As a matter of fact, one of the chief costs of generating electrical energy is the fixed charges on the plant investment, and this item for the ordinary hydroelectric plant amounts to nearly twice the same item for the steam plant.   The saving in coal and labor in generation by a hydroelectric plant is not sufficient to reduce the whole cost of generation much below that of the steam plant; besides, an auxiliary steam plant is usually necessary to supplement the hydroelectric plant during low flood stages, thus adding to the cost of hydroelectric generation.[7]

The ordinary newspaper reader, of course, cannot know much about "conditions" in Russia or Germany or India unless he supplements his newspaper reading considerably; but the reader of the newspaper is entitled to a true picture of his unseen environment, even though the picture be a bare outline.   Some news stories published by supposedly responsible American newspapers concerning "conditions" in Russia in 1929 and 1930 (not to mention during the hysterical period of 1917-1920) have been disgraceful examples of propaganda aimed at providing the reader with an unreal stereotype.   About all that the ordinary reader's "inside" and "close-up" information concerning many parts of his unseen environment amounts to is a visual image derived from news stories, cartoons, and editorials.

---

on elections and by no means a "control" of legislation.   For a surprising revelation of the Wall Street financiers' ignorance of the "inside" facts of national politics, see *They Told Barron,* the published diary of C. W. Barron, late publisher of the *Wall Street Journal,* who records his conversations with these men over a considerable period of years.

[6] *The Public and Its Problems,* p. 101.

[7] In connection with the Muscle Shoals controversy, it should be pointed out, the cost of construction of a hydroelectric plant must be calculated on a different basis for the reason that the Federal Government has already constructed the major portion of the plant and only a small additional capital investment would be required.

These images are sometimes distorted shadows of reality. Yet the reader acts upon them as if they were true.

3. *Detachment from Real Life.*—Sometimes a theory is not tested for its consistency with the real facts because the thinker is detached from real life—his experience-world has never comprehended the realities of certain aspects of life. The theories of intellectuals are frequently inconsistent with reality because of the limitation of their experience-world. It was the recognition of this truth that prompted Samuel Gompers and his associate founders of the American Federation of Labor to refuse the help of intellectuals and to proceed along the strictly practical lines that they had learned to trust in the seventies.[8] Much of our law, for example, is based on intellectual theories which are plainly not consistent with the realities of human nature; they are fictions which no longer have reality but have survived under the principle of *stare decisis* because the judges have not taken the trouble to make legal doctrines conform with the realities of life. The following editorial from the New York *World* exposes such a fiction:

> Down in Philadelphia a man has entered suit in the amount of $600,000 for alienation of his wife's affections, and once more we marvel at the law that it can entertain such a suit. In other situations, mind you, it exhibits a brutal common sense. It proceeds on the theory that human conduct is a matter of free will; that human beings, unless they are palpably lunatics, are responsible for their acts. Thus, without qualm, it can sit in judgment at York, Pa., and send a boy of fourteen to prison for life, although the murder he is alleged to have committed was most equivocal in its circumstances, and although many of us will doubt whether a person of his years can have any adequate comprehension of murder at all. That a murder was committed and that the boy was present are enough, and accordingly it passes sentence. But when it is confronted with the

---

[8] Samuel Gompers, *Seventy Years of Life and Labour,* Vol. I, Chaps. IV-XIII.

eternal triangle it seems to get giddy from romance and all its ordinary conceptions are changed.

The wife, as it happens to be in this case, is no longer regarded as a free agent, but as a sort of puppet to be pushed hither and yon, first by the husband, then by the tertium quid. So devoid is she of volition, of responsibility for what she does, that her affections are regarded as property, just as an automobile is regarded as property, and the person who appropriates her affections is liable to reprisals just as the person who appropriates the automobile is subject to reprisals. And in the course of time there is a suit, with the familiar hocus-pocus of the letters, the testimony of the private detective, and the impassioned oration of counsel.

This absurd show goes on every so often in every city in the country. It is a show that deceives nobody. The very loafers in the street are aware of its silly nature and read the testimony with ribald jeers. And it seems to us that the law does not add to its prestige when it pulls a solemn face and listens to it.

Wishful-Thinking.—The tendency of a thinker to champion a theory he has created (or of a passive reader to accept a novel theory he has read about) is often due not only to the thinker's ignorance of the real facts, but to his wish to believe the theory. The theory is true because he hopes it is. The thinker has a picture in his mind of his theory in operation, and he prefers to believe it is a real picture, though it is only a picture furnished by his imagination.

Since imagination is one of the elements in "sagacity," it is only natural, in problem solving, that some of the suggestions furnished by the imagination should emanate from the realm of the fanciful. Many suggestions that come to the mind are images. The mind sees a picture which represents the solution of the problem, as, for example, the Communist "observes" a society in which there are two classes—an exploiting and an exploited class. He visualizes a unity in the exploited class; he sees "labor" as an organism straining to break its chains. Although this picture is not true (for there are several social classes—not two—and workingmen do not wish for a classless society so much as they want higher wages, better working conditions, and an opportunity for their children to climb into a higher social class), the Communist insists that it represents reality; this is because he so earnestly wishes to establish a classless society.

An excellent illustration of wishful-thinking in connection with a public question was the movement within the Conservative party in Great Britain in 1930 (led by the so-called "Press Lords"—Rothermere and Beaverbrook) to put into operation what was called "imperial free trade." Since the beginning of the World War, Great Britain has been faced by the problem of her lost foreign markets. As a scheme to remedy the situation, the "Imperial Free-traders" and the "Crusaders" outlined programs which envisaged the enactment of a protective tariff on certain products by Great Britain and the dominions, but with preferential duties within the Commonwealth. Thus the Dominions would export to Great Britain surplus food products and raw materials, and Great Britain would export to the Dominions manufactured products. In addition, British surplus capital and population would be sent to develop the virgin parts of the various Dominions. To some extent, of course, this scheme could be made operative (e.g., by the arrangement of "bulk purchases" and "import quotas"), but it is essentially a beautiful picture in the heads of its innovators. Why this is so is explained by J. A. Hobson, the British economist:

> . . . No more foolish notion has ever entered the British mind. The value of our foods and raw materials imported from the Empire has grown since 1913, but our foreign supplies still greatly exceed them. The food imports from the Empire last year were 201 million pounds sterling as compared with 330 million from foreign countries; raw materials were 121½ million pounds sterling from the

Empire, 213 million from foreign countries. Certain essential materials, such as cotton, timber, iron ore and petroleum, are derived almost wholly from foreign sources. Even as regards foods, foreign supplies are incapable of replacement by Empire supplies. Last year nearly three-quarters of our imported wheat, and most of our imported meat, came from foreign countries. Indeed, it is evident that any attempt to rely upon Imperial resources would mean that we must pay more for an inferior and less secure supply. The reaction of such a policy upon our industries is obvious. Part of the protective policy is to enable our own farmers to grow wheat and other foods profitably, i.e., to get a higher price for them. Therefore, it is not expected that the Imperial supplies will compensate the loss of foreign supplies. Higher food prices and more costly materials will raise the cost of production in our mines, factories, and workshops, and the prices of their products must rise. This will operate most disastrously on our export trades, which are already outcompeted by cheaper continental products. Would the Empire compensate this damage by buying more of our high-priced manufactures? The supposition is ridiculous. Each Dominion is bent upon developing its own industries behind a tariff wall high enough to exclude all effectual competition. It only buys what it is not yet prepared to produce. Countries like Canada and Australia set no limit to their industrial development. It is simply inconceivable that their demand for British manufactures should increase within the near future, so as to compensate for the further loss of our foreign markets which would follow the adoption of this policy. . . .

The idea that this country can afford to pour vast resources of capital into "the vacant spaces of the Empire," and that the Dominions will eagerly welcome millions of unemployed Britons into their countries for the great work of opening up new areas of agriculture and mining will hardly bear the ven-

> tilation outside the area of Imperial sentiment
> which the business procedure of the [Im-
> perial] conference will secure.[9]

This tendency to do creative thinking without testing the theory honestly is indulged in by some of our greatest creative thinkers. Philosophers who have had the sagacity to pierce through a mass of data to select certain relevant factors sometimes are so in love with the new idea they have created that they continue to cherish it as reality even though critics point out its inconsistency with the real facts. Some of the panaceas devised by educators and reformers for remedying the multitude of social ills are brilliant conceptions which have a certain value, but as panaceas are not entirely consistent with the realities in human society.[10]

One who theorizes about society ought to know a great deal about society instead of cherishing a pseudo-picture of reality merely because the spectacle presented is a pleasant and desirable one. The English Liberals visualized the scene of men going to the polls to decide how they should be governed, and they were so in love with this picture that they assumed that universal political freedom would be followed by universal economic freedom. Yet the picture presented in their imagination did not represent reality. Some reformers, in studying about how to prevent war, encountered the suggestion that if only all the women in the world would refuse to sanction and support war, war could be entirely abolished; acting in accordance with the suggestion, the reformers proceeded in an attempt to organize women in peace societies. The mental image of the women

---

[9] *The Nation*, Vol. CXXXI (Oct. 1, 1930), p. 343. Regardless of the economic realities, a protective system for Great Britain seemed probable in 1931. Other countries had pushed their tariff walls so high that many British statesmen and economists calculated that Great Britain would have to enact tariff legislation for bargaining purposes, if not for revenue and industrial protection.

[10] Several such theories evolved by recent philosophers, psychologists, sociologists, economists, educators, and reformers (and even by investigators in the field of linguistics) are examined realistically by Henshaw Ward in an entertaining book entitled, *Thobbing*, the title being derived from a combination of the initial letters of the italicized words in the following sentence: "*Th*ink out the *op*inion that pleases us and then *b*elieve it."

of the world mobilized in opposition to war is a fanciful one, but to some peace fanatics it represents reality; to them it is so real that they expend money and time in "converting" others to their "program." Imagination, of course, is the supreme aid to creative thinking, but one must not mistake his mental images for reality: *he must so dissociate his wish from his reasoning that he can laugh at the ideas he himself creates.*

The Importance of Observation.—The natural scientist, as well as the philosopher and the social reformer, entertains fantastic hypotheses; but since the natural scientist is dealing with physical phenomena, he is able to make exact observations. As a consequence, he is more prompt in discarding untenable hypotheses. It was the great Darwin who said that no harm can come from entertaining a theory, but that making a wrong observation is a "crime." The social thinker, of course, cannot apply the exact tests that the natural scientist does, but is compelled to base his observation on his knowledge of the realities.

Classifying social thinkers with reference to the way in which they make observations, we can differentiate three classes, namely, theorists, cynics, and realistic thinkers. The theorist, whom we have already discussed, is one who sees in a problem only the factors he *wishes* to see and ignores those he prefers not to see. In many instances, he tries to apply a theory without reference to special circumstances. For example, he accepts the theory that "good government is no substitute for self-government" (which is true) and applies it to British India with reference to immediate and complete independence for the Indians, overlooking such difficulties as religious intolerance, the caste system, the Indian princes' ambitions, the budget requirements, taxation problems, and national defense. Most Britons desire a future for India that does not envisage civil war and the destruction of Indian credit by irresponsible borrowing.[11]

Cynical Versus Realistic Observations.—The cynic and the realistic thinker view a problem without wishing away the difficulties involved; but they pursue different methods when they

---

[11] These difficulties are examined realistically in Edward Thompson, *Reconstructing India;* the author favors dominion status for British India.

make observations. The difference between the cynical thinker and the thinker who observes the realities while refraining from cynicism is a difference in mental attitude: one has a closed mind, the other an open mind. The cynic, when a problem arises, tests the suggested solution with reference to his past observations, but with no open-minded attitude; that is to say, he makes no *new* observations. Having previously made a generalization in which he had given superior weight to the difficulties involved, he holds to this generalization as an eternal premise. The realistic thinker, on the other hand, is one who, without ignoring the difficulties involved, reëxamines his past observations with an open-minded attitude, regarding his former generalization only as a tentative premise. The realistic thinker may revise, the cynic always dogmatizes, his past observations. For example, it has always been held by students of proletarian movements (who took their cue from Marx, the founder of Communism) that Communism could never succeed in a country that was primarily agricultural. Experience, indeed, may show this generalization to be true; but since 1929 some students have been considering a revision of their past observations in the light of new observations made in Russia: it is quite possible that an agricultural people which has never been exposed to the ideology of the French Revolution, as have western peoples, may, under the compulsion of a determined, doctrinaire government, learn how to live under a Communistic régime and prefer it to the former régime even though the Marxian ideal of a purely Communist state is never realized.

In the past, policy-molding officials of imperialistic states have realistically applied certain generalizations and have found them to be sound; but the time has now come when they may find it necessary to revise some of their observations. It may still be true, of course, that "the tropical man (e.g., the Filipino and the Central-American) prefers to submit passively to tyranny than to fight for his right to govern himself" and that "Asiatic mankind, having never in its long history evolved a free government, will continue to submit to tyranny"; but policy molders of imperialistic states who adhere to such generalizations without reëxamining their observations must bear responsibility in history for the effects of the current bad conditions which these suppressed peoples are protesting against.[12]

Reality and Myth.—Although most of the foregoing section is a warning to the editorial writer to beware of wishful thinking, the point should be made here that, in so far as the naïve mind is concerned, it sometimes makes no difference whether or not an hypothesis is consistent with reality, for the naïve mind sometimes *acts upon* an hypothesis regardless of its foundation in reality. This is frequently true of the hypotheses that relate to the future organization of society, as, for example, the catastrophic general strike envisioned by Syndicalists and revolutionary Socialists. This psychological phenomenon was first explained clearly by the anti-intellectualist, George Sorel. It does no good, says Sorel, for intellectuals to argue about whether or not the general strike will follow from the concentration of wealth in the control of a few, or about what sort of Socialist tactic is to be employed in the general strike— these are factors in the future about which we can not reason scientifically. All that matters is that the workers accept the "myth" of the general strike; that is, that "the men who participate in the great social movements envisage their immediate action in the form of images of battles assuring the triumph of their cause." [18]

Experience shows [says Sorel] that the *framing of a future, in some indeterminate time,* may, when it is done in a certain way, be very effective, and have very few inconveniences; this happens when the anticipations of the future take the form of those myths, which enclose with them all the strongest inclinations of a people, of a party, or of a class, inclinations which recur to the mind with the insistence of instincts in all the circumstances of life; and which give an aspect of complete reality to the hopes of immediate action by which, more easily than by any other method,

---

[12] The term *realistic thinker* is used here to differentiate a certain attitude of mind from the attitude habitually assumed by the theorist and the cynic. It is probably a pure idealization. There may not be living anywhere such a thinker; for the differentiation of the idealist and the theorist, on the one hand, and of the cynic and the realistic thinker, on the other hand, can seldom, if ever, be made with reference to all public questions. The following chapter, which discusses "values," may be more helpful in explaining these attitudes of mind.

[18] *Reflexions sur la Violence* (2nd ed.), pp. 26-27.

men can reform their desires, passions, and mental activity. We know, moreover, that these social myths in no way prevent a man profiting by the observations which he makes in the course of his life, and form no obstacle to the pursuit of his normal occupations.

The truth of this may be shown by numerous examples.

The first Christians expected the return of Christ and the total ruin of the pagan world, with the inauguration of the kingdom of the saints, at the end of the first generation. The catastrophe did not come to pass, but Christian thought profited so greatly from the apocalyptic myth that certain contemporary scholars maintain that the whole preaching of Christ referred solely to this one point. . . . In our own times Mazzini pursued what the wiseacres of his time called a mad chimera; but it can no longer be denied that, without Mazzini, Italy would never have become a great power, and that he did more for Italian unity than Cavour and all the politicians of his school. . . .

To estimate, then, the significance of the idea of the general strike, all the methods of discussion which are current among politicians, sociologists, or people with pretensions to political science, must be abandoned. Everything which its opponents endeavour to establish may be conceded to them, without reducing in any way the value of the theory which they think they have refuted. The question whether the general strike is a partial reality, or only a product of popular imagination, is of little importance. All that it is necessary to know is, whether the general strike contains everything that the socialist doctrine expects of the revolutionary proletariat. . . . To solve this question, we are no longer compelled to argue learnedly about the future. . . .

We know that the general strike is indeed what I have said: the *myth* in which socialism is wholly comprised, i.e., a body of images capable of evoking instinctively all the sentiments which correspond to the different manifestations of the war undertaken by socialism against modern society. Strikes have engendered in the proletariat the noblest, deepest, and most moving sentiments that they possess; the general strike groups them all in a co-ordinated picture, and, by bringing them together, gives to each one of them its maximum of intensity; appealing to their painful memories of particular conflicts, it colours with an intense life all the details of the composition presented to its consciousness. We thus obtain that intuition of socialism which language cannot give us with perfect clearness—and we obtain it as a whole, perceived instantaneously.[14]

---

[14] Sorel, *op. cit.*, pp. 133-137; translation published by B. W. Huebsch. Cited by Park and Burgess in *An Introduction to the Science of Society.*

The Value of Wishful Thinking.—In 1930 we were emerging from a decade of cynicism and complacency, and the ten or fifteen years following that date are likely to witness a more cordial reception to the ideas of the progressive thinker and even of the wishful thinker. The period following 1930 was one in which many novel and radical experiments in politics and economics were being launched. The intolerable economic situation, the dangerous international situation, and the living example of a virile régime of Communism were factors which induced men to pay attention to certain intellectual theories which had had no thorough examination prior to 1930. Some of these theories about social and industrial organization and some of these concrete remedies for the world's ailments will probably be found, by 1945, to be good, and others will probably be found to be unsound and unworkable. The open-minded editor, in the next few years, will give the creative thinker more encouragement than he has given him for many years. Editors ought to examine and encourage liberal ideas, for it is obvious that Western civilization has been passing "Danger" signs without paying heed. There is extreme social danger in inertia and narrow-mindedness.

CHAPTER XI

VALUES

When William James explained creative thinking as "a way of looking at things," he was establishing the basis of a philosophic system which has come to be called Pragmatism. This system—and Instrumentalism, as developed by John Dewey—was essentially a revolt against intellectualism (i.e., a conceptual logic which holds that truth resides in an ideal principle). Pragmatism and Instrumentalism have revolutionized our way of thinking about social problems. They have emphasized the value of scientific technique and, as a consequence, have caused us to be more critical of "first principles." This has led, of course, to an attitude of open-mindedness. Having come to regard our principles tentatively and provisionally, we are inclined to rely on social experimentation more than on the finality of logic.

Open-mindedness as regards principles ought not to lead us, however, to place our entire reliance on scientific procedure as a method of problem solving. As was pointed out in Chapter V, there are some social problems that cannot be solved by scientific technique alone.[1] Even a science, when it attacks some social problems, must proceed within a metaphysical setting. We must reflect on values as we proceed with measurement and interpretation, otherwise our results will lack meaning; for science itself is entirely neutral as regards values.

What Is a Value?—When we think in terms of values we think in terms of *ends*. We evaluate ends in terms of their values to ourselves individually, or to our group, our section, our country, or to society. That is to say, we do not think

---

[1] "It seems to us that science is a special technique developed for and applicable to the control of physical nature, but that the ideal so constantly preached and reiterated, of carrying its procedure over into the field of the social phenomena rests on a serious misapprehension."— F. H. Knight in *The Trend of Economics* (R. G. Tugwell, ed.), p. 254.

objectively. For example, in an objective discussion with a friend regarding the merits of two different makes of automobiles, it is easy enough for me to convince him that a Cadillac—let us say—is a better automobile than a Ford: it has more power, less vibration, better upholstery, more speed, more accessories, etc. These are facts, and, because the end is agreed upon by both parties to the dispute, proof can be readily adduced to demonstrate that a Cadillac is a better automobile than a Ford. All scientific discussion is of this character; for, in science, there is no disagreement as regards the ends desired —the only end desired is the truth. Scientific discussion, as a consequence, is confined to *facts*. But in a dispute with a salesman who wants to sell me a Cadillac there enter certain values, which, *to me,* are ends. Are the chief ends desired cheapness in price and low cost of maintenance? Or is the chief end comfort? or durability? or speed? Some of these ends—cheapness and low maintenance cost, let us say—enter into my decision as to which automobile I shall purchase and, of course, into my controversy with the salesman. These ends, or desires, are values. They control my decision: since it is cheapness and low maintenance cost that I want, the Cadillac salesman assuredly would lose the argument. He would not have so much difficulty, however, in convincing another prospect who had in mind different ends—say, comfort and speed.

Oftentimes, however, men do not perceive the highest values. This is true not only in controversies regarding social ends, but in instances in which the individual is permitted a preference as to his own best interests. Some men are not sufficiently enlightened to know what is good for themselves as individuals. This is illustrated by the following news story from a Chicago newspaper:

> While building programs in most cities have slumped to a considerable degree during the last six months, the construction activities in New York have continued at a brisk pace. Those conversant with labor conditions in the nation's building industry assert that when the volume of building in any large city is large and continues un-

abated, the building mechanics are wont to ask for higher pay rates and more time to spend their earnings.

August 26 has been set as the date for the establishment of the forty-hour, or five-day, week for New York's 150,000 building workers. It is said the building workers have agreed to forego any general demand for increases of pay in order to procure the five-day week.

In Chicago, however, when agreements were negotiated last year between the unions and the contractors, there was no mention of the five-day week. . . . Practically all the trades which had agreements to negotiate accepted an increase in wage rates.

Then came the movement to start the five-day week in New York for the workers in that city. Chicago contractors have now been asked to give the five-day week consideration, and are doing so.

Labor representatives of the local trades maintain that the forty-hour week would aid the unemployment situation that now confronts practically all Chicago building trades.

The secretary of the Contractors' Association, however, says that the unemployment angle is not held forth by President William Green of the American Federation of Labor in his advocacy of the five-day week.

"Mr. Green," he said, "has championed the forty-hour week because he believes it would aid in the spiritual uplift of the working-man."

The foregoing news story illustrates how differently men conceive their own interests. One group of workers, when it was given an opportunity to have its wish fulfilled, merely accepted higher wages for themselves; another group preferred that the interest of their union be advanced by the creation of more jobs; another group—the highest leaders in trade unionism—perceived the advantage of more leisure; the latter's preference recognized the fact that there are higher values in life than mere material things which wages buy.

Social Values.—The values which the foregoing section discussed are selfish values. But it is not that type of value that this chapter will discuss; we are concerned here with social values. Social ends are not those which we ourselves desire so much as they are ends that *we ought to desire*. To the extent that social values are ethical values, they have moral content. We are not concerned, however, with the moral valuation that pertains to individual conduct; for the editorial page of the newspaper is devoted almost exclusively to the discussion of social conduct—of the ends that individuals ought to desire in a collective sense.

Which Social Values Are Highest?—The editorial writer sometimes meets with a difficult moral situation. A proposal has been made for the achievement of a good social end, but the editor, on reflection, perceives that the end is incompatible with another social end. He then faces a moral situation: which is the higher end?

Sometimes only a minimum of reflection is required to determine which is the higher of two social ends. For example, it was perfectly plain to the intelligent and conscientious Louisiana editor in the late nineties that the three million dollars contributed to the Louisiana school fund as a result of the legalizing of lotteries was a less desirable social end than the discontinuance of the lotteries; for lotteries, it was plain, contributed to human degradation and ought to be abolished, even though they contributed to the state's revenue. It was still necessary, however, for Louisiana editors to explain to some naïve readers the social consequences of lotteries, but their task was mainly one of exposing an antisocial practice whose defenders were justifying it on the ground that it contributed to a good social end, the school fund. In most instances, the editorial writer does not have to perform much reflection about values: he has only to expose antisocial forces and agents, some of which are easily identified. In such cases the sound moral judgment of the reader is assumed, and the task of the editorial writer merely consists in identifying plainly and making conspicuous those forces and agents which are opposing an effort to attain a definite social end. The editorial writer's task, in other words, is one of stripping the Devil of his monk's hood and leaving the rest to the moral judgment of the reader.

In many other instances, however, the editorial writer is confronted by a conflict of social ends about which it is difficult for both him and his readers to make a preference. In such an instance, he must reflect deeply.

The Need for Reflection.—When one reflects upon ends, he clarifies values. As a consequence, he may elaborate new ends: he may perceive that what at first had appeared to be an end itself is merely a means to a *further* end.

Illustration: Order vs. Liberty.—Thus it is only by reflection upon ends that we can begin to attack the central problem of all political theory, namely, the reconciliation of sovereignty and individual liberty. Since the World War, dictatorships based on violence have been established in several European countries on the ground that the preservation of social order requires the restriction of the individual's liberty to criticize government. Few persons dissent from this conception of government when it is apparent that the dictatorship reflects merely a policy of expediency; but when such governments consolidate their power with a view toward permanency and when they construct a philosophy to justify the character of their government, they meet with dissent from those persons who hold that the individual's liberty to criticize government is a further end than the preservation of social order. When the Italian Fascists exalt the state above the individual and assert that the individual can realize himself only through the state (i.e., by renouncing the right of free speech and assemblage), they are setting up the proposition that the ultimate end of government is the exaltation of the state. Because this view is now echoed all through the world—even, in one sense, in certain American municipalities which have been experiencing corrupt government —it is necessary that we reflect upon this asserted end of government to determine whether or not it is the ultimate end.

It is recognized, of course, that the first function of government is to provide stability; but stability is only a means to a further end. To argue, as do the Fascist philosophers, that Italians do not deserve liberty, is to deny to Italians the opportunity to learn how to govern themselves. The greatest degree of free government is found in the Anglo-Saxon countries, and there are two reasons for the phenomenon. Anglo-Saxons, in the first place, have had the longest period of training in how to make their free institutions work. In the second place, reflection and experience have shown them that freedom of discussion is an *ultimate* value, and they have fought to attain it and preserve it: whenever the common man comes to be satisfied with a sop of economic prosperity cast down to him by a benevolent dictatorship, then will he cease to fight for an abstract idea. Yet, unless he reflects on this value, he will not attain or preserve his freedom.

Illustration: Liberty vs. Social Justice.—In the foregoing discussion we observed how reflection upon two conflicting social ends led us to decide that one of the social ends (the preservation of social order) was, in final analysis, merely a means to a further social end (the liberty of the individual citizen). Reflection will also show that individual liberty itself is a means to the attainment of a still higher social end, namely, social justice. We shall now analyze a value conflict in which we shall observe how insistence on regarding individual liberty as the ultimate social end may defeat the end of social justice. That is to say, in a conflict between the ideal of freedom of contract and the ideal of social justice, reflection will show us that the latter is the higher social end.

This controversy is to determine whether the preservation of freedom of contract is more desirable as a social end than is the intervention of the state in industry to guarantee social justice to the workers. It is a conflict of ideals which has lain at the foundation of much of the social legislation for the regulation of working hours and working conditions. Social reformers and labor unions have obtained the passage of laws that are in the interest of the worker, and afterward have had to meet arguments in the law courts that the legislation violates the constitutional liberties of the worker. In some instances, the opponents of this kind of social legislation have averred that it is the constitutional liberties of the employer that have been violated, but more often they have argued that it is the constitutional liberties of the worker himself that were interfered with. The nature of this conflict of ideals is well illustrated in the judicial reasoning involved in the decision of the United

States Supreme Court, in 1923, which declared unconstitutional the District of Columbia minimum wage law.[2]

The Fifth Amendment to the Federal Constitution provides that no person shall be "deprived of life, liberty, or property without due process of law." The Fourteenth Amendment provides that no state shall "deprive any person of life, liberty, or property without due process of law." The Constitution itself does not define "due process of law." The only definition we have is that one which the United States Supreme Court has been engaged in defining for nearly a century. The court has been refining its definition by the "gradual process of judicial inclusion and exclusion."[3] That is to say, the Court, as various cases have come before it, has decided by judicial reasoning whether or not the particular case is one in which a citizen has been deprived of his liberty without due process of law, and future cases are examined to determine whether or not they are *essentially like* those cases which have been "included" within the definition. By the principle of *stare decisis*, each decision about a particular case is a precedent for deciding future cases. The practical result of this protean method of making a definition of "due process of law" is that the general rule is distorted within certain limits according to whether or not the justices who happen at the time to be sitting agree with the social end that a particular statute is calculated to attain. Several laws which undoubtedly interfered with freedom of contract have been held constitutional. In the case of Muller *v.* Oregon, for example, a law restricting the working hours of women was held constitutional on the ground that it was a protection of public health which government could enforce by reason of its "police power."

In spite of this and many other precedents, however, the United States Supreme Court, in 1923, in a five-to-three decision, held that the District of Columbia minimum wage law was unconstitutional because it deprived female employees of their right to make any contract they desired with an employer.

---

[2] Adkins *et al. v.* Children's Hospital, 261 U. S. 525, 43 Sup. Ct. 394.
[3] Justice Miller in Davidson *v.* New Orleans, 96 U. S. 97. For the historical definition of "due process of law," see L. P. McGehee, *Due Process of Law,* and R. L. Mott, *Due Process of Law.*

That is to say, the law which forbade an employer to pay less than a fixed wage actually prevented an employee from accepting less than the fixed wage. One of the plaintiffs, for example, was an elevator operator in a hotel who had been discharged after the passage of the act because her compensation—$35 a month and two meals a day—was below the wage scale fixed by the minimum wage board; her employer was able to employ a male operator for less than the wage fixed by the board, but he could not legally continue to employ the girl at that scale.

This law undoubtedly interfered with the plaintiff's freedom to enter into a contract. But in many previous cases the court had held that exceptional cases deserved to be held constitutional because the Government has the right, by its police power, to conserve the health and morals of the public. That is to say, in a choice between ends to be served, the Court had held in several prior cases that violation of freedom of contract was justifiable because of the higher end to be served by the particular statute. The question before the Court in the minimum wage case, therefore, was to determine *whether the statute was essentially like the other statutes which had been held constitutional (i.e., justifiable), or whether it was so novel as to merit being held unconstitutional.*

Mr. Justice Sutherland, who wrote the majority opinion, asserted early in his argument that "freedom of contract is . . . the general rule and restraint the exception, and the exercise of legislative authority to abridge it can be justified only by the existence of exceptional circumstances." This proposition is the major premise of Justice Sutherland's argument; for in judicial reasoning the jurist starts from a general principle (called a "rule") and applies it to the particular case at hand to deduce a conclusion. What Justice Sutherland did, then, was to assert a minor premise and try to prove it. If he could prove it, he would have succeeded in establishing his conclusion. Syllogistically, his argument would be arranged about as follows:

Freedom of contract should not be abridged by legislation unless the legislation is calculated to remedy an exceptional social evil (such as those which were prohibited as the result of former decisions).

This case is not like the other (exceptional) cases which the court has decided were justifiable abridgements of freedom of contract. This case is a violation of freedom of contract, and hence is unconstitutional

A great part of Justice Sutherland's decision is devoted to proving his minor premise, namely, that the minimum wage law is *unlike* the former laws that had been held constitutional. In summarizing his explanation of these previous cases, he says:

If now, in the light furnished by the foregoing exceptions to the general rule forbidding legislative interference with freedom of contract, we examine and analyze the statute in question, we shall see that it differs from them in every material respect.

[First] It is not a law dealing with any business charged with a public interest or with public work, or to meet and tide over temporary emergency [such as *Louisville & Nashville R. R. Co. v. Mottley, Munn v. Illinois,* and *Wilson v. New,* which had been held constitutional].

[Second] It has nothing to do with the character, methods, and periods of wage payments [as did *McLean v. Arkansas, Knoxville Iron Co. v. Harbison,* and *Erie R. R. Co. v. Williams*].

[Third] It does not prescribe hours of labor or conditions under which labor is not to be done [as in *Holden v. Hardy* and *Bunting v. Oregon*].

[Fourth] It is not for the protection of persons under legal disability or for the prevention of fraud [as *Muller v. Oregon*]. It is simply and exclusively a price-fixing law, confined to adult women . . . who are legally as capable of contracting for themselves as men.

The method employed by Justice Sutherland in proving his minor premise was the comparative method. He compared the minimum wage case with the other cases and found that there was an *essential difference* between the former precedents and the minimum wage case. As was said in a previous chapter, one's ability to think depends chiefly upon his ability to perceive *resemblances* in things. Did Justice Sutherland think clearly in this instance? Was he correct in deciding that the minimum wage case was different from the preceding cases? In the opinion of Chief Justice Taft and Associate Justices Holmes and Sanford, Justice Sutherland did *not* think clearly. Justice Holmes said in a dissenting opinion:

Without enumerating all the restrictive laws that have been upheld, I will mention a few that seem to me to have interfered with liberty of contract quite as seriously and directly as the one before us. Usury laws prohibit contracts by which a man receives more than so much interest for the money that he lends. Statutes of frauds restrict many contracts to certain forms. Some Sunday laws prohibit practically all contracts during one-seventh of our whole life. Insurance rates may be regulated (*German Alliance Insurance Co. v. Kansas*). Contracts may be forced upon the companies (*National Union Fire Insurance Co. v. Wanberg*). Employers of miners may be required to pay for coal by weight before screening (*McLean v. Arkansas*). Employers generally may be required to redeem in cash store orders accepted by their employees in payment (*Knoxville Iron Co. v. Harbison*). Payment of sailors in advance may be forbidden (*Patterson v. Bark Eudora*). The size of a loaf of bread may be established (*Schmidinger v. Chicago*). The responsibility of employers to their employees may be profoundly modified (*N. Y. Central R. R. Co. v. White* and *Arizona Employers' Liability Cases*). Finally women's hours of labor may be fixed (*Muller v. Oregon, Riley v. Massachusetts, Hawley v. Walker, Miller v. Wilson, Bosley v. McLaughlin*) ; and the principle was extended to men with the allowance of a limited overtime to be paid for "at the rate of time and one-half of the regular wage" (*Bunting v. Oregon*).

Thus Justice Holmes perceives a *similarity* between the exceptional abridgments of contract and the minimum wage case, whereas Justice Sutherland thinks there is an *essential difference* between the minimum wage case and the former cases.

Why do these judges fail to perceive the same resemblances and differences? Is one judge less "logical" than the other?

The reason why the judges disagree is that they have made a preference between two different social ends: Justice Sutherland has the viewpoint of the legal formalist and Justice Holmes the viewpoint of the social philosopher. Justice Holmes has written: "Inasmuch as the real justification of a rule of law, if there be one, is that it helps to bring about a social end which we desire, it is no less necessary that those who make and develop the law should have those ends articulately in their minds." [4] In other words, Justice Holmes would infer that Justice Sutherland and others of his type of mind are not

---

[4] *Collected Legal Papers*, p. 238.

enlightened as to the realities of industrial labor. They have
not *reflected* sufficiently on the ends to be served. The end is
not clear in their minds because they are detached from the
realities of industrial life.

We cannot say that Justice Sutherland, in the way he looked
at the minimum wage case and the various precedents, was
illogical; we can only say that if he had reflected more upon
the social end to be served he might have had a different sense
of values. For when one examines, in its entirety, the opinion
written by Justice Sutherland, he perceives a considerable
amount of bad logic which is the consequence of his viewpoint.
Much of his reasoning is pervaded with his preference of the
end to be served; to make his reasoning seem logical he has
rationalized his viewpoint. Specimens of Justice Sutherland's
logic have already been referred to on pages 189-190; we shall
notice one other specimen.

When Justice Sutherland attempted to prove that the minimum wage case was unlike the case of Muller *v.* Oregon, he
met with difficulty. In that case, and also in the cases of Riley,
Miller, and Bosley, the Supreme Court had held that a statute
forbidding the employment of any female in certain industries
for more than ten hours during any day was constitutional.
But Justice Sutherland said:

The decision [in the Muller case] proceeded upon the theory
that the difference between the sexes may justify a different rule
respecting hours of labor in the case of women than in the case
of men. It is pointed out that these consist in differences of
physical structure, especially in respect of the maternal functions,
and also in the fact that historically woman has always been dependent upon man, who has established his control by superior
physical strength. The case of Riley, Miller, and Bosley follow
in this respect the Muller case. But the ancient inequality of
the sexes, otherwise than physical as suggested in the Muller case
(p. 421) has continued "with diminishing intensity." In view
of the great—not to say revolutionary—changes which have taken
place since that utterance, in the contractual, political and civil
status of women, culminating in the Nineteenth Amendment, it is
not unreasonable to say that these differences have now come
almost, if not quite, to the vanishing point. In this aspect of the
matter, while the physical differences must be recognized in appro-

priate cases, and legislation fixing hours or conditions of work may properly take them into account, we cannot accept the doctrine that women of mature age, *sui juris* [that is, those who have no legal disabilities and do not need guardians to act for them at law], require or may be subjected to restrictions upon their liberty of contract which could not lawfully be imposed in the case of men under similar circumstances.

This particular piece of reasoning (which, incidentally, was applauded as sound by a distinguished St. Louis newspaper) was refuted by Chief Justice Taft, as follows:

If I am right in thinking that the legislature can find as much support in experience for the view that a sweating wage has as great and as direct a tendency to bring about an injury to the health and morals of workers, as for the view that long hours injure their health, then I respectfully submit that Muller v. Oregon, 208 U. S. 412, controls this case. The law which was there sustained forbade the employment of any female in any mechanical establishment or factory or laundry for more than ten hours. This covered a pretty wide field in women's work and it would not seem that any sound distinction between that case and this can be built up on the fact that the law before us applies to all occupations of women with power in the board to make certain exceptions. Mr. Justice Brewer, who spoke for the court in Muller v. Oregon, based its conclusion on the natural limit to woman's physical strength and the likelihood that long hours would therefore injure her health and we have had since a series of cases which may be said to have established a rule of decision. Riley v. Massachusetts, 232 U. S. 671; Miller v. Wilson, 236 U. S. 373; Bosley v. McLaughlin, 236 U. S. 385. The cases covered restrictions in wide and varying fields of employment and in the later cases it will be found that the objection to the particular law was based not on the ground that it had general application but because it left out some employments.

I am not sure from a reading of the opinion whether the Court thinks the authority of Muller v. Oregon is shaken by the adoption of the Nineteenth Amendment. The Nineteenth Amendment did not change the physical strength or limitations of women upon which the decision in Muller v. Oregon rests. The Amendment did give women political power and makes more certain that legislative provisions for their protection will be in accord with their interests as they see them. But I don't think we are warranted in varying constitutional constructions based on physical differences between men and women, because of the Amendment.

Justice Sutherland's reasoning on this point, which was characterized by Justice Taft as "formal rather than real," represents almost an utter detachment from the real concerns of life, and is characteristic of many jurists and college professors. It is this application of a general rule to a specific case which furnishes the example for that group of persons who often assert that they prefer to trust the sense of justice that is possessed by a jury of farmers than to trust the sense of justice of a judge.[5] General principles, such as freedom of contract, are broad and vague, and their application is broad and vague unless those who apply them are enlightened as to the realities of the particular case to which they are applied.

It is one of the tragedies of life that the men who control affairs do not always *understand* the consequences of their acts. Financiers, lawyers, judges, statesmen, and publishers, because of their failure to reflect on social ends, frequently do much harm to society and to themselves. The "official mind" is nearly always one that considers the immediate consequences of a policy and not the ultimate social end. The "official mind" seldom tries to "understand" a situation in all its social consequences. Mr. Alfred E. Zimmern has made this plain in an explanation of why Englishmen have shown an aptitude for governing:

> The distinctive qualities required for such work may perhaps be summarized in two characteristics, public spirit and judgment.
> What we call "public spirit" is a moral quality, a particular and highly specialized form of unselfishness. . . . What we call "judgment," on the other hand, is an intellectual quality, a particular and highly specialized form of intellectual activity. It involves the power of taking a mass of facts, together constituting a "political situation," surveying them as a whole and framing a practical decision—a decision leading to action. To have a good judgment about a situation is not the same thing as to have an *understanding* of such a situation in all its bearings. Englishmen have not governed India by understanding her, nor did they quell the Great Mutiny in 1857, which would assuredly have proved fatal to

---

[5] Most newspaper men seem to have a sense of reality like that of the jurors in the John Peter Zenger libel case, but the history of journalism reveals some editors who did not have it. The intellectual Godkin, for example, came perilously near to formalism when he was thinking about social economics.

their rule had they been differently constituted, by their power of comprehending the motives which produced it. They held their ground by their power to comprehend not the underlying facts, but the urgent facts, and by their ability to decide as to the "next step." Just as public spirit in its most concentrated form involves a certain emotional abdication, so judgment, especially in an emergency, involves an intellectual abdication. The statesman, faced by the necessity of framing a political decision, cannot afford to look too deeply or to cultivate too nice a sense of intellectual consistency.[6]

Social Experimentation.—We have tried to show in the preceding sections of this chapter that all problems cannot be solved by the same method. Scientific technique, in the first place, can solve only those problems about which we can reason objectively: it cannot solve problems which involve a choice of values, either selfish or social values. Conceptual logic, in the second place, cannot solve some problems because the premises from which the reasoning begins causes the thinker to accept unhesitatingly an end as a good end without reflecting on the incompatibility of that end with another end. The danger which ensues from deciding social questions as Mr. Justice Sutherland decided the minimum wage case is that we can never know which of the values is the higher. For even reflection cannot always decide: *we must sometimes rely on social experimentation* to make our final decision.

The method of thinking that is reflected in the majority opinion in the minimum wage case is one that cannot always be employed in the modern world. The effect of the court's decision in this case is to shut the door on social experimentation. Having reasoned formally that a minimum wage is unconstitutional and against the principles of economics, the court forbids the legislative branch of our government to experiment

---

[6] "The Politics of Martha," *Century Magazine,* Vol. CVI (September, 1923), p. 678.

When we assess the blame for the world's ills we must never fail to assign a considerable share to the world's governors, who are frequently stupid, selfish, and narrow-minded; but we must also take into account that public officials are frequently compelled to follow policies dictated by the mass of unenlightened people. In this connection, read Ray Stannard Baker, *Woodrow Wilson and World Settlement,* Vol. I, and Louis Fischer, *The Soviets in World Affairs,* Vol. I, Chaps. III and IV.

with it. The question of whether or not a minimum wage is economically sound cannot be decided by armchair thinking: it must be decided by actual experiment.[7] When the Supreme Court forbids such experimentation, there are only two alternatives: we must either forego the experiment or we must resort to the procedure of securing the adoption of a constitutional amendment. The latter procedure, as the prohibition amendment seems to have demonstrated, proves the unwisdom of conducting social experiment within such a tightly locked laboratory: if the experiment fails, the experimentors must smash down the walls of the laboratory in order to have an exit.

---

[7] Several economists have already interpreted our experience with the minimum wage, as it has operated in some of the states that adopted it, as an unsound economic policy which is not in the interest of the workers themselves.

CHAPTER XII

REFUTATION

Present-day editors do not contradict their opponents as much as did nineteenth century editors. An examination of editorials of the last quarter of the century shows that a large proportion of the editorials were destructive in their purpose. It was as if those editors, conceiving themselves to be debaters rather than teachers, searched the speeches of politicians of the rival party and the editorials of rival editors for points which they could contradict or refute. Today, however, editorial controversy is less in the nature of dual debate; editorials are more constructive in their purposes, and destructive argument is more frequently embodied in constructive argument merely as an auxiliary part of it. The art of refutation, however, is by no means a lost art among editors of today.

WHAT TO REFUTE

The success of refutation often depends on how much one tries to refute. We can safely lay down two rules which ought to be followed.

1. *Do not try to refute too much.* Editorials, in the first place, cannot run to great length because the reader is not inclined to read long editorials. In the second place, the answering of petty arguments gives such undue emphasis to them that the reader may be confused as to the really important points at issue.

If one tries, first of all, to make clear to the reader exactly what he is trying to refute, he is not likely to refute too much; for it is not usually necessary to pay any attention to the less significant points if one will make clear to the reader what is the main issue. When Lincoln, as a criminal lawyer, desired to refute testimony regarding the occurrence of certain events on a moonlight night, he merely produced an almanac which showed there was no moonlight on the night in question. A refutation that was remarkably effective because of its simplicity was the reply of Mr. S. K. Ratcliffe, the British journalist, to an address by an advocate of immediate and complete independence for India. The speaker had announced Mahatma Gandhi's five-fold program for India, which, he said, was quite "practical" and "suited to the situation," and would make Indians capable of governing themselves. The five objectives were: "to do away with the terrible religious differences between Hindus and Muslims"; "prohibition of all drink and drugs"; "woman's equality with man"; "removal of untouchability"; and the introduction of *Khadder,* or the spinning wheel, to provide industry for idle peasants. Mr. Ratcliffe replied, in part, as follows:

You have had Mr. Andrews' outline of Mahatma Gandhi's program for his own people. Hindu-Muslim unity is the first. Mahatma Gandhi has noted again and again how terrible are the obstacles to that. Second, prohibition. Need I say one word before an American audience of its difficulties? Third, woman's equality in India, and our honored speaker of this afternoon [Mrs. Sarojini Naidu] is, I believe, the only Indian woman in public life. Fourth, the abolition of untouchability, equal rights for the great Indian masses. Again, is even one word necessary about that? And fifth, *Khadder,* the spinning wheel, as the way to liberation of India. Well, if freedom is not granted to India within this calendar year, Mrs. Naidu reminds us, there will be a strong movement for complete independence. . . .[1]

2. *Do not refute too little.* One cannot usually dismiss an opponent's argument with a mere flourish. If the opponent has prestige or if his argument is at all deserving of refutation, it should be sincerely refuted, not dismissed with a scornful gesture. Scorn and mere dissent are no substitutes for argument.

METHODS OF REFUTATION

Refutation may be accomplished by three methods: (1) refuting the facts; (2) attacking the opponent's reasoning; (3) using rhetorical devices.

---

[1] Quoted from Foreign Policy Association, Pamphlet No. 57, Series 1928-9 (May, 1929), p. 17.

1. **Refuting the Facts.**—The truth of arguments about important questions is determined finally by the facts. Arguments, of course, usually concern a principle or a policy, but the truth of the principle or the justification of the policy is usually determined by the facts in dispute. We want to know, "What are the facts about prohibition?" "What are the facts about public utilities' profits?" "What are the facts about the relative size of our navy and the national need for a navy?" "What are the facts about real wages in the United States?" A great part of editorial argument, therefore, consists in trying to establish, or in trying to refute, certain facts, the truth of which will determine the adoption of a policy or the adherence to a principle.

One method that editorial writers employ is to disprove the facts by citing contrary facts, as in the following editorial entitled, "The Free Coinage of Falsehood," from the New York *World,* in 1896:

> The Denver *Republican* echoes a common assertion of all the free-silver advocates when it says:
> "The reopening of our mints to the free coinage of both metals at the ratio of 16 to 1 would do a great deal to right the wrong of demonetization. It would put an end to the existing money famine which is forcing lower prices every day."
> Now, first, there is no "existing money famine." We have in use the enormous sum of $2,197,000,000 of gold, silver and paper money. Our actual per capita circulation is $24.34, against Great Britain's $18.42, Germany's $18.54, and Austria-Hungary's $9.75. To talk of an "existing money famine" in this country is simply to talk nonsense and falsehood.
> Secondly, neither a money famine nor anything else "is forcing lower prices every day." About a year ago cotton was at 5 cents. It is now worth 8⅛. Wheat, which was 50 cents a bushel, is now 70; silver bullion, which sank a while ago to 55 cents, is now worth 68

> and more. These are samples. It is simply
> not true that anything "is forcing lower prices
> every day."

Facts do not always admit of so simple a statement as the foregoing editorial provides. Often it is necessary to comment on the facts one by one as they are listed in the argument. The following editorial from the Milwaukee *Journal,* entitled "Farmers Are People," illustrates how sarcastic comment may emphasize the truth that the facts are supposed to contain. This editorial cites numerous facts in reply to a single assertion:

> It has been many years since Calvin Coolidge left the farm and began his life of holding public office. But even his natural unfamiliarity with present day farming does not explain his statement in his message to Congress that "Everything the farmer uses in farming is already on the free list." Mr. Coolidge's purpose was to oppose a revision of the tariff for the benefit of agriculture. As a thoroughgoing New Englander that was to be expected. But it was hardly to be expected that his opposition should go the length of saying that the tariff costs the farmer nothing.
>
> Farmers live in houses, and window glass isn't on the free list. Farms have barns and stables and sheds, and corrugated sheet iron for barn roofs is tariff taxed. A farmer who cares anything about his home and his other buildings and equipment uses paint; and paints are taxed 25 per cent.
>
> Many farmers still have horses. Horseshoes and horseshoe nails are tariff burdened. Fences are a part of the equipment of farming; steel wire fencing is taxed. And iron pipes, which farmers must use in piping water; and wire for baling hay, jute bags, barrels and packing boxes.
>
> When the weeds start up, the farmer takes down his scythe, and his scythe isn't on the free list. Nor are his pruning shears, or sickles. If he must replace a board on his pig pen, the nail he drives and the hammer

he drives it with, and the cheap cotton glove he wears on his hand are on the tariff list. The woollen blanket he throws over his horse these cold days, or over the flivver, carries a tariff.

On the free list we do find plows, harrows, harvesters, reapers, drills, and planters, mowers, horserakes, cultivators, threshing machines and such agricultural implements. But this doesn't mean anything. We make the world's farm implements. There is no foreign competition. Nevertheless, the steels, the chief materials used in the manufacture of these articles, are on the tariff list.

Harness, too, is on the free list, but on all saddlery and harness hardware, buckles, rings, snaps, bits and swivels there is a tax of 35 per cent of their cost. Fertilizers, too, are "free"—except the ingredients which go into making most of them.

This only begins to tell the story of what the tariff does to the farmer. For the list is confined to some of the things the farmer may be said, in the President's words, to use "in farming." We have not taken up the crockery, chinaware, jars, kitchen and table utensils, linoleum, and the hundred other things that go into the farm home, nor the hosiery, knit goods and other wearing apparel which, after all, are as necessary to operating a farm as shovels and spades. For farmers live like other people, and they pay the tariff on everything.

Surely the President cannot be so uninformed.

Sometimes the facts themselves are not directly refuted, but the authority who asserted them is attacked. The refutation consists in showing that the authority is not an expert or that he does not sincerely believe his assertions.

Another effective method of attacking an authority for a statement, when the point in dispute cannot be determined empirically, is to cite an authority for a contrary statement who possesses more prestige. The following editorial from the Balti-

more *Evening Sun,* entitled "Different Standards," is an
example:

> The Nebraska State Conference of the
> Methodist Episcopal Church, meeting yester-
> day in Kearney, adopted a resolution which
> said in part that
> "the political record [of Al Smith] is of such
> a character that his election to this office
> would be a moral and political calamity."
> This is the first time so far as we can
> learn that the Nebraska State Conference of
> the Methodist Episcopal Church has shown
> any concern over the political welfare of the
> country.
> Our records do not show that the confer-
> ence ever saw any moral and political calamity
> in the wholesale robbery of wounded veterans
> during the Harding administration.
> If they were conscious of any moral or
> political calamity in the descent of the Ohio
> gang upon Washington, they did not express
> their feelings in any public resolution. If
> they felt that the friendship of the late Presi-
> dent Harding with Jess Smith and Harry
> Daugherty was a moral and political calamity,
> they did not say so.
> When the Falls, Dohenys, Sinclairs and the
> rest worked out their scheme for despoiling
> the public domain, the Nebraska State Con-
> ference of the Methodist Episcopal Church
> was as silent as Mr. Herbert Hoover.
> But the Democratic party, in convention at
> Houston, nominated by an overwhelming ma-
> jority a man of whom Charles Evans Hughes
> recently said:
> "He is one who represents to us the ex-
> pert in government . . . and a master of the
> science of politics. . . . In the highways and
> byways of the law, particularly of the statu-
> tory law . . . while we go haltingly and with
> much study, he threads his path with perfect
> familiarity, for to him the administration of
> government is not a study but a life. If we
> had the customs of other countries, he would
> long ago have been elevated to the peerage.

. . . But we do better than that. He long since became a member of high distinction of the fine aristocracy of public service. We have watched him, some of us carefully, all with fascination. The title that he holds is the proudest that any American can hold, because it is a title to the esteem and affection of his fellow-citizens."

And this is the man whose election, in the opinion of the Nebraska State Conference of the Methodist Episcopal Church, would be a moral and political calamity.

The only comment which we care to make on this strange situation is that the political standards of the Nebraska State Conference of the Methodist Episcopal Church and those of Charles Evans Hughes are not quite the same.

2. **Attacking the Opponent's Reasoning.**—An opponent's reasoning may be unsound either because the substance of his argument is unsound or because the form of his argument is unsound. Usually it is the substance of an argument that is attacked; the editorials quoted above which refuted argument by citing a contrary set of facts illustrate how the substance of an opponent's argument is refuted. When we speak of attacking the form of an opponent's argument, we usually mean one of the forms, such as argument from analogy, *a priori* causal argument, etc. We also attack the form of an opponent's argument when we point out a fallacy in his argument, that is, when we show that the argument is invalid because it violates some rule of the syllogism such as an unwarranted assumption or a substitution in the meaning of a term.

3. **Rhetorical Devices.**—There are four rhetorical devices for refuting argument which include most of the methods discussed in previous sections. These are (*a*) "turning the tables"; (*b*) *reductio ad absurdum;* (*c*) dilemma; and (*d*) the method of residues.

(*a*) *"Turning the Tables."*—Sometimes it is possible to take an opponent's argument and use it to prove your own contention. The writer who argues a question without making a thorough analysis of his subject lays himself open to such a method of refutation. The following example is an editorial entitled "Sauce for the Goose," from the Chicago *Tribune:*

> Sir William Joynson-Hicks, Home Secretary in the present British Ministry, suggests, now that Mr. Kellogg has put through his treaty outlawing war, it is unseemly and inconsistent for us to add to our navy. Prime Minister Baldwin told Parliament he is in general accord with Sir William's line of thought.
>
> If so, Mr. Baldwin's government, having signed the outlaw treaty, will see that no additions to the British navy are made, and we suggest that he ought at once take up with Washington negotiations for turning over the British Islands of Bermuda and the Caribbean.
>
> These are nothing but bridgeheads or bases for attack upon us, and following the British Home Secretary's cogent reasoning we can see no reason for either Great Britain or France, also a signatory to the outlaw treaty, to retain these military threats upon our shores.

A variation of the method of "turning the tables" is called *tu quoque* ("you, too"). By this method, one does not try to answer charges made by one's opponent, but presents a countercharge; it is mere recrimination. Although not always a fair argument, it is sometimes an effective way to answer an unfair accusation. It seldom appears in editorials, but is a frequent type of appeal in politics; as, for example, in the Illinois senatorial primary of 1926, when Senator McKinley was charged by his opponent, Frank L. Smith, with casting a vote in the Senate for America's adherence to the World Court, he replied that Mr. Smith himself had voted for a declaration in the party platform urging adherence of the United States to the World Court.

The following quotations illustrate the use of *tu quoque* argument:

(1)

Lord Ponsonby, who replied for the Government, said his purpose was not to defend the Soviet system of labor conditions but to defend the British Government against such serious charges as had been made by the Lords. Replying to the Bishop's accusation of British indifference to the suffering in Russia, the Labor party's spokesman recalled the report to the Russian Duma in 1908 which gave authentic details of cruelty under the Czarist régime and asked the Bishop of Durham and Lord Newton if they had denounced the British Government then in power for being silent in the matter.

(2)

The Madison *Journal* wants to know where to find that 5-cent glass of beer that Senator Blaine promised the people. Answer:
On the same cake of ice where reposes the 5-cent glass of beer promised by former Senator Lenroot.

(*b*) *Reductio ad absurdum.*—This rhetorical device consists in accepting the opponent's proposition and then, by carrying it out to its logical conclusion, reducing it to absurdity. It is an "if . . . then" type of argument which is effective if the logic employed in reducing the opponent's proposition to absurdity is sound. That part of the argument which consists in proving the opponent's proposition an absurdity is usually equivalent to argument from analogy. The following editorial from the Grand Rapids (Mich.) *Press,* entitled "Clinical Advertising," is an example of *reductio ad absurdum:*

The Illinois Medical society has upheld on appeal the expulsion of Dr. Louis E. Schmidt by the Chicago Medical society. He was convicted of being what might be called unethical in the second degree. He had not advertised himself. But he had performed paid service for a free clinic which had advertised. Therefore he had violated the code of ethics of the medical profession; or so, at any rate, the Illinois Medical society believed. Dr. Schmidt is appealing to the American Medical association.

The medical societies, like bar associations or other professional groups of the kind, have a right to establish their own group of ethics, make their own interpretations and expel whomsoever they please. But this particular decision will be a puzzling one for many laymen.

How far would it logically carry? If an accident insurance company advertised, and maintained on fee a special group of doctors, to whom its policy-holders would be sent, would that violate medical ethics on the part of the doctors retained, even though their own names were never advertised?

It happens that the work Dr. Schmidt performed in Chicago was supported by a high-minded and responsible group of philanthropists who objected to quack treatment of social diseases and to the spread of these diseases through society because of indisposition or inability of victims to pay the cost of reliable treatment. Suppose a state or city similarly determined to offer free treatment as was the case in Michigan during the war and is still the case with respect to juvenile cases handled at the institution in Kalamazoo at state expense. Suppose the state or city favored and supported such treatment as a matter of general protection to public health, and advertised the service. Would a physician retained by state or city on fee be a violator of medical ethics?

Since, by *reductio ad absurdum,* one reduces an opponent's argument to absurdity by argument from analogy, the logic is reënforced when the analogies chosen to illustrate the absurdity are themselves ridiculous. The editorial just quoted cited examples of what might actually happen in the practice of medicine, but the ordinary *reductio ad absurdum* argument supposes conditions and facts that are too absurd to happen or to exist logically. The following editorial is an example in which absurd comparisons are made:

> The assurance of President Hoover that he will not countenance the plan to propagandize the nation's public schools on behalf of prohibition will prove gratifying to both friends and opponents of the eighteenth amendment. Leaving the merits or demerits of prohibition entirely out of the picture, and waiving all discussions as to the manner and necessity of its enforcement, it should be perfectly obvious to any unbiased individual that the undertaking of any such function by the Federal Government would be highly improper, and that the fruits of any such policy of Government intrusion upon the public schools could only be those of bitterness, controversy and dissension.
>
> Offhand we can think of no government official or group of government officials enjoying the public's confidence to such an extent that they could prepare universally acceptable school propaganda on any subject, let alone the moot subject of prohibition. Nor can we think, offhand, of any good reason why one Federal statute or constitutional amendment should be propagandized in the public schools to the exclusion of a great many other Federal statutes and constitutional amendments. Let us assume for a moment, that the Federal Government should suddenly inaugurate a thorough-going policy of school propaganda. The Navy Department would conceivably seize upon the cruiser program, which a great many sincere and conscientious taxpayers heartily deplore, as an excuse for persuading the young idea that the nation could spend the sum of $274,000,000 in no better way. And the Department of the Interior would conceivably seize upon the Hoover-Wilbur oil conservation policy, which offends a great many sincere and conscientious taxpayers, as an excuse for suggesting to juvenile America the plan's complete impeccability.

> Such examples may seem exaggerated but
> they point, nevertheless, to the fundamental
> folly of the Federal Government assuming the
> rôle of school propagandist.

(c) *Dilemma.*—The method of dilemma consists in dividing an opponent's proposition into two alternatives, and then destroying them both. The two alternatives are called "horns" of the dilemma. It is as if one says, "If your proposition is true, then there are two horns: either horn *A* is true, or horn *B* is true; neither is true, so your proposition is not true." This method may be distinguished by its "either . . . or" form. The following editorial from the Chicago *Tribune* of June 6, 1892, entitled "Thomas Lied," is an example of the method of dilemma:

> "Washington, May 27 (By The Associated Press)—The silver convention met again this morning. An address was made by P. K. Thomas of Pennsylvania, who said that ten years ago his farm was worth $10,000. By the labor of himself and family he had been able to save $500 a year since. But his farm had continually depreciated in value and now was worth only $5,000. This shrinkage, he said, was due entirely to a pernicious financial system, operated in the interests of money-lenders, corporations, and monopolies."
>
> This rot was uttered in the hearing of the reporters for the purpose of having it published throughout the country. But see what a falsehood it becomes when it is analyzed and its assertions tested.
>
> Ten years ago was 1882. If his farm has shrunk in value one-half since then, its cause must be [either] that he has impoverished his land by overcropping, undermanuring, and bad farming, or that prices of farm products in Pennslyvania have declined one-half since 1882, and this tremendous fall in agricultural prices has knocked down the selling value of his farm products one-half.
>
> Now it is not true that farm products in Pennsylvania have fallen one-half since that year; and it is not true that they have de-

clined one-quarter. We greatly doubt if farm products in that State brought any higher prices in May, 1882, than in May, 1892.

Why, then, has his farm declined in value one-half in the last ten years? The answer is that it has not, unless he has botched it by bad farming, or put an inflated price upon it in 1882. He himself declares that the shrinkage was due to a pernicious financial system operated in the interest of money-lenders, which is silly bosh; but on his own confession he is making a clear ten per cent a year on his $5,000 of capital invested in his farm in addition to his family living and spending money for himself to visit silver conventions to make harangues in favor of 67-cent dollars.

In this editorial the Pennsylvania farmer asserted that his farm had shrunk in value one-half in ten years and that the cause was the single-standard currency system. The editor attacks this argument by dilemma. The two "horns" are: *either* his farm has been impoverished in productivity because of bad management *or* because the prices of farm products have fallen. The editor then destroys both "horns": he shows, on the one hand, that the farm has not deteriorated, because the farmer has been able to make 10 per cent on his investment plus his and his family's living; and, on the other hand, that the prices of farm products in Pennsylvania have not fallen to any great extent. Obviously, then, the value of his farm has not shrunk one-half in ten years. Thomas's argument is destroyed.

Since it is not always easy to divide an opponent's argument into two alternatives and then to disprove both of them, one must guard against presenting a dilemma that is not conclusive. Refutation by dilemma may be unsuccessful for two reasons: (*a*) it may not be possible to divide an opponent's argument into only two possibilities; and (*b*) it may not be possible, after a division has been made, to disprove both of the possibilities. Ordinarily, however, the failure to disprove one of the "horns" is the result of one's failure to exhaust all the possible alternatives.

In trying to divide an opponent's argument into two alternatives, one must be sure there is not a third alternative. The following editorial furnishes an example of how certain fanatical prohibitionists were unsuccessful in dividing their opponents' argument into only two mutually exclusive alternatives. The editorial is a refutation of a refutation.

> The fanatical prohibitionists only reveal their hypocrisy when they assert that the proposal for modification of the Volstead law is an appeal to a man's stomach, not his head —in other words, that all the persons who favor modification are of two classes, the so-called whiskey interests and the thirsty citizens.
>
> There is no logic in such argument. These fanatics pretend that there are only two horns to the dilemma, whereas there are several. Even admitting for the sake of argument that there does still exist what the fanatics call a "whiskey trust," it is not true that the man who favors modification of the prohibition law necessarily wants to be permitted to drink liquors. There are millions of Americans who desire to see the law modified because they realize that it cannot be enforced and is therefore breaking down our respect for law generally.

The argument of the fanatical prohibitionists represents what is called in logic the fallacy of *imperfect disjunction.* A proposition which presents an alternative, as, for example, "All voters are either Democrats or Republicans," is called a "disjunctive" proposition, as distinguished from a "hypothetical" or a "categorical" proposition.[2]

An illustration of imperfect disjunction is the following editorial from *Harvey's Weekly* of August 9, 1919, in opposition to the adherence of the United States to the Covenant of the League of Nations without reservations concerning Article X.

---

[2] A hypothetical proposition is one which contains both a condition and a consequent, as in, "If he passed the examination, he will be eligible"; a categorical proposition is one which is all inclusive, as in, "All men are mortal."

It restricts the possibilities regarding the interpretation of Article X to two.

If Article X of the League Covenant means what Mr. Wilson says it means, then it means nothing. If it means nothing, then its proper destination is the wastebasket. It should be stricken out *in toto* as so much sheer surplusage.

The first sentence of the Article provides that "the members of the League undertake to respect the territory and existing political independence of all members of the League." The second sentence provides that the League Council shall advise upon the means by which the obligation involved in the first sentence shall be fulfilled.

Mr. Wilson's interpretation of this second sentence, as presented in his message transmitting the Franco-American alliance treaty, is that after the League Council's advice has been duly given, the League members will do precisely as they please about following it. In the first sentence the members of the League solemnly agree to respect and protect each other as against external aggression. In the second sentence—according to Mr. Wilson's interpretation—a League member will act upon the League Council's advice in a given aggression case "only if its own judgment justifies such action." In other words, the second sentence of the Article completely cancels the first sentence, leaving zero as the remaining total.

Mr. Hughes said of Article X that it was an "illusory engagement." Mr. Wilson goes Mr. Hughes one better. He says, in substance, that it is no engagement at all, illusory or otherwise. The League Council may advise until it is black in the face, and the League members may go serenely on their respective ways without giving the slightest heed to this advice. And both League members and the League Council will equally have done their full duty under Article X.

> If Article X be interpreted to mean any-
> thing, that meaning necessarily is that we
> engage to send our armed forces wherever
> and whenever a super-government of for-
> eigners sitting in Switzerland orders us to
> send them. If it be interpreted as Mr. Wil-
> son interprets it, the foreign super-govern-
> ment's powers extend only to the giving of
> advice which we agree to heed or ignore as
> our judgment dictates. One interpretation is
> an insult to our self-respect as a nation. The
> other reduces the whole Article X to a
> vacuum.
>   The way to treat Article X is to strike
> it out.[3]

The proposition in dispute in the foregoing editorial is
whether or not the United States should join the League of
Nations without subscribing its dissent to Article X of the
Covenant. The writer of the editorial—probably Colonel
George Harvey, afterward Ambassador to the Court of St.
James—asserted that Article X could be interpreted in one
of two different ways: either it meant that the United States
was obligated to send soldiers across the seas at the behest
of the League Council in Geneva, or it meant nothing at all.
He argues that neither interpretation ought to be acceptable
to the United States. His refutation of President Wilson's
proposition that the United States should join the League of
Nations without making reservations regarding Article X depends, first, upon his success in proving that there were only
two interpretations, and, second, that neither of these two interpretations ought to be acceptable to the United States—in
other words, that the United States should join the League only
on condition that a special interpretation be placed on Article X
so far as the obligations of the United States were concerned.
Obviously, he did not prove that the United States would be
obligated to send troops across the seas on the orders of the
Council; he merely made this assertion. Nor was he successful
in proving that Article X was a meaningless phrase. The fault
of his argument was in his attempt to restrict the interpretation

---

[3] Quoted from Allan Nevins, *American Press Opinion*, pp. 556-557.

to two possibilities. There is a third interpretation which more nearly comprehends the truth: it is that Article XVI, when considered in connection with Article X, provides for sanctions other than military sanctions—economic sanctions (trade and financial boycott and blockade of the ports of an aggressor nation) and the sanctions of public opinion. Thus far—up to 1931—the Council has not had to invoke economic sanctions, but it has prevented war on at least one occasion by invoking the sanction of public opinion and by exerting diplomatic pressure. The Council is a body which meets three times a year and can be assembled on instant notice to mediate or to use its good offices in the prevention of war. Prior to the founding of the League of Nations, quarrels between nations merely smoldered until eventually a spark set them off. The Council probably could not now prevent a general war, but efforts are being made to "put more teeth" into Article X through the setting up of certain permanent agencies such as an arrangement for rendering financial assistance to a nation waging a defensive war while the members of the League were conducting a financial boycott of the aggressor nation.[4]

Strictly, the method of dilemma requires that one reduce an opponent's proposition to two alternatives. Sometimes, however, an opponent's proposition cannot be reduced to two possi-

---

[4] At the Fourth Assembly, in 1923, the following interpretation of Article X was proposed by a committee of jurists, and received twenty-nine affirmative votes and one negative vote (Persia's), with thirteen states abstaining:

"It is in conformity with the spirit of Article X that, in the event of the Council considering it to be its duty to recommend the application of military measures in consequence of an aggression or danger or threat of aggression, *the Council shall be bound to take account, more particularly of the geographic situation and of the special conditions of each State.*

"It is for the constitutional authorities of each Member to decide, in reference to the obligation of preserving the independence and the integrity of the territory of Members, in what degree the Member is bound to assure the execution of this obligation by employment of its military forces." Etc.

That the words *existing independence* mean "existing" at the moment of a dispute, and not "existing" at the time of the signing of the Treaty of Versailles; that Article X simply means that no annexations should result from warlike action—a principle that must be accepted before a real international community can be established—is now well understood. See R. L. Buell, *International Relations* (1st ed.), p. 557.

bilities. Then one must list all of the possibilities and go to the
length of disproving all of them. This, strictly, is not dilemma,
but a refutation of an argument by example (generalization).
It is an effective method of refutation, provided that one
contradicts all of the examples cited by his opponent. The following example of such a method of refutation is from an article
by Walter Lippmann, entitled "The Greatness of Mr. Mellon."

It is often a puzzle to know just how a popular idea gets into
circulation. There is, for example, the idea that Andrew W.
Mellon is a very great Secretary of the Treasury. Where did that
idea come from? Not, I venture to suggest, from any close
popular appreciation of the conduct of the Treasury, for the work
of the Treasury is for the most part too technical to be appreciated by more than a few members of Congress and a small circle
of financial experts. The man in the smoking car who says
Mr. Mellon is the greatest Secretary since Alexander Hamilton
would find it hard to describe either the greatness of Alexander
Hamilton or the greatness of Andrew W. Mellon. The idea of
greatness has been put into such extensive circulation, however,
that it has now become one of the sacred cows of American public
thinking. . . .
    I am told that he has dealt skilfully with the domestic floating
debt of the United States and has taken good advantage of the
money market. That is excellent, but any first-rate banker could
have done it. Mr. Mellon advocated a reduction of taxes. That
is popular and most welcome to those of us who pay an income
tax. But nobody, I suppose, would argue that it is greatness in a
Secretary of the Treasury to reduce taxes when there is a surplus
of money in the bank. Mr. Mellon's plan was worked out by his
two Democratic predecessors at the Treasury. Mr. Mellon has
also had some odd jobs like Prohibition Enforcement. If he had
handled that job well it would not make him a great Secretary of the
Treasury, although it would make him a very great man. As a
matter of fact Prohibition Enforcement under Mr. Mellon's titular
leadership has been just what everybody knows it is: a dismal
failure surrounded by foolish promises that nobody any longer
believes.
    The test of Mr. Mellon's greatness as a Secretary of the Treas-
ury must certainly lie in his policy on the international debts.
[From here Mr. Lippmann goes on to show that the foreign debt
policy has been unwise.] [5]

[5] In *Men of Destiny*, Chap. XIV, *passim.* Reprinted by permission of
The Macmillan Company, publishers.

(*d*) *Method of Residues.*—This is not really a method of refutation, but a method of constructive argument. It is discussed under the subject of refutation, however, because it is destructive in method though constructive in purpose. It consists in dividing a question into two or more parts and then destroying all of the parts except one. The part left standing constitutes the constructive part of the argument. It is for the purpose of proving this part that the other parts are disproved. The following editorial, although not entirely sound, illustrates the method of residues:

There are but four attitudes we can adopt with regard to the prohibition question. We can assume that the Volstead Law represents perfection in the method of curbing drunkenness and crime and reducing the ill physical and social effects of intemperance; we can repeal the Eighteenth Amendment to our Constitution and then proceed with a modified experiment in which certain states would be allowed to adopt their own liquor laws; we can, as individuals, adopt a policy of nullification; or we can attempt to modify some of the stringent provisions of the Volstead law and some of the harsh methods of enforcement without changing the Constitution. Whatever action is taken with regard to the prohibition question must be along one of these lines—there are no other courses open to us.

But some of these courses cannot be followed. We cannot assume that the Volstead law represents a satisfactory settlement of the question. It is not possible to eliminate the Eighteenth Amendment from the Constitution; thirteen recalcitrant states would prevent it. Nor can individuals adopt a policy of nullification without our scheme of self-government ending in failure. The only course open to us is to modify some of the stringent provisions of the Volstead Act, and then to wait patiently for a time before proceeding to further changes in the "noble experiment."

In arguing by this method it is not only important that one refute all the parts except one, but *it is necessary that the part left standing be reënforced with strong positive proof.*[6]

Nor should one always be so eager to disprove a contrary point that he puts too much emphasis on it as compared with the emphasis he places on his constructive proof. He may antagonize a large group who already believe in the contrary point before he has reached the place at which he can prove his own point. Thus, if one desired to prove that all forms of life have descended from a common ancestry, he could—if he desired—show, first, that there can be only two explanations of the existence of life, and that one of these—special creation —is untrue. But if one should devote most of his argument to proving that the account of special creation in Genesis is untrue, many persons who believe in a literal interpretation of the Bible would not remain open-minded long enough to enable one to enforce his own argument for the evolutionary explanation.

Refutation in a Series of Editorials.—The following editorial from the New York *World* of May 1, 1896, is for the most part destructive. It not only urges the Democratic party convention to adopt a single-standard currency plank, but warns it not to adopt a plank advocating the free coinage of silver.

> The Democratic party marched to victory in 1892 over this plank [no free coinage of silver or gold].
> Is it not good sense to "trust the bridge that has carried us safely over" in politics as in other things?
> This platform was Democratic in 1892. What has happened to make it less so now? Has the price of silver advanced, so that

---

[6] For example, it is this fault in Dr. Sigmund Freud's *Totem and Taboo* that makes his thesis unconvincing. His thesis is that the "beginnings of religion, ethics, society, and art meet in the Œdipus complex"—that is to say, he traces social origins to the alleged incestuous relation of parent and child. In order to make his own argument strong, he first refutes more than a score of hypotheses which had previously been advanced to explain the origin of totemism and exogamy (that is, the tribal taboo against marriage outside the clan), and thus leaves the way clear to enforce the truth of his own explanation, namely, the recurrence of totemism which is observable in children.

free coinage would be less dangerous now than it was then? No. The average price of silver in 1892 was 87 cents an ounce. It is now 68.

Has the supply of silver dollars been cut down since 1892? No. The Treasury has coined $15,000,000 since the present administration came into power.

Has the cause of free silver so strengthened in the country that it is more politic to indorse it now than it was four years ago? No. It has just been defeated in the House by a majority of 125—the largest ever recorded against it.

Have the States in the East and Northwest that helped to elect President Cleveland and a majority of Congress in 1892, and upon which the party must depend for success now, shown any signs of receding from their opposition to free coinage? Emphatically, no. Their Democratic conventions are stronger and more explicit than ever in favoring the highest standard, the best money, and an honest discharge of all national obligations—one of which is the continuance of bimetallism by maintaining the parity of the money metals and the equality and exchangeability of all our dollars.

These being facts beyond dispute, why urge a departure from the safe path? Why desert the bridge that has carried the party safely to victory?

Although this editorial could have been more convincing if positive argument had been adduced in favor of a single-standard currency plank, one must remember that newspapers frequently publish editorials in series. In advocating important propositions, newspapers frequently employ the method of residues, using some of the editorials in a series for the purpose of refuting the untrue possibilities and some for proving positively that the remaining point is true. In this particular case that was the method employed by the *World*.

The Value of Refutation.—On the whole, there is too little refutation in editorial pages today. Although editorial writers realize that their readers do not desire them to be incessant grumblers, they ought, nevertheless, to take more opportunity to puncture the unsound arguments advanced by demagogues and other selfish crowd-leaders. Many dangerous and ridiculous arguments that gain wide acceptance can be so easily demolished that one cannot help wondering why their refutation is so often left to the weekly and monthly critical journals.

CHAPTER XIII

READERS' ATTITUDES

It has long been recognized by publicists that the response which the human mind makes to suggestion is not always an intellectual response. It is often emotional. This fact determines in great measure the technique that is employed by advertisers, politicians, clergymen, and others who desire to enforce an idea or a program of action upon the mass of men and women. It is a significant factor in the formulation of editorial policy and sometimes in the presentation of editorial thought.

One's mind is the product of all his experiences, intellectual and emotional. Any new experience, therefore—any suggestion—that is presented to the mind is interpreted by the mind in terms of what has previously been deposited there. These deposits in the mind are called by psychologists the "apperceptive mass."

They are not, however, wholly first-hand and concrete experiences. In some measure they are the experiences gained from reading and from conversation with one's associates in the home, in the school, and at the factory, office, club, or street corner. In some measure, also, they are the ideas that the race and the group have long treasured and have bequeathed to the individual member; every mind, that is to say, has a social heritage of ideas as to what is right and wrong, what is true and false. With respect to many ideas, the apperceptive mass of all the individuals in the race or in the group is identical. It is this consensus of mind that makes possible the group.[1]

---

[1] "Culture," Professor C. A. Ellwood says, "is nothing more than a series of mental patterns passed along from individual to individual in a group by means of the process of intercommunication. So far as these patterns are passed along as ideas, standards, or values, we call them 'tradition.' So far as they are passed along as objective action, we

Attitudes and Opinions.—When the publicist desires to elicit a particular response to his suggestion, he tries to formulate the suggestion with reference to the apperceptive mass of the individual or group to which he is appealing. That is to say, he tries to take into account the *attitudes* and the *opinions* of the individuals, for these are the units in which the apperceptive mass is crystallized.

An attitude is the mobilization of the individual's will with reference to a situation. It is a tendency to response, moreover, which is habitual. Having been built up by suggestion, it habitually responds to the suggestions that built it up. Thus, the publicist who understands the basic attitudes of individuals in the mass and who knows how to release these attitudes by appropriate suggestions has the power to control large masses of people.[2]

An opinion, in the strict sense, is an intellectual judgment; but men's opinions, as all publicists know, are often only their attitudes which have been conditioned in small degree by their intellects. The philosophers of the "rational" eighteenth century made opinion the corner stone of their theory of democracy, but recent investigation has revealed its artificiality.[3] For an individual's opinion is frequently only a justification of his attitude; that is to say, a rationalization.[4]

Wishes, Desires, and Interests.—How is the publicist to know what are the attitudes and opinions of the individuals to whom he wishes to appeal? How can he calculate in advance

---

call them 'custom.' The best sociological usage adheres to the distinction made by Professor Ross between these terms; namely, that tradition is a way of *thinking* and *feeling* handed down from the past, while custom is a way of *action* handed down from the past. . . . Indeed, the tradition and custom of a group together make its 'culture'."—*Recent Developments in the Social Sciences* (E. C. Hayes, ed.), pp. 34-35.

[2] For an expanded discussion of attitudes with reference to social response, see Park and Burgess, *An Introduction to the Science of Sociology*, p. 438, and F. H. Allport, *Social Psychology*, pp. 244-247. Both "radical" and "conservative" attitudes have a basis in the "subconscious"; for an explanation of the displacement of "subconscious" drives on political motives, see Harold D. Lasswell, *Psychopathology and Politics.*

[3] A sentiment, as distinguished from an opinion, is a feeling about some object, usually a person or a place.

[4] See J. H. Robinson, *The Mind in the Making*, pp. 40-48.

whether or not a specific appeal will release the desired response from certain groups of individuals? How does the politician, for example, know how people generally, or certain groups of people, "feel" about a specific issue? How does he divine the "currents of opinion" that determine the direction of events? Is he gifted with a peculiar sixth sense of understanding that is nearly clairvoyant?

There are publicists who seem to sense popular "feeling." Their understanding of so-called public opinion, however, is, at bottom, merely an apprehension of the fundamental desires and interests of the individual or of the group. If the publicist knows what these desires and interests are, he can probably calculate whether a specific suggestion will result in a positive or a negative attitude as regards the suggestion. An attitude, after all, is only a state of mind that has reference to a definite situation. The state of mind is either positive or negative; the attitude is either one of approach or one of withdrawal as regards the specific suggestion. Fear, for example, is not an "instinct"; it is simply the individual's attitude of withdrawal from a specific suggestion—a negative attitude. Deeper than fear in the individual's psychological make-up are his primary desires or interests that are affected by the suggestion. The individual considers the situation with reference to his primary desires or interests, and habitually (i.e., "instinctively") adopts an attitude of approach or withdrawal.

What are these primary desires or interests?

"*Interests.*"—As is to be expected, there is considerable disagreement as to what are the primary desires of the individual, but sociological thinking has now got so far away from the metaphysical approach to the problem that several classifications are regarded as satisfactory for purposes of analysis, even though they are different classifications.

The late Professor Small, for example, asserted that the individual has six "interests" that determine his behavior. An "interest" he defined as a "plain demand for something regardless of everything else." [5] The "interests" are these: (*a*) *Health,* which is inclusive of what we are accustomed to think

---
[5] A. W. Small, *General Sociology,* p. 201.

of as self-preservation. (b) *Wealth,* or the desire for lordship over things. (c) *Sociability,* which is inclusive of the individual's craving for reciprocal personal valuation. (d) *Knowledge,* which includes both the knowledge that is necessary as a means of attaining the standard of life and the knowledge which provides a "vision of the meaning of life." (e) *Beauty,* that is, the esthetic desire in the individual. (f) *Rightness,* which includes that impulse in man—both the naïve and the reflective man—to do what he "ought" to do; to be "right with God," as the evangelical preachers urge; to be adjusted to that larger and superior self that is imagined or posited by the individual.[6]

"Wishes."—A second classification is Professor Thomas's [7] four "wishes." They are as follows: (a) *The desire for new experience.* This desire is expressed in the individual's tendency to break away from the conventional standards of the group. (b) *The desire for security.* This desire is opposed to the desire for new experience, and is expressed in the individual's tendency to seek security within the group. (c) *The desire for recognition.* This wish expresses itself in ways that are too numerous to mention; for the purpose of this discussion, we merely note how it finds expression in the individual's group pride. (d) *The desire for response.* This wish is different from the desire for recognition in that it refers to the individual's wish to be appreciated and loved by a few individuals rather than by the public.

These "wishes" and "interests" appear to comprehend all of the so-called "instincts" of which we hear so much. These "wishes" and "interests" in themselves are neither positive nor negative: they are values (or the objects of values) concerning which the individual has positive or negative attitudes. Fear, hate, sympathy, gregariousness, acquisitiveness, and curiosity, for example, are merely prepotent tendencies which are expressive of attitudes toward or away from a suggestion that seems calculated to frustrate one of the four "wishes" or one of the six "interests."

---

[6] *Ibid.,* Chap. XXXII, *passim.*
[7] Cited by Park and Burgess, *An Introduction to the Science of Sociology,* pp. 489-490.

These Drives Too Elemental.—These "interests" and "wishes" are *primary* drives. As such, they are too elemental to be of great assistance in predicting and controlling human behavior.[8] All individuals are motivated by them, but in nearly every other respect individuals are different and will react differently and erratically to a given stimulus. It is only when we consider how these primary drives are conditioned by intellectual factors that we can really approach an understanding of how to control attitudes. By studying various types and groups of individuals, we can in some measure calculate what are their attitudes. Some light, too, can be thrown on the technique of the propagandist if we examine certain types of negative and positive appeals and certain attitudes that are peculiar to specific groups.[9]

---

[8] They are of much value to the advertiser, who makes an individual appeal to such elemental drives as appetite, vanity, etc. "American life and customs," says the Baltimore *Evening Sun,* "more and more are being guided by fear and the advertising man. It began, the historians report, some years ago when a bright young man rediscovered the perils of halitosis and covered the billboards and the street car posters with lurid pictures of its dire results. 'Always a bridesmaid but never a bride' set other bright young men to thinking, and accordingly four out of five of us have so-and-so; all of us, poor critters, have b.o., etc., etc. Not to keep that schoolgirl complexion is to be relegated to the wall flowers; one is too thin or too fat according to advertising standards—and as a consequence, we are becoming a nation of mild hypochondriacs, all doing our daily dozens, garglings, soapings, and eating our yeasts and vitamins in unison."

[9] In an effort to determine the motives of voters in the 1924 presidential election campaign, Mr. Norman C. Meier, of the University of Iowa, studied the attitudes of 1,088 voters in five middle western states. ("Motives in Voting: A Study in Public Opinion," *American Journal of Sociology,* Vol. XXXI, pp. 199-212.) With the exception of a few replies which he could not classify, the reason given by voters for casting their vote for President were interpreted as expressions of the following springs to action: (*a*) self-interest; (*b*) sympathy; (*c*) fear; (*d*) safety motive. Mr. Meier points out that although the "safety motive" is identical with the fear motive, it is necessary to distinguish between that spring of action which reflects a real fear (say, of a "Red menace") and that which merely reflects a desire to rely on the tried and true ways of living as opposed to more adventurous ways.

The great majority of the voters who preferred Coolidge stated the following reasons: His record of tax reduction (self-interest); he is "safe and sane, while La Follette and Davis are uncertain" (safety motive); he is against our joining the League of Nations (safety motive); the election of Davis or La Follette may mean a business depression—"Coolidge or Chaos" (fear and self-interest).

The great majority of the voters who preferred La Follette seemed to be actuated by rational rather than irrational motives; as, for example,

Negative Appeals.—Propagandists often direct appeals to the individual's desire for security by formulating the suggestion that certain *institutions* are endangered. Prohibitionists, for example, have made effective use of the appeal which suggests that the home is endangered. The following passage from a pamphlet of the South Dakota Anti-Saloon League is an example:

The liquor traffic is in the crisis of a death struggle for supremacy over the American Home. God is silently but surely sifting the American people into two classes—Home Defenders . . . and Saloon Defenders. . . . Protect the Home from the Saloon or the Saloon will destroy the Home.[10]

The Republican party, which championed prohibition, used this danger-to-the-home appeal successfully in the 1928 presidential election campaign, especially with respect to the women's vote. The party propagandists adopted the slogan, "Hoover, Homes, and Happiness," and distributed thimbles bearing the slogan. Agitators against Communism make appeals which warn the American public that Communism endangers not only the institution of the home, but several other institutions as well.

---

those voters who believed there had ceased to be a real difference between the two major parties and, therefore, desired to see a new alignment along realistic lines of conflict. Many replies of La Follette supporters, however, were actuated by the sympathy motive: they saw La Follette as "the true friend of the common people." In instances in which the voter for La Follette was conscious of belonging to the "common people," the motive of "remote self-interest" was combined with the sympathy motive. Mr. Meier's conclusion is that the successful outcome of the 1924 election was based "not on appeals to sound judgments so much as to the arousal of instinctive, emotional, and habitual sets" [i.e., attitudes].

Virtually the same conclusion is drawn by Mr. G. W. Allport, of Dartmouth College, from a study based on the 1928 presidential election campaign, in which the subjects were 375 undergraduates. ("The Composition of Political Attitudes," *American Journal of Sociology,* Vol. XXXV, pp. 220-238.) Mr. Allport concluded that "the political character of the men in certain extreme groups is bound up with many generic traits (i.e., race, religion, family tradition, etc.) in their personalities"; and that "a man's political opinions reflect the characteristic modes of his adjustment to life." The investigator also stated the following conclusions: (*a*) Radicals show "decidedly less" prejudice than conservatives—they consider the more ultimate national issues. (*b*) Radicals, while possessing no more information than do conservatives, have less misinformation. (*c*) The scholarship of radicals is higher than that of conservatives.

[10] Quoted by P. Odegard, *Pressure Politics,* p. 42.

The following quotation is from a speech by a professional "Red-baiter":

> Communism is a method of Bolshevism which eventually intends to destroy all such institutions as the home, inheritance, religion, property rights, government, and morality.[11]

The Supreme Court is an institution that is also frequently said to be endangered by the election of radicals to federal office. Republican propagandists and editors were quite successful in the 1924 presidential election campaign in appealing to voters against Senator La Follette's candidacy because the Wisconsin Senator favored an amendment to the Constitution which would have prevented five-to-four decisions from overturning legislation passed by Congress. Certain racial minorities in the country who are ordinarily inclined to vote for radical candidates were convinced by propaganda that the Supreme Court, as the guardian of their constitutional rights, should be preserved in its present form, and, accordingly, they voted against La Follette.

Certain appeals to the voters' desire for *national security* are frequently successful. Much of the argument against the adherence by the United States to the World Court protocols was a nonrational appeal to the voter's desire for security. The following editorials are examples. The first one relates to the Senatorial primary election in Illinois in 1926, in which one of the candidates was attacked because he had voted for the adherence of the United States.

(1)

> Country-wide indignation exists against McKinley and his colleagues. More than a dozen of these Senators, including McKinley, are running for renomination and reëlection. Defeat a few of them and the new Senate in December will heed the warning. It will

[11] See, also, the speech of Representative Hamilton Fish, Jr., chairman of a Congressional committee to investigate Communist propaganda in the United States, as reported by the New York *Times* of November 30, 1930.

vote us out of the League's Court before the Court gets its hands on cases that affect our vital interests, such as war debts, Japanese immigration, tariffs, and shipping.

(2)

... And by the way, Mr. American Citizen, have you met your new overseas bosses? Do you know the names of the men who, as members of the World Court, are to settle in the future the destinies of the American nation? Now that we have ditched Washington, John Quincy Adams, Monroe, and Jefferson, you should become acquainted with the new directors of American policy and tradition. You probably will never learn to pronounce the names of these members of the World Court, but they are going to have something to say about the future life of America:

Dinoisio Anzilotti
Rafael Altamira y Creves
Bernard Cornelis Johannes Loder
Didrik Galtrup Gjedde Nyholm
Robert Bannatyne Viscount Finlay
Dimitri Negulesco
Hans Max Huber
Charles André Weiss
Yorozu Oda
Machael Yovanvitch
Frederick Valdemar
Nikolai Beichmann
Epitacio da Silva Pessoa
Antonio Sanchez de Bustamente y Sirven
Wang Chung-hui

Agitation for a big navy is frequently formulated in an appeal for the protection of our national wealth and our relatively high standard of living. The following editorial is an example:

For the year 1914 the following estimate of the national wealth of the great nations shows how much ahead the United States is over the others:

United States	$150,000,000,000
Great Britain & Ireland	85,000,000,000
Germany	80,000,000,000
France	50,000,000,000
Russia	40,000,000,000
Italy	20,000,000,000
Spain	5,400,000,000
Netherlands	5,000,000,000

What insurance have we for that $150,-000,000,000 worth of property?

None worth mentioning!

What insurance have the 25,000,000 American homes against the torch of the greedy invader?

The policy has lapsed.

What insurance have our tens of millions of women and children that they won't be the victims of the cruel hordes who, lured to the attack by our riches, bring the horrors of war to our shores?

Very little insurance.

The best insurance is the biggest navy.

If we are attacked, notwithstanding, the biggest navy in the world is our best defense!

The technique of setting off negative attitudes in the public is usually a subtle one, but sometimes the technique consists simply in rearing, out of a pseudo-situation, a Satan. This Satan, the public is told, is a menace to individual and social welfare. Thus, the Kaiser and "Prussianism" were painted as beasts, and alcoholic liquor was termed "Demon Rum." "Fears," says an enlightened editor, "are the foundation of every tyranny in the world. There never was a tyrant, there never was a despot, there never was a demagogue whose power did not rest finally on the irrational and superstitious fear of his followers. We must emancipate this generation from fear. . . . We must cure them with conscious understanding." [12]

This discussion of the technique of setting off attitudes of withdrawal in individuals is not meant to be a complete explanation. An entire volume would probably not suffice to explain the technique thoroughly. The present explanation

---

[12] Walter Lippmann in *Social Forces*, Vol. VI (September, 1927), p. 4.

aims only to suggest a few points which the student may use as a foundation in analyzing nonrational appeals.[13]

Positive Appeals.—Propagandists sometimes formulate an appeal that is calculated to elicit a positive response from the hearer or reader. If the propagandist has correctly estimated the latent attitude of the individuals to whom he is appealing, his suggestion is successful in releasing it. Such appeals usually have one of two different purposes: they either flatter the individual or his group, or they promise a reward.

It is difficult, of course, for a propagandist who is appealing to the public with reference to a public question to flatter the individual. What the propagandist does, therefore, is to flatter the group to which certain individuals belong. The crowd insists on being flattered. It wants to be told that it is morally superior to other crowds. This is especially true of racial, occupational, and religious groups, and the principle extends even to national groups.

Perhaps the most effective appeal that is calculated to make the individual adopt a positive attitude is the suggestion of reward. By holding out a promise of reward, propagandists induce individuals and groups to react in the way desired. Usually the suggestion is in the form of myth rather than reality. For example, the myth of Republican prosperity—the "full dinner-pail"—has been a powerful argument for that party. It failed to succeed, however, in 1916, because the Democratic party not only had the good fortune to be in office during a period of prosperity, but implied in its campaign propaganda a counter-promise, namely, that the administration would keep the United States out of war.[14] The public often reacts to some of these appeals in quite the same way that the naïve worker responds to certain types of advertising of which the following is an example:

SUDDENLY I TURNED THE CORNER

For years and years I was always up against it—either I was out of a job or I was holding some kind of a position which gave

---

[13] The student should read H. D. Lasswell, *Propaganda Technique in the World War,* and Edward Bernays, *Crystallizing Public Opinion.*

[14] Another important factor in the 1916 election, of course, was the continued schism in the Republican party.

me such a meagre salary that I could scarcely make ends meet.
. . . Then one day I saw an article telling about a new book entitled, "THE SCIENCE OF GETTING A JOB, OR THE WHAT, WHERE, AND
HOW OF WINNING THE POSITION YOU WANT." . . . I sent for the
book immediately.   When it came I sat right down and read it.

Orr in Chicago Tribune

WHAT SUGGESTION IS GIVEN TO THE READER HERE?

. . . The next morning I immediately proceeded to do the things
which the book had told me.   It was so easy and so interesting
that I wondered how it was possible that these great secrets had
remained unknown during all these years.   Well, it was just one
week later—the seventh day after I received the book—that I
landed a wonderful job. . . . *You, too, can find this same success!*

Appeals of this kind always imply a *quid pro quo*. Thus, the public was told in 1917 that enactment of prohibition would "speed the end of the war and of all war"; and the readers of the Chicago *Tribune* were told in 1898 that "the healthy gale" of a war with Spain would "stimulate business." In its purest form, however, the reward appeal is illustrated by the following address of Congressman De Armond to his mortgage-ridden constituents in rural Missouri at the time an income tax measure was enacted by Congress (1893):

The passage of the bill will mark the dawn of a brighter day, with more of sunshine, more of the songs of birds, more of that sweetest music, the laughter of children well fed, well clothed, well housed. Can we doubt that in the brighter, happier days to come, good, even-handed, wholesome democracy shall be triumphant? God hasten the era of equality in taxation and in opportunity! And God prosper the Wilson Bill, the first leaf in the glorious book of reform in taxation, the promise of a brightening future for those whose genius and labor create the wealth of the land, and whose courage and patriotism are the only sure bulwark in the defense of the Republic.

Propagandists who organized farmers' coöperatives in some of the Southern states in the early post-war years were adept at telling farmers how the fruit- and nut-growers' coöperatives enabled Californians to "send their children to college."

One should not assume, however, that any appeal that is directed to the economic self-interest of the individual will be successful. A man has other selves than the economic self.[15] The crowd-man at times reacts positively to idealistic and altruistic suggestions, just as he does to suggestions that are calculated to appeal to his self-interest.[16] Indeed, this side of the crowd-man is sometimes so responsive to suggestion that it is easy to exploit it for selfish ends, as witness the ideal of "service" applied to profit-making. It was a rhapsody of words about "preserving the liberties of (Continental) Europe" that enabled the British Government to make an alliance with the "unspeakable Turk"

---

[15] For a criticism of economic determinism from the point of view of individual psychology, see Walter Lippmann, *Public Opinion*, Chap. XII.

[16] See E. D. Martin, *The Behavior of Crowds*, and Gustave Le Bon, *The Crowd*.

in the Crimean War without losing the confidence of English people. Patriotism, although at bottom a desire for security, is inclusive of other fundamental human wishes.[17] Patriotism, however, is a wholesome expression of attitude wherever it has not become confused with artificial values. Once a unifying force in Western countries, patriotism, as it is expressed in "nationalism," is tending to become a disintegrating force. It is sometimes confused with trade opportunities and is frequently exploited by selfish interests who know how to flatter the crowd-ego and how to appeal to national pride.

Appealing to Group Attitudes.—The propagandist who desires to enforce an idea or a program of action on the public must not only understand the attitudes that are common to nearly all individuals: he must know the attitudes that certain individuals have as a consequence of their occupation or profession, their social status, their economic status, their geographical location, their isolation and contacts with others, their religion, their race, etc. He must know, in other words, what are the attitudes of farmers, lawyers, wage-earners, Southerners, Methodists, Catholics, Polish-Americans, etc. Every individual has an "expanded" personality;[18] that is to say, the character of the sum-total of his attitudes is determined not merely by the congenital traits in his individuality, but also by the associations he has in group life and by his industrial function. Propaganda oftentimes fails to accomplish its purpose because the propagandist—a city man, say—makes the wrong appeal to farmers, of whose attitudes he is entirely ignorant. While we do not have sufficient space here to examine the attitudes of numerous types of individuals, the following explanation of the farmer's attitude shows the necessity for the publicist's understanding of types:

Farmers are opposed to many measures fostered by the laboring classes, because their property holdings, their occupational and economic status, as a class, and the essential nature of their lives makes them different. They oppose the laborers on measures

---

[17] See Walter Lippmann, *The Stakes of Diplomacy*, F. Delaisi, *Political Myths and Economic Realities*, and C. J. H. Hayes, *Essays on Nationalism.*

[18] See Hornell N. Hart, *The Science of Social Relations*, Chap. **VIII.**

which tend to abrogate property rights. Since the rural classes are entrepreneurs, they can see few objections to a long working day. Further, they do not understand the nervously debilitating nature of much of urban labor. Farmers have strong family units. As a rule, they accumulate some real property. The cost of living is cheap. For these reasons and others they are able to take care of themselves in old age. As a result they object to pensions for old age, etc. Further, pensions mean higher taxes and farmers pay direct taxes. Other classes, especially the laboring classes in cities, pay primarily indirect taxes, where they pay any. Farmers can see their tax money go out.

The moral idealism of farm political attitudes arises out of the religious and family organization of rural life. It is not only in America that farmers vote "dry." The Swedish "dry" party, as already shown, gets most of its support in rural districts. . . .

The farmer vote on military justice, abolition of the death penalty, and concerning the initiative and referendum, is a result of many factors: greater rigidity of farmer-peasant moral convictions, greater unanimity in the ideas of what is good and what is bad, and other factors discussed in the chapters dealing with the rural family, religion, and criminality. To these the influence of agricultural occupation is to be added.[19]

Since the intelligent publicist knows that a single blanket appeal is not always adequate for his purposes, he formulates several different appeals, each of them directed toward a particular type of individual. He appeals first to one group and then to another, using a different appeal for each group or each type of individual. Taken as a whole, these appeals make up what the publicist calls a "campaign." The following excerpt from an editorial is representative of the appeals made to various groups in behalf of various ideas or objectives of the editors:

> It is to you, the business men of the Northwest, that the *Tribune* is particularly addressing itself today.
>
> You represent, in large measure, the dominant opinion and the informed opinion of the Northwest. You are, naturally, interested

---

[19] P. A. Sorokin and C. C. Zimmerman, *Principles of Rural-Urban Sociology*, pp. 473-474; reprinted by permission of Henry Holt & Co. See also C. C. Zimmerman and C. A. Arnold, "Attitudes of Rural Preachers Regarding Church Union and Science," *Sociology and Social Research*, Vol. XII (November, 1927), pp. 144-150.

in the future of the Northwest. You are,
therefore, interested in agriculture, and in the
pending tariff bill supposed to be conceived
for the purpose of aiding agriculture. Whatever harms agriculture harms you. *Whatever harms the Northwest harms you.* The
pending tariff bill is a matter of extraordinary serious concern to the Northwest. The
Tribune urges you to familiarize yourself
with this bill in order that you may properly
do your duty by the Northwest.

[Then follows a column and a half of explanation of how the tariff bill harms the
farmers of the Northwest.]

The *Tribune* asks you business men of the
Northwest to ponder and reflect upon this
proposed tariff bill. You are accustomed to
thinking in terms of costs. You are better
fitted than any other class to comprehend and
digest the meaning of the changed rates.
Your influence, when exerted, is far-reaching
and bound to make itself felt in Washington. You have the economic well-being of
agriculture at heart, and you are the cus-
todians of the economic future of this part
of the country. The *Tribune* believes that
a plain obligation rests upon you to study the
Hawley bill painstakingly, and to put the
weight of your authority behind the movement to see that justice is done the farmer
and the Northwest. It feels certain that at
this juncture you will not fail, either.

The following editorial is addressed to the city renter to
obtain his alignment against a proposed income tax in Illinois:

No part of a man's income is derived
from the home he owns if he occupies it
himself. Therefore, he may make no deduction from his income tax for the taxes he
pays on his house. This provision works
in favor of the flat owner, however. His
tenants pay the taxes on his property, but
he and not they will get the benefit of the
refund. Of course, the farmer gets off scot-

free. His farmhouse no doubt will be considered as a source of his income as it is an integral part of his farm. Unquestionably his farm itself will be exempted. The full weight of the income tax foreshadowed in this Senate resolution must fall upon the home owners and flat renters of the urban communities of Illinois.

No one can pretend that the city home owner now escapes taxation. He pays, and he pays heavily. There seems to be a popular notion that the wage and salary earners who do not own but rent their houses and flats do succeed in evading their share. Nothing could be farther from the truth. More than 10 per cent of the money which is paid in the form of rent on most Chicago flats is a tax payment. The landlord has to add that much to the rent to meet his tax bill. The rent payer makes his contribution to the cost of government as certainly as any farmer pays his taxes on the land he owns. The city man commonly pays a fourth of his income in rent. If he earns $4,000 a year, he pays $1,000 for his flat, which means that he pays at least $100 in taxes or 2½ per cent on his gross income, but, unlike the farmer, he would get no exemption from income tax on that score. Nor could he look forward to any profit from his appreciation of property values. When city property goes up in value, rent and taxes go up. When farm property goes up in value, taxes may increase but the profit on the investment belongs to the farmer.

This proposal would exact a tax on the home owner's and the rentpayer's earnings in addition to the real estate tax which they now pay. It would force these city dwellers to add to their already disproportionate share in maintaining the State Government and in addition would take the city man's money to pay the cost of local government in rural communities. Cook County's money would be sent downstate to pay the salaries of downstate job holders and to build downstate court-

> houses as it now builds downstate roads.
> These results would obtain whether the state's
> share of the total income tax collection is 10
> per cent or 25 per cent or any other per
> cent. It is impossible to believe that any of
> the Cook county members or, for that matter,
> the members from East St. Louis, Rockford,
> Peoria and the other urban centers in the
> state, can for a moment consider voting favor-
> ably on this resolution.[20]

For some years the Progressive-Republican party in Wisconsin championed the interests of the farmer, the laborer,
and the small business man, and the Conservative-Republican
party was primarily the representative of the interests of manufacturers. In the course of events, however, the small business
man (local merchant, local banker, etc.) came to align himself
with the Conservative-Republicans. In 1930, however, as the
result of the growth of chain stores and chain banks and of
agitation against public utilities, the small business man class
returned in large numbers to the Progressive ranks. The following editorial, from the chief organ of the Progressive party,
addressed to the local merchant class in Wisconsin, is characteristic of the appeals made to these interest groups:

> Yesterday The Associated Press carried a
> story that the Standard Oil Company is plan-
> ning to sell tires at its thousands of gasoline
> stations throughout the country.
> For several weeks the Madison Gas and
> Electric Company and the Wisconsin Power
> and Light Company have been announcing in
> ads that they have taken on the sale of radios
> at their various offices throughout southern
> Wisconsin.
> Here we have further evidence of the con-
> tinuing encroachment of the big monopoly
> interests in the field of retail merchandising.
> Standard Oil (Rockefeller), Madison Gas
> and Electric (Mellon), and the Wisconsin
> Power and Light (Insull) represent the in-

---

[20] This editorial is, in some respects, fallacious. Read in connection
the discussion on pp. 198-200.

terests recently named by ex-Ambassador Gerard as among the 59 powerful personages who are ruling this country.

Slowly but surely these big monopoly interests are taking on the sale of one new line after another with the result that hardware dealers, electrical dealers, tire dealers, household appliance distributors, and furniture men are standing by helplessly while they are losing thousands of dollars in business because of the invasion in their fields of the big monopoly interests.

The Progressive movement in Wisconsin and in the nation has always been the friend of the small business man. From the day when Old Bob La Follette began to fight to get a square deal for the small shippers and the small manufacturers and stopped the rebates which the railroads were giving to the big fellows, the Progressive movement has fought steadily for the interests of the little fellow.

How long is the small business man going to continue to fight the political battles of the big monopoly interests which are slowly putting a halter around the necks of the small business man?

These few examples are probably sufficient to indicate how various classes are appealed to by publicists. Some publicists are very successful in their appeals, even being clever enough to convince wage earners and farmers of their self-interest in such unfamiliar phenomena as sea power. *The success of the publicist consists chiefly in his knowledge of which of several attitudes to appeal to.* The country weekly editor, for example, who uses the appeal of local pride in his buy-at-home propaganda, will not be nearly as successful as the editor who demonstrates how dollars that stay in the community really benefit the community.

The Laws of Conviction.—There is a psychology of conviction which has an emotional as well as an intellectual basis. The ordinary reader adopts an attitude toward a public question which is a compromise of logic with his own wishes. His opinions are weighted with values, with egotistic wishes. He finds "good" reasons for voting the Republican or the Socialist ticket without much regard for the real reasons as to why he should vote this or that ticket. This type of thinking does not always decide; usually it merely inclines. It gives rise to "attitudes" and "beliefs"; it is wishful-thinking.[21] An experiment by F. L. Lund shows that in the human mind belief and desire are nearly identical. After submitting a list of questions to his subjects, Lund found a correlation coefficient of .88 between "desire" and "belief," whereas the correlation coefficient of "belief" and "evidence" was only .42.[22]

There are at least three laws of conviction that will repay our examination.

1. *One does not need to understand an idea, a process, or a proposal in order to believe in it.* An experiment made in connection with advertisements illustrates the truth of this law. In 1921, a safety-razor company, its patent right on the original type of razor having expired, placed on the market a "new triumph of American inventive genius of startling interest to every man with a beard to shave." The advertisements contained diagrams which illustrated the new patents—the "fulcrum shoulder," the "channeled guard," and the "overhanging cap." These devices, the advertisement declared, had been made possible for the first time by "micrometric control of blade position"; a diagram showed how the blade is "biflexed between the overhanging cap and the fulcrum shoulder." These devices provided for an exactness of adjustment of one thousandth of an inch, and a "major flexure" and a "minor flexure" made for "easy gliding action and play of the wrist in shaving." A copy of this advertisement, together with seven questions, was submitted to a group of fifty-seven subjects to determine whether or not they understood it. The results showed that all fifty-seven subjects believed the advertisement; they declared they would prefer to pay five dollars for the new type of razor rather than one dollar for the old type. None

---

[21] See Joseph Jastrow, *The Psychology of Conviction.*
[22] "The Psychology of Belief," *Journal of Abnormal and Social Psychology,* Vol. XX, pp. 63-81, 174-196.

of the subjects, however, could explain how the "micrometric control" was obtained or what was its advantage.

If the human mind is credulous about such simple matters as the one just described, it is no wonder that it accepts and lives by hazardous social hypotheses that are highly emotionalized. It is only natural for some minds to believe in myths like those described by Sorel in a preceding chapter.[23] These myths are the only explanations of things that the experience-world of the naïve man can account for. He not only lacks the knowledge that is requisite for a complete understanding of things, but he lacks the knowledge that is requisite for submitting the fanciful explanations to critical analysis. Yet his own experience can account for them, and he believes them.

"Stereotypes."—Nor can the uninformed man be held in scorn who possesses and acts upon an unreal picture of his unseen environment. Given the opportunity, he would probably acquire a true picture of "conditions in Russia" just as his well-informed fellows have acquired it. When the press, however, presents an unreal picture, or when it fails to present any picture at all, we ought not to assess the entire blame on the man who is not a student of affairs. The ordinary man often holds a false conviction which is traceable to the unreal picture in his head. Mr. Lippmann has called these unreal pictures in the apperceptive mass "stereotypes."

"Stereotypes" account for many of the mistakes made by democracies. For example, both Americans and Spaniards were possessed of stereotypes in 1898, and the result was a war. The average American envisioned Spain as a despotic monarchy and its public men as being like Cortez, Pizarro, and Philip II; his picture of Spain had been obtained from the histories of Motley and Prescott. The Spaniard, on the other hand, could not understand how America or any other country could desire freedom for the Cuban people without desiring also possession of the island; the tradition of the "European system" had too firm a hold on his imagination for him to believe that Americans could have disinterested motives.

---

[23] See pp. 220-221.

"Stereotypes" are usually developed in our minds slowly and while we are unaware of them. It is possible, therefore, to counteract them before they are full grown. Indeed, it is this fact of psychology which provides almost the only prophylactic against antisocial propaganda. At the present time, for example, there is evidence of two developing stereotypes which, if they are not counteracted, may some day have unfortunate consequences for the peace of America and Great Britain. Alanson B. Houghton, former Ambassador to Great Britain, has clearly described them:

> Between Britain and America [he says] I see only one reason for distrust. And that is the existence of two mental hobgoblins. One of these hobgoblins appears from time to time in America to assure us that Britain is a predatory power, cynically careless of right and wrong, indifferent to the interests of others, greedy, cunning, and waiting only for a favorable opportunity to strike us down. The other appears from time to time in Britain to assure you that as America becomes more conscious of her strength she will inevitably become more imperialistic and, ruthlessly and brutally seeking to exploit others, will use that strength merely to play the bully and become a danger and a menace to the peoples of the world. . . . There are no such peoples as those described. . . . The real peoples are wholly different. They are made up of kindly, decent, hard-working, God-fearing men and women who possess innate common sense, who are busy about their own affairs, who do not fear one another, who want to live in peace and who mean, God willing, to do so.[24]

A kind of "stereotype" that is more conceptual than visual is the one which reflects a deep-seated prejudice that had its inception in authentic experience. The Irish-American's stereotyped conception of the British nation and the Soviet Russian's conception of France and England are such concepts; the ordinary American's prejudice against any form of government ownership is another. Some of these "stereotypes" are difficult to root out of men's minds unless men are forced to analyze the counter-idea very thoroughly. America's policy of isolation, for example, will continue to rest on public assent so long as individual Americans fail to perceive the absolute

---

[24] *Current History*, Vol. XXX (May, 1929), p. 205.

necessity in the machine age for nations to attend more to their community of interests and less to their "vital national interests." President Wilson realized this difficulty in 1922, when he said, "The poison of untruth has gone so deep into the wells of popular thinking that it will be thirty years, at least, before a rational public opinion as to the true foundations of our security and as to our national duty is restored." [25]

"Absolutes."—The crowd-minded person not only possesses "stereotypes" of the kind described above, but sometimes thinks in terms of ambiguous symbols, which we may term "absolutes." A "stereotype" is an incomplete picture or an incomplete concept in one's mind, but an "absolute" is a concept which has no objective meaning whatever, but an intense subjective meaning. That is to say, it is a concept presented by a propagandist who realizes that each person hearing or reading it will give to it his own peculiar meaning. Each member of the public sees in the concept exactly what he wants to see. Such a catch-word is "democracy." To one member of the public—an unsophisticated immigrant in America—it is a symbol of his own personal aspirations; to another—a crowd-minded employer—it is a symbol of his right of private property and a bulwark against Communism. To an American it may mean equality and social justice in America, but not necessarily equality and social justice for the peon in Mexico or Nicaragua. "Fatherland," "100 per cent American," "Liberty"—these are concepts which possess no objective meaning whatever, but are potent stimulators of response used by leaders appealing to certain crowds.[26]

These catch-words are discussed here because they help to describe how the public sometimes thinks. The editor who desires to perform the rôle of instructor as well as leader will discover that the only prophylactic against such nonrational appeals is an editorial or a series of editorials which analyze the

---

[25] Quoted in address by Bainbridge Colby, Associated Press dispatch of April 28, 1930.

[26] Much of the controversy over the slavery question turned on the "absolute"—"Liberty"; for a recital of how it was interpreted by the different factions, see Herbert Croly, *The Promise of American Life*, pp. 77-80.

"absolutes"—editorials which break them up into their component parts, which expose their lack of objective meaning.[27]

2. *Even though an idea be true, it may not necessarily gain public acceptance.* "A new idea, in order to gain currency," says James Harvey Robinson, "must seem to be good and noble and beautiful. . . . If it is ugly, wicked, or discouraging, or seriously disturbing to the conventional plan of life, it is likely to be shown the door. Ideas, like kisses, go by favor. The truth of an idea proposed for acceptance plays an altogether second rôle." [28]   Dr. Robinson has in mind great and comprehensive ideas like the theory of organic evolution, but his statement holds true of even less important ideas and proposals.[29] The chief reason why persons refuse to accept true ideas is the reason intimated by Dr. Robinson—that they do not wish to believe it. A second reason—one which has been discussed in preceding chapters—is that the idea conflicts with one's experience.

3. *A conviction once acquired is not easily relinquished.* This law is merely a corollary of the other two laws. Once an idea has become freighted with egotistic meaning, the individual will defend it to the death. "Every man," said David Lloyd George, "has a little House of Lords in his head—a man's prejudices, predilections, dispositions, wrong ideas, misconceptions of fact. These were the hereditary peers. They came from far beyond the Norman Conquest. They had descended from a Garden of Eden and from generation to generation and age to age. They were there and they had to

---

[27] "Absolutes" are not to be confused with mere euphemistic catchphrases which obscure meaning, such as "full-crew" law for the regulation which requires railroads to have an extra brakeman on every train; "safeguarding duties" for protective tariff rates; "American plan" for "closed shop" plan, "dole" for the public charity provided for workers not entitled to the full unemployment insurance benefits; etc.

[28] *The Humanizing of Knowledge,* pp. 19-20.

[29] Advertisers have discovered that an idea may be even "too true" to be believed. In an experiment by a psychologist, subjects were shown an advertisement containing an affidavit certifying that a certain make of vacuum bottle had been dropped from an eight-story window without breaking. Although the advertisement was true, one-third of the subjects refused to believe it.

sanction every idea—first, second, and third reading, and committee stage. But once that conservative element of the Briton had passed a thing he would never go back on it." [30]

The Editor: Crowd-Leader or Teacher?—To what extent is the newspaper justified in using nonrational appeals in an effort to mobilize the public will for the achievement of specific social ends? Some newspapers, in championing a cause, do not always direct arguments at the intellects of their readers, but frequently employ certain literary and graphic devices (e.g., cartoons, the iteration of slogans, etc.) for the purpose of releasing attitudes in readers. Is this practice ethically justifiable? Leaving out of consideration the nonrational appeals for such obviously "good" ends as poor relief, the raising of "fresh air funds," etc., which are primarily appeals to the attitudes of sympathy, civic pride, etc., we find, on analysis, that the question resolves itself to one of whether or not the end justifies the means. That the end sometimes does justify the means is self-evident; but that as a safe rule to follow in every case it has been proved true in experience is not yet admitted. One can only say that it is a dangerous doctrine.

Despite the danger to democracy inhering in such a rule, there is nevertheless so much argument for it that we are compelled to examine the argument.

The theory of democracy, as it was expounded by eighteenth century philosophers, assumed that men were reasoning animals and that they could form sound opinions from first impressions. In the world as it is today, however, things are so complicated that men who would have right opinions must rely on a few of their well-informed fellows; either they must do that, or they are likely to have wrong opinions. If the mass of uninformed men were willing to accept the opinions of their better-informed fellows, the problem of public opinion would not

[30] Address before the Liberal Party's Summer School, Cambridge, reported in *Manchester Guardian*, August 2, 1927.

The foregoing discussion is not meant to be a complete exposition of the nonintellectual factors in individual and social psychology. The extremely important phenomena of imitation, for example, is not discussed. The reader who desires to study the subject further should consult bibliographies contained in the various textbooks on social psychology.

appear so discouraging to social reformers. But the mass of men refuse to do this. They refuse because the correct opinions that are offered to them are frequently opposed to what the mass of men wish to believe. This fact opens the door to the demagogue, that is, to one who tells men only what pleases them.

What can be done about this? The alternatives appear to be two. They are: (1) We may persist in trying to educate the mass of men; that is, try to provide them with more and more information so that their nonrational attitudes will be conditioned more by their intellects. (2) Instead of trying to teach them to think, as the first alternative suggests, we can try to condition their attitudes merely by nonrational suggestions; that is, we can adopt the technique of the demagogue, wherever it is possible to do so, as a means to a good social end. The first remedy is based on the assumption that the mass of men can be taught to think; the second rests on the assumption that the mass of men are impervious to education in the true meaning of the term.

The second remedy, though it may turn out to be a mistaken one, nevertheless has a sound basis in psychology. The best presentation of this remedy has been given by Professor Ross L. Finney.[31] Most of the learning process (so the argument runs) is unconscious. We are inclined to assume that the ordinary man's *individual* learning is his whole apperceptive mass, whereas the greater content of his apperceptive mass, like the unseen portion of the iceberg, is his *social heritage* (that is, the beliefs passed down to him by tradition). Education, therefore, ought to be directed toward the transformation of his social heritage rather than his individual thinking. That is to say, we should try to change his attitudes *without* trying to teach him to think; we should restock his "social mind with a new outfit of popular beliefs that harmonize with the best modern knowledge." This is a "big job; perhaps an impossible one"; yet it is "infinitely easier than teaching every manjack, moron and flapper iconoclastic skepticism" about their sets of false

---

[31] See *A Sociological Philosophy of Education*, Chap. XX, and "The Unconscious Social Mind," *Journal of Applied Sociology*, Vol. X, pp. 357-365.

values. Perhaps a sounder social apperceptive mass can be secured through "systematic social suggestion." In other words, since the apperceptive mass that now exists has been built up through rote learning, it will be easier to change it by the same process rather than by conditioning it intellectually. Teach men by rote; they now believe that "virtue is its own reward," that "you can't make people good by law," and that "honesty is the best policy" simply because they learned it by rote. Teach men sounder truths in the same way: induce them to parrot these truths. "Teach the *what* to all; but to the bright also the *why*."

Those who believe in this method probably mean that it be applied in the elementary schools. As to whether or not the method should be applied by newspapers, opinion is divided. Indeed, the method is being employed, and nearly always has been employed, in the news columns of the newspaper. Mr. H. L. Mencken, for example, observes that the methods used by newspapers in reporting many events are hysterical and orgiastic. He maintains, moreover, that it is only by such means that newspapers can achieve social reform; for "the morality subscribed to by that public is far from the stern and arctic morality of professors of the science."

> The newspaper [he says] must adapt its pleading to its clients' moral limitations, just as the trial lawyer must adapt *his* pleading to the jury's limitations. Neither may like the job, but both must face it to gain a larger end. And that end, I believe, is a worthy one in the newspaper's case quite as often as in the lawyer's, and perhaps far oftener. The art of leading the vulgar, in itself, does no discredit to its practitioner. Lincoln practiced it unashamed, and so did Webster, Clay, and Henry. What is more, these men practiced it with frank allowance for the naïveté of the people they presumed to lead. It was Lincoln's chief source of strength, indeed, that he had a homely way with him, that he could reduce complex problems to the simple terms of popular theory and emotion, that he did not ask little fishes to think and act like whales. This is the manner in which the newspapers do their work, and in the long run, I am convinced, they accomplish about as much good as harm thereby.[32]

---

[32] *The Profession of Journalism* (W. G. Bleyer, ed.), pp. 65-66; reprinted by permission of Little, Brown & Co. See Ralph Pulitzer's reply, pp. 68-78.

The contrary opinion is that the newspaper should not adapt the technique of the demagogue even in a righteous cause. This argument asserts that propaganda cannot settle problems in a democracy: that only logic and social experience can settle vital issues, and that the use of propaganda to gain public acceptance of an idea is, therefore, abortive: it not only leaves the bulk of men no further advanced in their power to reflect on values, but eventually it so exhausts their "floating capital of social-motive forces" that they are left morally bankrupt.[33] Assuming that this latter argument is the sounder one, it will nevertheless be difficult to make it prevail in the future. As long as there are men who understand the technique of exploiting human attitudes, the tendency will be for realism to disregard ethics.[34]

Practical Purpose of the Editorial.—With specific reference to the editorial page as distinct from the newspaper in general, the argument against applying propaganda technique rests on other factors than those mentioned above. Those who advocate the view that editorials should be intellectual in their appeal declare that it is not the function of the editorial to mobilize the individual wills of all classes of readers with reference to public questions. The function of the editorial, they say, is to analyze public questions for those readers who have sufficient intelligence to understand them, and to trust to other modes of communication to carry these opinions to the minds of those who are less well equipped to understand them and less interested in reading about them. The editor himself ought not to function as a crowd-leader. He ought, of course, to argue a question in as clear and as forceful a manner as possible, and he ought to take into consideration the fact that many of his readers do not possess a large fund of information about the question he is discussing; yet he ought not to descend from the intellectual level.

---

[33] Raymond Dodge, "The Psychology of Propaganda," *Religious Education*, Vol. XV, pp. 241-252.

[34] With special reference to political campaigns, another point can be made for what it is worth; namely, is it more important in a democracy that the editor's candidate and the issues advocated by the editor be victorious in a given campaign, or that men develop a sense of political values? See the author's *Newspaper Reporting of Public Affairs*, p. 328.

The impelling reason alleged for this practice is not merely the necessity for preserving the newspaper's dignity. There is a more practical justification. It is simply this: that in any conflict involving the determination of policy by the public there must be a division of labor among the advocates of a policy. There must be an intellectual fountain-head to furnish arguments, and there must be crowd-leaders to repeat these arguments to the masses with whom they are in intimate contact. The function of each type of leader is quite distinct from that of the other. Thus, the newspaper editor who argues a question does not intend his arguments for the whole body of the public so much as for those influential leaders who will accept the opinions inculcated by the newspaper and then pass them down to others in either intellectual or nonintellectual form (e.g., by their personal prestige, by catchwords, etc.). In a political campaign, this is precisely what happens. Political "mass meetings," which are seldom attended by any except partisans, are usually addressed by the chief leaders who put "arguments" into the mouths of those who will pass them along at the work-bench, on the street corner, etc.

This view of the function of the editorial coincides with Godkin's view, although in Godkin's time publicists but little realized the possibilities for exploiting human motive-forces. In discussing the phenomenal circulation of the New York *Herald,* a paper for crowd-minded readers, Godkin said:

A good editorial is the earnest address of an exceptionally able and an exceptionally well informed man to some fifty thousand, more or less, of his fellow citizens. . . . When the world gets so intelligent that no man shall be more intelligent than any other man, and no man shall be swayed by his passions and interests, then there will be no need of editorial expressions of opinions, and editorial arguments and appeals will lose their power. . . . If influence and not money [i.e., circulation and advertising revenue] makes success, . . . [the *Herald*] is the least successful journal in the country. Horace Greeley edits a hundred, yes, a thousand newspapers in America where James Gordon Bennett edits one.[35]

What Godkin said of Greeley's *Tribune* he might have said a few years later of his own *Nation.* Although the *Nation's*

---

[35] *Nation,* Vol. II (May 8, 1866), pp. 584-585.

circulation was never large, it was an editorial fountain-head for newspapers, teachers, and social reformers throughout the country.

Regardless, however, of whether or not the editor deliberately makes use of nonrational appeals, he cannot exert his greatest influence unless he is acquainted with human motive-forces and, especially, with the customs and *mores* of the readers in his community. They will resist his intellectual arguments, and he will fail to enforce any desirable idea that conflicts with these forces, unless he takes them into account as limiting factors. The editor at least ought to understand thoroughly the attitudes which he is trying to change.

CHAPTER XIV

EDITORIAL POLICY

It is not sufficient that the editorial writer think straight: he must also exercise the function of leadership. Some men whose function it is to find solutions for social problems fulfill their function when they discover and announce a solution. They are scientists and investigators. The editorial writer, however, is a leader as well as an investigator. He is a publicist. He must try to enact right solutions into practice. Logic does not make its way unimpeded. It is opposed by indifference, self-interest, prejudice, and politics. It can make its way forward only by debate.[1]

The Rôle of Experts.—Recent years have witnessed a reaction against newspaper leadership because propaganda was being frequently substituted for debate. In 1922, for example, Mr. Lippmann published his *Public Opinion,* an argument advocating that social decisions be made in a preliminary way by experts—"that public opinions . . . be organized for the press . . . not by the press as is the case today." [2] This excellent suggestion, coming immediately after the American referendum on the League of Nations and during the postwar period of crimination and recrimination—a period of social unrest, of uncertainty, and hysteria—received in some quarters an interpretation which is not entirely justified by the realities

---

[1] There is, of course, the "logic of events" which is even stronger than debate. Repeal of the British corn laws, in 1846, would not have succeeded at the time, even though an abundance of statistical facts had proved its necessity, had not the Irish famine intervened. And, in 1931, the forces inherent in Great Britain's economic condition seemed perhaps strong enough to establish a protective tariff policy, even though it had little justification in economics.

The "lessons" of the last war, in which it was demonstrated that a general war is not profitable even for the victors, are probably not strong enough to overcome the forces of racial prejudice, greed, pride, and ambition in European peoples.

[2] P. 32.

inherent in social organization. This method, if carried to its logical conclusion, would paralyze leadership; for it underestimates the value of debate which, in controversies that rest on a philosophic basis, is necessary for the clarification of premises. Experts, for example, can determine what is wrong with our criminal code and can suggest a reformed code, but leaders are necessary to obtain the enactment of the reformed code into law; for many lawyers have a professional interest in the preservation of the old code and have large representation in legislative assemblies.[3]

It has long been recognized that the car riders ought not to have to bear the whole cost of the construction of new rapid transit lines, but that the abutting property owners whose unearned increment is increased ought to bear a fair share; yet, in every instance of new construction, the entire cost is recovered from the passenger revenue. Again and again experts are appointed to discover solutions for public problems, but the solutions are never enacted into law or practice.

The Value of Debate.—The expression of opinion in a controversy is one of the most effective ways of arriving at the truth; for the truth, as Renan has said, can only be presented in dialogue. When sincere leaders, therefore, stand off from debate to await the ascertainment of the "whole truth," they are relinquishing the function of leadership to charlatans and demagogues. Especially is this true of the foremost type of modern social leader, the newspaper. The editor of a newspaper is not a scientist, but a publicist. If he expresses a genuine opinion—not a catch-phrase aimed at drawing followers to his banner, but a rational reason for preferring a certain point of view—he is helping, not hindering, the search for truth.

Genuine opinion [says a writer in a "journal of opinion"] is not cold, logical judgment nor is it irrational feeling. It is scientific hypothesis, to be tested and revised as experience widens. Opinion is a view of a situation based on grounds short of proof. In a valid opinion they must be *just* short of proof. . . .

---

[3] See Chicago *Tribune* editorial, August 5, 1930. The same point can be made, in the opinion of the author, with reference to the United States reducing the Inter-Allied war debts.

[A good opinion] is a provisional conviction to be held as a conviction until new light alters it. It is an interpretation with a definite slant and bias. But it presses hotly for proof. It strains constantly toward the accuracy of proof. Good opinion, although firm, is the direct opposite of dogma. Dogma is hard and un-yielding, a sort of petrified emotion. It is constantly masquerad-ing as proof, as genuine opinion never does. You do not revise dogmas. You smash them. . . .

We are stunned by the volume of what there is to know in the human world. We are overwhelmed by the mass of sociological data, and brought to despair even more by the great gaps which must be filled. We have every day set before us infinitely more than we can possibly digest. . . . The result is often an excessive caution among those whose business it is to know. The universi-ties remain esoteric through the refusal of those who have the wide survey to commit themselves. Those who have the "grounds just short of proof" will not form opinions. Those who will loosely express their opinions have not the grounds. This treason of the intellectual class has neutralized the effects of public educa-tion. Discussion and universal reading have not really made popular opinion any more intelligent or reliable. They have merely made great masses emotionally articulate, rendered prejudice more vociferous and varied. The need for interpreters, for resolute expressers of opinions, becomes therefore more urgent.[4]

The Methods of "Personal Journalism."—At such times as the leadership of the press is hesitant, we hear the wish expressed for a return of the great personal editors who lived

---

[4] Randolph Bourne, "What is Opinion?" *New Republic Book,* pp. 359-360.

The freedom of the university professor to express opinions based on grounds "just short of proof" is restricted by his fear of what his colleagues may think of his "scholarship." This situation does not exist in journalism except to the extent that the newspaper, obviously, must maintain its reputation for expressing sound opinions. The distinction has been pointed out by Harry Elmer Barnes, who resigned a university professorship in 1929 to become an editorial writer for the Scripps-Howard newspapers. "There is," he says, "a thrill and a drive to the game which is a thing unknown to the class room. In Scripps-Howard I find an intellectual freedom and an air of challenge and combat. Moreover, in journalism one can be human without a sense of fear. There is a straightforwardness and frank interchange between newspaper men which does not exist in the halls of learning. . . . A professor is currently regarded as valuable in proportion to the absence of any ideas and opinions. . . . In writing for these papers one's success depends upon the possession of sound and positive opinions and the ability to express them in lucid and cogent form."—*Scripps-Howard News,* Vol. IV (August, 1930), pp. 17-18.

and wrote in a presumed "golden age" of journalism. It is true, of course, that "there were giants in those days," but these editors often expressed their opinions in a violent and intolerant manner which would find no place in modern institutional journalism. A brief review of some of these opinions is necessary to provide a setting for our examination of editorial leadership. The editorial written by Benjamin Franklin Bache in the Philadelphia *Aurora* at the time of Washington's retirement, although not typical of the editorials of the day, illustrates the intemperate and acrimonious expression in which the editors of his time often indulged.

> . . . The man who is the source of all the misfortunes of our country, is this day reduced to a level with his fellow citizens, and is no longer possessed of power to multiply evils upon the United States. If ever there was a period for rejoicing, this is the moment—every heart in unison with the freedom and happiness of the people ought to beat high, with exaltation that the name of Washington from this day ceases to give a currency to political iniquity, and to legalized corruption. . . .

Of the author of the foregoing editorial, William Cobbett, a rival editor, wrote in a tone of acerbity, as follows:

> This atrocious wretch (worthy descendant of old Ben) knows that all men of any understanding set him down as an abandoned liar, as a tool and a hireling; and he is content that they should do so. . . .
>
> If [our readers] have read the old hypocrite Franklin's will, they must have observed that part of his library, with some other things, are left to a certain *grandson;* this is the very identical Market-Street scoundrel. He spent several years in hunting offices under the Federal Government, and being constantly rejected, he at last became its most bitter foe. Hence his abuse of General Washington, whom, at the time he was so-

> liciting for a place, he panegyrized to the
> third heaven. . . .
> He is an ill-looking devil. His eyes never
> get above your knees. He is of a sallow
> complexion, hollow-cheeked, dead-eyed, and
> has a *tout ensemble* just like that of a fellow
> who has been about a week or ten days on
> a gibbet.

This acrimonious and personal tone in editorials persisted for a whole century, although to a much less extent than during the early years of the Republic. During the "moral war" of 1840, for example, the following epithets were hurled at James Gordon Bennett, of the New York *Herald,* by James Watson Webb, Park Benjamin, and Mordecai Noah, rival editors: "infamous blasphemer," "loathsome and leprous slanderer and libeler," "venomous reptile," "pestilential scoundrel," "venal wretch," "habitual liar," "veteran blackguard," "contemptible libeler," "caitiff," "rogue," "ass," "rascal," "cheat," "common bandit," "turkey-buzzard," "unprincipled conductor." [5]

In the late thirties, too, George D. Prentice, of the Louisville *Journal,* was writing the following paragraphs:

> Messrs. Bell and Topp, of the North Caro-
> lina *Gazette,* say that "Prentices were made
> to serve masters." Well, Bells were made
> to be hung, and Topps to be whipped.
> James Ray and John Parr have started a
> Locofoco paper in Maine, called the *Demo-
> crat.* Parr, in all that pertains to decency
> is below zero; and Ray is below Parr.
> The *Globe* says that Mr. Clay is a sharp
> politician. No doubt of it, but the editor
> of the *Globe* is a sharper.[6]

When the foregoing paragraphs were written, politics was a strenuous profession and the American Government was being democratized by Andrew Jackson with the editorial assistance of such effective writers as Amos Kendall and Francis P. Blair.

---

[5] F. Hudson, *Journalism in the United States, 1690-1872,* pp. 459-460.
[6] These paragraphs and the editorials of Bache and Cobbett are reprinted in Allan Nevins, *American Press Opinion.*

But even as late as 1892, after politics had become tamer, the distinguished and intelligent Chicago *Tribune* was referring to Grover Cleveland as "the fat coward of Buzzards Bay," and to the Democratic vice-presidential candidate as Ad*lie* Stevenson.[7]

In appealing to a group of voters to defeat John P. Altgeld, Democratic candidate for Governor of Illinois, the *Tribune,* in the same year, said:

> Do the German Lutherans, who are proud of their morality, their honesty, and their consistency, propose after this exposé of rascality to vote for John P. Altgeld, that incarnation of political mendacity and dishonesty? Can they vote for such a copperhead snake with the approval of conscience or self-respect? Can they look at the reflection of their faces in a glass after doing such a thing?[8]

Editorials today are seldom so violent. Frequently they are sarcastic, oftentimes they are denunciatory of men who deceive and exploit the public, and generally they are vigorous; but they are usually restrained and exhibit the writer's sense of humor. The reasons for this change have been explained by Senator Arthur Capper, publisher of the Topeka *Capital,* as follows:

. . . The day of the great editorial personalities had its own errors and failings. We cannot understand their status in the community without regard to the conditions of the times. And we cannot fully understand them and their power apart from the one overshadowing public concern during the entire period from 1830 up to the Civil War and its aftermath. That was the slavery controversy. It is difficult to realize today how that great issue subordinated and submerged all other interests, nor, what is important, how the ultimate abolition of slavery as well as the long controversy itself affected the thought of the leading publicists of the time.

Since the problem of American persistence as a nation had been

---

[7] Adlai Stevenson.

[8] Even more violent were the *Tribune's* characterizations of the "Anarchists" arrested after the Haymarket Riots. See issues of the second week in May, 1886.

finally settled, even though in blood, it was not unnatural, in the sense of triumph over that terrible issue, to feel that all major problems were now solved, or if not, that this country had only to turn its hand to them to solve them. It was a period of inordinate cocksureness, complacency, and optimism. Both the controversy itself and its final settlement tended to convert opinions into fixed convictions. So differences of opinion were generally violent and intolerant. Moreover, the era of the natural sciences had scarcely dawned, so far at least as affecting common opinions and beliefs. Perhaps never in history was there a time when men felt that everything was already known that was necessary. As to the long future of the United States there was a rampant optimism.

Today we live in different times, in a new world of which it may be said generally that uncertainties have replaced certainties. Diversity and complexity have succeeded general optimism on religious, political, social, industrial, moral, and economic questions. It is not a time for dogmatism or the closed mind. The old-time editorial writer, however effective for another age, would not fit well, and would perhaps not readily adjust himself in an age of widening knowledge and of bewildering change.[9]

PRINCIPLES AND THEIR APPLICATION

The older editors often were champions of a principle. This was partly due to the prevailing assumption that great problems could be solved by dialectic. The chief reason, however, was the conflict of principles inhering in the nature of the new government and in the slavery question. Although recent historians have noted that the conflicts between Federalists and Anti-Federalists and between North and South were, at bottom, as much concerned with economic realities as with juristic and political principles, editorial expression, for the most part, dealt with principles.[10] Today, public controversy is less enveloped in polemics; the problems that press for solution are more technical in their nature and cannot, therefore, be solved by

---

[9] *Editor and Publisher*, April 27, 1929, p. 27. Senator Capper's remarks do not refer to editors prior to Greeley, but the same explanation —i.e., the great issues of the time—attaches to the early editors also.

[10] Concerning the arguments relative to the constitutionality of Hamilton's national bank, John Marshall said, "The judgment is so much influenced by the wishes, the affections, and the general theories of those by whom any proposition is decided, that a contrariety of opinion on this great constitutional question ought to excite no surprise."— Quoted by C. A. and M. R. Beard, *The Rise of American Civilization,* Vol. I, p. 356.

logic—a fact which accounts for much of the hesitant editorial leadership evidenced in recent years. Yet, this is by no means true of all our current problems; some of them rest on a philosophical foundation, and no solution, outside of conflict, can be discovered unless there be an expression of opinion which clarifies the social values involved in them. The editorial policy that does not have some basis in principles cannot merit the respect of enlightened leaders.

Where We Get Our Principles.—Men come by their principles both by learning and by inheritance. Those principles that they learn are derived from direct contact with life and from reading. From the time that he reads stories of moral heroism in the fifth grade to the time that he studies social problems in college or in the newspapers, a man is learning principles of individual conduct and social relations. At some time or other these principles assume the form of convictions and become to him general principles. Sometimes they are modified by his subsequent study and experience, but often they are adhered to rigidly, and of some men it may be said, as Mr. D. C. Somervell said of Macaulay, "He forgot nothing, and after the age of twenty-four he learned little."

But it may be said of principles learned from contact with life, no less than of principles gained from reading and study, that they also may be either modified by reasoning or adhered so rigidly. Principles acquired from reading often are excellent, for they are the thought of great minds and, in this technical age, are frequently the most reliable principles. But they are often second-hand experiences for the one who adopts them and, in so far as they relate to the deep concerns of life, may be less reliable than the principles that one derives from living at close quarters with the world. The Socialistic views of Philip Snowden, Mr. H. J. Laski tells us, "were born not of reading Marx, but from the direct contemplation of the life about him." The convictions of conservative John Marshall as to centralization in government, as to the sacredness of contract, and as to stable institutions "were not made; they grew." His nationalistic convictions ran back to his youthful experience at Valley Forge where Continental soldiers starved and froze because of the lack of coöperation among the Colonial Governments, and his opinions respecting the sacredness of contract and the stability of institutions traced back to his early experiences in the Virginia legislature where he witnessed (and opposed) the passage of resolutions to repudiate honest debts.[11]

Of principles that are inherited, we ought to be more skeptical. At least we ought to examine them in the light of reason. Our ancestors, when confronted by a specific situation, lacking the scientific knowledge that we now have, often fabricated imaginary solutions which served their purposes. Out of these solutions, however, they derived general rules and principles, and eventually came to live by them as eternal truths. Some of these "eternal truths," which originated out of guesses by our ancestors, have survived through social heritage. Some of them, indeed, are eternally true: they are generalizations about living which the race has derived from its arduous experience. But some of them are not true, though a great part of society continues to live by them.

The Application of Principles.—The question of whether or not the editor should militantly champion a principle depends upon the stage that has been reached in the controversy that involves the principle. Controversies pass through one or both of the following stages: (1) the stage of discussion; (2) the stage of conflict.

On the first level, the question is open to argument. The application of an old principle under novel conditions, or the assertion of a new principle as relating to a new situation, is under discussion. Investigation by scientific method and editorial debate are resorted to for the purpose of laying open the situation to solution. The public is too busy and too indifferent to examine the question. It may at first envisage the problem in so simple a way that it decides the issue off-hand on the basis of some stereotype it possesses. As discussion proceeds in the press, however, the public is presented with new aspects of the problem, and perhaps comes to put aside the stereotype. In this stage of the controversy, the editor ought not to insist that the question can be expressed only in blacks and whites.

---

[11] A. J. Beveridge, *The Life of John Marshall*, Vol. I, pp. 147, 231.

He should examine the other side. Cicero has left on record, says John Stuart Mill, that he always studied his adversary's case with as great, if not with still greater, intensity than even his own. "He who knows only his own side of the case knows little of that." [12] Only the editor who has such an attitude ought to take part in debate. To discuss principles in an intolerant way obscures rather than clarifies.[13]

When an issue reaches the stage of conflict, however, the editor ought to be militant. Some issues arrive at this stage because debate has not been able to settle them. Logic has been found inadequate. They can be settled only by force or by propaganda. Fanatics, obsessed with a concept to which they assume false universality, have succeeded so well in attracting converts that the editor must change to stouter armor and meet the enemy on equal terms. Public questions do not often descend from the stage of discussion to the stage of conflict, but every so often in history there are such crises. The slavery question passed from the discussion level to the conflict level, and the prohibition question in 1931 seemed to have arrived nearly at the conflict level. At the latter stage, either force or propaganda decides the issue—not discussion. But the editor ought not to decide too quickly to abandon the method of debate.

Another type of public issue—usually a very old one or a permanent one in a new form—is settled from time to time (or

---

[12] *On Liberty* (People's Edition), p. 21.

[13] One great editor of the Civil War and Reconstruction period was so tolerant that he seems to have belonged to the present rather than to his own time. Henry J. Raymond, of the New York *Times*, was accused by his fellow Republican editors and statesmen of being too eager to see the other side of a question. Greeley said of him, "He saw both sides of a controverted issue, and, if one of them seemed juster to-day, the other might nevertheless command his preference to-morrow." Of himself, however, Raymond once said, "If those of my friends who call me a waverer could only know how impossible it is for me to see but one side of a cause, they would pity me rather than condemn me; and however much I may wish myself differently constituted, yet I cannot unmake the original structure of my mind." Yet Raymond was a man of principle. When other men were hysterical, he stood by Andrew Johnson's reconstruction program even though he realized he was signing his own political death warrant. He was deposed as chairman of the Republican National Committee and was refused renomination to Congress. For a description of this affair, see C. G. Bowers, *The Tragic Era,* Chap. VI.

temporarily) on the conflict level without having passed through the discussion stage. Such questions are those which concern permanent ideals, as tolerance, the sacredness of contract, and questions of simple justice and honor. When, as the consequence of the efforts made by selfish interests or by fanatics, such a question arises, the editor should not long hesitate in drawing his sword. When the freedom for social inquiry is restricted, when injustice is done to the unprotected, when the strict provisions of a treaty are deliberately misinterpreted to serve self-interest (as in the case of the Panama Canal tolls question of 1913-1914), there is only one right side to the question; and the editor whose sense of values does not tell him which is the right side has no business being an editor.

The Editor as Critic.—Editorials that defend principles are often only indirect defenses. That is to say, they are timely editorials which criticize a wrong social act or the act of an institution, and only imply the defense of the principle underlying the social offense. Thus, many editorials are mere judgments of *approval* or *disapproval*. Such editorials applaud or deplore a judicial or administrative decision, an official appointment, a public address, or an individual act. The following editorials are examples, although there are innumerable types: [14]

(1)

> It is such small, petty tricks as that which members of the Women's Christian Temperance union felt called upon to play on the Pennsylvania railroad that makes the prohibition fight such a bitter affair fraught with so much violent difference of opinion and difficulty of enforcement. Because the president of the Pennsylvania, a personal "wet," appeared before the house judiciary committee in Washington and advocated repeal of the eighteenth amendment, W.C.T.U.

---

[14] This section perhaps emphasizes the critical more than the constructive function of the editor. Few constructive examples are cited because of lack of space, but most of them fall within a single category. For example, when the editor supports the movement for old age pensions, he is really defending the underlying principle that society ought to recognize human dignity, not merely a particular piece of legislation.

members enroute to present the "dry" side of the controversy to the judiciary committee cancelled reservations which they had made upon the railroad—apparently in high dudgeon. Dispatches did not state whether the exacting "drys" ascertained whether all of the crew, passengers and officials of the railroad they did use to Washington were arid beyond all question. It is such tactics, practiced nearly equally by the "wets" and "drys," that make prohibition the problem it is today. Action of the W.C.T.U. in the case of the Pennsylvania is nothing less than bigotry and intolerance which has no license in this country. We all should have outgrown such evidences of "smallness."—Rockford (Ill.) *Morning Star*.

(2)

While great questions are hanging in the balance at London, Washington, and other centers, it is gratifying to note a victory for plain justice, public convenience, and sound economy right here in New York. This victory took place when Justice John Ford, in the state supreme court, rendered a decision in favor of lower rates for taxicabs.

As has been pointed out on this page, the adoption of lower rates for small taxicabs would not only give the taxi using public a considerable saving but would relieve traffic congestion, for the smaller taxis could turn more easily and work their way through traffic more quickly. But when a certain Eugene Piantoni applied for a hack license for a cab equipped with a lower rate meter the police department turned him down. The taxicab companies already in the field, presumably afraid of the competition of lower rates, favored the stand of the police department.

The police commissioner let it be known that the lower rates would bring about a bitter war among the cabmen in which the public might suffer greatly. There may be some truth in this. Undoubtedly some drivers would be tempted to resort to Chicago tactics and ram the cheaper taxis when they got a chance. To allow one's self to be terrorized into accepting the present rates, however, is something which will not appeal to most citizens, nor does the fear of such a rate war speak well for the valor of the police.

Justice Ford granted Piantoni's mandamus to compel the police department to license his cab, pointing out that it does not lie with the police commissioner to fix minimum rates. The commissioner, however, may appeal this decision. Moreover, a bill has been introduced into the board of aldermen establishing the present rate as the minimum. Several obstacles placed in the path of economy and convenience by the city authorities have thus to be overcome before the public can be certain of paying far less for taxi fare than they do now. Justice Ford's action is, however, a commendable step in the right direction.—NEW YORK *Herald Tribune.*

(3)

The only questions admissible concerning an applicant for office are, according to Thomas Jefferson: "Is he honest? Is he capable?" But there are those in this city who would change all that. In connection with the election of the borough president of Manhattan to succeed Mr. Julius Miller, strong appeals have been made to the Mayor and to Mr. Curry of Tammany Hall to name a Jew. The petitioners flatly state that retention of "a Jewish appointee in the office of borough president" is something which the Jews of this city have a right to insist upon; and they add that "failure to appoint a Jew would be an unpleasant reflection either upon the integrity or the ability of the Jew to hold important public office." But the real disparagement is cast by the very tone of this statement. It implies that a Jew might not be selected were he not able to press the claim of his race or religion. There could hardly be a more "unpleasant reflection" than that.

We do not forget that such a demand may have been fostered or encouraged by the course of the appointing power in this city for many years past. Tammany is made up of many heterogeneous elements, and has been anxious to ingratiate itself with each one of them. As a consequence, the officers have often been divided according to national origins. When the mayor has had, for example, to choose a city magistrate, his stipulation has virtually been that the endorsers must bring him the name of a German-American, or an Irishman, or an Italian, or a Jew, as the case may be. This plan is supposed to convey a special compliment to a specified group of voters in this city. The method is one intended to cater to the "Italian vote," the "Jewish vote," and so on. Strictly speaking, it is an affront to such a vote. It suggests that the groups singled out for favoritism cannot produce a man whose qualifications would be so outstanding and superior that he could be chosen for office without any favoritism at all.

It is much to be hoped that the man elected by the Manhattan aldermen to succeed Borough President Miller will come somewhere near measuring up to his abilities and records for public service. But the search for such a man should not be limited by any cramping requirement of locality or of religion or race.—NEW YORK *Times.*

The criticism of acts cannot, and indeed ought not, to be always directed to the act alone; for the actor, especially if he be a public official, can be corrected as well as the act. Yet it is usually more important to society to correct the wrong than the wrongdoer. In American newspaper practice, however, the wrongdoer, more often than the wrong, is attacked. According to Mr. H. L. Mencken, this practice has a sound basis in American popular psychology. The American newspaper man, says Mr. Mencken, "knows very well that a definite limit is set . . . upon the people's capacity for grasping . . . moral concepts," and, therefore, the newspaper must correct

YET THE WORLD CALLS HIM LAWLESS

Orr in Chicago Tribune

THE END DOES NOT JUSTIFY THE MEANS

wrong "by translating all argument for a principle into rage against a man." [15]   Indeed, this is a true rule, but to follow it always is for the newspaper to confine its function to that of reformer.   The newspaper is an educator also; by discussing

---

[15] "Newspaper Morals," *The Profession of Journalism* (W. G. Bleyer, ed.), p. 54.

moral values, it should help to establish a sounder moral judgment in its readers.

Criticism of Institutions.—The editor can serve as both corrector and educator by criticizing institutions; for modern civilization must produce institutions to meet the needs of human nature. An institution, Professor Sumner has explained,

consists of a concept (idea, notion, doctrine, interest) and a structure. The structure is a framework, an apparatus, or perhaps only a number of functionaries set to coöperate in prescribed ways at a certain conjuncture. The structure holds the concept and furnishes instrumentalities for bringing it into the world of facts and action in a way to serve the interests of men in society. Institutions are either crescive or enacted. They are crescive when they take shape in the mores, growing by the instinctive efforts by which the mores are produced. Then, the efforts, through long use, become definite and specific. Property, marriage, and religion are the most primary institutions. They began in folkways. They became customs. They developed into mores by the addition of some philosophy of welfare, however crude. Then they were made more definite and specific as regards the rules, the prescribed acts, and the apparatus to be employed. This produced a structure and the institution was complete. Enacted institutions are products of rational invention and intention. They belong to high civilization. Banks are institutions of credit founded on usages which can be traced back to barbarism. There came a time when, guided by rational reflection on experience, men systematized and regulated the usages which had become current, and thus created positive institutions of credit, defined by law and sanctioned by the force of the state. Pure enacted institutions which are strong and prosperous are hard to find. It is too difficult to invent and create an institution, for a purpose, out of nothing.[16]

Some institutions, originally organized to meet some necessary social situation, have by now outlived their usefulness; they have become ends in themselves and are mere depositories for concepts which now impede social progress. Some institutions, originally organized for the attainment of a social end, have been so modified as to pervert the purpose they were organized to serve; and some institutions, though still, on the whole, socially useful, have not been modified to meet new

---

[16] W. G. Sumner, *Folkways*, pp. 53-54 (Ginn & Co.); reprinted by permission.

conditions. Such institutions ought to be criticized so that they can be corrected.

The newspaper, however, ought not to be too eager to denounce the purpose of a good institution; more often the newspaper can criticize the means employed by the institution for the attainment of the social end, rather than the institution itself. If this is done, the newspaper is more likely to offer constructive criticism and is less likely to offend and alienate individuals whom it is the desire of the newspaper to educate. One may criticize, for example, the intolerance of a church— its censorship of opinion, say—without attacking the good end to which the institution is dedicated.

Of equal importance, though, is the help rendered by the newspaper in modifying old institutions and in trying to establish new (enacted) ones. The institution of the law, for example, should be made more sociological, and likewise, to a greater extent than it now is, the institution of private property. The establishment of a new institution of diplomacy, such as the League of Nations, is absolutely necessary, for the old-time methods of diplomacy are not adequate for modern conditions: international organization and international law today are in the same stage of development as was the English constitutional law in the thirteenth century.

Scolds and Pucks.—It is expressing a truism to say that editorial criticism should have a constructive purpose. Some newspapers, however, because there is so much falsehood and evil to expose and denounce, acquire unconsciously a combative habit which is resented by their readers who are inclined to be, in this day in America, optimists. Some newspapers thus become petulant, adopting a sniping attitude toward whatever persons and institutions they oppose; they come eventually to be regarded as scolds. It is to this type of newspaper that Carl Magee, of the Oklahoma City *News,* a courageous editor who has been sent to jail because of his denunciation of public wrongs, and one of the men chiefly responsible for the disclosures in the notorious oil scandals in President Harding's Cabinet, addresses a warning: "Don't go around with a chip on your shoulder. When the time comes to fight in a good cause and when you know you're right, fight and fight hard. . . . Character, not belligerency, is the quality to develop if you would become successful and influential editors." [17]

Other newspapers are veritable Pucks, stirring up discord or thumbing their noses at persons and institutions merely for the sake of amusing their readers. It is difficult, of course, to draw the line in journalism where we can dispense with puckishness without surrendering the duty to criticize, but the present tendency of some important newspapers to walk softly is probably just as harmful at the moment as is the tendency of sensational newspapers to indulge in irresponsible criticism. Eternal vigilance is the price of liberty.[18]

THE DETERMINANTS OF EDITORIAL POLICY

The editorial policy of a newspaper is determined by several factors which, for purposes of convenience, we shall classify as internal and external. When we speak of internal factors, we mean simply the viewpoint of the newspaper's owners and editors independent of any external influences. These factors are discussed under two heads: (1) ownership; and (2) the control of editorial policy. By external factors we mean the influences of the newspaper's readers and of others on the views held by the owners and editors. The external factors are distinctly limiting factors on the newspaper's freedom to say what it wishes.

External factors are discussed under three heads: (1) the ideology and economic interests of the readers; (2) the competition of the newspaper with other newspapers; and (3) economic pressure and subsidy.

---

[17] Quoted in *Editor and Publisher*, Dec. 1, 1928, p. 16.

[18] The most interesting personalities in journalism have usually been Pucks, and the young man who is entering journalism cannot help admiring them rather than the "stuffed shirts" of journalism who are so engrossed in upholding "respectability" and "stability." The "heroes" of journalism nearly always have been St. Georges. "Even Munsey and Curtis," says Mr. Mencken, "though they appear to be fish have this puckish quality concealed in them. They are, among fish, somewhat rash and reckless—salmon with vine-leaves in their hair. Pulitzer was a gorgeous porpoise with red, blue and purple spots, streaking through phosphorescent seas, forever lashing his tail."—*American Mercury*, Vol. II (February, 1925), p. 252.

Internal Factors: 1. Ownership.—In the first instance, of course, the editorial policy of a newspaper is determined by the proprietors. Although their control of policy is not usually exercised in a purely arbitrary or capricious manner, the character of the owners and the fact that the owners have a large capital risk may have a considerable effect on the determination of policy.

American newspapers are seldom dedicated to the advocacy of a single idea or ideal, as is the case with many Continental newspapers and of American newspapers of a few generations ago. The American newspaper, from a partisan standpoint, is more or less independent and tries to serve the whole public. Why this is true is discussed in following pages; it suffices here to point out that editorial opinion, on the whole, tends to reflect the cleavage of class interest in the economic order, and that differences of editorial viewpoint among newspapers, wherever they occur, rest not so much on a basis of principle and ideal as on the economic realities in American life.[19] A few newspapers overtly champion a philosophy of "liberalism";[20] but

---

[19] Mr. G. R. Bauer, who investigated the editorial policies of leading American newspapers from 1895 to 1923, using as touchstones outstanding decisions of the United States Supreme Court, found that editorial policy tended to reflect sympathy for an economic class more often than a philosophical viewpoint. In instances in which a clear-cut principle was involved—for example, the principle of state's rights *versus* centralization, or of individualism *versus* collectivism—the newspaper which had traditionally championed a principle deserted the principle in order to argue for the interests of a specific economic class.—Master's Thesis, University of Wisconsin (1929).

[20] Among these are the twenty-six Scripps-Howard newspapers. In explanation of their policy, George B. Parker, editor-in-chief, said: "In matters of general editorial policy, about which there can be no local exception, we do achieve what we consider to be a strong degree of uniformity. . . . We achieve it, simply because our organization is made up of men whose journalistic philosophy, generally speaking, accords with those upon which the organization is founded. I don't like labels, but they are handy. The one most fitting for Scripps-Howard Newspapers is 'Liberal.'

"To be specific, if we could conceive of two men in political life as being in newspaper work rather than in politics, we could say that it would be impossible for Reed Smoot, for instance, to be a Scripps-Howard editor. Now Reed Smoot is a very capable man. He possesses certain very fine intellectual qualities and a very large element of strength. But his philosophy just wouldn't fit in our family. On the other hand, it would be easily conceivable to me that Justice Brandeis would be welcomed—if he were a newspaper man—as a Scripps-Howard

most papers, although asserting their policy to be eclectic, reflect a distinctly conservative viewpoint. This fact is due to several factors which are discussed below.

The Newspaper as Property.—Not only is the newspaper a great capitalistic enterprise; it is one of the most hazardous of the modern types of business. It is more hazardous frequently than is the theatrical business to which it bears several resemblances. The theatrical producer who desires to present a play rents a theater for six months, expends a certain amount of money for scenery, employs a cast, and promises contingent royalties to a playwright. If he fails to gauge the public's current desire for entertainment, he may, after several unsuccessful performances, sublease the theater, discharge the cast, and store the scenery for possible use in the future. The newspaper has a much greater risk and a much larger stake; yet, like the theatrical producer's play, the newspaper publisher's property derives its value almost entirely from what business men term "goodwill." Another name for "goodwill" in the newspaper business is "circulation." When a great Chicago newspaper was sold a few years ago for $11,000,000, only $1,000,000 of the sale price was for "fixed assets" (i.e., plant, unused paper stock, etc.) ; the real value of the newspaper consisted in its 400,000 readers who were valued at about $25 each. The purchasers of these readers bought nothing that was tangible, but they assumed that they could continue to give the readers what they wanted in the way of a newspaper.

The big newspaper is compelled to make money.

The Chicago *Daily News* four years ago [Mr. W. P. Beazell relates] issued $8,000,000 of 6 per cent debentures to cover the purchase of the property from the Lawson estate. It has 60,000 shares of 7 per cent cumulative preferred stock outstanding, and

---

editor. That wouldn't mean that we would expect on every occasion and on every issue to agree with everything that Brandeis thought or that all of the other Scripps-Howard editors would be in accord with every one of his ideas. But his general objective would be ours."—*Editor and Publisher,* August 30, 1930, p. 9.

For an account of a confused application of the Scripps-Howard philosophy of "liberalism" in a presidential campaign, see R. D. Casey, "Scripps-Howard Newspapers in the 1928 Presidential Campaign," *Journalism Quarterly,* Vol. VI, pp. 209-231.

400,000 shares of common. It provides $250,000 a year for a sinking fund, so that now it has only $7,000,000 of debentures outstanding. Interest on these debentures calls for $420,000, which, with the $250,000 for the sinking fund, makes a total of $1,090,000. For the five years immediately preceding the issue the net profits of the *Daily News* averaged a few dollars less than $1,500,000. These new *fixed* charges, then, require 75 per cent of the net profits before any provision may be made for common stock dividends or any of the other demands resulting from the change in organization. All the old obligations remain, payrolls, materials, replacements; these charges are additional.[21]

"Business Ethics."—As a consequence of this capital risk, newspaper proprietors are naturally motivated—often without much philosophical examination of values—by a safety-motive. The natural inclination of the newspaper proprietor (oftentimes a joint stock company) is to operate his business on the safe plane of "business ethics" rather than on the more hazardous plane of moral ethics. "Business ethics" does not necessarily imply a lack of moral standards in the conduct of a business. It is merely a code which emphasizes the "sanctions" of morality as opposed to the doctrine that the morality of an act resides in the motive of the act—an emphasis on externals which the Utilitarians made so much of. The code proceeds according to the maxims, "Honesty is the best policy" (i.e., "Be honest because it *pays* to be honest") and "The customer is always right." It says: "We shall have only decent and truthful advertisements in our paper because our readers demand it; if we have 'reader-confidence' the advertisements will get better 'results' and we shall make more money. We shall publish only truthful news in our paper: we shall cause our paper to be relied upon by readers—and our circulation will be stable." [22] This "pain-pleasure" conception of ethics con-

---

[21] *The Quill,* February, 1930, p. 17.

[22] The Scripps-Howard newspapers, although not really motivated by this standard of morality (their purchase of the Albuquerque, N. Mex., *State Tribune* is one of the proofs of their sincerity), nevertheless direct advertisements to business men which are calculated to "sell" them on the efficacy of the "business ethics" policy. "Each Scripps-Howard editor," says an advertisement in the *Saturday Evening Post,* "strikes or stays his hand as he sees fit. No class, party, or outside pressure determines his action. But he is never silent on questions that involve his city's welfare. He fights even when he is certain to be

tains more of realism than of morality, but it is a significant fact in modern journalism, and only the future can tell whether or not it will profit society. In criticizing it, one can only point out that Kant's doctrine—that the morality of an act is located in the actor's motive—likewise has much justification in experience: that only "men of principle" ought to conduct newspapers.[23] This doctrine is interpreted even more broadly by the school of thinkers that believes that all newspapers should champion causes; thus, we hear the *Nation*, a critical review, complaining of the New York *Times* that it expresses no opinions and gives no judgments on conflicts of principles and of social classes:

> A good editorial [according to the *Times'* standards] . . . is rather a summary of the background of the daily news than a penetrating analysis or a call to action. The *Times*, by its own theory, does not attempt to mold history; it pleads no cause and wages no wars, it simply reports. The result is that although able men have collaborated in it the *Times'* editorial page is one of the dullest and most wobbling in America. Dull, because it never knows the passion of an ideal; wobbling, because after a period of impartiality any crisis is sure to find it upon the side of the possessing classes.[24]

The Publisher's Associations.[25]—It is inevitable that the social and business relations of the publisher with other men will affect his viewpoint. It is this subtle fact which explains

---

beaten, always on the side of honest public service. . . . *Idealism? . . . Yes, and a sound successful business formula, as every advertiser knows."*

[23] The reaction against this doctrine, which, of course, is not a thoroughly reliable one since it justifies blundering idealists and intolerant fanatics, led to a wide acceptance of Utilitarianism in the nineteenth century—an era of great social and political reform in England—because it was apparent that the Victorian statesmen, landlords, and manufacturers who sincerely *thought* they were acting as men of principle were producing *results* that were decidedly immoral. If the student is interested in examining criticism of these two schools of ethics, he will find an excellent explanation in Dewey and Tufts, *Ethics, passim.*

[24] Vol. CXXXIII (Sept. 29, 1926), p. 287.

[25] For purposes of emphasis, we discuss this "external" factor as if it were an "internal" factor.

the property-mindedness of many American newspapers more realistically than the oversimplified explanation of M. Siegfried that advertisers determine the editorial policy of great newspapers.[26] Mr. William Allen White, himself a publisher, has noted this fact with relation to editorial policy:

I know of no editor so low that he would take direct dictation from any advertisers. I know of no editor so high that his mind is not affected by his industrial environment. The fact that he lives in daily contact with the rich people of his community, whether the community be large or small, that he gangs with them at the country clubs, eats with them at the leading hotels, and, indeed, prays with what might be called a plutocratic congregation, colors his mind and he sees things as his friends and associates see them.[27]

It is related of Joseph Pulitzer—perhaps apocryphally—while he was publisher of the St. Louis *Post-Dispatch* in the eighties, that when he read in a New York newspaper the account of a sumptuous entertainment given by the city's most dominant international financier and the first American millionaire to marry his daughter into European aristocracy, he recognized in the list of guests the names of every New York newspaper publisher. "By God!" he cried, "there is room in New York for an editor that doesn't go to the Vanderbilt Ball." Sir Henry Campbell-Bannerman, the Liberal British Prime Minister, who was among the most sociable of men, never disguised his opinion, says J. A. Spender, "that London society was bad for Radical politicians. You couldn't, he used to say, be perpetually in the company of people who thought your opinions disreputable without wishing to tone them down to prove yourself respectable."[28]

---

[26] See pp. 173, 179-182.
[27] *Editor and Publisher*, French Advertising Supplement (July 7, 1928), p. F-10.
[28] *The Public Life*, Vol. I, p. 147.
It is only the unusual publisher whose view of life is not affected by those factors which develop his "expanded" personality. It was one of the strange traits in the character of William Randolph Hearst that in his early days as publisher he cared nothing for the opinion that San Francisco's social and business leaders held of him. He frequently attacked their actions in public and business life, although some of them were the friends and intimates of his wealthy parents.

Some of the explanations of editorial policy are to be found in such subtle factors as these: the newspaper publisher or editor is the golf partner of a railroad president;[29] or his wife, a former Englishwoman, was snubbed in London society; or he derives satisfaction from being thought of as the "adviser" of the governor.[30]

The Publisher's Outside Interests.—Recent years have witnessed the purchase of newspapers by wealthy men who possess no professional newspaper background. They have been bankers, lawyers, or manufacturers. Their motives, in a few cases, were dictated by their desire to exert an influence on public affairs, but, in most cases, they were merely seeking profits just as they would in any other business. Although some of these former business men turned publisher have pursued an enlightened editorial policy, the entrance of business men into journalism cannot be regarded as a wholesome development.

An equally unhealthy situation has ensued from the practice of successful newspaper publishers diverting some of their surplus capital and personal interest to other business enterprises.[31] Thus we see newspaper publishers on the directorates of banks, public utility companies, and real estate companies. Some successful publishers, however, have deliberately avoided making "entangling alliances" with business by using their surplus

---

[29] It would be an interesting fact in the history of journalism if we knew whether William T. Laffan, publisher of the New York *Sun* subsequent to Mr. Paul Dana's resignation, determined the paper's policies because of his personal intimacy with J. P. Morgan (both were connoisseurs of art) or solely because Mr. Laffan sincerely believed in the ultraconservative policies of the *Sun*. See E. P. Mitchell, *Memoirs of an Editor,* Chap. XII, *passim,* and Mark Sullivan, *Our Times,* Vol. III, p. 236.

[30] After reading H. H. Kohlsaat's *From McKinley to Harding,* and studying the editorial efforts made by the Chicago *Record-Herald* to avert a war with Spain, one could speculate as to a possible motivation of the publisher.

[31] The number of publishers who are directors in banks, investment companies, and manufacturing companies, and who hold an appointive or elective political office, is much too large from the point of view of independent thinking. A study made by Miss Elizabeth Maier, at the University of Wisconsin, of 162 biographical sketches of editors and publishers, which were printed in *Editor and Publisher* from 1929-1931, reveals that 30 per cent of the men interviewed were directors of business corporations.

profits for the construction of new buildings and for the purchase of additional newspaper properties. Thus we see the wealthy Chicago *Tribune* building a Gothic skyscraper and establishing the New York *Daily News* and the *Liberty* magazine. It has always been a Scripps-Howard policy to avoid what one of their editors calls "journalistic bigamy" by setting aside a certain percentage of the profits of the organization for the purchase of additional newspapers.

Likewise, the newspaper proprietor who seeks political appointment cannot maintain that fiduciary relation to his readers that the publisher can who eschews political office and honor. Although the tendency for newspaper publishers and editors to seek political office has grown less as the years have passed, it is significant that President Hoover, within the period of a few weeks, appointed six newspaper men to diplomatic posts.

The type of ownership—that is, whether the property is owned by an individual, a family, a joint stock company, etc.—appears to make little difference in the formulation of editorial policies. The increasing tendency for employees to own a newspaper property is a healthy sign of the character of ownership that we may have in the future; but even this plan does not guarantee an open-minded independence of outside influence, for the mutualization of newspapers is often accomplished with bank loans, which, in at least one instance, have seemed to have resulted in a silent influence during the period of the loan.

Internal Factors: 2. The Control of Editorial Policy.— The actual work of formulating editorial policy is delegated to men whose profession is journalism—men who give no thought to the profits side of newspaper publishing and whose minds are wholly occupied with studying public affairs. The extent to which this power is delegated to a professional class varies with different newspapers. On the smaller papers and on a few larger ones the proprietor actually commands that a certain policy be adopted and adhered to.[32] On a few other

---

[32] There appears to be an insufficient basis for the alarm expressed' by some Americans that our press is destined to fall into the control of a few "press lords" as has happened to a great extent in Great Britain. In the prewar period, readers of British newspapers looked to certain

papers, the proprietors make little or no effort to dictate policy. For example, the late Van Lear Black, a banker and capitalist who was chief proprietor of the Baltimore *Sun* newspapers, assumed that only professional newspaper men knew how to conduct a newspaper and, accordingly, left the formulation of editorial policy entirely in the hands of the editors. As a consequence, the *Sun* at one time championed the side of striking miners employed in a coal mine controlled by Mr. Black; yet the proprietor made no protest.[33]

It is not possible, of course, to generalize about types of control, for any classification would have to be based on numerous case studies which are not now available.

The Editorial Writer's Freedom.—It is no longer possible, except in the country newspaper field, for a man without a great deal of money to establish a medium for the expression

---

great editors for guidance in matters of public policy, such as J. A. Spender of the *Westminster Gazette,* Sir Robert Donald, of the *Chronicle,* J. L. Garvin, of the *Pall Mall Gazette,* A. G. Gardiner, of the *Daily News,* and C. P. Scott, of the *Manchester Guardian.* Today the control of the British press is almost entirely in the hands of a few wealthy men who often determine their editorial policy capriciously. For a severe criticism of the situation, see address by the Rt. Hon. Stanley Baldwin, reported in New York *Times,* March 17, 1931.

[33] An exceptional instance of the freedom permitted by a proprietor to his editorial employees is evidenced in the following letter written by W. T. Anderson, proprietor of the Macon (Ga.) *Evening News* and *Telegraph,* to Ben B. Johnson, whom he had appointed as managing editor of the *Evening News* after Mr. Anderson had purchased it:

"DEAR BEN:

"You are hereby appointed managing editor of the Macon *Evening News,* effective from this date.

"Your duties will consist of seeing to it that the *News* is made the best afternoon newspaper it is possible to make it, exigencies considered. You will be expected to write the editorials according to your own views and reactions to public questions.

"We must bear in mind that there is a substantial element in Macon that have opinions that differ with those of the *Telegraph,* and while I don't want to suggest what argument you shall offer or side you shall espouse, leaving that to your intelligence and your conscience, I shall have no criticism of or quarrel with you if at any time you are found opposing the views of the *Telegraph.*

"I hope you agree with my idea that publishing a newspaper is a trusteeship, and will treat it as such. A newspaper is an institution, if it measures up to the high ideals the public sets for it. It goes on and on, generation after generation, building and serving, and establishing itself in the hearts and confidence of the people—if it is a good newspaper—while those who publish it are transitory; they are here today and gone tomorrow."

of his personal opinions. Prior to 1850 the cost of establishing a newspaper was small, but today it is prohibitive. The writer of editorials, therefore, must express the opinions of an entity—the editorial council. There is one exception, however; a few editorial writers have been able to exploit their personalities in such a manner that they are always permitted to express personal opinion. Such writers as Heywood Broun, Arthur Brisbane, Glenn Frank, Walter Lippmann, and H. L. Mencken, because of the peculiar attraction of their style or of their manner of looking at life, possess absolute editorial freedom.[34]

The editorial writer on the large newspaper does not usually feel that his freedom is restricted, for the following reasons: (1) If he is a "liberal," he does not seek employment on an ultraconservative newspaper, and *vice versa;* this fact is not satisfying, however, to the liberal-minded men not engaged in writing editorials who would probably go into that work if there were more liberal papers to write for. (2) The men who usually determine editorial policy are the writer's professional associates who hold a philosophy quite like his own. (3) The writer himself usually has a voice in the determination of editorial policy. (4) He is not required to write an editorial which embodies a view contrary to his own: there is always some other writer on the staff who can sincerely express the opinion dictated by the editorial council.[35] (5) Many of the

[34] There are limitations even upon the opinions expressed by some of these men, although the editorials of some of them are so innocuous that there can be no objection to what they write. Among them, however, Heywood Broun, although writing a column which appeared opposite the editorial page of the New York *World*, was compelled by the *World* either to resign or to conform to the policy laid down by the editorial council with reference to the Sacco-Vanzetti case. Broun resigned. See *Editor and Publisher*, Aug. 13, 1927, p. 5.

[35] This demand was not often made of editorial writers of strong character even in the days of personal journalism and under the most arbitrary of publishers. "Robert Lyman . . . recalls a council called by the Commodore [James Gordon Bennett, Jr.] to determine the *Herald's* course a few days before the national election of 1888. Bennett was inclined to come out for Benjamin Harrison as against Grover Cleveland, who was running for reëlection. . . . Lyman and S. J. E. Rawling . . . were added to the conference largely because Bennett wanted to test their judgment. Doctor Hepworth, Charles Nordhoff, Doctor George W. Hosmer, and John Russell Young were the elders. Bennett stated his views and called on Lyman and Rawling first for opinions. Both were adverse. Hepworth and Young were acquiescent—eager to bend

editorials are not controversial, and their preparation is left entirely to the individual editorial writer. Because of these factors, the editorial writer does not usually feel cramped. In the case, however, of the doctrinaire who is incapable of considering the various limitations forced upon a newspaper by its readers, there are no satisfying compensations.

In six Central European countries and in Sweden, countries in which newspapers are chiefly organs representing a distinct point of view or class interest rather than the interest of the whole public, as in the United States, and where personal journalism has not given way to institutional journalism, editorial writers are safeguarded in their freedom by contracts which the governments have legalized. Thus, if any newspaper changes its editorial policy during the period of the writer's contract, the writer is entitled to annul the contract and to receive indemnity of approximately a year's full salary. The contract provisions vary in the different countries, but in some instances arbitration boards have been established.[36]

External Factors: 1. The Readers' Influence.—Sir Martin Conway has suggested a classification of crowd-leaders that is applicable in many respects to newspapers.[37] There are, he said, "crowd-compellers" and "crowd-exponents." [38] Crowd-compellers are "men who achieve a great idea or far-reaching plan, who fashion and master a crowd big enough to give effect to it, and who drive the crowd to do the work they determine that it shall do." Men like Disraeli, Napoleon, and Joseph Chamberlain are examples of the crowd-com-

to the imperial will. Bennett accordingly ordered Nordhoff to write a leader coming out for Harrison. He quietly declined, remarking that the agreement under which he came to the *Herald* prescribed that he should never be asked to write in support of things to which he was opposed. To this Bennett gave cheerful assent and instructed Young, a Republican, to produce the editorial. This he did. It was put into type, but never printed."—Don C. Seitz, *The James Gordon Bennetts* (The Bobbs-Merrill Co., Indianapolis), p. 242; reprinted by permission.

[36] These agreements between publisher and writer are described by Albin E. Johnson in *Editor and Publisher*, May 18, 1929, p. 30; Aug. 3, 1929, p. 11; Sept. 21, 1929, p. 22; and by Harold B. Johnson, in *Editor and Publisher*, Oct. 1, 1927, p. 11. Contrast this freedom of the writer with the incident described by Paul Y. Anderson in the *Nation*, Jan. 1, 1930, p. 9.

[37] *The Crowd in Peace and War*, Chaps. VI-VIII, *passim*.

[38] Also, "crowd-representatives," a category not discussed here.

peller. The crowd-exponent, on the other hand, is a "man who feels by sympathetic insight and mere sensitiveness of nature as the crowd feels or is going to feel, and who expresses in clear language the emotion of the dumb organism. . . . He is the voice of the crowd and his utterance is really theirs. He in fact borrows his thunder from them and gives back to them what he has himself received from them." Lloyd George is an example of a crowd-exponent. In modern times, few politicians can be anything but crowd-exponents.

The ordinary American newspaper, in the sense that it voices a more or less settled opinion, is essentially a crowd-exponent. This is not the same, however, as to say that the newspaper is merely the echo of crowd-mania. A few newspapers, it is true, make little effort to assert a public leadership. They devote themselves entirely to entertaining the public in their news and nonnews columns, their editorials being only echoes of crowd-thinking.[39] These newspapers, when they take a stand on a vital public question, deliberately voice the traditional policy—the time-honored opinion of the nation or the community. Assuming that public opinion about a question lags behind advanced thought to the same extent that legislation lags behind public opinion,[40] they wait until public opinion has been crystallized by other agencies or by events, and then they attack with vigor whatever opposition remains.[41]

---

[39] When Mr. A. J. Kobler succeeded to the directorship of the New York *Daily Mirror* in 1928, he described the kind of paper it would be. "It will be nonpartisan," he said. "It will print facts without flavor or personal opinion. When a reader reads an editorial which expresses something that is on his own mind but which he has been unable to express, an editorial that causes him to exclaim, 'Well, that is right!'— that is what I mean by a newspaper merchant supplying the goods his customers will like."—*Editor and Publisher,* Sept. 15, 1928, p. 8. Mr. Kobler is by no means the first exponent of this theory of editorial policy; James Gordon Bennett adopted it in 1835, and Mr. Hearst is said to be the author of the editorial instruction, "Get excited when the crowd gets excited."

[40] See A. V. Dicey, *Law and Opinion in England, passim.*

[41] A distinction, however, should be made between journalistic demagoguery and mere conservatism. John T. Delane, the great editor of the London *Times,* was a representative of the latter attitude. "Kinglake likens Delane to a Tudor king; careful to mark the growth of public sentiment or opinion, he went up to a cause that was waxing strong, offered to lead it, and reigned." He did not "start public opinion in the direction of abolishing Corn Laws, or disestablishing the Irish Church, or

The newspapers that are quick to advocate advanced policies and extreme measures are few. This class of publication, in fact, is almost wholly limited to weekly "journals of opinion" and organs that are special pleaders for a group or an interest, as, for example, the organs of associations and "movements." [42]

The bulk of American newspapers, although representing different sets of opinions about politics and economic and social questions, have one characteristic in common: *as shepherds, they do not jeopardize their leadership by getting too far in advance of their flocks.* The newspaper of general circulation is compelled to recognize the fact that its readers possess a social heritage and a group loyalty which exert a powerful resistance to novel or radical ideas. The newspaper must have mass acceptance; otherwise it is not a newspaper. It is never true of the editor, said the late Dr. Talcott Williams, that,

like the drum-major, he leads the procession along a predetermined route, from which he cannot vary. . . . But it is true that the instant the journalist turns into a side street and the procession leaves him and goes its own way, as has happened to many an independent journalist, he ceases to be a journalist and becomes that admirable but costly person, to himself and to his publisher, the pamphleteer. . . . If men leave his newspaper he may be publishing a most admirable history of the world for a day freighted with the wisest opinion ever uttered, but the publication is not a newspaper. It is, instead, a book published daily by its author and creator at an extravagant cost.[43]

Nor can one conduct a newspaper with the same obstinate attitude with which the Stuarts tried to rule the English nation; nor can the editor obtain social reform in the manner of Joseph II, the enlightened despot of Austria.

It is the discovery of what they can *not* do, and ought not to attempt [said a great reformer] that transforms reformers into

introducing large measures of parliamentary reform; yet sooner than many others he rendered stout assistance to all those causes."—Sir E. Cook, *Delane of The Times*, pp. 297-298.

[42] Many Continental European newspapers, however, are of this type, each of them expressing a shade of opinion different from the others. In Paris, for example, they range from *Action Française,* organ of the Royalists, to *L'Humanité* organ of the Communists.

[43] *The Newspaper Man,* pp. 31-32.

statesmen. . . . No statesman dreams of doing whatever he pleases; he knows that it does not follow that because a point of morals or of policy is obvious to him it will be obvious to the nation, or even to his own friends. . . . [Reformers] have found office a veritable cold-water bath for their ardor for change.[44]

Partisanship.—To some extent, newspapers are limited in their editorial freedom by the partisanship of their readers. Many newspapers, of course, are entirely free from this restraint, but some of the older newspapers which were once party organs have acquired a reader constituency. This fact has tended to institutionalize the newspaper and to place it in a fiduciary relation to a large number of its readers. In some instances, the ghosts of former editors walk in the editorial sanctums of today,[45] but usually it is the ghosts of party loyalty and prejudice that stalk the minds of readers.

The conditions that limit a politician's freedom also limit the editor's freedom, although to a much less extent. Politics is a coöperative enterprise in which the individual politician must conform to the party's will and must support the party's candidates. Few statesmen have succeeded in making themselves bigger than their party—not even Roosevelt and La Follette in recent times; and not many editors of institutionalized newspapers have been able to change parties and at the same time retain their influence on their clientele of partisan readers. This was especially true in 1884 when the Democratic New York *Sun,* because of Dana's dislike of Cleveland, supported an impossible independent candidate, Ben Butler, and lost nearly half of its subscribers.[46] It was also true in 1896, as Henry Watterson learned when his Democratic papers supported the Gold Democratic ticket instead of the regular nominees. This policy almost wrecked the newspaper property of Watterson and Haldeman.

---

[44] Woodrow Wilson, *When a Man Comes to Himself,* pp. 23-30.

[45] For example, Joseph Medill, prior to his death in 1899, inserted the following instruction in his will: "I desire the *Tribune* as a party organ, never to be the supporter of that party which sought to destroy the American Union or that exalts the State above the nation."— *History of the Chicago Tribune,* p. 2.

[46] See Don Seitz, *The James Gordon Bennetts,* p. 359.

Their newspapers were literally proscribed and physically burned. Threats were made against their printing plant. The four years which followed 1896 were the most difficult in the history of the famous newspaper institution; and it required all the business sagacity of the one and the editorial genius of the other to keep the ship afloat.[47]

Newspapers today, though still bound to some extent by the partisanship of their readers, are more independent on the whole than are statesmen—more independent than the greatest statesmen. Mr. Taft and Mr. Hughes, for example, the biggest men in the Republican party, were the leading champions of the League of Nations idea not only when it was an academic proposal but even after it had become identified in the public mind as a Wilsonian idea. In the presidential election of 1920, however, Mr. Taft and Mr. Hughes, in order to retain their party influence, advised voters to support Mr. Harding, the Republican nominee who was opposed to the League of Nations. Some of the Republican newspapers which had supported the League of Nations idea, however, maintained a consistency of principle by supporting the Democratic candidate who was a champion of the League. On the other hand, some Republican newspapers which had supported the League of Nations idea up until the campaign had begun, felt compelled, like Taft and Hughes, to support the Republican candidate. One of these newspapers had come to be regarded as the Republican oracle of the Northwest. To desert its constituency because of a single plank in the party platform would, it believed, imperil its prestige of leadership for all the future on many other important issues. The question that confronted the editors was, "Shall we imperil and possibly wreck this great institution because of a single issue? Is it worth while to sacrifice our power to influence this community in the future in many things merely because we believe in this one idea?" It is not

[47] Arthur Krock, *Editorials of Henry Watterson*, p. 87.
"At that time Mr. Watterson had expected to retire from active journalism, and was supervising the education of his children abroad. But so serious was the financial effect of the *Courier-Journal's* bolt of Bryan and support of Palmer and Buckner that Mr. Watterson returned to his desk and the next four years of his life and those of his partner were the busiest and most anxious in their careers."—*Ibid.*, p. 75.

always easy for an editor to answer this question; it is not always easy to perceive the vital importance of an issue. When the issue is slavery, or when the financial structure of the nation is threatened by an unsound proposal for currency reform, as it was in 1896, it is not difficult for a newspaper to perceive its duty; but not always does the "paramount issue" appear to be so vital as to justify partisan apostasy.[48]

More and more, however, partisanship as a determinant of editorial policy is losing its force. Voters are coming to realize that neither of the old parties represents a set of distinctive principles, but, instead, certain economic and sectional interests. A new alignment of parties is in prospect, but if this does not come about (because of the limitations inherent in our peculiar constitutional system), editorial policy will tend to reflect economic and sectional interest instead of political philosophy and loyalty.

Sectionalism.—A very definite and significant fact in editorial policy is sectionalism. Some historians regard sectionalism as the central fact in American history,[49] and it is now being predicted that the present divisions in national politics will give way in the future, in large measure, to sectional alignments. In a cultural sense, some of our sections are equal to some of the European nations, a fact which—despite all our unity—cannot escape significance for the politician and the editor. It is a significant fact that certain cities and certain regions in the United States owe much of their prosperity to

---

[48] Not partisanship, but a sincere point of view determined the attitude of some Republican editors in 1924 after a Senate investigating committee had revealed gross corruption by Republican party leaders and cabinet members. "But we must hasten to liquidate the war," these editors decided. "That is more important right now than the repudiation of corrupt party leaders. Tax burdens are depressing industry; business is just beginning to recover from the depression of 1920-21. Only a Republican administration can get us back on the road to normalcy. The bribery and corruption of Republican officials is disgraceful and ought to be punished severely and quickly, but that is no reason for putting an inefficient Democratic administration back in Washington. Come, let us liquidate the war! Mr. Coolidge personally is honest, and he will reduce taxes. Business and the future economic position of the United States demand his election." This view may have proceeded from false observations and inferences, but it was held sincerely by some Republican editors.

[49] See F. J. Turner, *The Frontier in American History*, Chap. XII.

the leadership of their newspapers. The regional newspapers are largely responsible for the building up of cities in the Northwest and on the Pacific coast, for the diversification of farming in the South, and even for the large volume of business transacted at certain ports. These things were accomplished in large measure by earnest and consistent programs of education and propaganda in the news and editorial columns.[50] The following editorials illustrate how the newspaper tries to awaken its readers to a comprehension of their sectional interests:

(1)

As things now stand in Congress it may be possible, says a Washington dispatch, to obtain an extension of the Mississippi barge line to Peoria without much delay. Later on, when the Illinois waterway is opened, the line may be extended to Chicago.

If there is any money left after other sectional projects are accommodated, and provided congress feels like it, barges may be run on the Illinois river. If other parts of the country are satisfied with all the white meat, both drumsticks, and all the stuffing, Illinois may get the neck.

As the government engineer has apportioned the river and harbor money for 1929, $7,225,000 goes to the Mississippi river, $4,590,000 to the Ohio river, $3,630,000 to the Missouri river, $1,700,000 to the Hudson river, $1,200,000 to the East river, $1,150,000 to the Delaware river, $1,000,000 to the waterway from the Delaware river to Chesapeake bay, $800,000 for Savannah harbor, $800,000 to the Beaufort–Cape Fear waterway, $650,000 for Miami harbor, and $1,025,000 for the Sabine-Neches, Tex., waterway. In addition, Maj. Gen. Jadwin is suggesting

---

[50] Some of those who have observed that the newspaper, with respect to national and international affairs, can only be a "signalizer" of events, are inclined to underestimate the power of the newspaper in local and regional affairs. The factors that limit the usefulness and influence of the American newspaper in national and international affairs are not so potent with respect to the nearer environment.

that $24,000,000 be spent for deepening the Great Lakes connecting channels, and $3,400,-ooo for lakes compensating works, Chicago paying $1,750,000 of the latter sum.

Illinois, in the meanwhile, is to be showered down upon with these generous amounts: $750,000 for the Illinois river, $45,000 for the Calumet river and harbor, $20,000 for the Chicago river, $120,000 for the Chicago harbor, and $10,000 for the Waukegan harbor —a total for Illinois of $770,000, or slightly less than the allotment for the Savannah, Ga., harbor.

Other states somehow are invited in or elbow their way in to a seat and pick of the menu. Illinois is left on the sidewalk, clutching a nickel and the admonition to go buy itself a cup of coffee.—CHICAGO *Tribune.*

(2)

The [Minneapolis] *Tribune* has been stressing the necessity of developing in our part of the world an informed and intelligent sectional consciousness. Again and again it happens that we fail to defend our own best interests because we do not know where our best interests lie. And we wake up too late to discover either that we have missed an opportunity for expansion or that we have been victimized in a bad intersectional deal.

The tariff affords us with several such cases in point. Not only the Northwest farmer, but the Northwest business man, would have profited substantially had the Hawley tariff bill imposed a duty on the vegetable oils and fats coming in from the Philippines. And not only the Northwest farmer, but the Northwest business man, will continue to operate at a certain disadvantage so long as copra and cocoanut oil from the Philippines take away from the Northwest farmer a part of the American market for his butter-fat, his lard, his tallow, and his soya bean. Yet the average Northwest citizen is not acutely conscious of the fact that he has any interest in the imposition of a duty upon the vegetable oils and fats coming in from the Philippines. He regards the whole subject as remote, academic, and, doubtless, rather dull. This is because he is deficient in informed sectional consciousness.

Blackstrap molasses affords us another case in point. Here is an issue which our entire Minnesota-Wisconsin-Iowa-North Dakota-South Dakota-Montana-and-Nebraska area should be treating as a matter of importance. We have already pointed out that industrial alcohol can be made from either American corn or Cuban and West Indian blackstrap molasses, that foreign blackstrap molasses now has almost complete command of the American industrial alcohol market, and that this market, if given to the American farmer, would mean about 35,000,000 bushels of corn at once, and that very shortly it would mean 50,000,000 bushels of corn a year to him. He now puts on the market only about 450,-000 bushels of corn per year, and the stabilizing effect which an assured outlet for 50,000,000 bushels would exert upon the price of his corn is obvious at a glance. . . .

The very fact of sectionalism, however, is a limitation on the freedom of expressing editorial opinion. Bound up as it is with the economic well-being of its region, the newspaper usually is a special pleader for economic advantages for its section. If the newspaper is located in the Central states, it is likely to plead for a reduction in freight rates on farm products; it is likely to oppose construction of a new oceanic canal in Nicaragua or the lowering of toll rates by the Panama Canal because of their effect in reducing freight rates between the East and West coasts; it is likely to oppose the raising of rediscount rates by the Federal Reserve Board to the advantage of Eastern exporters and to the disadvantage of the farmer; it is likely to oppose federal appropriations for public improvements in other sections (as, for example, the purchase of the Cape Cod Canal by the Federal Government, the development of Boulder Canyon Dam, or the rehabilitation of the Muscle Shoals power plants) ; it is likely to oppose the construction of new naval yards and the voting of subsidies to a merchant marine. If the newspaper is located on the seaboard, we observe that it is likely to advocate or oppose nearly every one of the sectional projects opposed or advocated by a newspaper in the Central states. Newspapers thus are inclined to take a position on many public questions without consideration for the welfare of the whole country, and sometimes their demands stimulate Congressmen to engage in wasteful "logrolling."

Sectionalism is reflected in the newspaper in another form that is less natural but sometimes more harmful to the section itself. This is a sectionalism that is based not upon economic interest, but on the local *mores* or ideology of the region. This form of sectionalism is too indefinite to admit of precise definition, but its manifestations are easy to discern. It reveals itself in connection with moral, religious, and political questions. It is a limiting factor, for example, in the editorial policy of Middle Western newspapers that desire to advocate improved naval defense; of newspapers in some Southern states that desire to adopt a liberal attitude toward the prohibition question or a tolerant attitude toward the teaching of biological science in the public schools; of metropolitan newspapers with a large country circulation that desire to adopt the urban point of view on any of the current issues that divide city and country. A majority of newspapers are complacent as regards these sectional sanctions, but some are courageous enough to stand out against the ideology of the region. The Chicago *Tribune,* for example, has a nationalistic policy, although most of its readers are more pacifistic than militaristic; the Scripps-Howard newspapers published in Southern cities were brave enough to oppose prohibition in some of its forms several years before public opinion evidenced any reaction against the law; the Baltimore *Evening Sun,* located in a state that is 50 per cent rural, does not hesitate to adopt the urban point of view in the city-country conflict.

Ideology of the Readers.—Sectionalism and partisanship are manifestations of a people's ideology which operate to limit freedom of editorial utterance, but there is an ideology that is common to the majority of the American people irrespective of party and section. Just what this ideology is and how it is manifested in attitudes as regards morals, social justice, patriotism, law, and institutional life cannot be explained in a brief space. Several penetrating analyses of American character, however, have been made by competent scholars and keen observers, and the editor should become familiar with them.[51] Editors who are not aware of this ideology are likely to meet resistance in advocating a policy that conflicts with it. As to how far an editor can go in opposing the ideology or *mores* of a people is a question for which there is no ready answer. The Stuart kings taxed the English people heavily and violated many of their customary constitutional rights, but the throne was never put in jeopardy until the Stuarts began to flirt with Catholicism.[52]

Thomas Paine was a successful pamphleteer who learned how far it was possible to go in attacking British institutions. When he published, in February, 1791, the First Part of his *Rights of Man,* in which he advocated the radical ideas that government was derived from the people, that government could be altered at their will, and that it could be carried on only through a system of popular representation, it was eagerly and sympathetically read and studied by Englishmen. But in the Second Part, published a year later, Paine asserted that "all the hereditary elements in the constitutions, both Monarchy and House of Lords, ought to be abolished, and the country governed by its representatives alone, sitting either in one or two chambers"; and that "pensions on the taxes now granted to the rich would be diverted, and used, together with a graduated income-tax, to

---

[51] Some of these studies are: James Bryce, *The American Commonwealth;* André Siegfried, *America Comes of Age;* Harvey O'Higgins and O. M. Reede, *The American Mind in Action;* Hugo Münsterberg, *Die Amerikaner;* Douglas Woodruff, *Plato's American Republic;* Charles Merz, *The American Bandwagon;* Walter Lippmann, *American Inquisitors;* Vernon Parrington, *The Beginnings of Critical Realism in America;* James Truslow Adams, *Our Business Civilization;* Herbert Croly, *The Promise of American Life.*

[52] For the text of the House of Commons protest, see Adams and Stephens, *Select Documents of English Constitutional History,* pp. 346-347.

give education to the poor, old-age pensions, and maternity benefit." [53] These statements aroused violent alarm, and Paine was forced to flee for his life to France.

Few editors have found it possible to oppose the national sentiment when the nation enters a war or is near to a war. Some editors have adopted the course of John Walter, of the London *Times,* with reference to the Crimean War as being one of "common sense." This policy is described in John Bright's journal, as follows:

MARCH 24. Conversation with Mr. Walter of the *Times* on the war—urged him to seize any chance of preserving or making peace—remarked upon the *Times* being brow-beaten into a support of the war. He said when the country would go for war, it was not worth while to oppose it, hurting themselves and doing no good.[54]

The Manchester *Guardian,* on the other hand, opposed the Boer War and, as a consequence, its very existence was threatened; but afterward, because of its steadfastness, it came to be regarded as great.[55] "The soundest editorial policy," says Col. R. R. McCormick, of the Chicago *Tribune,* "may be temporarily the most unpopular with the readers upon whose support the newspaper depends. It may at times conflict with the interests of those upon whom the newspaper depends for another kind of support. And that is why I say it takes a very definite kind of courage to succeed in newspaper editing."

The newspapers that were slow to combat the Ku Klux Klan in 1920 and the hysterical measures taken against the rights of free speech during the time of the "Red menace" (1920) over-

---

[53] G. M. Trevelyan, *British History in the Nineteenth Century,* p. 65.
[54] G. M. Trevelyan, *The Life of John Bright,* p. 233.
[55] We cannot insist too strongly that the influence of a newspaper on its readers is governed by the same psychological factors that determine the influence of an individual personality on other individuals. The mercuric, wavering newspaper, in its relation to its readers, has precisely the same influence as the mercuric, wavering politician or business man in his relation to other men. A reputation for steadfastness in a newspaper is acquired in precisely the same way that the individual personality acquires prestige. Bright and Cobden, who opposed the Crimean War, Campbell-Bannerman, who opposed the Boer War, and Ramsay Mac-Donald, who opposed Britain's participation in the World War, came, in a few years, to be thought of as "great men," although for a time they were ostracized.

looked an opportunity for making their influence count in a permanent way; and the newspapers that have complacently observed the development of an exaggerated materialistic ideology since the war without making the least effort to correct it have surrendered their prestige of leadership to other agencies of communication and to the weekly journals of opinion. The spirit of the postwar era has been well described by Marlen E. Pew:

> In the pursuit of quick, unearned wealth, the national ideal, very few of the old American pillars have been allowed to stand. The Big Boys, sometimes referred to as Big Shots, have had their sweet will in almost everything for some 15 years. Government, acting for the common welfare, has had little to say. Control, regulation, rational economics fitted to human service, whenever proposed, have been spat upon and ground into the dust. If a man were audacious enough to raise his voice against any of the prevailing evils, such as crazy inflation, headlong speculation, cockeyed overproduction, bank control of industry, ticker-tape management of railroads, private power propaganda in public schools and the press, exaggerated tariff ideas, excesses of organized labor and industrial monopoly, overcapitalization, or dozens of other evidences of an age of ruthless gambling and hogging, he would immediately be seized upon as a disturber of the peace, an eccentric freak, and run out of the community, showered with epithets, if not bricks. We have worshipped profit, and now that a little bit of it has deserted us we are as a people shorn and chastened by mystical gods whose anger we seem not to understand.[56]

The Journalist's "Marching Orders."—This abdication of journalistic leadership constitutes a disobedience (in at least

---

[56] *Editor and Publisher*, Nov. 15, 1930, p. 72.

this one respect) of what a distinguished former editor [57] called the "journalist's marching orders," found in Ezekiel 33:1-9:

1. Again the word of the Lord came unto me, saying,
2. Son of man, speak to the children of thy people, and say unto them, When I bring the sword upon a land, if the people of the land take a man of their coasts, and set him for their watchman:
3. If when he seeth the sword come upon the land, he blow the trumpet, and warn the people;
4. Then whosoever heareth the sound of the trumpet, and taketh not warning; if the sword come, and take him away, his blood shall be upon his own head.
5. He heard the sound of the trumpet, and took not warning; his blood shall be upon him. But he that taketh warning shall deliver his soul.
6. But if the watchman see the sword come, and blow not the trumpet, and the people be not warned; if the sword come, and take any person from among them, he is taken away in his iniquity; but his blood will I require at the watchman's hand.
7. So thou, O son of man, I have set thee a watchman unto the house of Israel; therefore thou shalt hear the word at my mouth, and warn them from me.
8. When I say unto the wicked, O wicked man, thou shalt surely die; if thou dost not speak to warn the wicked from his way, that wicked man shall die in his iniquity; but his blood will I require at thine hand.
9. Nevertheless, if thou warn the wicked of his way to turn from it; if he do not turn from his way, he shall die in his iniquity; but thou hast delivered thy soul.

External Factors: 2. Competition.—The policy of a competitor ought not to determine the editorial attitude of a newspaper, and today it seldom does. Yet the tendency persists for editors to study their competitors' policies with reference to their own. In some American cities there is still observable the phenomenon of one newspaper adopting a negative attitude toward a particular proposal simply because its competitor has adopted a positive policy, and *vice versa*. This policy may be traced to either of two motives. The first is a desire to prevent the competing paper from obtaining credit for the success of a particular program. This motive, how-

---

[57] Talcott Williams, *The Newspaper Man*, pp. 33-34.

ever, does not result in the newspaper openly opposing the policy of its competitor as often as it results in its adopting a policy of noncoöperation, of silence, or of damning by faint praise.

The second motive is not so palpable to the layman. It is the recognition by the newspaper of the fact that profit and influence will accrue from its posing as the champion of a group that is antagonistic to the policy advocated by the competing newspaper. Realizing that readers even today are divided into opinion groups, some newspapers try to make themselves the representative of a particular reader constituency. An excellent illustration of this policy was the attitude of Mr. Hearst's New York *Journal* during the presidential election of 1896. In the opposition of all of the other New York newspapers to Bryan's candidacy, Mr. Hearst saw an opportunity to make the *Journal* the leading Democratic newspaper of the country.[58] Entering also as a factor in the decision of a newspaper to adopt a policy contrary to that of its competitor is the desire to exploit the reader's interest in a conflict; a large section of the public delights to read charges and countercharges, criminations and recriminations; it must have its St. Georges and its Satans.

External Factors: 3. Economic Pressure and Subsidy.— The question of the external control of editorial policy through economic pressure or subsidy has already been touched upon in preceding sections. The question, naturally, is a subtle one, but sufficient evidence is available to justify our making a few generalizations.

In the first place, actual subsidy of a metropolitan newspaper can be said not to exist. One seldom hears of a subsidized newspaper or of an effort made to subsidize a newspaper. The very commercialization of the press has freed it from reliance on subsidy by a political party or a business interest. Few of the business men who have the desire to deceive the public are so ignorant as to believe that the public can be influenced by a subsidized newspaper. The Bourne Law of 1912, which requires semi-annual postal statements, makes it ex-

---

[58] John K. Winkler, *Hearst: An American Phenomenon*, pp. 122-123.

tremely difficult for a subsidy to be concealed, and the public, being aware of the source of opinions expressed in a subsidized newspaper, are not influenced by them.[59]

In the second place, advertisers, when they desire to do so, exert very effective pressure on the majority of small dailies and country weeklies. The publisher of the small newspaper frequently lacks the fine sense of understanding of the place of the press in society that the more important publishers have acquired. Because of his lack of education, his lack of stimulation through broad contacts, and the necessity for his performing so much routine work, the small publisher often has the soul of the merchant. He does not comprehend, moreover, that he can best serve his self-interest by resisting an advertiser's pressure. Although there is no real necessity for a publisher to acquiesce in the unethical demands of advertisers (the sanctions of "business ethics" usually decree that the honest publisher is more successful than the publisher who acquiesces), many small publishers are so human as to tire of the continual pestering by advertisers and grant their demands in much the same manner as they would give in to a nagging wife or child.

As to the economic pressure directed against metropolitan newspapers, no generalization is a sufficient explanation. Only a thorough case study could produce sufficient evidence to justify general conclusions. From time to time we hear of newspapers being influenced by banks, and of boycotts organized by department stores. It is doubtful if the editorial policy of the great newspapers is often affected by the newspapers' relations with advertisers, but the indifference of newspapers to some of the dangers in our materialistic age and the policy of refraining from the exposure of certain sharp practices in finance and commerce which are indulged in by private corporations is doubtless due to the publishers' unreflective acceptance of the ethics of modern business. This point, which is probably the chief explanation of a situation which lay critics of the press find so easy to "explain," is discussed by Mr. John T.

[59] For an exception, see Oswald Garrison Villard, *The Press Today*, Chap. VIII.

Flynn, former managing editor of the now defunct New York *Globe:*

> The newspaper today represents the interests of the advertiser. It represents the commercial civilization which the advertiser supports and fashions. . . .
> To all this the average publisher replies feelingly that no advertiser would dare to dictate the policy of his paper. That is true. The publisher is under the influence not of the advertiser but of *advertising.* Of course the advertiser does not tell him what not to print. But because his paper lives by it, the publisher knows there are certain subjects he must not touch. He may think he is right when he says he is free. What he overlooks is that he himself is the product of this system.[60]

THE NEWSPAPER AND COMMUNITY CONFLICT

In its rôle of reporter, the newspaper emphasizes conflict; for the best news story is the one that describes a struggle.[61] In its rôle of leader, however, the newspaper ought to strive to minimize conflict in the local community whenever it is obvious that the conflict is socially wasteful. Conflicts, for example, between racial and religious groups in the local community ought not to end in the superordination of one group and the subordination of the other: they ought to end in accommodation. The newspaper, as one of the agencies of social control, ought to lend its influence toward such solutions. As to the precise rôle that the newspaper should assume in other types of conflict and in those conflicts which take place on the outer fringes of the reader's environment, no rule can be laid down; for we have not yet arrived at an understanding of all the factors in society which make for maladjustment, and we know even less about how to control them.[62] The fol-

---

[60] "News by Courtesy," *Forum,* Vol. LXXXIII, p. 140.

[61] "Human nature demands the stimulating effect of conflict, thrives on issues, problems and the clash of opinions. This is vividly illustrated by the fact that whenever a community lacks something big to talk about it will invariably work itself into a passion over something little. . . . France turns from the reparations problem to a discussion of bathing suits, and with quite as much zest. . . . We are quite as apt to get excited over a neighborhood scandal as an international controversy."— New York *Telegram.*

[62] For a fundamental guide, the editor should consult the procedure suggested in Walter Lippmann, *The Phantom Public.*

lowing discussion, therefore, is concerned only with the newspaper's relation to conflict within the local community and that type of conflict which is socially wasteful.

How Conflict Arises.—A community conflict usually arises in this manner: A new policy or a readjustment is suggested. The party that proposes it does so in a manner which provokes dissent. The parties who are provoked to dissent (persons, groups) react in a manner which provokes a distrust in the proposing party. Thus a circular behavior ensues which mounts in intensity. As the conflict proceeds, the original suggestion becomes confused with collateral issues. Other groups are drawn into the conflict. Old sores are reopened. Irrelevancies creep in. Attitudes harden.

The Rôle of the Newspaper.—In such conflicts, the newspaper can act in at least four ways that are socially useful:

1. *The newspaper can try, during the course of a conflict, to keep the debate centered on the intrinsic issues.* It can rebuke (usually without calling names) those who deliberately bring in irrelevancies and collateral issues.

Example.—Ames and Marlowe had been warm friends since Marlowe, as President of the Board of Education in Crowellton, had sponsored the move to invite Ames to take the job of Superintendent of Schools in the town. But difficulties soon arose: A teacher had been discharged for immoral conduct, both Ames and Marlowe concurring in the discharge. Later, however, Marlowe was won to sympathy by a visit from the young woman's father and asked Ames to take her back. Ames, standing firm upon his original decision, refused. Marlowe pressed; Ames grew adamant. The old cordial relationship between the two men now became strained. Marlowe was reported to have said that he would "get Ames" and clamored for his dismissal. The dispute between the faction supporting Ames and that behind Marlowe then ramified to every phase of the community life. Several years before, there had been considerable heat aroused over the choice of the site of the new school building. Marlow had favored the site which was finally chosen. Those who had likewise favored it now took up the battle against Ames, while those who had opposed it came to Ames' support. Similarly, Marlowe's intimacy with the Kleagle of the Klan brought the Klan forces to his side, and turned the Catholics to the support of Ames, though he was himself a Presbyterian. At the same time, Baker, an old political rival of Marlowe from the other side of the town, came to the defense of Ames with his colleagues, and the situation was further involved by local political intrigues. Enemies of long standing took sides with whomever the other happened to oppose. The original question [i.e., the dismissal of Ames] . . . ceased almost at once to be the chief factor in determining alignments.[63]

2. *The newspaper can act at every stage of the conflict to minimize the importance of certain acts and declarations so that both sides will be able to "save face."* One side to a controversy can become so committed to a plan that its *amour propre* forbids that it compromise or give in. (This fact is just as significant in the world community as in the local community. A small question is permitted to assume the proportions of a question of "national honor.")

Example.—The town of Marvin had been split for months over the necessity of changing the zoning and building regulations as a result of the influx of large numbers from the near-by city. The old home-owners fought all change in an effort to hold fast to the charm and leisureliness of the olden days. Merchants and real estate operators sought to build apartments in order to attract new residents, to stimulate trade, and to increase business. The old zoning commission had intensified the conflict; the backs of the Board of Aldermen were up. They resented the peremptory demands of the commission and the notices of the press which exposed them to public criticism before time had been given them to examine the recommendations. Bitterness grew until at length the commission was appointed. It was composed of some of the members of the earlier commission; but the chairman, who had antagonized the board, was replaced by a more temperate, detached spirit. His plan of procedure effected a change at once; no releases were given to the press until after they had been submitted to the board. The old attitude of superiority was abandoned. In its place came an assumption of unity of aim and comradeship which was carried out to its least implication. The members of the commission became "the boys" to the aldermen; they discarded their polished phrases for the homely talk of the City Hall, and were met with friendliness and confidence which smoothed the way for the suggested changes. Although the commission derived from the county legal power to enforce these changes, this power was never mentioned, much less resorted to. They moved slowly, taking the

[63] *Community Conflict* (Preliminary edition), pp. 71-72; reprinted by permission of The Inquiry.

board along with them in their thinking, discussing all situations with them. When the old conflict attitudes between the board and themselves had died down, they were able to proceed to the essential issues between the home owners and the merchants. Their budget was tripled by the board, making it possible for them to employ experts to draw up a master plan. This plan provided for the development of the town at logical points, such as railroad centers, thoroughfares, etc. Important streets were to be widened, and all future buildings would be made to conform to a general plan. Apartment houses were not decried in themselves, but were seen as economic necessities for some types of small family, and when properly placed, fitted into the plan. In this way, the charm of the residential section was safeguarded, the false economy of creating a business section many times too large for this type of community was recognized, at the same time that far-sighted growth was encouraged.[64]

3. *The newspaper can determine and point out those who are representing private interest as being identical with public interest, and try to align the public against them.* Mr. Lippmann believes this is about the only rule that can be applied to resolve industrial and international conflict.[65]

Example.—The small town of B. saw a bitter struggle over the building of a new school auditorium. The superintendent came out in favor of the auditorium, not only for the school but for the town meeting as well. Every public meeting that didn't properly belong in the churches had to be held in an old fire-trap, called the opera-house. Although the auditorium was finally built, the proposal stirred trouble. The man who owned the opera-house had five brothers in town and more cousins than you can count. He had been making five dollars a night renting his hall. Once there was a free meeting-place there would be less business. So he got his father-in-law elected on the school board. He stirred up his whole family, and they fought. They called it a fight against additional taxes, but behind that was a fight to make five dollars a meeting for the owner of the opera-house.[66]

4. *The newspaper can refrain from intervening in a conflict when there is no good purpose to be served.* Now that sincere community leaders have learned more about the technique of

64 *Ibid.*, pp. 91-93; reprinted by permission.
65 *The Phantom Public, passim.*
66 *Community Conflict*, pp. 65-66; reprinted by permission.

conference and have come to appreciate the harm involved in conflict, most incipient conflicts can be settled in early stages without resort to publicity.

Example.—In Banning, an aristocratic colony near a large Eastern city, prevailing harmony was disrupted when a local community house was established and it was decided to exclude from membership in the house the colored boys, many of whom were participating freely and winning honors in the activities of the local high school. The reason given by the board was the fear of jeopardizing the building campaign then in progress, and the colored group was asked to wait until some plan could be worked out. They waited for a year and when no action appeared forthcoming, one of the leaders wrote a letter to the local paper demanding a declaration of policy on the part of the board. There followed several days' controversy in the columns of the paper in which the points made by the colored leader were not disproved and several letters from white sympathizers came to his support. Yet the incident achieved no alteration in the minds of the board members. From that time on the board declared that the colored group had broken the pledge to wait for their decision. And they have since refused to consider the problem of colored membership.[67]

Leadership Based on Knowledge.—The newspaper editor ought to understand community organization—the group anatomy of his community and the types of leadership in it.[68]

---

[67] *Ibid.*, pp. 50-51; reprinted by permission.

[68] The most significant classification of types of urban groups is that made by Nels Anderson and E. C. Lindeman:

1. Functional groups, organized primarily on behalf of a specific and objective interest: trade unions, manufacturers' associations, chambers of commerce, etc. (Conflict groups.)

2. Occupational groups, organized on behalf of a professional interest, but less concerned with directly objective issues: medical societies, engineering societies, etc.

3. Philanthropic and reform groups: organized to protect the unfortunate members of society, or to propagate such constitutional changes as will improve society.

4. Religious groups: held together by virtue of a common subjective goal of interest.

5. Nationality groups: clusters of immigrants who fall into natural groups because of language, culture, etc.

6. Memory groups: organized for the purpose of projecting a past experience (pleasant or unpleasant at the time but somehow since risen to importance) into the present and future: war veteran societies, alumni associations, etc.

7. Symbolic groups: formed about a set of symbolisms or rituals which

He ought to understand human nature. He ought to analyze the community's needs and the agencies available for realizing the needs.[69] He ought to keep informed about improvements and conflicts in other communities so as to apply their lessons in his own community. If the editor has this social knowledge, he will be in a position to interpret what is the community's purpose with reference to the various proposals that are made for improvement and readjustment.

---

often are valued in direct proportion to their inappropriateness to the present environment: lodges, fraternal societies, secret societies.

8. Service-recreational groups: informally organized about the wish for playful adult activity coupled with a sense of doing good: Rotary, Kiwanis, Lions, etc.

9. Political groups: clubs or societies which are often, at least in part, memory groups, but which exist for the purpose of perpetuating a set of political principles: Tammany Hall, Jefferson Clubs, Lincoln Clubs, etc.

10. Feminist groups: women organized in the interest of cultural, educational, civic purposes: women's clubs, leagues for women voters, etc.

11. Atypical groups: groups which exist in all cities, and lend color to the urban scene, but which must be regarded as departures from the norm; on the positive side, bohemians, intellectuals, esthetic groups, etc.; and on the negative side, "gangs," or groups organized for effective law v olation.—*Urban Sociology* (Alfred A. Knopf), pp. 298-299; reprinted by permission.

The following references are helpful: J. F. Steiner, *Community Organization* and *The American Community in Action;* W. Pettit, *Case Studies in Community Organization;* R. M. Maciver, *Community.*

[69] See E. C. Lindeman, *The Community,* and R, S, and H. M. Lynd, *Middletown.*

CHAPTER XV

THE STRUCTURE OF THE EDITORIAL

The Structural Pattern.—When the student prepares to write his first editorial, he is usually confused by the lack of a few standard patterns which he may imitate. Sitting down to write, he explores his memory in vain in an effort to recall the set form of one or more editorials he has read. If he has read many editorials attentively so that some of them have remained in his consciousness, he usually produces a fair imitation of conventional editorial expression. Upon analysis, however, he observes that the effect he has striven for and in some measure achieved has been the result not of imitating a particular structural pattern, but rather the result of imitating the conventional editorial style and editorial tone. Strictly, there are no formal requirements as to the structure of an editorial as there are with regard to some of the other literary forms. But tentatively, for the purpose of assisting the novice in analyzing editorial technique, it is possible to classify editorials according to their structure.

A Simple Pattern.—The editorial pattern is the simplest of literary forms. It is simpler, of course, than the various narrative forms, and even simpler than the other journalistic essay forms such as the special feature article and the news story. Lacking the elements of narrative and description, the editorial need follow only a logical course from the opening sentence to the final sentence. It frequently consists of nothing more than the statement of a subject and a comment about the subject, as in the following example:

Subject Stated

A vigorous campaign by the St. Louis Chamber of Commerce resulted yesterday in the voting of a $2,000,000 bond issue for the establishment of a municipal airport.

The example might well be followed by the Chicago Association of Commerce. The

338

Comment | talk of Chicago public officials has been getting us nowhere; the "plan" for an island airport off Grant Park is moribund. But the vigorous support of the Association of Commerce would be of great value in compelling public officials to a realization of their duty and opportunity.

The foregoing editorial consists of nothing more than comment hung upon a "news-peg." This is the form that many editorials assume, the chief variation being a division of the comment into sections arranged in the order that is most likely to penetrate the reader's mind—that is to say, in a logical manner.

The following examples illustrate a simple structural pattern:

(1)

According to advices from Havana the Cuban Government proposes to remove restrictions on the sugar crop for 1928-29. The proposal at once meets with sharp criticism from Royal D. Mead, an official of the Domestic Sugar Producers' Association. Mr. Mead is alarmed over the possibility that cheap Cuban sugar will flood the country to the ruination of domestic production. Therefore, he warns that the Cuban proposal should be met by removing Cuba's preferential tariff or by increasing the tariff rates.

It seems the irony of fate that no sooner is a proposal put forward to save the consumer money than some one rises to present cogent reasons why that saving cannot be allowed. It is the case, not only with sugar but with other staple products and manufactures. It would seem invariably that the welfare of the country rests upon the consumer buying from the domestic producer in a protected market. Perhaps the high price of sugar is a good thing. But it does seem a pity that once in a while the welfare of the country cannot depend upon the consumer saving money on the things he has to buy.—BALTIMORE *Evening Sun.*

(2)

> "My message to Mr. Strawn and his millionaire clients, the bankers, is that in his program to destroy the confidence of the people in elected public officials he is sowing the seed of Communism."—ALD. OSCAR F. NELSON, (46th).
>
> "The public officials will never get together with Strawn. They will not stand for creating a lack of confidence in the elected officials. It is improper that public distrust of public officials should be built up."—H. WALLACE CALDWELL OF THE BOARD OF EDUCATION.
>
> This requires words by Gilbert and music by Sullivan.—CHICAGO *Tribune.*

A More Complex Pattern.—Sometimes, however, editorials may be said to consist of three separate parts: (1) the statement of the subject; (2) the expansion of the subject by means of comment; and (3) an application or conclusion drawn from the comment. The following editorial from the Chicago *Tribune* is an example:

1. Subject Stated

> Judge Thompson, the Democratic candidate for governor, is making a determined campaign for votes by the direct method of appearing before audiences—groups as large as can be corralled by the local organizations—to project his thoughts about himself, about Mr. Emmerson, and about an administration as it would be conducted under a Thompson régime.
>
> Mr. Emmerson, the Republican nominee, is making an equally determined campaign for votes, thus far by the more indirect method of appearing before groups of precinct captains, chairmen of county committees, and other titled Republicans, to project his thoughts about himself, about Judge Thompson, and about an administration as it would be conducted under an Emmerson régime.
>
> Whether the candidates have selected these

diverse methods of campaigning or whether they are proceeding under the direction of political advisers, each seems to be following a system dictated by his own capabilities. Judge Thompson is a facile student of forensics. He warms to his subject, improvising now diatribes, now encomiums, with oratorical feeling. He has the ability to swing votes by oratory.

2. Expansion of subject by comment

Mr. Emmerson excels, perhaps, in directing a campaign by more intimate and casual contact. The platform rapture of the younger man is somewhat lacking in Mr. Emmerson's manner, and his custom of reading his address detracts from its delivery. Among a group of party workers, however, he is skillful and confident. In such a capacity he fits easily into the rôle of the chairman of the board directing a meeting of directors.

3. Application:
(a) Both methods of campaigning are satisfactory to party enthusiasts

(b) But Emmerson ought to discuss the issues of the campaign

We have no quarrel with either method of campaigning. Both candidates seem to be conscientiously busy in collecting votes for their own advantage. Party leaders and party enthusiasts in the state should be gratified at the zeal of their respective candidates.

We are confident that Mr. Emmerson will, during the course of the campaign, make public appearances to discuss freely and fully the issues of the contest. Although he may be deficient in spontaneous eloquence, the electorate is entitled to hear from his own lips a statement of the management he expects to give to Illinois and a complete discussion of his past and present attitude to the disorders of the Small administration.

The following are examples of a more complex structural pattern:

(1)

A short paragraph reported the death of James Ryan, a mailman with a defective heart, from overexertion in carrying the Christmas mail.

The letter carriers perform their services

unobtrusively and we are disposed to take them for granted. But the fate of Mailman Ryan should cause the citizens to reflect on the hardships of these loyal government employes. It is well to remember that the physical burden of the work increases with the hazard of the weather.

The mailmen are not adequately compensated for their responsible and often arduous service. That injustice should be corrected, and there is before Congress a bill for an increased pay schedule among postal employes which will correct it, if it is adopted. That is an expense which the nation can well afford.—CHICAGO *Tribune.*

(2)

The headlines read, "Small to give Lincoln Park board to mayor." A good head, because a copy reader is not supposed to editorialize.

But what it might have said was, "Small to sell Lincoln Park board to mayor." There is nothing philanthropic about it; there never is. Politics as played by the gentlemen in question is a business and both are shrewd bargainers.

Small, so says the political talk, will meet Thompson's demand that he split with Lundin to the extent of letting the mayor name the head of the Lincoln Park board and one commissioner. Furthermore, he will give the word that the Thompson president of the board is to be the boss. That is what Small has to offer.

On Thompson's part is offered doubtless the support of the Chicago administration machine for Small's third term campaign. It is barter and trade, and report has it that the deal is on.

It is a buying and selling proposition, but with this characteristic. In the end the public foots the bill.—CHICAGO *Tribune.*

Editorials that develop an idea by the use of concrete assertions, apt examples, and literary references are more interesting than editorials that omit these units, but the editorial writer must guard against expansion of an idea to any great length. Success in editorial writing is often due to the ability of the writer to compress a great deal of argument into a small space and at the same time give it concreteness. Care in preliminary planning often helps to achieve this objective.

Directness and Compactness.—The simplicity of editorial structure does not imply, however, that the writing of editorials is an easy task. What gives the editorial its conventional form—that is to say, what makes it effective—is not the structure alone, but the skill of the writer in achieving directness and compactness. The ordinary editorial does not weave in and out and around a central theme or a "thread of interest," as in a short story or a special feature article; and it does not pack all of its interest in the beginning, as the news story does. The editorial leaves its mark and marches logically on-

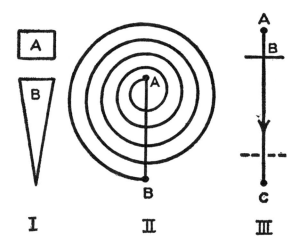

ward in a straight path to its objective. There it halts abruptly. The accompanying diagrams contrast, in an inadequate way, the directness of the editorial with the news story and the special feature article.

The conventional news story (Fig. I) states the important facts in the "lead," then proceeds to give the details in the order of their interest until the least interesting detail has been related. The conventional special feature article (Fig. II), like the editorial, begins at a point (*A*) and travels toward an ending (*B*). But it does not travel in a straight line; the straight line (*AB*) is the "thread of interest," and the actual story weaves around the "thread of interest" so that characterization, explanation, and anecdote may be included. It always comes back to the "thread of interest" at some point in time to prevent the reader from losing interest in the article. The editorial (Fig. III) travels straight from its beginning (*A*) to its ending (*C*). It has a beginning (*AB*) somewhat similar to the "lead" of a news story, but after the subject has been announced it progresses logically step by step to its conclusion. The conclusion (*C*) may, or may not, be a separate element in the structure. In the simple form of editorial, the conclusion is integral with the second or amplifying part (*BC*) and is not distinguishable from it; but in the complex editorial it is frequently a distinct third division.

Editorials are effective chiefly because of their directness and compactness. The effective editorial is closely reasoned and compactly written. To write it requires a great deal of practice in the marshaling of one's ideas, a considerable amount of preliminary analysis, and a knowledge of how the reader's mind works in the absorbing of connected ideas. The editorial usually tries to make one point—and only one.

Beginning the Editorial.—Nearly all editorials begin with the statement of the subject. Usually the subject concerns a current event, and the beginning paragraph announces the event in much the manner of a news story "lead." Editorial writers call this kind of beginning a "news-peg" beginning. Some examples follow:

(1)

A sentence of two to fourteen years in the penitentiary and a fine of $1,000 has been imposed upon William Nelson of Hammond, Indiana, who was convicted of conspiracy to bomb his own motion picture theatre. . . .

(2)

John Steele [a special correspondent] reports that the Amir of Afghanistan is about to visit London, a bit of news more significant than the casual American reader will realize. . . .

(3)

The announcement that the oil companies owning wells in the western hemisphere are uniting on a program of conservation will cause a good deal of eye rubbing. . . .

Sometimes, however, it is assumed that the reader has knowledge of an event that is still in progress, and there is no need for the beginning to be specific. Examples follow:

(1)

America had better look to her sport titles. A few years ago every newspaper in the country proudly flaunted the fact that Americans were supreme in every field of sport, amateur and professional. [Written at the time when "Bobby" Jones, "Bill" Tilden, and the American channel swimmers were losing their titles and records to European athletes.]

(2)

At this writing Kansas is still negotiating with the forward looking convicts who want a brighter social life. The incident seems to be peculiarly one of the American scene, etc. [Convicts in a Kansas state prison had been "on strike" for several days and had barricaded themselves against attacks by guards because of the alleged poor food and tobacco furnished them.]

In an argumentative editorial that is based on an event, the writer sometimes states the proposition he is going to prove in the same sentence or paragraph in which he announces the "news-peg." The following are examples:

(1)

The state department should not let up
until it has obtained complete satisfaction
from France for her treatment of Harold
Horan, Paris correspondent for the Hearst
newspapers. Suddenly set upon at one of
the busiest corners of the French capital, the
American correspondent was hustled off and
held incommunicado for more than seven
hours while the secret police subjected him
to inquisition. . . .

(2)

Let it be said no more that the intelligence
of the war department is muscle-bound or
otherwise incapacitated. It has proved its
ability to learn by experience. Three times
in as many years it has attempted to organize
a Mobilization Day, with attending unpleas-
antness, opposition, and indifferent results.
Three being a perfect number, it is now
satisfied the endeavor is a mistaken one. Announcement is made that there will be no
Mobilization Day this year. The effort has
been abandoned. . . .

(3)

It so happens that it is Volsteadism which
is responsible for the charges of police graft
and corruption in the city of Philadelphia. . . .

(4)

There can be nothing but condemnation for
the United States treasury department em-
ploye who gave out information as to the
amount of tax that Colonel Lindbergh paid,
indicating approximately the income he received last year. The proceeding was most
underhand. . . .

The element of timeliness is almost indispensable in editorials.
Some editorials are nothing more than news reviews with a
fresh slant given to the news by the editorial writer. Some
newspapers have adopted a policy of trying to make their

editorial pages as fresh and newsy as their front pages, selecting for editorial subjects only those events and subjects which they believe the public is interested in at the time, and treating them in a newsy and interesting manner. It has been said by a professor of applied psychology that the most powerful words in our language are "now" and "new." If the statement is true, it justifies the policy of that particular school of editors which aims primarily at furnishing a newsy editorial page.

Many editors, however, do not construct their editorial pages upon the newsy principle. Newspapers that have specific policies or platforms which require many years of discussion to realize devote a considerable portion of their space to advocating their proposals and principles regardless of whether or not the editorial subjects furnish a news-peg upon which to hang editorial comment. When such editorials are written, they usually begin with the statement of the subject or the proposition that is to be discussed. Sometimes the subject is merely a restatement of the principle or proposal that the newspaper is advocating, but frequently it is a new aspect of the same subject. Examples follow:

(1)

The old saying, "loan a man your money and you lose his friendship," cannot aptly be illustrated in the war debt controversy between France and the United States, as so many think it can. . . .

(2)

Whether or not Baltimore should spend $2,500,000 for park purposes is not a matter for the legislature to decide. It is the just right of this city. . . .

There are no specific rules about how to begin an editorial. The conventional beginning, which has been described in foregoing paragraphs, is the best beginning because it is simplest. In the editorial, the purpose of the beginning is not, as in the beginning of a special feature article or in the title of an advertisement, to attract the reader's attention or to arouse his interest. The assumption is that no "entering wedge" need be driven into the reader's mind as is necessary in long articles and in advertisements. The purpose of the beginning of an editorial is simply to state the subject; if the comment that follows is interesting, the reader will be pleased; but if the comment is uninteresting, then an attention-getting, interest-arousing beginning will not make the reader more pleased.

A clever or witty or whimsical beginning is absolutely necessary in only one instance: when the editorial is to be written in an unconventional manner or in an unconventional tone the writer should give the reader a signal at the beginning to indicate that the editorial is to be ironical, sarcastic, mock-serious, or whimsical. In such an instance, the beginning sets the tone for the whole editorial and serves the same purpose as does the opening of a symphony composition or of a narrative of atmosphere.

The Ending.—Technically, the editorial pattern does not require a separate division called an ending. For the sake of unity, however, the editorial cannot usually be permitted just to taper off at the last sentence. There must be a logical stopping place.

Unity in the editorial is most frequently obtained by the use of an ending that *sums up* the editorial. Ordinarily, the summary ending tries to clinch as well as to summarize the points the writer has been discussing, and frequently it tries to reduce the writer's arguments to a single pungent statement, usually an epigram, an analogy, a rhetorical question, or an otherwise clever and forcible expression. The chief requisite of an effective editorial is that the ending have "punch," that it drive home the point the editorial is trying to make. Some examples follow:

(1)

With reference to the political principles held by two rival candidates for President of Nicaragua, one of whom called himself a "Liberal," the other a "Conservative":

> The difference between Sacasa and Diaz is less than the difference between Tweedle-dum and Tweedle-dee.

(2)

With reference to a proposed solution of Chicago's traffic problem:

> If it is mass hysteria to object to this, then a householder bolting his door at night should be arrested for disorderly conduct.

(3)

With reference to the rebuke to General Summerall implied in President Coolidge recalling him from a speaking tour during which he was critical of the army's administration, and shortly afterward, a compensating promotion in rank:

> Having been sent away from the table as an example to the younger children, his dessert is going to be sent up to him.

(4)

With reference to the increasing use of aspirin:

> Two courses are open to him. He must either stop having headaches or draw up his will.

(5)

With reference to the number of young girls who go to Hollywood to "break into" the "movies":

> The times demand a feministic parallel to Horace Greeley's famous phrase. Here it is: "Young woman, stay home!"

(6)

With reference to the propriety of seriously rebuking Mayor Thompson's censorship of histories in the Chicago public library:

> What use? There isn't any. You cannot argue with a bunk artist.

(7)

In answer to a North Carolina Democrat's criticism of Governor Alfred E. Smith's presidential candidacy in 1928:

> Since when has Senator Simmons become the valiant foe of the "forces of privilege and license"?

(8)

With reference to Mussolini's policy of advocating population increase and its imperialistic implications for Italy:

> Mussolini is swatting the ball over the backfield fence and the outfield will have to be extended.

The summary ending sometimes takes the form of an expressed or implied exhortation to the reader to act in a certain way. An example follows:

With reference to politicians arousing racial prejudice during a local election:

> Let there be as much criticism of unpatriotic sentiment for England, or Germany, or France, or Italy, or Poland, as the case warrants. It is the right of every American to speak his mind. But let his mind be spoken as an American and for the sake of America, not as a German, or an Irishman, or an Italian, or an Englishman, and for the sake of a foreign country.

In a few cases, the final sentence in an editorial is so closely related in thought to the rest of the editorial that it really is not a separate division of the editorial in the sense that it summarizes the argument or exhorts the reader to act. In such an editorial, the final sentence is usually climactic, and in that sense has "punch." An example from the Decatur (Ill.) *Herald* follows:

> Bruno Bodgon, Chicago boy, told a story of a man who had seized his playmate, Johnny Pyrek, and locked the boy up in a box car. Police and railroad officials, spurred on by the alarm of frantic parents, searched thousands of box cars in the Chicago yards without result.
>
> Bruno, confronted with the fact that his story would not hold water, promptly presented another one. The Pyrek boy was not put into a box car, he said. That was all a mistake. He was playing on the side of

a sand pile, when the sand began to slide down and covered him over. Immediately volunteers and paid workers attacked the gigantic sand pile. A steam shovel was brought up. Ten thousand tons of sand was moved, without uncovering a trace of the boy.

Now Bruno Bodgon, undismayed and resourceful as ever, retracts both previous statements and assures the police that Johnny Pyrek was drowned in the river. Dragging of the river has begun.

There is no doubt at all that the changeable nature of Bruno's testimony is very annoying to the Chicago police. Probably he has been told that he is a bad boy and that if he persists in such conduct he will come to a bad end. Bruno might admit the first part of the statement with a smile. The prediction about his future he could set aside by appeal to distinguished precedent. "I am preparing," he might say, "to grow up and be head of a big oil company."

The Title.—The chief purpose of the title is to tell the reader the subject of the editorial. A secondary purpose is to arouse the reader's interest. Whenever possible, the two purposes ought to be combined. The writer, in his effort to be clever, ought not, however, to conceal the subject of the editorial in a pun or other kind of clever phrase, especially if the editorial is an important one.

The conventional title is one which merely tells what the editorial is about. Whenever the subject is of importance, it is assumed by the writer that the reader will be interested in reading the editorial. Such titles are "The Maine Election," "Mr. Hoover's Acceptance Speech," and "The Chinese Treaties." Sometimes, however, the subject cannot be stated in a short title, and the title can only suggest the subject, as, for example, "M. Briand Salutes Mr. Kellogg," and "Soviet Russia Condescends." Illustrating how varied are the titles placed upon an identical subject are the following titles of editorials that discussed Henry Ford's apology for his attack upon Jews:

"Amende Honorable"
"A Gain for Tolerance"
"Mr. Ford in Reverse"
"The Ford Retractor"
"Creditable Recantation"
"Henry Ford Can Change"
"Henry Ford Owns Up"
"A Needed Repudiation"

The titles in each instance reflect the tone of the particular editorial, some of which rejoiced in Mr. Ford's high sense of honor, some of which criticized his original lack of sense in attacking the Jewish race, and some of which hinted that the purpose of the retraction was to sell more Ford automobiles.

Editorial Style.—It is not the structural matter, we repeat, that is so important in editorial writing. Of more importance is editorial style. We turn to that subject in the following chapter.

CHAPTER XVI

EDITORIAL STYLE

Considered as a literary form, the editorial is a special form of the essay. More particularly, it is a journalistic essay: its subject matter is concerned with the events of today. This definition does not imply, however, that the editorial treats of purely ephemeral matters. Its subject matter, although of contemporary interest because of the focus of the news of the day, may have its roots in the past and its sequel in the future. It is, in other words, a *serious comment in essay form about those present happenings which are important and significant to society.* Such happenings concern policies of government, social problems, economic phenomena, international relations, and many other matters of public and quasipublic concern.[1]

The editorial, of course, is not the only kind of journalistic essay. The news story, for example, is an essay which combines the elements of exposition and narration but which seldom contains opinion; the special feature article is an essay which combines the same two elements of style, but is longer, contains little or no opinion, and is a looser and freer form of composition. The editorial, however, is a compact essay of exposition or argumentation, is seldom more than three or four hundred words in length, contains virtually no elements of narration, and represents the opinion of an institution—the newspaper—rather than that of the individual writer.

This definition of the editorial as a journalistic essay and the foregoing differentiation of the types of journalistic essay do not, however, define the editorial with the exactness that is necessary. What finally gives the term *editorial* a distinctive

---

[1] This definition does not take into account the entertaining type of editorial; that type is discussed in the next chapter. In all other sections of this book, only the serious editorial about public affairs is discussed.

meaning is not merely the form of its composition, but the tone or manner.

Editorial Manner.—Every literary composition has a distinctive tone. A sermon, for example, does not have the tone of a textbook, and a textbook does not sound like an editorial. The tone of a literary composition is determined, in the last analysis, by two factors, namely, the character of the subject matter discussed and the point of view of the writer. The subject matter of editorials is concerned with disarmament conferences, legislative proposals, public engineering projects, diplomatic notes, etc.; the point of view of the writer results from the fact that he is expressing not his own opinion but that of a respected institution and from the fact that he poses as a leader and teacher. Both the character of the subject matter discussed and the point of view of the writer determine that the editorial shall be *judicial* and *authoritative* in manner.[2]

Since the editorial writer's style is conditioned by his responsibility to the reader for interpretation and leadership, he does not express himself in the manner of an evangelist exhorting sinners, or like a college professor shaking his gray beard at his students, or like Mr. Will Rogers "wisecracking" flippancy and homely philosophy, or like the editor of the *American Mercury* clubbing his opponents on their heads. He seldom writes with religious fervor or with righteous indignation or with his tongue in his cheek. He does not pretend to infallibility. Yet he poses as an authority and expects his opinions to be respected; he discourses about serious matters and expects to be taken seriously; he expresses the opinions of a composite entity—the newspaper—not the opinions of a free-lance. He is, in other words, judicial and dignified, but not didactic or pedantic; he is positive, but not oracular or cocksure; he is

---

[2] When we say that the editorial writer expresses the opinion of his newspaper rather than his personal opinion, we are, to some extent, idealizing the situation. Quite often the editorial writer does not express the opinion of the editorial council, but his personal opinion; and, in some instances, he even expresses the personal opinion of a superior. Nevertheless, editorial manner must be authoritative. What the judge, the preacher, and the philosopher say has the ring of authority because they are wrapped in the robes of authority, and—in the case of the judge and the preacher—because they pretend to speak for an entity which transcends their personality. Yet what they say is only their personal opinion.

dynamic and earnest, but he does not write "at the top of his voice."

The Qualities of Editorial Style.—The textbooks that treat of composition and rhetoric list three qualities of style: clearness, force, and beauty (sometimes called elegance or ease). This last quality is ordinarily absent from journalistic composition, but clearness and force are its distinguishing characteristics. In the news story and frequently in the special feature article, force is subordinated in the effort to obtain clearness; and in the editorial composition, clearness is by no means lacking. Clearness is requisite to journalistic writing because the journalistic composition is addressed to an audience of busy and indifferent readers upon whom there is no compulsion to read slowly and carefully. Clearness is obtained by the use of short paragraphs, short and medium-length sentences, anticlimactic sentences and paragraphs, simple words and—sometimes—colloquial words and expressions. Nearly the whole effort in some forms of journalistic composition— notably the news story—is directed toward making the composition intelligible and adaptable to rapid reading. In editorial writing, however, though clearness is necessary, it is not the most important quality of style. The quality that differentiates the editorial as a literary composition, the quality that helps to create the editorial tone, is force.

Force.—In the editorial office of a certain New York newspaper hangs a framed legend which is supposed to provide the chief rule and challenge for those who write the newspaper. It proclaims, "They Don't Want to Read It," which, interpreted, means, "Most of our readers are busy, tired, or indifferent people without much background of knowledge of public affairs; they are not going to read and enjoy and continue to buy our newspaper if the news stories and editorials are not written in a plain and easy style and if they have no stimulus or animation." Translated into classroom jargon, the legend means, "Strive for clearness and force." By force is meant that quality of discourse which gives vigor and virility to style, which attracts and holds the reader's interest. Clearness means merely writing intelligibly; force means stimulating the reader's interest by requiring him to use his own intellect as he reads. For example, Emerson's maxim, "Hitch your wagon to a star!" while at first not intelligible, becomes, upon slight reflection, more stimulating than an extended discourse advising the reader to "aim at the unattainable so that your work will have an ideal direction even though it never achieves perfection"; the very brevity and unusualness of Emerson's statement, and the figurative expression given to it, stimulate even the dull mind and make an idea imprcssive that might not otherwise have sunk into the consciousness. This is what is meant by force.

Vigor.—A characteristic of force that is evident in editorial writing is vigor. Vigor, however, is not the equivalent of force: it is only one characteristic of force. Vigor is one of the chief characteristics of force in editorial composition because editorials are so frequently argumentative and so frequently concerned with moot questions and proposals. Vigor is especially apparent in those newspapers which aim to exert a strong leadership in public affairs.

Some newspapers devote their editorial space almost exclusively to the discussion of policies which the newspaper regards as its special purpose to have adopted—even to the extent of neglecting to comment about many of the important events in the news. Other newspapers have very few pet policies that they advocate, but, instead, use most of their space for an interpretation of nearly all the important events in the daily news; this type of newspaper—at least, the extreme type—as one great editor has remarked, is like a boresome guest at the breakfast table who converses on nearly every subject under the sun. Most editorial pages, however, regardless of the number of subjects that they discuss, aim first at exerting a positive leadership in public affairs. Their editorial style, consequently, is vigorous.

The Instruments of Force.—Force in editorial style is obtained in three ways: (1) by the choice of expression; (2) by the arrangement of words for emphasis; and (3) by the writer's own character for force. Under these headings the textbooks list several methods for obtaining force, but the discussion here will treat of only those methods which affect editorial style.[3] In discussing these methods, we must bear in mind that we are not only discussing literary style in general, but editorial style, and that we must consider at all times the point of view of the writer: that he is writing about contemporary events in flux, that he is expressing the opinion of a corporate entity, that he is writing in the newspaper to a busy and perhaps an indifferent audience, and that he is frequently trying to inculcate his readers with the ideas he is advocating.

1. **Choice of Expression.**—The editorial writer chooses words of brevity and vigor; he usually prefers Anglo-Saxon words to classical words because of their forcible brevity, their plain and simple connotations, and their imitative character.[4]

---

[3] Herbert Spencer, in his essay on "The Philosophy of Style," resolved all the rules that concern force and clearness to the single principle of economy in style, by which he meant that the writer should aim to attain a style which would yield its meaning with a minimum of effort on the part of the reader.

"Regarding language as an apparatus of symbols for the conveyance of thought, we may say that, as in a mechanical apparatus, the more simple and the better arranged its parts, the greater will be the effect produced. In either case, whatever force is absorbed by the machine is deducted from the result. A reader or listener has at each moment but a limited amount of mental power available. To recognize and interpret the symbols presented to him, requires part of this power; to arrange and combine the images suggested requires a further part; and only that part which remains can be used for realizing the thought conveyed. Hence, the more time and attention it takes to receive and understand each sentence, the less time and attention can be given to the contained idea; and the less vividly will that idea be conceived. . . .

"Hence . . . in composition, the chief, if not the sole thing to be done, is, to reduce this friction and inertia to the smallest possible amount. Let us then inquire whether economy of the recipient's attention is not the secret of effect, alike in the right choice and collocation of words, in the best arrangement of clauses in a sentence, in the proper order of its principal and subordinate propositions, in the judicious use of simile, metaphor, and other figures of speech, and even in the rhythmical sequence of syllables."

[4] The necessity for choosing the right expression has no better illustration than the famous "Angel of Death" passage from one of John Bright's speeches—a speech of which Disraeli said, "Bright, I would give all that I ever had to have made that speech." In the middle of a speech denouncing the Crimean War, Bright said, "The Angel of Death has been abroad throughout the land; you may almost hear the beating of his wings." After the speech Cobden said to Bright: "You went very near that time. If you had said '*flapping*' instead of '*beating*' of his wings,' the House would have laughed." But Bright, says his biographer, could no more have said "flapping" than Mr. Gladstone could have made a false quantity (G. M. Trevelyan, *Life of John Bright*, p. 385). The editorial writer must also guard against a *lapsus linguæ*. Many

He prefers specific, concrete words to generic words because of the quick images they evoke.

He chooses, whenever they are in good taste, new and colloquial words because they are the language of the people, rich in connotative meaning. The editorial writer, in this respect, has more license than the literary artist; he can freely and effectively employ the new terms that have popular meaning.

Of the other languages I know little [says H. L. Mencken], but of English I have learned something. Its charms and its infinite complexity, its impenetrable mystery. Do not suspect me of rhetoric when I say that it seems to change from year to year. Or maybe those of us who write it change. We hear new melodies, sometimes far below the staff. We are tripped by strange, occult surprises. A new and rich color appears. . . . My advice, if you would do honor to our incomparable tongue, is that you pay little heed to books, even the best. Listen to it on the street. It is there that it is alive.[5]

The necessity for using in newspaper editorials words of everyday meaning is appreciated if we examine the ponderous style of editorial writing in the last century. In imitation of British leader writers, American editorial writers for a long time seemed to shun vigor, directness, and pungency. The old style, as practiced in England, is well described by J. A. Spender:

In those days the jargon which is called parliamentary style was built up into a kind of professional language. The Member and the Minister used it, and the leader-writer revelled in it. No one ever talked in this way on any subject under the sun except politics, but in politics the use of the common tongue would have been thought a kind of levity which stamped a speaker as a man of vulgar origin.[6]

Charles A. Dana was the first great editor to declare an American independence of this British editorial style,[7] and

unfortunate phrases have undone a fine effort. Woodrow Wilson was often the victim of unfortunate phrases, as, for example, "too proud to fight" and "peace without victory."

[5] Baltimore *Evening Sun*, Sept. 7, 1925.
[6] *The Public Life*, Vol. I, p. 32.
[7] See W. G. Bleyer, *Main Currents in the History of American Journalism*, pp. 296-298.

since Dana's time editorial style is more attuned to the rhythm of American life. The modern editorial has less of Burke and Madison and Macaulay and Jonathan Edwards in it, less of the pulpit, the seminary, and the front-bench well; but it has more of the tone of the street, the office, the factory, and the field. This is not to say that the modern editorial is vulgar or light or crude: it is only livelier, franker, more vigorous, more pungent, more direct.[8]

Not only in the choice of words, but in the choice of longer expressions, the editorial writer employs those which evoke specific images in the mind of the ordinary reader. Frequently these expressions are epigrams and homely analogies which express the writer's thought more forcibly than half a dozen sentences. In choosing these expressions, however, the editorial writer must guard against the use of those which may destroy the tone of his composition; for the use of a single flippant expression within a context of serious discourse may destroy the whole effect that has been built up in the reader's mind. William Allen White, who makes much use of colloquial and bucolic expressions in addressing a rural Kansas audience, succeeds admirably in adapting his expressions to the tone of his composition; the student will profit from studying his editorials.[9]

The following examples from the Chicago *Tribune,* although they have been separated from their context, are effective analogies :

(1)

With reference to the failure of the Geneva naval conference wherein Great Britain, possessing more cruisers than the United States, was not willing to scrap any of them:

> If Great Britain won't cut down its ulster, certainly we are not going to reduce the size of our umbrella.

---

[8] The student who hopes to be an editorial writer ought, by all means, to read Dr. Talcott Williams' chapter on "Newspaper English" in *The Newspaper Man.*

[9] See collection entitled, *The Editor and His People,* selected by Helen O. Mahin.

(2)

With reference to a proposition to give the city of Chicago increased representation in the Illinois State Senate provided the city would agree not to demand more members in the Assembly; suggested by a story once told by Dana:

> It is plain what we'd lose on the damma banan, but where's the assurance of profit on the peanutta?

(3)

With reference to the methods by which professional politicians have turned the direct primary election system to their own advantage:

> For the political leaders the direct primary is coal in the bin and music on the radio. The special session [called to pass a new primary election law] will have the outer garments of high public morality. It is to re-establish the people in their political rights. In fact, it will be to give them back the knife with which they generally whittle their fingers.

(4)

With reference to the 1928 Pan-American Congress at Havana in which it was apparent that the Latin-American nations were as jealous of each other as they were afraid of the United States:

> But the massed attack against us never came. The Latin-American delegates failed to bunch their hits. There was no unity of command. So about all our delegation had to do was to watch its step and to let nature take its course. Even the one admittedly outstanding accomplishment at Havana was mostly cold turkey served over as fancy-looking croquettes.

It is not only by such figures as these that an editorial composition is made effective; the pungency and positiveness of the expression also help. It is from pungency and positiveness that editorials derive their authoritative sound. The editorial writer expresses his opinions without using many "ifs," "buts," and "howevers." He omits, whenever possible, such expressions as "we think that" and "in our opinion," and makes positive affirmations. There is a wide difference, however, between being positive and being dogmatic. The editorial writer uses expressions that carry conviction, but he does not usually give a tone to his expressions that suggests narrow-mindedness and intolerance. Some examples follow:

(1)

Nobody but an idealist expects the movies to be anything but a phase of eastern capital and industrialism.

(2)

Mr. Lewis' theory is interesting. The only trouble with it is that when viewed from the angle of actual results it doesn't hold water.

(3)

This is not the record of a man of principle.

(4)

It was not an agreement to limit armaments; it was an agreement not to limit armaments.

(5)

The members [of the Ku Klux Klan] enjoyed being told they were the intellectual leaders of a great nation. No doubt they really think they are. . . .
The klan, in short, speaks for our rural slums. Its tactics and its ideology reflect its origin. Its pretensions to leadership in American thought will not be taken seriously outside the narrow circle of its membership.

(6)

The reason is the opposition of union labor which fears that the constabulary [state police force] will be used to suppress strikes and prevent picketing. . . . It is unfortunate that so much of the discussion has turned upon

> the question of strike duty. . . . It is not for riot duty, but for everyday duty that a state police force is needed. The fact is that life and prosperity are not adequately safeguarded in the rural districts.

The use of concrete instead of general expressions likewise gives force to an editorial. An excellent example is in an editorial by the late Frank I. Cobb, in which he was arguing that the granting of the suffrage right to women would not destroy domestic tranquillity. In this editorial, Mr. Cobb might have said, "The home, which has withstood the vicissitudes of centuries, is not likely to have its peace disturbed *because women exercise the right to vote.*" Instead, he said, "An institution that has withstood the vicissitudes of centuries is not likely to collapse *because the women of a community spend half an hour in a voting booth on the first Tuesday after the first Monday in November.*" [10] Much of the force in H. L. Mencken's style is due to his very frequent use of concrete rather than general expressions; although the concrete expressions are often gross exaggerations, the point the writer tries to make sinks into the consciousness of the reader and remains there long after the exaggeration has been forgotten.

2. Arrangement for Emphasis.—Not only the choice of words and expressions, but their arrangement within the sentence or within the whole composition helps to give the editorial its authoritative and judicial tone. Words, phrases, and sentences, by their mere order within a composition, either intensify or soften affirmation and negation so that the reader's will is enlisted and his emotions are delicately aroused.

The devices discussed below, however, are artificial, and their conscious use by a writer is no substitute for the writer's earnestness and sincerity. "The ability to appeal to, to impress and to stir the reader," says Roy W. Howard, "must be in the writer. It isn't in the dictionary."

The Periodic Sentence.—In the news story and in the ordinary expository editorial, sentences are often anticlimactic in structure; but in argumentative editorials, more use is made

---

[10] Italics not in original.

of climactic sentences. The ordinary sentence is one in which the substantive subject with all its modifying elements is put first and is followed by the main verb with its modifiers. A sentence in which there is no apparent effort to distribute emphasis is technically called a *loose* sentence. When, however, a sentence is ordered in such a manner that the element of main significance is withheld until the end, it is called a *periodic* sentence. The periodic sentence is constructed on the psychological principle that when a series of ideas is presented to the reader, the first and last make the strongest impression. The following sentence from an editorial by Frank I. Cobb illustrates the effect of the last idea in the sentence:

> If the fruits of recent political activity are to be gathered; if popular rule is to be spared another staggering blow; if fresh energy is not to be given to all socialistic and revolutionary influences which even now are undermining representative government, the President cannot fail to perceive that it is his highest duty to call the new congress in extra session in March.

According to the same psychological principle, the elements in a sentence are sometimes *inverted* in order to give emphasis to the first idea presented, as in, "Great is the mystery of space, greater is the mystery of time."

Climax.—Whole sentences, as well as the elements within a sentence, may be arranged in a climactic order in order to obtain force. That is to say, the details are enumerated in an order the pattern of which becomes familiar to the reader before the end of the section is approached, and the order is such that the details increase in importance and intensity toward a culmination. A simple example is Cæsar's, "I came, I saw, I conquered." The following example is from William Allen White:

> Smith is honest. Smith is consistent. Smith is wise in his day and generation, and he has the courage of his convictions. And because he is wise and honest and brave, as President of the United States, he will

> menace American ideals and threaten the institutions of our fathers.

The example below is from the New York *World:*

> In the name of "social justice" it is proposed to erect a replica of Prussian institutions upon American soil. It is proposed that a government of bureaucrats shall regulate the activities of ninety-five million people. It is proposed to make the national government a priceless prize for plutocracy to take possession of and administer for its own profit. It is proposed to turn a great republic into the theater of a class war, and every election into a battle for wages, dividends, and spoils.

Sometimes the mere enumeration of details without regard to the order of their relative importance or intensity adds force to an editorial. The following is an example:

> Such a management assume that the only durable influences in Chicago political action are the influences of racketeers, bombers, machine gunners, kidnapers, beer needlers, panderers, joint keepers, gamblers, pay-roll mendicants, and petty thieves, fee robbers, habitual criminals . . . immunized murderers.

Iteration.—In editorial writing, force is obtained by the repetition of words, phrases, and constructions. Extended repetition, however—because it is so obviously artificial—gives an editorial too much of the oratorical manner; repetition in editorials must not be permitted to destroy the judicial tone.

Usually the repetition of merely a word or a phrase gives force to a composition, especially when the word or phrase is rung as a *refrain.* In the following example from an editorial in the Milwaukee *Journal,* the repeated words recur with the regularity of a refrain. The editorial is in answer to Mr. White's indictment of Governor Smith's candidacy, a portion of which was quoted above.

> Whose fathers, Mr. White? It is the boy who likes garlic with his meat, asking you.

> In the Argonne he earned the right to ask it.
> Whose fathers, Mr. White? It is the mother
> of the boy whose father came to this coun-
> try in the steerage asking you. At Chateau-
> Thierry she laid her sacrifice on her coun-
> try's altar. Whose fathers? Those of us
> whose progenitors were Tories in the Revo-
> lutionary war; and those of us whose pro-
> genitors stood with Washington at Valley
> Forge, or unhappily, were cursed by Wash-
> ington for deserting him in his hour of need
> for the price of a gun? Let's talk turkey,
> Mr. White.

The most common form of repetition is *parallel construction;* that is to say, the repetition of the same parts of speech or the same form of phrase or clause. The following example repeats a clause in a forcible manner without suggesting artificiality:

> No political boss brought about his nom-
> ination. No political machine carried his
> candidacy to victory. No coterie of Wall
> Street financiers provided the money to
> finance his campaign. He stands before the
> country a free man.

For the sake of rhythm, however, the writer should not have too many phrases of the same structure. Because sing-song is somewhat monotonous, the writer should change the structure of the last member of the series—as in the following example:

> Thus Harding was elected. Thus Coolidge
> was elected. Thus Hoover will be. Thus
> Kohler, in business tweed, may inherit the
> seat of the mighty.

Antithesis.—The setting off against each other of opposing ideas, either in a balanced form of structure or in a less obvious form, gives vigor and life to editorial style. We usually call this contrast antithesis. The more marked the contrast between the ideas, the stronger is the effect of the antithesis.

Antithesis frequently takes the form of *balanced structure—* as in the following examples:

(1)

> It is one thing when industry maintains tariffs to encourage industry; it is another thing when industry maintains tariffs to debauch government and oppress the people.

(2)

> How can it do better than to match sanity against lunacy; statesmanship against demagogy; the historian against the Rough Rider; the educator of public opinion against the debaucher of public opinion; the first term against the third term; the tariff-reformer against the stand-patter; the man who would prosecute against the man who protects trusts magnates; the man with clean hands against the man who draws his campaign funds from Wall Street; the supporter of constitutional government against the champion of personal government; law against lawlessness; Americanism against Mexicanism; the Republic against dictatorship?
>
> Who better represents these issues than Woodrow Wilson?

Sometimes the *repetition* of a balanced structure gives added force to the antithesis, as in the following example:

> It is not the Taft administration which the Senate has injured. It is the Senate itself.
> It is not the President who has been betrayed, it is a great cause of civilization.

A subtle form of antithesis is *paradox,* wherein there is a contrast not between two stated ideas, but between one stated idea and the reader's credulity or sense of congruity. Similar to paradox—so similar that here it is not worth while to make a differentiation—is *epigram.* The essence of epigram is that it surprises the reader. It states an idea and then gives it an unexpected turn, as in, "You can always tell a Harvard man—but you can't tell him much." Sometimes, but not always, epigram may embody paradox. The following are examples of epigram, some of which contain a paradox:

(1)

What we learn from history is that men learn nothing from history.

(2)

The majority in New York is a shackled majority—unless it happens to be a Republican majority.

(3)

The only antidote to the influence of some women upon government is the influence of all women upon government.

(4)

The Constitution of the State of New York prohibits representative government.

(5)

The high cost of living is arranged by private understanding.

(6)

Liberty is still liberty.

Effective though it is, antithesis should be employed sparingly in editorials. For it tempts the writer to exaggeration, especially the young writer who is likely to place a premium upon cleverness. The most valid criticism directed at the journalist and the essayist is that they too often sacrifice truth for the sake of literary form. Epigram and paradox are not difficult to write if the author does not value truth; it is a simple matter to fill in the antithetical element of a balanced sentence with a half-truth if the writer cares only for clever effect.

There is one circumstance, however, in which a partially true antithesis can be used with sincerity; it is in a composition in which the writer, having established a tone that warns his reader to expect a bit of exaggeration, anticipates that the reader will discount sufficiently his exaggeration. For example, Macaulay, who was accused by historians of exaggeration because he wrote in his *History of England,* "The Puritans hated bear-baiting, not because it gave pain to the bear, but because it gave pleasure to the spectators," probably stated enough of the truth to justify his clever statement. Editorial writers, however, do not often write with the tongue in the cheek.

Aphorism.—Any short, pithy sentence is not technically an epigram unless it contains the element of antithesis. *Aphorism* is the name given to a short, pithy sentence regardless of whether or not it contains antithesis. The sententious sentence —that is, one which is crowded with thought and is made of the "pith and heart of sciences"—is one of the hall-marks that identifies a thinker. There are no rules that govern the creation of sententious sentences except the warning uttered by Sir Francis Bacon, "No man can suffice, nor in reason will attempt, to write aphorisms, but he that is sound and grounded."

It is not possible for the ordinary editorial writer to fill an editorial with aphorisms; an aphorism, being a distillation of much thought, is not always ready to hand. Nor is it desirable to fill an editorial with aphorisms, for the mind of the ordinary newspaper reader is not attuned to Baconian essay. Aphorisms are employed best at the end of an editorial or a section of an editorial in summarizing and giving point to the whole content of the editorial. An example follows:

With reference to the large crowd that attended the Dempsey-Tunney prize fight at Philadelphia one hundred and fifty years after the signing of the Declaration of Independence (sesquicentennial):

> It is easy to achieve political independence of a British king, not so easy to become independent of animal forces locked up within us 10,000,000 years ago.—BRISBANE.

Platitudes.—If aphorisms exhibit in the writer a depth of learning and a philosophical mind, platitudes expose a writer's shallowness. A platitude is a statement so commonplace that it need not have been expressed for all that any reader cares. The most common platitude is the *truism,* that is, a statement whose truth is self-evident. Editorials that contain little more than platitudinous statements—and there are a great many written every day—are not worth the paper they are printed on or the time consumed by the reader in reading them. Mr. James M. Cain, himself an editorial writer, has burlesqued the platitudinous editorial as follows:

> ### THE NEW PLAYGROUND
>
> Every resident of the city must rejoice at the opening of the Evergreen Park Playground. Coming as it does at the beginning of the warm weather, it means that thousands of little tots will have the opportunity for fresh air and play all through the summer. Wholesome frolic in such surroundings means that when school opens in the fall, thousands of sturdy, sunburned scholars will be on hand to take up the more serious business of life with renewed vigor. . . .
> Happy the official who can spare an hour or two during a busy day to romp with the kiddies at a time like this. *Parva leves capiunt animus.* It is well so, and it would be well for all of us to realize it more often. We salute you, Mr. Mayor, as one who has not forgotten the happy days of childhood. And we freely confess that our salutation is slightly colored with envy.[11]

Intensifying the Negative.—It is not always easy to say "not." Negation, because it implies a contrast, gives greater or less distinction to the idea expressed than does affirmation. Writers, therefore, sometimes have to intensify and sometimes soften a negation. One way of intensifying a negation is to forego the use of "not" and to use "no" to negate the subject of the whole sentence, as in the following example:

Simple negation: Herbert Hoover is not merely an engineer.
Intensified negation: No mere engineer is Herbert Hoover.

Other examples are:

(1)

> The tariff is in *nowise* the reason for our prosperity.

---

[11] *American Mercury,* Vol. I (April, 1924), p. 436.

(2)

> *No* corporation tax law should be enacted which leaves the matter of publicity to the discretion of any federal official, whether President or departmental clerk.

A second method of intensifying negation is by the use of *irony* and *litotes*. Irony is a figure of speech which affirms or suggests the opposite of what is intended, the clew to the real truth of the statement being embodied in the tone or context, and the effect intended being innuendo. Some editorials are ironical compositions, but some are merely given an ironical touch. The following are examples of ironical editorials:

(1)

> Municipal ownership at its worst! An Associated Press dispatch from Colby, Kansas, reports:
> "Colby citizens will have to worry along another year with no municipal taxes to grow indignant over. For the third successive year the city council voted to let the municipal water plant wash away the city's bills. During two years, earnings of the plant have paid administration bills, provided $200,000 for pavements, paid for new equipment, and placed a balance of $45,000 in the city treasury."
> We know nothing about this nefarious enterprise except what appears in this dispatch, but it looks like outright bolshevism and ought to be stopped. Cannot the public-relations committees of the esteemed National Electric Light Association protect us against such pernicious propaganda?—THE *Nation*.

(2)

> The people of New York may think that they are in the midst of a traction strike, but they are mistaken. There is no strike.
> We know there is not, because we have been reading Mr. Hughes's speeches attacking President Wilson and the eight-hour law.
> Mr. Hughes proved conclusively that if the

President "had stood firmly for the principles of arbitration," as the railroad presidents demanded, there would have been no general railroad strike. It follows, therefore, that there is no street-car strike in New York.

We have a Republican public service commission appointed by a Republican governor under a public service law drafted by Charles E. Hughes himself. In consequence, we are as near the millennium as fallible human beings can expect us to be.

This public service commission talks about arbitration from morning till night. It has immeasurably more power over the traction companies and the employes of the traction companies than the President had over the railroads and brotherhoods, for he has no legal power at all. It is inconceivable that there could be a traction strike under such benevolent Hughes auspices. What the people of New York regard as a traction strike is something else, because Mr. Hughes has proved that a strike cannot happen except through Wilsonian timidity and vacillation.

It is true that the surface cars are not running, that the elevated service is much muddled, that there is great public inconvenience, with heavy incidental business losses and no little disorder. It is true also that conditions are getting worse rather than better, but there is no strike.

We have read Mr. Hughes's speeches and know that a strike cannot possibly take place when government remains "firm," as Republican government always does.

It follows, then, that the Interborough did not refuse to arbitrate the "master-and-servant" contracts, that the employes of the Third Avenue Line did not break their agreement with the company, that neither the traction interests nor the union leaders wanted a strike, and that the Federation of Labor has not meddled with the situation. Mr. Hughes's speeches demonstrate that there is not an industrial cloud on New York City's horizon.
—NEW YORK *World.*

Ironical editorials often misrepresent the view that they are written to refute. Irony is a difficult device to employ because one is so likely to be contemptuous of the opposing point of view. The writer, therefore, ought to guard against an irony that is too "biting" under the circumstances.

Litotes, like irony, negates the opposite of what is intended. But, unlike irony, it takes the form of understatement. The understatement is made so obviously that it intensifies the idea in the reader's mind. Some examples follow:

(1)

Our mental defectives are the products of *no ordinary* social carelessness, and the children of *no decent* poverty.

(2)

The loan sharks are *not so unfortunate.*

(3)

A war that has wrecked vast empires, overthrown dynasties, and brought about sweeping revolutions is not likely to leave society *just as it was before.*

Softening the Negative.—The vigorous editorial does not always obtain the reader's assent. When the editorial writer is arguing for a point of view about which many of his readers have deep convictions to the contrary, he designedly couches his arguments in mild terms. He does not try to carry his readers along with him in a vigorous sweep of argument, but appeals calmly to the reader's common sense. To some extent this attitude is adopted in nearly all editorials because editorials must have a judicial as well as an authoritative tone; usually, however, it is reserved for the editorial discussion of questions about which readers have deep convictions, such as prohibition and religious tolerance. This attitude is also required for the discussion of such questions as judicial decisions, sectional disputes, and the personal character of revered national heroes. In arguing about such matters, a restrained tone carries more conviction than a vigorous tone.

The simplest device for softening the tone of an argumentative composition in which negation is expressed is the *double negative*. For example:

(1)

It is *not improbable* that we shall yet regret the passage of this law.

(2)

Although Judge Willis has reversed his former attitude, he is *not unashamed* of his decision in the Murray Transit case.

Ordinarily, a judicial tone is achieved in editorials simply by the use of mild terms and qualifying expressions, such as "it seems to us," or "in the opinion of The *Times*." In the following excerpt from an editorial that deals with prohibition and morality, the first paragraph has an authoritative ring, the second a mild tone:

The prohibitionist has not turned to Christ, but to Caesar. He has decided upon his own grounds that teetotalism is essential to morality and to Christianity, and he calls in Caesar to impose his conviction by force upon all who do not agree with him.

In our opinion, this is justified neither in morality nor in Christianity, and neither is it moral nor Christian to assume, as the prohibitionist ministers assume, that disagreement with them is evidence of immoral or unChristian character.

One of the best examples of a dynamic style that is also thoroughly judicial in tone is that of Justice Oliver Wendell Holmes of the United States Supreme Court. Editorial writers who study his phraseology will find it nearly always adaptable to editorial writing. An example follows:

This case is decided upon an economic theory which a large part of the country does not entertain. If it were a question whether I agreed with that theory, I should desire to study it further and long before making up my mind. But I do not conceive that to be my duty, because I strongly believe that my agreement or disagreement has nothing to do with the right of a majority to embody their opinions in law. It is settled by various decisions of this court that state Constitutions and state laws may regulate life in many ways which we as legislators might think as injudicious, or if you like, as tyrannical, as this, and which, equally with this, interfere with the liberty of contract. Sunday laws and usury laws are ancient examples. A more modern one is the prohibition of lotteries. The liberty of the citizen to do as he likes so long as he does not interfere with the liberty of others to do the same, which has been a shibboleth for some well-known writers, is interfered with by school laws, by the post office, by every state or municipal institution which takes his money for purposes thought desirable, whether he likes it or not.

The fourteenth amendment does not enact Mr. Herbert Spencer's Social Statics. The other day we sustained the Massachusetts vaccination law. United States statutes and decisions cutting down the liberty to contract by way of combination are familiar to this court. Two years ago we upheld the prohibtion of sales of stock on margins, or for future delivery, in the constitution of California. The decision sustaining an eight-hour law for miners is still recent. Some of these laws embody convictions or prejudices which judges are likely to share. Some may not. But a constitution is not intended to embody a particular economic theory, whether of paternalism and the organic relation of the citizen to the state or of laissez-faire. It is made for people of fundamentally differing views, and the accident of our finding certain opinions natural and familiar, or novel, and even shocking, ought not to conclude our judgment upon the question whether statutes embodying them conflict with the Constitution of the United States.

General propositions do not decide concrete

cases. The decision will depend upon a judgment or intuition more subtle than any articulate major premise. But I think that the
proposition just stated, if it is accepted, will
carry us far toward the end. Every opinion
tends to become a law. I think that the word
"liberty" in the fourteenth amendment, is
perverted when it is held to prevent the natural outcome of a dominant opinion, unless
it can be said that a rational and fair man
necessarily would admit that the statute proposed would infringe fundamental principles
as they have been understood by the traditions of our people and our law.[12]

Rhetorical Question.—An effective device used in editorial
writing is the rhetorical question, wherein the writer, instead
of expressing an affirmation, states a question which the reader
is supposed to answer for himself in the affirmative. Examples of the rhetorical question range in intensity from the
familiar affirmative-interrogative, "Can a duck swim?" to such
bombast of eloquence as, "Are we slaves to endure longer
this terrible oppression?" Some editorial examples follow:

(1)

Who better represents these issues than
Woodrow Wilson?

(2)

Is it [the electrocution of Sacco and Van-
zetti] any vast improvement over the massacre of St. Bartholomew, the wrecking of
art treasures in monasteries by Henry VIII,
the cry of "No Popery!" by Lord Gordon, or
the dragging of Garrison through the streets
of Baltimore?

(3)

What must be the judicial conscience and
sense of propriety of Judge Eller when he
not only consents to act in the proceedings
against his associate, Kaplan, but takes action
in his favor against the vigorous objection
of counsel for the state?

[12] Dissenting opinion in Lochner *v.* New York, 198 U. S. 45.

As the foregoing examples show, the principle of contrast contained in the rhetorical question gives greater distinction to the affirmation than the writer could express in a declaratory manner.[13]

3. Force Through Character.—The Man Who Doesn't Care cannot be an effective editorial writer, even though he is able to apply the various instruments of force we have just discussed. Force in style, as related to the writer himself, is the result and evidence of "some strong emotion at work infusing vigor in his words." [14] The writer

realizes vividly the truth of what he says, and so it becomes intense and fervid; he has a deep conviction of its importance, and so it becomes cogent and impressive. Along with this fervor of feeling his will is enlisted; he is determined, as it were, to make his reader think as he does, and to make his cause prevail. Every employment of word and figure is tributary to this.

Genuine force in style cannot be manufactured; if the style has not serious conviction to back it, it becomes contorted; if it has not a vivifying emotion, it becomes turgid. Force is the quality of style most dependent on character.

The writer's culture for force, therefore, is in its deepest analysis a culture of character. To think closely and seriously; to insist on seeing fact or truth for one's self, and not merely echo it as hearsay; to cherish true convictions, not mere fashions or expedients of thinking,—these are the traits in the culture of character that make for forcible and virile expression.[15]

It was character as well as literary ability that made Greeley, Bowles, and Godkin effective editorial writers. "With these men, their personality, in the sense both of *distinctness* of character and *weight* of character, was an outstanding element in their success," says Professor Allan Nevins.

They could be trusted. People believed in them. It was because they inspired trust that they could play an important rôle in the formation of public opinion. Finally, all these eminent men were men of action, as well as men of advice. They had a constructive

---

[13] The use of figures of association as a means of attaining force is not discussed in this chapter; the figures were differentiated in Chapter VIII.

[14] J. F. Genung, *The Working Principles of Rhetoric*, p. 36.

[15] *Ibid.*, pp. 36-37.

faculty. They not merely warned the nation against fallacies, they not merely denounced bad officers and bad measures, but they were able to point out right courses of action. Greeley not merely attacked the iniquities of the Grant Administration; he led the Liberal Republican movement to replace that Administration.

Unquestionably, if an editor and his editorial page have these qualities; if they have the virtue of appositiveness; if they have a distinctive, salient personality, including weight of character; and if they have a shrewd constructive faculty, they may dispense with pretentious literary graces. Clarity and force in the use of English will suffice. They may serve the republic in the very highest degree with nothing more.[16]

Of such stuff, too, was the late Frank I. Cobb; and he made the editorial page of the New York *World* the most important and influential in America. A thorough democrat, he possessed a character of rugged simplicity. Writing in a period that was a bit more stirring than the present era, he gave to his newspaper that influence for social righteousness which today justifies our constitutional right of freedom of the press.

---

[16] *Journalism Quarterly,* Vol. V (March, 1928), p. 22.

CHAPTER XVII

MISCELLANEOUS TYPES OF EDITORIALS

For the most part, the work of the editorial writer is not self-expression. As the venerable Talcott Williams has said, "The prime end and office of journalism is not for personal expression, but the use of one's capacities, power, and will to express the tide of events for public ends and advance." [1] Yet, the editorial writer is not always compelled to choose subjects that are forced upon him by the news or by the demands of editorial policy. He often chooses subjects that permit of a modicum of self-expression. Such subjects are addressed to the individual reader for the purpose of entertaining, inspiring, or educating him, whereas the type of editorial that we discussed in previous chapters is addressed to the reader as a member of the public for the purpose of convincing or persuading him of the wisdom, expediency, or desirability of accepting or acting upon a specific principle or policy. The type of editorial examined in this chapter is seldom of social consequence, but is of much human interest.

The subjects of exposition are so many that it is not possible to classify editorials. In this chapter, therefore, we shall note only the following types: entertaining, inspirational, educational, critical, and occasional editorials.

Entertaining Editorials.—Since the earliest beginnings of journalism, one of the functions of the newspaper has been the entertainment of its readers.[2] This function is exercised in the editorial as well as in the news columns, and on many daily papers there has evolved the practice of writing each day at least one editorial of light tone for the sole purpose of entertaining the reader. The best British newspapers, for example, have had for decades three or four editorials, or

---

[1] *The Newspaper Man*, p. 21.
[2] See W. G. Bleyer, *Main Currents in the History of American Journalism*, Chaps. I and II, *passim*.

"leaders," the first two or three being polemic or interpretive discussions of current events and the last one an entertaining discourse in casual essay form. This practice has been imitated by many American newspapers. Some of these entertaining essays have been written so well and have touched so closely the intimate concerns of life that they have been reprinted in book form in numerous editions; the best known are the collection of "third leaders" from the London *Times*[3] and the "casual essays" of the New York *Sun*.[4]

Some of these editorials are the expressions of a mood that has been suggested by a personal observation of the writer. The following descriptive passage, by an editorial writer on the Chicago *Tribune*, is an example:

> ### APRIL SHOWERS AND MAY SNOWS
>
> The brown thrasher and the catbird have joined the cardinal in morning song as an April which had an affair with February flies into the West to join a March which was an illegitimate child of June. A north shore spring will do these unchurched things and, although wild and wanton, keep itself charming still. Possibly a proper spring behaving as a home girl, dependable about the place and always what she should be, would not be sufficiently piquant.
>
> Wood anemones run through the dead leaves of the woods. The trilliums are tall and white. Violets are on the banks. Wild geraniums are in the covert. Shad and wild plums are in blossom and the wind runs a cold knife along the back and sticks it in under the fifth rib.[5]

The types of editorials are as numerous and as varied as there are types of humor. The following treatment of an

---

[3] See George Gordon, ed., *Third Leaders from the London Times* (1928), and J. W. Mackail, *Modern Essays* (1915).

[4] *Casual Essays of the Sun* (1915); out of print.

[5] One of the best known editorials of this type was the famous editorial, "A Great Old Sunset," written in 1853 by S. S. Cox, a Columbus, Ohio, newspaper man and Congressman. Because of the unconventionality of this editorial and because of his initials, Cox was dubbed by the politically-minded editors of his time, "Sunset" Cox.

insignificant subject in a whimsical manner is illustrative of
the character of casual essay made famous by the editorial
writers of the New York *Sun* under the régimes of Dana and
Mitchell:

HAIRPINS

The comprehensive merits of the hairpin
are known to all observant men. Its special
value in surgery is asserted by a writer in
American Medicine. It seems that a surgeon
can do almost anything with a hairpin. He
can wire bones with it, probe and close
wounds, pin bandages, compress blood vessels, use it "to remove foreign bodies from
any natural passage," and as a curette for
scraping away soft material. And no doubt
the women doctors can do a great deal more
with that most gifted and versatile of human
implements. Anthropologists have never done
justice to the hairpin. It keeps civilization
together. In the hands of girls entirely great
it is much mightier than the sword or, for
that matter, the plough. What is the plough
but a development of the forked stick, and
what is the forked stick but a modification
of the hairpin? If there was any necessity,
a woman could scratch the ground successfully now. In fact, there is no work or play
in which something may not be accomplished
by means of it.

Dullards will tell you that women aren't
so inventive as men, don't take out so many
patents. They don't have to. With the hairpin all that is doable can be done. With a
hairpin a woman can pick a lock, pull a cork,
peel an apple, draw out a nail, beat an egg,
see if a joint of meat is done, do up a baby,
sharpen a pencil, dig out a sliver, fasten a
door, hang up a plate or a picture, open a
can, take up a carpet, repair a baby carriage,
clean a lamp chimney, put up a curtain, rake
a grate fire, cut a pie, make a fork, a fish-
hook, an awl, a gimlet, or a chisel, a paper-
cutter, a clothespin, regulate a range, tinker
a sewing machine, stop a leak in the roof,

turn over a flapjack, caulk a hole in a pair of trousers, stir batter, whip cream, reduce the pressure in the gas meter, keep bills and receipts on file, spread butter, cut patterns, tighten windows, clean a watch, untie a knot, varnish floors, do practical plumbing, reduce the asthma of tobacco pipes, pry shirt studs into button holes too small for them, fix a horse's harness, restore damaged mechanical toys, wrestle with refractory beer stoppers, improvise suspenders, shovel bonbons, inspect gas burners, saw cake, jab tramps, produce artificial buttons, hooks and eyes, sew, knit, and darn, button gloves and shoes, put up awnings, doctor an automobile. In short, she can do what she wants to; she needs no other instrument.

If a woman went into the Robinson Crusoe line she would build a hut and make her a coat of the skin of a goat by means of the hairpin. She will revolutionize surgery with it in time. Meanwhile the male chirurgeons are doing the best they can; but it is not to be believed that they have mastered the full mystery of the hairpin.

Although humorous editorials are often satiric, they are sometimes on the philosophical level of humor. Such editorials reflect the desire of the writer to play with ideas, and they are much appreciated by readers who laugh above the eyebrows. The following example is from the Baltimore *Evening Sun:*

WINNERS

This may, at first glance, offend ardent feminists. Feminists, therefore, are urged to apply a little logic before reaching a conclusion.

The happiest women are inferior to their husbands. This is no reflection on the wit of the women. It is, rather, a compliment. They are successful women, for they have attained a matrimonial relationship that is precisely what they desired.

The sex game—since the dawn of civilization, a matrimonial game—is not a man's game.

Man has many games—sowing, reaping, building, hunting, exploring, winning renown among his fellows. Love is his relaxation after the important business of life is finished for the day.

When he falls in love he is unassisted by his practical common sense. He falls in love with a pretty face, a dimple, a curl, a laugh.

He desires a woman for her own sake—a woman he can enjoy and pet and care for; a woman who will lean upon him.

He does not ask himself whether she is lower or higher than himself. He thinks she is higher in purity, gentleness and beauty, and other standards do not matter.

The prince may love a peasant maid; it is not in nature for the princess to love a peasant.

A woman looks up for a mate.

Whether she be a countess or a scullery maid, her dream is to find a mate more worthy than herself—a superior man to admire, to trust, to respect, almost to worship.

In short, she desires her superior. If her arts and wiles enable her to be captured by her superior, she is thereafter content.

She has won in woman's great game.

If she marries an inferior, contempt for him overcomes her every effort to be content. There isn't in America a happy woman who looks down on her mate.

Why are there so many divorces? Why so many unhappy marriages?

There are many reasons, perhaps. One usually overlooked, is that women have developed greatly and it is therefore increasingly difficult for them to acquire mates sufficiently superior to afford them happiness.

No effort is made in this section to list or even to suggest all of the types of entertaining editorials. On the contrary, what often makes an editorial of this kind entertaining is the fact that it is a fresh theme. The farther away the editorial writer gets from the themes of politics and economics the more likely he is to achieve originality and charm.[6]

Inspirational and Educational Editorials.—Some editorials have for their purpose not only the entertainment of the reader, but his inspiration and education as well. Such editorials are suggested by the news, by the season, or by some specific observation or experience of the writer. Sometimes the writer talks directly and intimately to the reader, sometimes he talks objectively. His themes range all the way from "How to Keep From Growing Old" to "Plan to Walk in the Country Next Sunday."

The following editorial from the Chicago *Tribune* mingles praise for an unsung hero with advice to a class of readers:

> Gottlieb Steek was a railway crossing guard at Niles Center. He saw a train approaching. He saw an automobile approaching. He stepped out into the crossing and signaled the automobilists to stop. They came on. They struck the flagman and knocked him into the path of the train. His body was found later forty feet away.
>
> It was not found by the automobilists. They had escaped the collision and speeded away. The man who had given his life to save theirs was nothing to them.
>
> These individuals are unknown. They are being sought by the county highway police, but they are safe, in all probability, from any punishment in this world unless they have consciences to apply the lash of shameful memory. That is not likely.
>
> The man who should have lived died a sacrifice for those who did not deserve the sacrifice. The exchange is a loss to the world, but not altogether. For Gottlieb Steek has added something to the dignity and glory of human life. If not the motorists he died for, at least many other men and women reading how he died have a richer sense of what

---

[6] In this connection, see the comment and the examples cited by Allan Nevins in "The Editorial as a Literary Form," *Journalism Quarterly*, Vol. V (March, 1928), pp. 19-27.

is brave and noble in human character. Gott-
lieb Steek held a very humble if also a very
responsible post, but he possessed something
higher than any place and more precious than
any material success.

The men for whom he gave his life represent the callous heedlessness of which there is
so much in the highways, a carelessness that
menaces the most careful and considerate and
piles up the tragic record of our motor casual-
ties, to our sorrow and our shame. Perhaps their example of ruthlessness may have
some effect in reminding us all of the folly
and wickedness of our motor manners.

The following editorial by Glenn Frank is of real value to
the reader because it reflects sound thinking:

FOCUSSED BUT NOT FIXED

Lately I have been bootlegging certain biographies into my boy's library, hoping he
might, without too obvious direction from
me, catch their significance.

All of these biographies I have been leaving about in my boy's room tell of men
whose minds managed to be unusually effective without becoming chained to a specialism.

I want him to become acquainted with
Benjamin Franklin who somehow managed
to be a craftsman, a tradesman, a philosopher,
a journalist, a diplomat, a statesman, an inventor, and a few other things, and withal
a very effective man.

I want him to become acquainted with
Leonardo da Vinci who somehow managed to
be an artist, a scientist, an inventor, a philosopher, a canal builder, a writer, and several
other things, and withal a very effective man.

I am leaving the biographies of such men
lying about in my boy's room because I want
to inoculate him against the worship of
specialization I know he will encounter when
he outgrows boyhood and enters a modern
university and later when he leaves the university and enters business or a profession.

I do not expect him to be another Leonardo, but I want him to catch something of Leonardo's spirit, for I am convinced that, by the time he must take his place in the affairs of his adult world, he will find that there will be no place for the narrow specialist save among the regimental routineers who will be ordered about by the few leaders who have managed to rise above the religion of specialization that grips our time and become men who can see things in their relation.

I want his mind to be like a searchlight—focussed, but not fixed.

The capacity to concentrate upon the job in hand is something far different from slavery to a narrow specialization.

The searchlight does not fritter its light away until it illuminates nothing.

At any given moment the light of the searchlight is concentrated upon the thing that needs illumination, but it can sweep the countryside as well.

Unless man can combine specialization of mind with sweep of mind, specialization will mean suicide in this complex age.

Editorials of this type are often so platitudinous that the intelligent reader wonders that they are read. Apparently they are read, however: the writers of certain syndicated editorials, such as the late Dr. Frank Crane, received high reward for their work. When such editorials are written to supply a demand, it is likely that the writer cannot produce an excellent editorial every day. The result is an editorial not much better than this burlesque by Morris Bishop:

OUR SYNDICATED EDITORIALS

"Art is Power," said the poet Longfellow long ago in his Hyperion. This is a truth that too many of us today are prone to forget.

Indeed, how many people, in their daily occupations, ever pause to reflect that Art in the highest and truest sense is Power, and that by devoting twenty minutes a day to the cultivation of Power we may attain to the fullness and beauty of Art? This is the Golden Mean of the Greeks.

When Michelangelo, the celebrated painter, was young he was too poor to pay a model. He therefore restricted himself to painting pictures of fish, garnished with lemons and fish sauce. After completing his painting, he would eat the fish, seasoning it with the lemon and the fish sauce.

He longed to do bigger things, but he could not afford to buy models and food as well. One day a society lady offered to pose for him, and Michelangelo thought his troubles were at an end. He painted his famous canvas, Nymph Playing With Pet Fish. But the nymph, to his despair, ate the fish.

There is a lesson in this for us all. Do we greet our associates in the morning and our customers when it seems proper? Are we genuinely interested in our customers and regard each as an opportunity for service? Do we betray scorn or humor when a customer asks a fool question?

The annual loss from insect pests alone in this country amounts to more than two billions of dollars. But insects should not invariably be destroyed, because they pollinate the flowers and other plant life.

If we should all bear these facts in mind this would be a better city in which to live.[7]

The editorial that discourses on ideals and virtues is more likely to be platitudinous and sentimental than stimulating to the spirit. Yet the intelligent writer can fill a great human need in this machine age by stimulating admiration for the ideals which the race has learned are worth seeking to achieve. Without being sentimental, he can bring the readers' thought to bear on the truly important values in life and momentarily lift readers out of their materialistic environment. The truth of the following editorial would probably be denied by the intelligent thinker, yet it is the same truth that Mr. G. K. Chesterton teaches in his *Orthodoxy*. The editorial is one of the most famous of the *Sun* essays:

---

[7] *Saturday Evening Post*, June 9, 1928.

Is There a Santa Claus?

We take pleasure in answering at once and thus prominently the communication below, expressing at the same time our great gratification that its faithful author is numbered among the friends of the The Sun:

"Dear Editor—I am 8 years old.

"Some of my little friends say there is no Santa Claus.

"Papa says, 'If you see it in The Sun it's so.'

"Please tell me the truth, is there a Santa Claus?

"Virginia O'Hanlon.
"115 West Ninety-fifth street."

Virginia, your little friends are wrong. They have been affected by the skepticism of a skeptical age. They do not believe except they see. They think that nothing can be which is not comprehensible by their little minds. All minds, Virginia, whether they be men's or children's, are little. In this great universe of ours man is a mere insect, an ant, in his intellect, as compared with the boundless world about him, as measured by the intelligence capable of grasping the whole of truth and knowledge.

Yes, Virginia, there is a Santa Claus. He exists as certainly as love and generosity and devotion exist, and you know that they abound and give to your life its highest beauty and joy. Alas! how dreary would be the world if there were no Santa Claus! It would be as dreary as if there were no Virginias. There would be no childlike faith then, no poetry, no romance to make tolerable this existence. We should have no enjoyment, except in sense and sight. The eternal light with which childhood fills the world would be extinguished.

Not believe in Santa Claus! You might as well not believe in fairies! You might get your papa to hire men to watch in all the chimneys on Christmas eve to catch Santa Claus, but even if they did not see Santa

Claus coming down, what would that prove?
Nobody sees Santa Claus, but that is no
sign that there is no Santa Claus. The
most real things in the world are those that
neither children nor men can see. Did you
ever see fairies dancing on the lawn? Of
course not, but that's no proof that they are
not there. Nobody can conceive or imagine
all the wonders there are unseen and unsee-
able in the world.

You tear apart the baby's rattle and see
what makes the noise inside, but there is a
veil covering the unseen world which not the
strongest man, nor even the united strength
of all the strongest men that ever lived, could
tear apart. Only faith, fancy, poetry, love,
romance, can push aside that curtain and
view and picture the supernal beauty and
glory beyond. Is it all real? Ah, Virginia,
in all this world there is nothing else real
and abiding.

No Santa Claus! Thank God! he lives, and
he lives forever. A thousand years from now,
Virginia, nay, ten times ten thousand years
from now, he will continue to make glad the
heart of childhood.

Occasional Editorials.—A type of editorial that appears
less often than any of the types discussed above is the occasional editorial, one that is written on an anniversary date,
on the death of a person, on the dedication of a monument, on
the opening of a vehicular tunnel, on the completion of a personal achievement, or on a day that calls to mind the progress
of a movement.

The following editorial from the Minneapolis *Journal,* although based to some extent on misapprehensions, is representative of the type that is written on an anniversary date:

LABOR'S SOLID GAINS

Labor Day of 1926 finds the American
workingman living in a better home, wearing better clothes, eating better food, enjoying better facilities for recreation, than ever
before. His life now is fuller of good things,

is pleasanter, yields more happiness, than any worker's life in any past era, either here or abroad.

What has brought this about? A number of things, but there are three prime factors that stand out from the rest.

First, there is labor's discovery, possibly overslow in the coming, that sensible negotiation is as superior to the strike weapon, as a means of improving the worker's condition, as honest arbitration is superior to costly warfare in the settlement of international differences. The strike spells loss to both employee and employer, through interruption of production.

A second prime factor in the present era of good feeling in most industrial sections of America is the ownership by hundreds of thousands of workers of shares of stock in the great corporations that employ them, stock usually bought on terms more advantageous than those granted the general public.

A third prime factor, and possibly the most important, is the great strides made recently in speeding up production without any proportionate increase in operating expenses. Industry is producing more per man, and labor is getting a liberal share of the gain. Efficient management, improved processes, the advantage of standardized mass production, substitution of machine for muscle, and the realization by the workers that they can earn more as they produce more, all have contributed to this peculiarly American advance.

Inasmuch as certain anniversary dates have been so long observed, it is not always easy for the editorial writer to find something new to say each year. Some writers, therefore, often shirk the task by reprinting a particularly good editorial that has appeared in a previous year. When this is not possible, however, they have to think hard in order to freshen the theme. The famous editorial writer, Isaac H. Bromley, once attached a note to an editorial submitted to Whitelaw Reid, of the New York *Tribune:*

Here is a bit of Fourth of July. I consider it a triumph in this respect: that I was running into the "embattled farmer" and the "shot heard round the world" every other line, but as every other paper in the country has rung several changes on both quotations I avoided them. I think it is the only article on the subject that steers clear of the "embattled farmer" and the "shot." That is its only merit, but if you knew how I had to wriggle and twist to avoid the two quotations you would agree that it is an absolute stroke of genius.[8]

The obituary editorial is often difficult to write for reasons that are obvious. If the writer, however, will devote adequate time to research in the life and career of the subject, he will probably produce a creditable editorial, as is shown in the following example from the New York *Times:*

COOPER OF WISCONSIN

In 1870 the Alerts, a baseball nine of Burlington, Wis., defeated the Milwaukee Stars three out of five games for the championship of the state. The catcher and captain of the Alerts was Henry Allen Cooper. That was about the last time he was ever on the winning side. As a member of the House of Representatives from March, 1893, to last Sunday—with an interval of but one term—Mr. Cooper was a dauntless leader of the insurgent minority [i.e., the LaFollette Republican group]. He never flinched and he never quit, and he lived to see forlorn hopes grow into laws and political customs.

Twice his congenital opposition to the majority opinions of his party and his fellow-countrymen cost him chairmanships. It was the late Speaker Cannon who made an insurgent of Mr. Cooper, and the Wisconsin leader never forgot it. Appointed on a Philippine commission by President McKinley in 1899, Mr. Cooper became the champion of wide measures of immediate self-government for the people of the islands. For this the speaker declined to appoint him chairman of the new committee on insular affairs, al-

---

[8] Royal Cortissoz, *The New York Tribune*, pp. 40-41.

though under the normal customs of the House the place was his.

From that time forward Mr. Cooper was Speaker Cannon's untiring, intelligent foe. When the revolt against the House system flared up in 1910, the Wisconsin member, with Mr. Norris of Nebraska and Mr. Murdock of Kansas, led the fight not only to take the power from the speaker, but to unseat "Uncle Joe" himself. The second part of the plan failed, but not because Mr. Cooper faltered in support of it.

In 1917 by seniority Mr. Cooper was in line for the chairmanship of foreign affairs. But he had been a champion of the McLemore resolution and of other proposals tending to permit the Central Powers to do what they would on the high seas. Accordingly, in response to general opinion, the House organization gave the chairmanship to another. Mr. Cooper voted against the declaration of war against Germany, explaining, however, that, once war was declared, he would support the government to the utmost. He proved his consistency by voting in favor of the war declaration against Austria-Hungary. Long years of devotion to the late Senator LaFollette were crowned by Mr. Cooper's speech at the Cleveland convention of 1924, putting the Wisconsin candidate in nomination against Mr. Coolidge. His cause was lost before he stated it. But, as on many previous occasions, the insurgent, by that time approaching 80, won a personal triumph.

The Racine district is conservative. The only trace of his constituency about Mr. Cooper was his extremely dignified person. Tall, broad-shouldered, frock-coated, with long white beard and resonant voice, he typified the elder statesman of his party. But when he spoke, it was invariably an assault upon the party and its leaders. A House wit once said of the contrast between Mr. Cooper's appearance and his views: "It's like seeing Lord Salisbury on a soap box in Hyde Park on a Sunday."

Editorials are often written on the occasion of a great or an interesting achievement, such as the rescue of a submerged submarine crew, the rescue of entombed miners or lost explorers, or the completion of a feat in aviation. Such editorials are meant to be a recognition of ability or of service and are of value to the reading public because of the exemplary suggestion they contain. Although not typical of this kind of editorial, Harold MacDonald Anderson's editorial, for which he was awarded a Pulitzer prize, shows how an intelligent writer may express the applause of a nation without indulging in sentimentality:

> ### "LINDBERGH FLIES ALONE"
>
> Alone?
> Is he alone at whose right side rides Courage, with Skill within the cockpit and Faith upon the left? Does solitude surround the brave when Adventure leads the way and Ambition reads the dials? Is there no company with him for whom the air is cleft by Daring and the darkness is made light by Emprise?
> True, the fragile bodies of his fellows do not weigh down his plane; true, the fretful minds of weaker men are lacking from his crowded cabin; but as his airship keeps her course he holds communion with those rarer spirits that inspire to intrepidity and by their sustaining potency give strength to arm, resource to mind, content to soul.
> Alone? With what other companions would that man fly to whom the choice were given?

Other Types.—In this chapter we have tried to discuss a few miscellaneous types of editorials that represent a free choice of subject by the writer as distinguished from the editorials about social and political questions which the news or the paper's policy compel the writer to discuss. Except for the occasional editorials, most of the examples have been of this character. In addition to these types, there are one or two other types which include nearly all editorials.

One of these is the editorial of criticism. Some editorial writers who love and understand literature and the drama write editorials that comment on current plays and books. Such criticism appears in the editorial columns rather than in the space usually devoted to criticism; although on many of the smaller papers the editorial writer is also the regular literary and dramatic critic.

Under the head of "essay-editorial" we can classify nearly all of the editorials that editorial writers compose for the' sole reason that they enjoy writing about topics that have little connection with the news. Such essays are about every topic under the sun, such as "Fashions," "Doctors," "Silence," "Left-hand Turns," etc. The following editorial from the Baltimore *Evening Sun* is typical of the kind of editorial that *Evening Sun* editorial writers contribute nearly every day:

> ### ENVIRONMENT
>
> The flint hardness of a city man's exterior is not inherent. His cynicism, reserve, and coldness are developed by necessity. They are similar to the protective coloration of a jungle cat and the hard shell of the turtle.
>
> When a country man hears steps behind him and feels a hand on his shoulder, he does not start or whirl about with resentful countenance and suspicious eyes. He turns slowly, with a smile on his face, for he knows the hand belongs to somebody who loves him.
>
> The habit of greeting callers brusquely and disposing of them promptly isn't the result of any peculiar trait in the city man's cosmos. Necessity made the habit. The city man has no time to waste.
>
> To the country man a stranger is an event. He brings a breath from the outside world. He relieves the monotony of existence. He affords entertainment, and as an entertainer is welcome, though he may be a book agent.
>
> The city man thinks more quickly than the country man—not because Nature endowed him with a superior mind, but because a hard environment required him to think quickly or go under.

The country man has unlimited time to chew a mental cud, and failure to reach a decision today will cost him nothing. Tomorrow is a day also.

The city man is not by birth more enamored of liberty than his brother in the country. He talks more concerning liberty, and more quickly and hotly resents the suggestion of any statute that might threaten his liberty; but if he carries a chip on his shoulder, it is because he is at all times surrounded by evidences of authority. There are within sight agents to enforce the law that is designed to hobble him. He cheers lustily for liberty because he lives in an atmosphere of tyranny.

The country man thinks seldom of liberty, just as a man with a good digestion seldom is aware of it.

In the country men are free. There are none to molest or make them afraid. They may at all times do as they please. Theirs is the only freedom America affords, and they take freedom for granted as they take for granted the rising sun.

The country man doesn't crave liberty; he merely enjoys it.

Although editorials like the one just quoted are appreciated by the readers, they are often written merely because the writer desires to express some thought that is on his mind or some mood that he feels. Editorial writers, too, have hobbies and subjects of special interest such as fishing, femininism, yachting, lawyers' ethics, and architecture, which they like to write about. Solely for their own pleasure, they think and read a great deal about these matters, so that when they write about them they are able to give them historical and philosophical setting. The opportunity thus to express themselves makes up in great measure for the drudgery involved in discussing other subjects forced upon them by the news.

EXERCISES

CHAPTER I

Why and How Editorials Are Written

1. Select from the New York *Times* a nonargumentative editorial and answer the following questions about it:

(*a*) What apparently was the occasion for writing the editorial?

(*b*) What is it that the writer undertakes to explain?

(*c*) What are the evident sources upon which the writer drew in preparing the editorial?

(*d*) Does he accomplish his apparent purpose?

(*e*) Would the editorial have been more effective if the writer had taken up fewer points?

(*f*) How many words does the editorial contain?

(*g*) Is it longer or shorter than the average editorial on the page?

(*h*) Does the writer waste time in getting under way in his editorial?

(*i*) Is the beginning an announcement of a piece of news, or is it a general statement?

(*j*) Does the editorial end effectively?

2. Select from the New York *World-Telegram* an argumentative editorial and answer the following questions about it:

(*a*) What is the proposition that the editorial attempts to prove?

(*b*) Is the point which the writer undertakes to make one that is worth making?

(*c*) Does the writer deal with the subject broadly or pettily?

(*d*) Would the editorial have been more effective if the writer had taken up fewer points?

(*e*) Do you think the argument convincing?

(*f*) Could you change the order of the ideas and thereby make the editorial more effective?

(*g*) Does the editorial end effectively?

3. Analyze the editorials in the Chicago *Tribune* and the Detroit *News* over a period of three or four weeks. Which newspaper seems to have the newsiest editorial page? Which appears to contain more policy editorials than editorials that discuss news events?

4. Write an editorial for Armistice Day in which you summarize those events of the past year which you interpret as being steps toward peace. Do not write a sentimental, uplifting, or cynical editorial, but a calm survey.

5. Of all of the events reported in the newspaper of last evening, which four do you think ought to be discussed editorially this morning? Write out the definition of the standard you applied in making the selection of subjects.

6. What does Dewey mean by the statement, "An event implies that out of which a happening proceeds"?

7. Why is there "no irresponsibility in the unsigned editorial"?

Chapter II

Editorials of Definition

1. Referring to Isaiah Bowman, *The New World* (4th ed.), Chapter VIII, write an editorial of "geographical setting" on "Some Factors in Italy's International Position." Refer also to C. E. McGuire, *Italy's International Economic Position*, Chapters I-VII and XI-XII.

2. Write out answers to the following questions:

(*a*) Name the countries that touch the Adriatic Sea.
(*b*) Bound Poland on all sides.
(*c*) Name the "maritime" provinces of Canada.
(*d*) Where is the Sudan?
(*e*) Name the Baltic states.
(*f*) Where is Bessarabia?

3. To what books would you refer in order to find the following information?

(*a*) The amount of Russia's wheat exports in 1930. In 1913.
(*b*) The amount of manganese produced in the United States in 1929.
(*c*) The amount of Germany's pig-iron production in 1912.
(*d*) The value of the United States' exports of farm machinery in 1929.
(*e*) The name of the Japanese ambassador to the United States.
(*f*) The size of the French army in 1930.
(*g*) The treaty of Tirana (Italy and Albania, 1926).
(*h*) The Hay-Pauncefote treaty of 1901.

4. Write an editorial of "historical setting" based on an announcement by the Federal Treasury Department that henceforth the salaries of teachers in the state public schools will be taxable by the Federal Government. For a reference, read the decision of the United States Supreme Court, in 1871, The Collector *v.* Day, in *Wallace's United States Supreme Court Reports,* Vol. XI, pp. 1113*ff*, or *United States Supreme Court Reports,* Lawyers' Edition, Vol. XX, pp. 122*ff*.

5. Referring to Marriott and Robertson, *The Evolution of Prussia,* pp. 290-298, write an historical parallel editorial based on the following news dispatch:

> Amsterdam, July 12.—European dele-
> gates at the International Chamber of
> Commerce convention to-day demanded the
> organization of a European tariff union.
> Although the request emanated from in-
> dependent business men of various con-
> tinental countries, it is understood that
> certain statesmen in these countries look
> upon the formation of such a customs
> union as forecasting an ultimate political
> union of the continental states.

6. Write an historical parallel editorial on a subject which is suggested to you by a recent news story.

7. Distinguish technically between *arbitration* and *conciliation*. See P. B. Potter, *An Introduction to the Study of International Organization*. What, precisely, is the function of the World Court?

8. Define "war in self-defense" by differentiating it from other kinds of war (e.g., "war as an instrument of national policy" and war to enforce the provisions of the League of Nations Covenant).

9. Prepare a definition of news, contrasting it with free publicity.

10. The Republican Congressmen who were responsible for the drafting of the Smoot-Hawley tariff bill asserted in 1930 that the bill increased the average *ad valorem* rate on agricultural products 32 per cent and the average *ad valorem* rate on industrial products 18 per cent. Contradicting this assertion, the American Farm Bureau Federation asserted that the increase on agricultural products was 15 per cent and the increase on industrial products was 14.5 per cent. The conflict between the two sets of figures was due to the fact that the Farm Bureau Federation classified as an agricultural product for tariff purposes "one upon which the farmer is the prime beneficiary of a rate of duty," and an industrial as "one upon which a processor is the prime beneficiary of a rate of duty." Under this classification, all processed farm products such as flour, canned vegetables, and refined sugar are listed as industrial products. The framers of the tariff bill had classified as farm products all imports under the agricultural schedule such as sugar, tobacco, wool, and raw wool products.

Which classification do you think is the more accurate?

11. The following editorial is so thin that it is of no help to the reader. Try to put some substance into it by analyzing and defining (*a*) society; and (*b*) bureaucracy.

> A new voice of protest against the encroach-
> ment of government on the rights and freedom
> of individuals is being sounded. This time it is
> by organized labor.

Matthew Woll, vice president of the American Federation of Labor, is apprehensive that the present tendency of government will lead the country into a state of socialism no less oppressive than that espoused by Marx.

In an article in *Nation's Business,* Mr. Woll complains that governmental boards, bureaus, and commissions are intruding, inch by inch, on individualistic freedom.

"Everything that has been bred into me by America and by the trade union movement of America," he writes, "objects to this development of bureaucratic power."

Marx mistakenly thought that his socialistic program would help labor as much or more than any other class of citizens. Could he return in the flesh today and hear his theories of government and industry denounced by a leading apostle of organized labor, the great socialist advocate of the last century would be sadly disillusioned.

Mr. Woll warns that unless the people of the country guard vigorously against it this new form of state socialism will make of government a "blanketing incubus instead of a protecting force."

CHAPTER III

Editorials of Explanation

1. Write an editorial in which you try to explain the motives of the Senator mentioned in the following news dispatch (1930):

Washington.—A resolution calling upon the State Department to use its influence in the dispute between India and the British government was introduced today by Senator Blaine of Wisconsin, but no effort was made for immediate action.

The resolution cited charges of "atrocities" by Great Britain in her rule over India. It proposed that the Senate "deplore such acts of violence, infamy, and inhumanity committed by one signatory of the Kellogg Pact against another signatory of the pact; and that India is an original signatory of the Kellogg-Briand Peace Pact; the United States Senate instructs the State Department to use its best offices to insure peaceful settlement of the In-

> dian struggle with no abridgement of the
> just rights of the people."

Do you see any significance in any of the following factors? (a) the fact that no effort was made to obtain immediate action on the resolution; (b) that Senator Blaine was the only Senator who had voted against ratification of the Kellogg-Briand Pact; and (c) the character of the Senator's constituents?

2. When, in May, 1928, Professor John Bassett Moore resigned his judgeship in the Permanent Court of International Justice, the Chicago *Tribune* commented as follows:

> Mr. John Bassett Moore has sent his resignation to the secretariat of the League of Nations as a member of the League court. We congratulate our distinguished jurisprudent upon his retirement from a situation which must have been unsatisfactory if not embarrassing. He could not have cherished very seriously a theory that he had been invited to a place in this tribunal primarily because of his eminence as a master of international law, although that eminence will be conceded. He knew that he was offered his place because it seemed important in the interest of the court's prestige that it should have an American member even though he did not sit as a representative of the American government.
>
> Mr. Moore's membership was in fact a piece of tactics and we cannot believe, though he was induced to effectuate it, that as a loyal American he could be comfortable in a rôle inconsistent with his own loyal Americanism. The American nation had disclosed its distrust of the League of Nations and its unwillingness to be drawn into the system it represents, directly or by indirection. It had refused to adhere to the League's agency, the court, and there is no doubt that the invitation to Mr. Moore was not viewed in America in any other light than as a device to win opinion for the court and to give it a representative character more comprehensive than we are willing to lend it. Mr. Moore's acceptance had no sanction from American opinion, and while it was quite within his rights as an individual, it placed him in a situation subject to misinterpretation and inseparable from a sense of apology.
>
> We are sure that Mr. Moore will be better employed in the service of international law and the evolution of durable peace among nations in completing his work on international law rather

> than in occupying an anomalous and dubious
> place upon a tribunal to which his own country
> refuses to adhere for reasons explicit and well
> considered.

Look at this situation from all angles and then decide whether or
not the foregoing is a true explanation.

3. A study of the following editorial of explanation will help
the student to understand how editorial thinking is done. List
all of the factors in the situation which have caused the editorial
writer to believe that the action of the school board is a smoke
screen.

> The board of education, facing a desperate
> financial situation, has been devoting hours of
> its time to the discussion of a fantastic scheme
> to issue $50,000,000 in bonds for the purpose of
> building schools. Yesterday afternoon, with only
> two dissenting votes, the board adopted the
> scheme.
>
> It is to be hoped that parents and teachers
> will not be confused by this attempt to divert
> attention from the only matter to which the
> board should be giving attention at this moment.
> The discussion and adoption of the bond issue
> is merely a smoke screen intended to conceal the
> fact that between 1925 and 1931 school attend-
> ance has increased only 10 per cent, while the
> cost of administration has advanced 60 per cent;
> the cost of instruction, 30 per cent; the cost of
> the so-called coördinated activities, 85 per cent;
> the auxiliary functions, 83 per cent; the cost of
> operating the school plants, 106 per cent, and the
> cost of maintaining the plant, 206 per cent.
>
> A majority of the school board would prefer
> not to have much attention paid the fact that in
> 1926 it cost $4,406,000 to operate the school
> plant, while in 1931, when all commodities had
> declined sharply in value, the same item in the
> budget is placed at $8,132,000. Some of the mem-
> bers and their co-conspirators in raiding the
> school funds would rather divert public opinion,
> if possible, from the comparison brought out in
> the Cleveland bureau's audit, which shows that
> in Chicago 14.51 per cent of the current expenses
> on schools is devoted to the operation of schools
> as opposed to educational purposes, while in New
> York the comparative figure is 6.21 per cent, and
> the average in a dozen cities, including Chicago,
> is 8.99.
>
> It is cold facts such as have been recited which

prove the incompetence of the board for an able, not to say honest, administration of its funds. Naturally the members who are responsible for the waste, in conspiracy with those in a position to profit from it, would rather change the subject. If any teachers or parents are disposed to give a moment's attention to the $50,000,000 bond issue proposal which the board has now asked the legislature to authorize, let them consider the probability of floating such an issue now, at a time when the credit of Chicago's governments is at low ebb, when they are unable to borrow even short term money, when one government is already in default on its bond issues and others are headed in the same direction.

The members of the board who are making desperate efforts to conceal their own shortcomings, we are confident, will not succeed in hoodwinking the parents and teachers of Chicago. The board, as it is constituted, has lost the confidence not only of the present city administration but of the teaching force and the people of Chicago as well.

Chapter IV

How We Think

1. Prepare an example of an act of thought which you recall having performed at some time in the past. Explain thoroughly each step in the process.

2. Do you think that the following editorial from the New York *World,* published in October, 1930, reveals a clear insight into the realities of government?

In the last few months we have heard a lot about the desirability of preparing for bad times while good times are still with us. The President of the United States, with his plan for public works, was one of the first to enunciate this doctrine; the American Federation of Labor is the latest, and no doubt there will be others before the tide begins to turn. Unquestionably it is a sound idea, but it would run into a formidable snag if anybody tried to put it into actual practice. The snag is that in good times to talk about the possibility of bad times is a crime somewhat similar to imagining the king's death. A year ago the man who so much as wondered about bad times would have been denounced as a sort of public enemy. All sorts of arguments were advanced to prove that the boom would last forever; securities had acquired a "scarcity value" quite apart from their intrinsic worth, like the autographs of Button Gwinnett; the population was increasing; living standards were going up; the country had found an unlimited capacity to consume whatever was produced in it. What chance, at that feverish time, for the man who asked congress to appropriate money for dams, steamboat channels, and postoffices, frankly on the ground that their construction would provide jobs during the dark hours ahead? He would have been lucky to get out of the capitol alive.

3. Criticize the way you think about social problems:

Step 1.—Do you often start steps 2 and 3 without giving adequate attention to the necessity for defining and clarifying the problem itself?

Step 2.—Do your imagination and memory present many or few conjectures?

Step 3.—Are you quick or slow in testing a conjecture when it is presented?

Step 4.—Would you say that you are intellectually lazy and intellectually dishonest, or would you say that the reverse is true?

CHAPTERS V AND VI

V. Causal and Functional Relations
VI. Editorials Involving Causal Relations

1. Do you agree with the following statement by Gerard Swope, President of the General Electric Company?

It is confidently believed that if the fear of lack of work were removed from the mind of the workingman, he would approach his work with an entirely different attitude, his intelligence would be aroused, his interest stimulated and he would have enthusiasm and satisfaction from the work to be done. As a result the quality of workmanship would be better, he would feel free to suggest better methods, which would lower costs and be reflected eventually in lower selling prices to the public and assure a wider sphere of use for the article itself.

2. Analyze the following statement:

The unemployment insurance plan which provides that employers must bear all the cost of unemployment insurance would have serious consequences for the workers themselves. It is not difficult to see that such a scheme enacted into law would deter men from becoming employers and would result in the constant holding down of working forces to the minimum.

3. Senator James Couzens posed the following questions in a letter to the Chamber of Commerce of the United States in April, 1931. Do you agree with his insinuations?

Does the Chamber realize that to reduce wages would simply bring around a maladjustment of the distribution of the earnings of capital and labor that existed before the depression?

How will a reduction in wages increase the purchasing power, which is so badly needed at this time?

Does the Chamber, with the constant increase in productivity of man power, believe that the workers are to get less of their productivity rather than more?

Statistics show that the value of manufactured products in 1929 was $6,699,168,000 more than in 1927, and yet wages in 1929 were only $572,828,000 more than in 1927. They also show that wages paid in 1929 were $413,779,000 more than in 1923, and in the same period manufactured products increased by $8,887,941,000 for the same period.

Does not the Chamber believe that this development is drying up the springs of consumption?

4. Analyze the following statement made by the *New Leader:*

Figures of production recently published by the Department of Commerce show that factory production has increased 75 per cent from 1914 to 1925, while the number of factory workers increased only 13.5 per cent. This shows an increased exploitation of the workers of 54 per cent for the period.

5. The following statements have been made with .eference to installment selling:

(a) In 1930 the average family installment debt was $250.

(b) Installment buying costs the consumer an interest rate of about 25 per cent; the more money he pays for interest the less he has left to pay for other merchandise.

(c) When an industry goes on an installment basis, the cash price tends to rise somewhere near the installment price.

If these facts are true, what relation would they have to the business depression that began in 1929?

6. Analyze the following statement:

The Smoot-Hawley tariff act has caused Canada to establish a retaliatory tariff which has had the effect of causing 87 American manufacturers to establish Canadian factories within eighteen months after the signing of the Smoot-Hawley act. These American-owned factories will employ Canadians, not Americans. Still, Mr. Matthew Woll and his followers talk of the benefits of the tariff to American labor.

7. Have you made any observations which either bear out or challenge the following statement made by an American anthropologist?

In the course of social evolution, as in organic evolution, new patterns are formed, grow, realize themselves, and then give way to new forms. All life means growth and change. Nothing is static and permanent. Capitalist society cannot continue to exist. It has almost realized itself, and signs of disintegration are visible on all sides; and already a post-capitalist society has formed itself in our midst.

Imperialism, and hence capitalism, can exist only as long as it can exploit fresh markets and untouched sources of raw material. The markets are rapidly becoming industrialized, as in the case of China and India, and in turn they look for markets to exploit. And practically all of the world's raw materials have already been appropriated. It is obvious, then, that the margin upon which capitalism has been operating is rapidly diminishing and must soon disappear. The collapse is inevitable.

8. Along the line of thought contained in the following quotation concerning the effects of the invention of gunpowder, write an editorial on the possibility of electricity releasing man from so much of his present burdensome toil that he will have time in the future to develop a higher culture:

As Buckle points out, gunpowder, with its accompanying engines, made necessary the development of competent specialists in military affairs and released a large proportion of the population of every country from the responsibility of fighting which fell upon all freemen when pikes and bows and arrows were the weapons of warfare. "In this way immense bodies of men were gradually weaned from their old warlike habits and being, as it were, forced into civil life, their energies became available for the general purposes of society and for the cultivation of those arts of peace which had formerly been neglected. The result was that the European mind, instead of being, as heretofore solely occupied either with war or theology, now struck out into a middle path, and created those great branches of knowledge to which modern civilization owes its origin." . . . Moreover, gunpowder contributed to the downfall of the becastled, bewalled, shut-off and embattled feudal aristocracy and to the rise of modern urbanism with its world outlook and rich exfoliations.—C. A. and M. R. Beard, *The Rise of American Civilization*, pp. xi-xii.

9. Comment on the following statement:

The charge that the immigrant is responsible for the growth of crime in the United States is unjustifiable. The meager statistics that do exist indicate that the immigrant is less a criminal than the native American.

10. Do you agree with the following statement made in favor of the adoption of a state income tax in Illinois?

If taxes were levied upon the basis of income, voters would realize more readily that they were paying for increased expenditures for government and would consider with greater care the need for proposed new activities of government. As a general rule, the man who pays sees to it that his money is well spent. If we could get half a million more taxpayers in the city of Chicago, we need not worry about extravagance and inefficiency in our tax spending bodies.

11. What can you say about the following statement made by Samuel Crowther in the *Ladies' Home Journal?*

During the ten years which we have had prohibition the production of the country has increased between 25 and 30 per cent instead of the normal rate of about 15 per cent.

12. Do you believe this editorial is sound?

> There are a number of states that levy a five-cent gasoline tax. In Florida and South Carolina the tax is six cents. In Georgia, where it is four cents, the governor exhorts the legislature to double it. Let the tax be eight cents, says he, and after the state has no more need of so mighty a revenue as would be produced, let the tax be decreased. Fine chance!

13. What additional facts would have to be known in order for one to establish the truth or to challenge the accuracy of the following statement?

There are many reasons offered for the high rate of homicides in the United States, one of which is the lack of restraint upon the children of foreign-born parents. Yet the fact remains that Milwaukee has almost exclusively a population composed of immigrants or the children of immigrants, while the population of Memphis is almost exclusively native born. For every murder in Milwaukee there are twenty-two in Memphis.

14. On what generalizations about the organization of society does the following statement by a noted British economist rest?

If the Russian economic program succeeds, it will mean the end of Communism because it will bring the transmogrification of Russia from Communism to a liberal régime. If the plan succeeds, the towns will be able to pay for what they receive with goods. Once they are no longer starving, Communism will not have the same appeal.

15. How do you reconcile the statement quoted in Exercise 14 with the following statement by an American newspaper correspondent in Moscow?

Stalin has given up the idea of a world revolution. One of his reasons is his belief that the success of the Russian economic program will cause the exploited workingmen in certain European countries to try to emulate the Russian example.

16. A distinguished Western newspaper in 1929-1930 demanded a tariff for agriculture. Here is its suggested program. Analyze it.

(a) An adequate duty on blackstrap molasses would force the use of corn in the manufacture of industrial alcohol. That would take care of a part, at least, of the surplus of corn. (b) A duty on imported vegetable oils from the tropics would encourage the production of oil-bearing plants on our farms for use as food and in industry. (c) An adequate duty on hides might be expected to raise the value of the live-stock sold by American farmers. (d) A further effect of these duties would be in the encouragement which many of them would offer farmers to put their lands to new use, thereby decreasing the acreage planted to crops with which the market is already surfeited.

17. Which of Mill's methods is represented by the cartoon on page 94? In this cartoon, do you think the presence of the common factor, woman suffrage, is sufficient to establish the cause? Are other factors such as geographical position and manufacturing for export equally important as causal factors because they are present in or absent from the same groups of nations?

18. In the chain of causes described in the cartoon on page 117, which, if any, is the weakest link?

CHAPTERS VII AND VIII

VII. Argument from Example: Generalization
VIII. Argument from Example: Analogy

1. Explain the following news dispatch in the terms used in Chapter VII. Is the method described accurately?

Indianapolis, March 29, 1931.—Credit is given to the "hunch" or intuitive "flash of genius" for the solution of many difficult scientific problems by nearly 200 scientists of 232 whose answers to a questionnaire on the subject were given out today in a report to the American Chemical society, which opens its annual meeting here to-morrow.

The scientific hunch is defined as "a unifying or clarifying idea which springs into consciousness suddenly as a solution to a problem in which we are intensely interested."

"In typical cases," says the report, "it follows a long period of study, but comes into consciousness at a time when we are not consciously working on the problem. A hunch springs from a wide knowledge of

> facts but is essentially a leap of the imagination in that it goes beyond a mere necessary conclusion which any reasonable man must draw from the data at hand. It is a process of creative thought. . . ."
> There are four stages in research work, according to Professor Baker. The first is "preparation," in which the problem is investigated by reading and experiment. The second is "incubation," in which the mind, often unconsciously, goes over the information acquired in the first stage. The third is "illumination," consisting of the hunch. And the fourth is "verification," in which the hunch, or working hypothesis, which seems to unify and explain all known facts, is tested by experiment.

2. Comment on this description of the college graduate:

He has imagination and intelligence to master quickly what ordinary public men learn through their pores in the course of a lifetime.

3. Referring to P. T. Moon, *Imperialism and World Politics,* Chapter XIX, write an editorial based on the following excerpt from a speech by a former Vice-Governor of the Philippine Islands:

Although the Dutch in Java and the French in their colonies have made imperialism pay, England has made no money at it. Imperialism, in the long run, does not pay dividends.

4. Is the postwar experience of European countries with unemployment insurance sufficient proof by example that state-sponsored unemployment insurance, as a policy, is a mistake? In order to write an editorial about unemployment insurance as an American remedy, do your own research. (See partial list of references on p. 79.)

5. Is there a relation between illiteracy and political dictatorships? Write an editorial based on your interpretation of the following statistics on illiteracy: Hungary, 33 per cent; Italy, 35 per cent; Spain, 48 per cent; Greece, 57.2 per cent; Russia, 69 per cent; Switzerland, 0.3 per cent; the United States, 6 per cent; France, 14.1 per cent.

6. What is the relation between blood revenge, war, balance of power, and the League of Nations? Are they merely different forms of the same behavior pattern? Examine carefully the following discussion, which is taken from Chapter IV of Carl Murchison's *Social Psychology,* and write an editorial which embodies your analysis:

It is the thesis of this chapter that these four forms of social behavior are essentially identical in content, but may merge from one into the other in form. They are based largely upon identical motives and bring about almost identical social effects. In spite of presumptuous claims, all are equally the tools of the capable and strong, and all are equally destructive of the weak and incompetent.

(a) *Blood Revenge*. Blood revenge was not practiced within a tribe but always between tribes. Blood spilled by some member of an alien tribe must always be revenged by a spilling of blood in the tribe that has offended. The practice in ancient times was fairly general throughout those parts of the world where records are now available. It would be absurd to presume that the practice belongs only to ancient times, since modern wars have been caused by the same practice.

The practice of blood revenge was not necessarily engaged in by all of the members of a tribal community. The actual execution of the practice might lie within the hands of a very few individuals, even one individual. But the practice was supported by community approval and could not be avoided by the individual whose duty it was to avenge the spilling of blood.

There are obvious arguments in support of the practice. It gave community worth to individuals, resulting in increased community attachment and vigorous support of the community by the individual. It gradually increased the security of the individual—before the beginning of a feud. It resulted in the development of a conviction of social obligation on the part of the individual. It was probably the genesis of nationalism. The arguments against the practice are equally obvious. No issue was closed until one tribe or the other had been completely destroyed. The practice was all in favor of the stronger and more numerous tribe, and completely destructive of the weaker and less numerous community. From the point of view of the losing community, it was probably poor sportsmanship.

It is a very simple matter for us of the twentieth century to look upon this ancient practice as a sheer, barbarous evil. That is largely because we think too much of the blood that has been revenged, and not enough of the motives and the social effects. The surface of the earth obviously cannot support an unlimited population of human beings. In ancient times the average available resources of the world were far less than now. The food supply and available comforts were decidedly limited. The question of human survival was a very real one. This does not mean that primitive men were thinking about such matters very seriously. It was not necessary that they do much thinking on the subject—it was necessary only that they do or die. Blood revenge, like so many other practices of primitive man, played into the general problem of survival. It increased the probability that the stronger should survive and that the weaker would disappear. There is no intellectual reason why the stronger should survive in preference to the weaker, but it seems to be an obvious fact.

Where the contrast was limited to an open conflict between weak tribes on one hand and strong tribes on the other, the practice would persist without deviation or change in form. But when the conflict became one between two strong and numerous tribes, there would naturally arise a desirability on both sides for delaying the ultimate decision while better methods were being formulated and being brought into execution. This would result ultimately in truces, treaties of peace, watchful waiting, or inter-tribal combinations.

(*b*) *War.* War is blood revenge on a large scale. During the progress of war the only motive is to win at any cost. Of course, this is the same motive that functions during the practice of blood revenge. The motives that culminate in war, however, are as various and infinitely numerous as are the motives that culminate in the initiation of blood revenge. Two members of neighboring tribes might meet accidentally in the forest, and in the course of an argument over the fish supply might engage in a personal conflict resulting in the destruction of one of the individuals. The cause of the initial combat might be even more trivial. When once set in motion, the practice of blood revenge became stern, relentless, and destructive, regardless of the motive in the original combat.

It is true also that all wars are alike, after once beginning. After the first gun has been fired, all motives merge into one motive—to win at any cost.

The practice of war is accompanied by emotional outbursts of patriotic enthusiasm, of self-sacrifice, bravery, hero-worship, and desire to kill the enemy. All of these outbursts and forms of behavior have only one goal —to win at any cost.

The arguments in favor of war are identical with those in support of blood revenge. The social effects are identical. War is a tool for the strong and competent, and leads inevitably to the destruction of the weak and incompetent. There is no intellectual reason why the strong should win rather than the weak—it is merely a fact of nature and inevitably occurs.

If the resources of the world are limited, the practice of war means the strong and competent will enjoy these resources, and the resources will not be depleted by being shared with weaker communities or nations. There is a sophistry abroad in recent literature to the effect that the strong always lose in war and that the weak always win. This sophistry is based upon a stupid confusion of definite forms of strength and of definite forms of incompetence. A nation that is strong on the battlefield but weak off the battlefield cannot be listed only as a strong nation, but must be listed in both categories.

If war were always between the weak on the one hand and the strong on the other hand, there would never be any obstacle to the initiation of war, and the weak would eventually disappear. But when war is between two powerful nations, it becomes desirable that the ultimate decision be postponed while more effective methods are being formulated and being brought into execution. Each of the strong nations is willing to invite the weaker nations to come into the conflict on its side. In this way the weak survive and sit in the council chambers of the mighty. As a result, organizations come into existence that preserve the balance of power, and world politics gain in importance.

(*c*) *Balance of Power.* The phenomenon of balance of power has existed throughout most recorded history. It has gained in importance in recent times, and previous to 1914 was considered the most effective form of international relationships.

In recent times it has been the popular opinion that antagonistic organizations of nations, preserving a balance of power, existed primarily for the purpose of nurturing peace. This general belief has given prestige to the practice by making it possible for the practice to proceed undisturbed by undue excitement on the part of the general population. The motives behind the practice, however, are not even remotely concerned with the preservation of peace. It should be realized that, though peace may be a necessary condition for the accomplishment of certain things, it, in itself, has no social value. To imagine that great organizations of nations are brought about merely for the sake of preserving peace is an idea as comical as it is stupid.

The balance of power is merely a transient stage in the progress of war. It usually precedes open hostilities, but need not necessarily do so. The idea of "balance" is contributed from the side that is not yet equal in strength and efficiency to the opposing side. The idea makes further preparation and organization plausible and desirable. The process continues until one side or the other, or both together, begins open hostilities.

The practice is one for insuring ultimate victory after the hostilities begin. But, of course, the advantage is all with the side possessing superior diplomacy and physical resources sufficient to attract national accomplices.

If the practice of seeming to preserve the balance of power always resulted in the more stupid nations' banding and being together on the losing side, there would never be any important attempts made to destroy the practice. But if the practice results in an equal division of diplomacy and physical resources, that is, if the practice actually does what it has always claimed to do—make victory uncertain, then it becomes desirable that the ultimate decision be postponed in order that more effective methods may be formulated and put into execution. In this way is born the organization that absolutely guarantees that any war will be a world war—the League of Nations.

(d) *League of Nations.* It seems a far cry from the practice of blood revenge to the practice of such an organization as a league of nations. The content of the two forms of behavior, however, is essentially identical. Such an organization is generally thought of as being an engine of peace. It is an enterprise, however, that has been generated, developed, and put into execution by the strongest nations on the face of the earth. If it were an organization conceived and advertised by the weak nations of the world, it might be valid to label it as an engine of peace. But it has been conceived and advertised by the strongest and most warlike nations in the world, and is an enterprise which weaker nations may have been coerced into supporting. It is a most interesting enterprise for the social psychologist to observe. The paraphernalia and setting of a league of nations make possible a guarantee that what has been accomplished in the way of preparing for war will not be easily lost. It is a kind of mutual admiration and support of the *status quo.* Under ordinary circumstances, a nation that has succeeded in building a navy twice as strong as the navy of some other nation could guarantee a continuation of that superiority only by immediate hostility and early victory. If a league of nations is formed, however, the naval superiority can be guaranteed without the experience and danger of immediate warfare. Attention can then be turned to other fields where superiority is still uncertain, and where the authority of the league does not yet reach. It is undoubtedly one of the most brilliant enterprises of modern world politics. The affairs of any league of nations are bound to be controlled by those nations possessing the most able diplomats and the most effective means of coercing the support of other nations in the conduct of the league. Such an organization virtually guarantees that weak nations will not be exterminated from the face of the earth, but that they shall be partners in the long drawn out and complex contest between the mighty nations of the world.

It has been the thesis of this chapter that blood revenge, war, balance of power, and world-organization of nations are but different behavior patterns possessing the same general content. It is not important, as traditional social psychology has presumed, that we study these behavior patterns as such. It is of the greatest importance, however, that we understand the factors that determine which shall be the victor and which the vanquished. These factors are the real subject matter of social psychology, but have invariably been neglected by social psychologists. (Reprinted by permission of the Clark University Press.)

7. The following is a wise-crack by Ralph Barton in *Liberty* magazine. Who is right—Mr. Barton or Mr. Ford?

The "Sage of Detroit" releases another mouthful. "If booze comes back, I'm through with manufacturing. Drinking workers can't make perfect machines," says Henry Ford, referring apparently to such rattle-traps as the Rolls-Royce of England, the Hispano-Suiza of France, the Mercedes of Germany, the Isotta-Fraschini of Italy, and the Minerva of Belgium.

8. To what extent are there likenesses in these phenomena: (a) racketeering; (b) business as it is conducted under the capitalist system; and (c) economic imperialism?

9. What is the generalization, if any, which can be derived from the following relationships?

French investments (both government and private banking investments) in the Balkan states increased 242 per cent during the period of 1902-1914; France's investments in Russia, in the same period, increased 63 per cent; the total of French foreign investments, including those made in French colonies, increased in the same period only 83 per cent.

10. The following tables were published by Mr. Robert Marshall in the *Nation* for March 23, 1927. They indicate that in twenty-two cases out of twenty-five the quadrennial rainfall predicted the next president. If chance alone had operated, says Mr. Marshall, the probability of coincidence between precipitation and

presidential succession in twenty-two cases out of twenty-five would be only 1 in 14,603. Write an editorial analyzing the generalization, giving what you think is the correct weight for all factors.

PRESIDENTIAL SUCCESSION AND PRECIPITATION IN THE NORTHEAST

Date	Precipitation		Presidential succession
	Amount in inches	Relation to normal	
1825–1828	42.28	—	Change
1829–1832	46.08		Continuation
1833–1836	37.47	—	Continuation
1837–1840	37.98	—	Change
1841–1844	40.25	—	Change
1845–1848	40.36	—	Change
1849–1852	42.92	—	Change
1853–1856	43.59	+	Continuation
1857–1860	44.49		Change
1861–1864	45.10		Continuation
1865–1868	46.12		Continuation
1869–1872	47.89		Continuation
1873–1876	44.13		Continuation
1877–1880	43.38		Continuation
1881–1884	42.27	—	Change
Mean	42.95		

PRESIDENTIAL SUCCESSION AND PRECIPITATION IN THE WEST NORTH CENTRAL STATES

Date	Precipitation		Presidential succession
	Amount in inches	Relation to normal	
1885–1888	26.48	—	Change
1889–1892	26.21	—	Change
1893–1896	24.61	—	Change
1897–1900	27.88		Continuation
1901–1904	28.90		Continuation
1905–1908	29.61		Continuation
1909–1912	25.01	—	Change
1913–1916	27.95		Continuation
1917–1920	25.02	—	Change
1921–1926	26.24	—	Continuation
Mean	26.79		

11. In 1921 a campaign was waged in Cleveland for the adoption of a city manager form of charter. The advocates of the plan cited the experience of three other Ohio cities. Akron had adopted the plan in 1920, and Dayton and Springfield in 1914. Do you think the following relationships argue in favor of the city manager form of charter?

	Tax rate	Population	Per capita tax on income	Debt per capita
Cleveland	$9.63	936,485	$21.12	$103.00
Akron	6.63	208,435	11.14	73.44
Dayton	7.65	152,559	11.00	52.98
Springfield	6.95	60,840	10.84	31.72

12. Test each of the examples cited in the following editorial. Are they fair examples? Write out your answers.

The relations between Canada and the United States have served as an excellent model for all other countries. For more than one hundred years there has been peace and good feeling on both sides of the border. There has been an absence of international incidents of the sort that arouse animosities.

Not content, however, with the *status quo,* somebody recently proposed an exchange of diplomatic representatives. Pursuant to this proposal, Mr. William Phillips was dispatched as our first minister to Canada. What has happened? From an Ottawa dispatch it is apparent that Mr. Phillips is already in hot water. As the result of a speech delivered at Toronto he has provoked the criticism of several Canadian newspapers. Here is every ingredient for the making of an unpleasant situation.

One example, of course, does not prove the rule. But there are other incidents of diplomatic relations which may be cited to show that they do not always work as they are supposed to do. It will be recalled that Great Britain resumed relations with Russia. And what followed? The invasion of the Soviet headquarters in London, resulting in the engendering of bad blood. Likewise, France resumed relations with Russia, with the result that she has had to ask the recall of the Russian envoy. The United States, on the other hand, has so far declined to obey the im-

pulse to send diplomats to Russia. And, as every-
one knows, our relations with Russia have been
so excellent that for the last several years we
have enjoyed the lion's share of Russia's trade.

We offer no comment on these interesting
phenomena of international relations. Any one
is free to draw his own conclusions.

13. What form of argument is applied in the following editorial from the *Chicago Tribune Survey?* Is it sound?

A recent request was unusual even in the diver-
sified experience of the Business Survey staff of
The Tribune. A manufacturer of a product the
price of which was greatly depressed, and in
which competitive conditions are now rather
severe, asked us to suggest methods by which
these conditions could be overcome in his industry. He had in mind some sort of arrangement
with his competitors on price and output, and
he wanted us to supply him with examples of
industries which had secured improvement in
that way.

In these distressing times we like to be helpful.
But when schemes are likely to run afoul the law
we must decline to be of service in helping to
work them out. And here we have in mind not
only civil law—with which such a plan as our
interrogator had in mind must certainly conflict—
but also and particularly economic law. The
futility of attempting to defy the law of supply
and demand has been demonstrated so thoroughly
and so many times recently that it seems incomprehensible that any one now should have any
delusions about it.

English statesmen, who have, many is the time,
proved that they know economic law as Oliver
Wendell Holmes knows constitutional law, nevertheless made the mistake a few years back of
legalizing a scheme to put up the price of rubber.
They had some temporary success as long as they
kept down their output for the market while the
output of British Malaya dominated the market.

But they forgot that rubber stretches at least
as well as other things when the price is high
enough. The high price of rubber stimulated
increased production by the Dutch on the one
hand and the use of substitutes for rubber on the
other hand. The English had to back-water on
their Stevenson restriction plan. But they did
not do it soon enough. Rubber is now selling at

7 cents a pound, that comparing with $1.20 a pound at the peak. Present prices are the lowest in history, and stocks of crude rubber are also record breaking.

Copper production under ordinary circumstances is confined to a small number of producers. It was possible for the copper people to advance the price in 1929 to around 20 cents a pound. It was maintained at the high price through a great part of 1930. But price stimulated output. And the high price kept consumers out of the market, and those that didn't have to buy for immediate needs, didn't. The consequence was that stocks of copper on hand increased steadily to the highest point on record. Copper had to come down, and it did, with a thud. Recently copper has shown weakness at half the price at which the copper people attempted to stabilize their product.

An even better example of the futility of defiance of the law of supply and demand is provided by the government's experience with wheat. Uncle Sam willed that the farmer should get $1.18 a bushel for his wheat, backed his determination with a good many hundred millions, and what happened? Wheat stayed up as long as the government was buying, and then it came down. The following year output increased. Uncle Sam again tried to stabilize and again got stuck with a lot of wheat he doesn't know what to do with. Uncle Sam is obliged to back-water on his stabilization plan, and the farmer finds wheat prices the lowest in thirty-five years and has huge stocks of wheat yet to be sold, assuring low prices for the next crop. Need we mention coffee and Brazil?

Improvement in a number of industries has begun, but it has not come as a result of spurious schemes designed to get the better of economics. The law of supply and demand gets itself obeyed eventually and imposes a penalty for violation which bears a rough approximation to the extent of the violation.

14. Dividends paid to shareholders in American business corporations in 1930 were $350,000,000 greater (28 per cent) than in 1929, although it was a year of severe business depression. The dividends in many cases were not earned but were paid out of surplus earnings held in reserve. Wages paid to employes of American business corporations in 1930 were $707,000,000 less

(12 per cent) than in 1929. This is not right. Industry should be compelled by law to establish a reserve fund for the purpose of paying unemployment benefits to unemployed workers in time of business depression.

What form of argument is used in the foregoing paragraph? Is the argument sound?

15. What form of argument is used in the following editorial? Is it sound?

Efforts to hang a stigma upon old age pensions are odious.

The attempt to make them appear to be charity is an effort to hang a stigma upon them and also upon those who receive them.

A good part of what passes for charity is not charity.

Are children objects of charity?

If not, then recipients of old age pensions are still less so.

Children do not earn their living. They receive it from others.

They are not objects of charity for the reason that they are, in effect, borrowers from their own future.

They are some day to earn and repay to society what is spent upon them in their fledgling years.

When their earning years arrive, they not only repay what has been spent upon them in youth, but they also earn what is to be spent upon them in age. The old age pension is an earned right, not charity nor privilege.

16. In the following judicial opinion, what form of argument (reasoning) is used? Write a 500-word digest of the argument, explaining (a) what the decision was; and (b) the method of reasoning.

THE SCHOONER EXCHANGE v. M'FADDON & OTHERS
Supreme Court of the United States. 1812
7 Cranch 116

Appeal from the Circuit Court of the United States for the district of Pennsylvania.

[The Schooner Exchange, belonging to John M'Faddon and William Greetham, citizens of Maryland, while on a voyage from Baltimore to Spain in December, 1810, was seized in pursuance of the Rambouillet Decree by officers of the Emperor Napoleon, taken to France, converted into a public vessel, and given the name Balaou. The vessel having put into Philadelphia in July, 1811, her original owners filed a libel praying that she be attached and returned to them. Thereupon the United States District Attorney suggested to the court that the vessel was a public vessel, the property of a power with which the United States was at peace, and consequently not within the jurisdiction of the court. The decision of the District Court dismissing the libel having been reversed by the Circuit Court, an appeal was taken to this court.]

Marshall, Ch. J., delivered the opinion of the Court as follows:

This case involves the very delicate and important inquiry, whether an American citizen can assert, in an American court, a title to an armed national vessel, found within the waters of the United States.

The question has been considered with an earnest solicitude, that the decision may conform to those principles of national and municipal law by which it ought to be regulated.

In exploring an unbeaten path, with few, if any aids, from precedents or written law, the court has found it necessary to rely much on general principles, and on a train of reasoning, founded on cases in some degree analogous to this.

The jurisdiction of courts is a branch of that which is possessed by the nation as an independent sovereign power.

The jurisdiction of the nation within its own territory is necessarily exclusive and absolute. It is susceptible of no limitation not imposed by itself. Any restriction upon it, deriving validity from an external source, would imply a diminution of its own sovereignty to the extent of the restriction, and an investment of that sovereignty to the same extent in that power which could impose such restrictions.

All exceptions, therefore, to the full and complete power of a nation within its own territories, must be traced up to the consent of the nation itself. They can flow from no other legitimate source.

This consent may be either expressed or implied. In the latter case, it is less determinate, exposed more to the uncertainties of construction; but, if understood, not less obligatory.

The world being composed of distinct sovereignties, possessing equal rights and equal independence, whose mutual benefit is promoted by intercourse with each other, and by an interchange of those good offices which humanity dictates and its wants require, all sovereigns have consented to a relaxation in practice, in cases under certain peculiar circumstances, of that absolute and complete jurisdiction within their respective territories which sovereignty confers.

This consent may, in some instances, be tested by common usage, and by common opinion, growing out of that usage.

A nation would justly be considered as violating its faith, although that faith might not be expressly plighted, which should suddenly and without previous notice, exercise its territorial powers in a manner not consonant to the usages and received obligations of the civilized world.

This full and absolute territorial jurisdiction being alike the attribute of every sovereign, and being incapable of conferring extraterritorial power, would not seem to contemplate foreign sovereigns nor their sovereign rights as its objects. One sovereign being in no respect amenable to another; and being bound by obligations of the highest character not to degrade the dignity of his nation, by placing himself or its sovereign rights within the jurisdiction of another, can be supposed to enter a foreign territory only under an express license, or in confidence that the immunities belonging to his independent sovereign station, will be extended to him.

This perfect equality and absolute independence of sovereigns, and this common interest impelling them to mutual intercourse, and an interchange of good offices with each other, have given rise to a class of cases in which every sovereign is understood to waive the exercise of a part of that complete exclusive territorial jurisdiction, which has been stated to be the attribute of every nation.

1st. One of these is admitted to be the exemption of the person of the sovereign from arrest or detention within a foreign territory.

If he enters that territory with the knowledge and license of its sovereign, that license, although containing no stipulation exempting his person from arrest, is universally understood to imply such stipulation.

Why has the whole civilized world concurred in this construction? The answer cannot be mistaken. A foreign sovereign is not understood as intending to subject himself to a jurisdiction incompatible with his dignity, and the dignity of his nation, and it is to avoid this subjection that the license has been obtained. The character to whom it is given, and the object for which it is granted, equally require that it should be construed to impart full security to the person who has obtained it. This security, however, need not be expressed; it is implied from the circumstances of the case. . . .

2d. A second case standing on the same principles with the first, is the immunity which all civilized nations allow to foreign ministers.

Whatever may be the principle on which immunity is established, whether we consider him as in the place of the sovereign he represents, or by a political fiction suppose him to be extra-territorial, and, therefore, in point of law, not within the jurisdiction of the sovereign at whose Court he resides; still the immunity itself is granted by the governing power of the nation to which the minister is deputed. This fiction of exterritoriality could not be erected and supported against the will of the sovereign of the territory. He is supposed to assent to it.

This consent is not expressed. It is true that in some countries, and in this among others a special law is enacted for the case. But the law obviously proceeds on the idea of prescribing the punishment of an act previously unlawful, not of granting to a foreign minister a privilege which he would not otherwise possess.

The assent of the sovereign to the very important and extensive exemptions from territorial jurisdiction which are admitted to attach to foreign ministers, is implied from the considerations that, without such exemption, every sovereign would hazard his own dignity by employing a public minister abroad. His minister would owe temporary allegiance to a foreign prince, and would be less competent to the objects of his mission. A sovereign committing the interests of his nation with a foreign power, to the care of a person whom he has selected for that purpose, cannot intend to subject his minister in any degree to that power; and therefore, a consent to receive him, implies a consent that he shall possess those privileges which his principal intended he should retain—privileges which are essential to the dignity of his sovereign, and to the duties he is bound to perform. . . .

3d. A third case in which a sovereign is understood to cede a portion of his territorial jurisdiction is, where he allows the troops of a foreign prince to pass through his dominions.

In such case, without any express declaration waiving jurisdiction over the army to which his right of passage has been granted, the sovereign who should attempt to exercise it [i.e., territorial jurisdiction] would certainly be considered as violating his faith. By exercising it, the purpose for which the free passage was granted would be defeated, and a portion of the military force of a foreign independent nation would be diverted from those national objects and duties to which it was applicable, and would be withdrawn from the control of the sovereign whose power and whose safety might greatly depend on retaining the exclusive command and disposition of this force. The grant of a free passage, therefore, implies a waiver of all jurisdiction over the troops during their passage, and permits the foreign general to use that discipline, and to inflict those punishments which the government of his army may require. . . .

But if his [i.e., the receiving sovereign's] consent, instead of being expressed by a particular license, be expressed by a general declaration that foreign troops may pass through a specified tract of country, a distinction between such general permit and a particular license is not perceived. It would seem reasonable that every immunity which would be conferred by a special license, would be in like manner conferred by such general permit. . . .

[The learned Chief Justice now comes to the question that is before the Court.]

If, for reasons of state, the ports of a nation generally, or any particular ports be closed against vessels of war generally, or the vessels of any particular nation, notice is usually given of such determination. If there be no prohibition, the ports of a friendly nation are considered as open to the public ships of all powers with whom it is at peace, and they are supposed to enter such ports and to remain in them while allowed to remain, under the protection of the government of the place.

In almost every instance, the treaties between civilized nations contain a stipulation to this effect in favor of vessels driven in by stress of weather or other urgent necessity. In such cases the sovereign is bound by compact to authorize foreign vessels to enter his ports. The treaty binds him to allow vessels in distress to find refuge and asylum in his ports, and this is a license which he is not at liberty to retract. It would be difficult to assign a reason for withholding from a license thus granted, any immunity from local jurisdiction which would be implied in a special license.

If there be no treaty applicable to the case, and the sovereign, from motives deemed adequate by himself, permits his ports to remain open to the public ships of foreign friendly powers, the conclusion seems irresistible, that they enter by his assent. And if they enter by his assent necessarily implied, no just reason is perceived by the Court for distinguishing their case from that of vessels which enter by express assent.

In all cases of exemption which have been reviewed, much has been

implied, but the obligation of what was implied has been found equal
to the obligation of that which was expressed. . . .

[A public armed ship] constitutes a part of the military force of her
nation; acts under the immediate and direct command of the sovereign;
is employed by him in national objects. He has many and powerful
motives for preventing those objects from being defeated by the interference of a foreign state. Such interference cannot take place without
affecting his power and his dignity. The implied license therefore under
which such vessel enters a friendly port, may reasonably be construed,
and it seems to the Court, ought to be construed, as containing an exemption from the jurisdiction of the sovereign, within whose territory she
claims the rites of hospitality. . . .

It seems then to the Court, to be a principle of public law, that
national ships of war, entering the port of a friendly power open for
their reception, are to be considered as exempted by the consent of that
power from its jurisdiction. . . .

In the present state of the evidence and the proceedings, the Exchange
must be considered as a vessel which was the property of the Libellants,
whose claim is repelled by the fact, that she is now a national armed
vessel, commissioned by, and in the service of the emperor of France. . . .

The Exchange . . . must be considered as having come into the
American territory, under an implied promise, that while necessarily
within it, and demeaning herself in a friendly manner, she should be
exempted from the jurisdiction of the country. . . .

I am directed to deliver it, as the opinion of the Court, that the
sentence of the Circuit Court, reversing the sentence of the District
Court, in the case of the Exchange be reversed, and that of the District
Court, dismissing the libel, be affirmed.

Could the principle of international law laid down in the foregoing decision be extended with equal validity to private ships in
a foreign port? What is the "essential difference" involved?

17. In the following parts of an address delivered by Herbert
Hoover during the 1924 presidential campaign, list each form of
argument he employs and explain in detail whether or not you
agree with it:

Senator La Follette's party proposes government ownership and operation of railway and other public utilities. The Senator emphasizes this:
"I am for government ownership of railroads and every other public
utility—every one." This means all railways, power, light, telephone, and
telegraph. . . .

In its immediate form this is a proposition that the government should
buy and run the railways, electrical and other utilities, valued by official
commissions at $40,000,000,000, with 2,700,000 employes, requiring
$2,000,000,000 annually for bond interest, with an operating budget of
$10,000,000,000 per annum. . . .

Under government ownership, partisanship, "log-rolling," and politics
would be the inseparable accompaniments of administration. No great
business can be efficiently administered by such a board or such a basis

of choice. We shall convert business into politics, and surrender efficiency for spoils. If we distribute railway extensions as we distribute public buildings; if we locate electric power plants as we locate reclamation projects; if we divide up public industries generally as we share river and harbor improvements and army and navy stations—then, as surely as night follows the day, facilities will be wastefully provided for those districts or groups which are politically strong, and they will not be adequately provided for the districts or groups that are politically weak.

Also, under a régime of government ownership, these legislative bodies would have to deal with group pressures striving for favors in rates. The relative rates will affect the prosperity of every city and every section, every group, and every industry. States, counties, farmers, town dwellers, every group of manufacturers will press their representatives to secure an advantage, and legislators will inevitably honestly favor their constituents. Every experience to date indicates that the taxpayer will pay for the resulting concessions. Because the government had not the courage to increase railway rates during the war the taxpayer made up a $1,600,000,000 operation deficit. A neighboring government yielded last year to the demand for lower rates on the government railways; it is paying the deficit from taxes to-day.

If we embark on this vast venture we shall at once increase the total of national and local officeholders up to about six millions. The rightful interest of this group is in higher pay, constantly better conditions of service, and better standards of living. The rightful public interest will be to hold down rates and taxes. These interests will clash, and their clash must fight itself out, not on grounds of economic bargaining between laborer and employer, but in the political arena. The voting strength of this mass of officeholders, their wives and dependents, will be over 25 per cent of the whole. It is the balance of political power between parties in every district. Either every member of the legislative bodies will be elected to do the bidding of this bureaucracy or will be elected by a public in a rebellion against it. . . .

Moreover, the wasteful distribution of the $150,000,000 of capital invested annually in the Post Office, Reclamation Service, Shipping Board, rivers and harbors and roads, would not be a patch on the waste in appropriations when our legislative bodies get a chance to handle $2,000,-000,000 per year of new capital outlay. . . .

We can get some direct experience from government operated railways in foreign countries during the last ten years as to the results of these forces in this loading of employes. For instance, the number of employes of Italian railways has increased 50 per cent against an increase in traffic of 18 per cent. German employes increased 20 per cent against 5 per cent increase in traffic. Danish employes increased 48 per cent with 20 per cent increase in traffic. Swedish employes increased 10 per cent with a 25 per cent decrease in traffic. Norwegian employes increased 62 per cent with an increase in traffic of 37 per cent. Compare these figures with American railways, where the number of employes is about the same as ten years ago against a 10 per cent increase in traffic. . . . If we had increased our employes by such percentages it would cost $600,000,000 per annum or an increase of 10 per cent in rates. . . .

The classic domestic argument against all this is the postal service. There are, of course, conclusive reasons why that service must remain a public function. And it does carry the mails well, at a cost probably 25 per cent higher than private enterprise could do it. Its management and employes are the best that government can do; its faults are inherent in government ownership. But remember that the postal service pays no interest upon the vast sum of capital invested in its equipment and buildings. It pays no taxes on these structures. And how is that capital investment in public buildings distributed? Notoriously on the reverse side of business principles. How are the rates allocated to different classes of service? By the united pressure of organized groups; in all classes of mail for the lowest rates there is invariably a deficit in operating expenses piled upon the taxpayer. Postal employes are always in difficulties with their board of directors—that is Congress— as to pay adjustments. We are here proposing to amplify the shortcomings inherent in the postal service in the direct ratio of the Post Office budget of $600,000,000 to an annual budget of $10,000,000,000 in the utilities, not with 300,000 employes but with 2,750,000 and a business of infinitely greater technology.

Our national shipping is a daily sample of all the arguments I have given, and more. We paid $3,000,000,000 of the taxpayers' money for a fleet—some part of it was truly for war purposes—but we have written it down 90 per cent in six years to $300,000,000; and if the accounts were based upon the true costs with interest and depreciation, we should find that we are losing over $100,000,000 of the taxpayers' money a year in operating it. Yet private shipping is earning profits. Nor is this the fault of the Shipping Board: it is inherent in the system. . . .

18. List each form of argument used in the following editorial and state whether or not you think each is sound, stating your reasons fully:

> The Whitaker unemployment insurance bill is a sensible measure, and ought to be supported by all legislators who sincerely wish to remedy an unjust situation in our social order and who are desirous of being fair to employer and employe alike.
>
> The Whitaker bill, in brief, provides that the employer of ten or more full-time workingmen, on each regular pay-day, shall set aside a small percentage of each wage payment toward building up an unemployment reserve fund. This sum shall not be deducted from the wage but shall be in addition to the wage, and shall be reported to the state industrial commission at the end of every quarter. Any employe who is laid off by the company for more than four weeks in any one year shall be paid from the fund a sum not to exceed $18 a week for a period not in excess of 13 weeks. No employe shall be paid

from the fund who has not lived in the state one
year or who has been employed by the company
for less than nine months.

The bill is sound actuarially. It will guarantee
the means of subsistence to workingmen who may
become the victims of the usual depressions in
business. It will not, of course, support all or a
large part of the unemployed workers in a specific
plant during a time of extraordinary depression,
such as was experienced in the United States in
1929-1931 or in Great Britain and Germany where
a permanent unemployment problem has existed
since the end of the war.

The bill will correct a social injustice. Industry is responsible for the human material it uses.
No manufacturer would think of conducting his
business without setting up a reserve fund for
depreciation on machinery, and human beings,
certainly, ought to be treated no worse than machinery. This principle was recognized long ago
in 45 states of the union when industry was
compelled to assume the responsibility for injuries
received by workingmen in the course of their
work. The principle is so well established that
no employer to-day complains against the "injustice" of the workingmen's compensation laws.

It is, perhaps, true that the employer ought not
to be held responsible for all periods of business
depression since he does not have intimate and
actual control over the currents and cross-cur-
rents which affect the volume of production and
consumption. He cannot always prevent unemployment as he can prevent injury in his factory.
Society, not merely industry, should be held responsible for tremendous upheavals caused by
such agents of maladjustment as world wars.
Such conditions are to be remedied by scientific
planning, by the elimination of trade barriers,
and by coöperation and coördination. But the
Whitaker bill is a part of this process and is one
of the integral parts of an intelligent scheme.

The Whitaker bill will have the same effect in
preventing the usual unemployment that the workingmen's compensation laws have had in preventing injuries to employes. In order to
conserve the unemployment reserve fund, the
employer will plan his production along more
intelligent lines. He will try to stabilize employment instead of hiring men for rush periods and
discharging them shortly afterward. In every
industry it is practicable to do this. It has been

done successfully in the men's clothing industry,
in the soap industry, and in such seasonal industries as the greeting card industry and the date
packing industry.

The Whitaker bill was drafted after its authors had studied the experience of many industries which have installed such a plan. It is
sound in every respect, and employers will some
day thank this legislature for enacting it.

19. Write an editorial in reply to the following "letter to the
editor":

It is necessary to pay insurance on an automobile bought on the installment plan in order to
secure the firm from which it was purchased.

If a bank holds a mortgage on your property,
you must pay for a fire insurance policy. Should
the property be destroyed by fire, the bank collects.

Why not, therefore, demand a policy of your
banker, whereby your cash deposits are secured
100 per cent against loss?

Or, why not have the state guarantee your
deposits?

20. Apropos of the decision of the Federal Prohibition Bureau
to distribute pamphlets which purport to show the evil physio-
logical effects of drinking alcoholic liquors, an editor declared,
in substance, "The government has no business to engage in propaganda. Suppose the Navy Department would issue pamphlets to
convince the voters that we need a larger navy—no one would
approve of that."

A second editor, in reply, pointed out that the Department of
Agriculture issues bulletins for farmers and that the Department
of Labor issues bulletins on infant welfare and on the prevention
of accidents in mines. "This is not propaganda, but education,"
said the second editor. "The prohibition bureau is acting quite correctly."

Which editor, in your opinion, has overlooked the "essential
point of difference"?

21. Is this analogy true or false? What generalization under-
lies it?

I do not want to leave the regulation of business to the business man
any more than I want to leave the regulation of traffic to the motorists
when there are so many other interests on the highway.

22. Write an editorial in reply to the following editorial which
appeared in a Detroit newspaper during the famous Homestead
steel mill strike in 1892:

> The great employers of labor, whether they be corporations or individuals, are in no way responsible for the abundance of labor, or for its cheapness, and it is the supreme point of folly to demand or expect that they shall pay more for it than the lowest price at which it is offered. . . . There is not an editor in the land, nor a mechanic nor a laborer, how eloquently soever he may denounce big employers such as Carnegie or Frick, who does not follow precisely the same rule as they in every purchase he makes, whether it be merchandise or labor in which he is dealing.

23. With reference to a prohibition referendum in South Dakota in which the Drys won a 51 per cent majority, an editor remarked as follows:

If there is a majority either one way or the other we should be good sports enough to accept the results; for in a running race of men or horses, or any other mode of transportation, a win by an inch is as good as a win by a mile, and we accept the results of such a contest gracefully.

Do you agree with this view?

24. What is the logical force of the allegory embodied in the following speech by Mayor Hoan of Milwaukee?

The cause of this depression lies not so much in the fact that there has been too much produced, but in the fact that the consumers are unable to buy enough to keep up with production.

Let me give you an analogy. Assume that there is an island populated with 100 monkeys. They tire of collecting their daily cocoanuts and one enterprising chap suggests that cocoanuts be collected and turned over to him for storage. The monkeys turn over the cocoanuts and each gets a sea shell in return for each nut as negotiable security.

A large pile of nuts is collected, but some are lost by the keeper, others spoil in storage. The monkey in charge of the nuts finds himself in a hole and says he must charge two shells for each cocoanut he sells back to those who collected them. The monkeys see his predicament and agree that he must do that.

However, when all the shells have been collected, the holder of the nuts finds he still has some nuts left over. The people cannot buy them without shells. The monkey who holds them cannot sell them. The people bring in more nuts but he will not buy them because he already has a surplus.

What is to be done? Thereafter the monkeys must collect fewer nuts and should get more collateral for them. Without a consuming foreign trade, that is the only solution.

25. Analyze the following argument:

A lesson in the ethics of prohibition enforcement can be found in our experience with the XVth amendment. In that case the white population of the southern states was suddenly confronted with a constitutional mandate which they justly believed would wreck the foundations of their civilization. They did not seek to prove that the best way to get rid of it was to enforce it. They resisted it by any means at hand until they were able to find devices and legal fictions to outwit it. And the XVth amendment is still law. Forgotten, but not gone.

26. Write historical parallel editorials in which you compare (*a*) the Soviet and Cromwellian régimes; (*b*) the social classes in India in revolt against British rule and the social classes which revolted against British rule in the United States in 1775 and in Canada in 1837-8; (*c*) the State Department's policy of refusing to recognize those new governments in the Caribbean states which rest on revolution and the policy of the Quadruple Alliance after 1820 of intervening in European states which overthrew monarchic governments and replaced them with democratic régimes.

27. A form of argument similar to analogy is that which demurs to the "thin edge of a wedge." We must not do this, it is objected; for, if we did, we should logically be bound to do something quite similar which is plainly wrong or impractical. Once we start on this course, there's no knowing where we shall stop.

Analyze the following argument:

"I am opposed to the superintendent's plan of providing free breakfasts for undernourished school children," the chairman of the school board declared. "The time was when parents were required to educate their own children. But now, having been relieved of that duty, they are to be relieved of the necessity of feeding them. If we adopt this suggestion, we shall some day hear the plea that parents be relieved of the duty of clothing their children."

Has the "entering wedge" argument been logically employed in the debates about government operation of Muscle Shoals?

28. Do you agree with the generalization stated in the cartoon on page 130?

29. Do you think the analogy stated in the cartoon on page 148 is sound?

Chapter IX

How the Mind Falls into Error

1. Reduce the following argument to syllogistic form:

A millionaire may lose money in the stock market and cause no particular harm. The result of his gambling loss will be, in most cases, simply a transfer of surplus funds from his account to that of some one else.

Now a workingman or a man on a small salary undoubtedly has as much right to gamble in stocks as has a millionaire—that is, as much political and legal right. But the result of his losses is very different. When the man of limited means loses his money he is not losing surplus. He must deprive himself or his family of some necessity or luxury. It may be a new car. It may be an electric refrigerator. It may be some furniture. In any event, his inability to purchase the things he needs or wants injures the business of making and distributing these things. But as soon as merchandise cannot be sold, production must be curbed. This creates unemployment, and unemployment creates a further loss of buying power. This, in turn, results in further curtailment of production and still more unemployment, an ever-winding, vicious circle.

Workers who gamble in stocks may imagine that they risk nothing but their money, but when they lose their buying power they lose their work-giving power. Thus they create unemployment and, since this unemployment creates still further unemployment, they are actually risking their own jobs.—Edward A. Filene.

2. Identify the fallacies represented in the following arguments:

(*a*) Don't be deceived, voters. A certain little clique here is endeavoring to get in control of the city through the city manager plan. It is understood that if successful they will make a wholesale ousting of city officials and put in men of their kind regardless of capacity. Don't let them slip this over.

(*b*) The unconstitutional maternity act now in operation, which was signed by a lawyer-President after he had protested its unconstitutionality, was supported in Congress and out by lawyers. Senator Reed of Missouri opposed it vigorously but only the wilderness heard him. He called the roll of the powerful lobby of women, covering the country, which forced the measure through and showed that not one of them ever had borne a child.

(*c*) The United States ought to have an army and navy as large as any other nation's army or navy because no national impotence or weakness ever has developed as a boon to the world.

(*d*) We cannot accept President Hoover's assurance that our entry into the World Court will in no way involve us in the League of Nations. The judges of the World Court are appointed by the League, their salaries are paid by the League, and the decisions of the Court are essentially the decisions of the League. How is it possible, then, for us to be members of the Court without being involved in the League?

3. An editorial opposing compulsory unemployment insurance points out that responsibility for unemployment should be borne by society and not solely by industry. What is your opinion as to the logic of those who would require employers to bear the whole burden of unemployment insurance? What distinction should be made between the whole and the parts? Write an editorial in which you develop all the aspects of the problem.

4. Discuss the logic in Marx's theory of surplus value, basing your discussion on the following explanation by G. D. H. Cole:

. . . The amount of labour incorporated in production measures finally the "value" not of this or that particular commodity, but of the social product as a whole.

Here, yet, again, Marx's Hegelian affinities stand out clearly. The only One is, for him, more real than the Many; and he is always reaching out after a real Oneness underlying the phenomenal multiplicity of the capitalist world. He envisages a working class, which he had attempted to organize in the International Working Men's Association, in process of becoming one, and he sees the capitalists of the world as banded together against the working class. This Oneness alone is real. The prices of individual commodities are mere appearances. What is real is the one fact of exploitation—the appropriation by the capitalist class of the economic advantages of associated production. The "detail labourer" is a mere abstraction; not individuals, but only social classes, possess ultimate reality.

It is impossible thoroughly to understand Marx's thought without appreciating this mystical view of reality. Marx's view of social classes made him regard social classes as far more real and creative than individual persons. The theme of *Capital* is not the exploitation of individual labourers by individual capitalists, but of one whole class by another. He who would criticize Marx must begin by either accepting or attacking this fundamental concept. It conditions the entire Marx system. —Introduction to Everyman's edition of *Capital,* p. xxviii.

5. Examine carefully the following excerpt from an editorial published during the 1924 presidential campaign. Is the argument valid, or does it represent a fallacy of equivocation? Why?

. . . The Republican party cannot be held responsible for the corruption practiced by certain of its leaders. The Republican party is larger than any individual or group of individuals in it. The Republican party is not responsible for the deeds of Fall and Daugherty or Forbes and Miller or Hays and Harding. The Republican party is not responsible for the fraud connected with the leasing of our naval oil reserves, the graft connected with the veteran's bureau, the scandal in the office of the alien property custodian, or the acceptance of campaign funds from the alleged Continental Trading corporation conspirators.

Corruption is a personal, not a political matter. It must be remembered that a strong, courageous and honest man in the person of Calvin Coolidge sits in the White House and will continue to preside over the destinies of this republic.

> Our government is comparable to a great financial institution. Would you destroy a strong, successful bank because one or more employes had proved false to their trust? Would you wreck the institution and denounce the policies that made it great because the cashier or clerk or even the president had not measured up to all that was expected of him?

6. What is the fallacy involved in Mayor Walker's argument as reported in the following news story?

> Asserting that he was a "temporary target" for those who sought to discredit American governmental institutions, municipal, state, and national, Mayor Walker charged yesterday that the attacks on his administration and the charges against him were part of a Communist plot.
>
> The Mayor made this assertion in a speech with a dramatic setting at the annual communion breakfast of 2,000 members of the New York Fire Department Holy Name society in the grand ball room of the Hotel Astor after the Rev. Charles E. Coughlin, radio pastor of Detroit, had warned of the alleged Communist menace and made a vigorous defense of the Mayor.
>
> The Mayor mentioned no names but expressed scorn of "parlor Communists" and "certain high churchmen" who, he said, were fostering the attack on him and his administration. Father Coughlin mentioned pecifically John Haynes Holmes and Rabbi Stephen S. Wise of the city affairs committee, who signed the charges against Mayor Walker, and the mayor's references were interpreted as intended for them.
>
> The mayor warned his hearers that what he called Communist propaganda against him would be extended to other public officials and finally to business men in the campaign to undermine American institutions. He expressed confidence that right and justice would prevail when the fight was over.

7. What is the fallacy involved in the following statement reported by the New York *World* to have been made by Dr. John Haynes Holmes, pastor of Community Church, New York City?

When Nicholas Murray Butler will deliberately and openly violate the prohibition law, and voluntarily, on a plea of guilty, go to prison for his faith, as Roger Baldwin deliberately and openly during the war violated the conscription act, and voluntarily, on a plea of guilty, went to prison for his faith, I shall believe there is some moral principle in the wet revolt. But not before.

8. Here are two "labor" arguments concerning the tariff, one pro, the other con. Which do you think is more logical?

1. Only about 5,000,000 of our 25,000,000 wage earners are employed in tariff-protected industries. But tariff protection for these men has a reflex action on the prosperity of the remaining workers.

2. A tariff for the protection of 5,000,000 wage earners will raise the prices to be paid by the remaining 20,000,000 workers. As a consequence, the purchasing power of the 20,000,000 will be reduced and this will affect the volume of goods produced by the 5,000,000 tariff-protected workers.

9. An alderman introduced an ordinance in the city council which provides for the levying of a "wheelage" tax of $3.00 on every motor vehicle in the city, the revenues thus derived to be applied to the cost of paving boulevards and arterial streets. One newspaper in the city said the tax would be unfair; a second newspaper argued that the tax would be fair. Write an editorial expressing your view.

10. Analyze the following argument:

The United States has signed the Kellogg-Briand pact which makes war between nations illegal; there is no logic, therefore, in refusing citizenship to an alien on the ground that he refuses to promise to bear arms in defense of his country.

11. What is the fallacy inherent in the following argument which is the substance of the demurrer filed by the defendants in the famous Elk Hills naval oil reserve case?

President Harding had no authority to transfer jurisdiction of naval oil reserves to the Secretary of the Interior. Since President Harding's transfer was invalid, Secretary Fall had no authority to lease the reserve to Doheny. If Fall had no authority to lease the reserve, he could not be bribed into doing it. If he could not be bribed into doing it, then the charge of bribery should be dismissed.

Arrange the foregoing argument in syllogistic form.

Chapter X

The Creative and Critical Faculties

1. In the terms used in this chapter, write an editorial explaining the attitudes, "pollyanna" and "alarmist."

2. Write an editorial explaining the term *radical*. Refer to the following: A. B. Wolfe, "The Motivation of Radicalism," *Psychological Review*, Vol. XXVIII (1921), pp. 280-300; A. B. Wolfe, "Emotion, Blame, and the Scientific Attitude in Relation to Radical Leadership and Method," *International Journal of Ethics*, Vol. XXXII (1922), pp. 142-159; Lorine Pruette, "Some Applications of the Inferiority Complex to Pluralistic Behavior," *Psychoanalytic Review*, Vol. IX (1922), pp. 28-39; Harold D. Lasswell, *Psychopathology and Politics*, Chap. IX.

3. Write an editorial based on this statement by a manufacturer:

It seems that in the past the subject of taxation has largely been a matter of politics. It is an economic question, not a political one. Wisconsin and the entire nation will sigh with relief when taxation is eliminated from politics. No political party has a right to make an issue of taxation.

4. Write an editorial suggested by the following report by the New York *Times* of the eleventh plenary session of the executive committee of the Communist International at Moscow (April 24, 1931):

Finally the session approved the Comintern balance sheet for the year 1930, as follows:

Receipts carried over from the previous year totaled $14,733.24. Members' contributions from forty-nine sections, with 2,518,637 members, totaled $956,009.32. Other contributions totaled $65,481.74. Receipts from books, other publications and telegraph agencies were $60,006.80. The total receipts were $1,096,231.10.

The expenses were: (1) administrative, $321,469.05; (2) postal and telegraph, $24,-417.27; (3) traveling under orders, $48,-024.62; (4) for party papers and publications and for cultural and educational work (i.e., propaganda), $641,230.76. The carryover to the present year totaled $61,089.40, which balances the budget.

5. It has been estimated that it would cost approximately $300,-000,000 to construct the St. Lawrence waterway project. The annual interest charge would range from $12,000,000 to $18,000,-000 a year. Write an editorial which is suggested by the Canadian Government's report of traffic in the St. Lawrence canals during 1929. That report showed that purely Canadian traffic totaled 4,122,533 tons and American traffic 1,596,118 tons.

6. Comment on the following statement with reference to the discussion in this chapter:

It is high time the South was given credit for the soundness of its economic position. Whenever cotton prices drop, "The South is ruined" is the cry. Whenever there is a flood, however small a fraction of the land may be involved—"The South is ruined."
Last year [1927] it was cotton.
The price dropped and the old cry went up. The fact that cotton constituted less than eight per cent of the South's income was utterly disregarded. But the South was not ruined. In fact, its income for the year was the highest in all history.
This year it is the flood.
The present flood area covers only .009 per cent of the South's area. The population involved is only .007 per cent. The destroyed property is only .0025 per cent of the total. Only .04 per cent of the crops for 1927 are affected, and even that is the most pessimistic estimate.
But does any one pay any attention to that? No, "The South is ruined," as usual.

7. The International Chamber of Commerce met in the United States on May 4, 1931, during the height of the worldwide economic depression, when Germany was thought to be within a few months of a revolution, and the disarmament conference was only nine months in the future. On May 4 the New York *Times* published an editorial, and on May 5 the Chicago *Tribune* published an editorial. Examine both editorials and try to discover which exhibits the keener insight into the realities of the world situation. Do you think that the New York *Times'* editorial reflects wishful-thinking, or does it have a sound basis in reality?

(1)

COÖPERATING WITH EUROPE

Whatever one's opinion may be on the subject of armament limitation or reduction, as to the measure of its practicability or the pace at which we may reasonably hope to move in that direction, the President has done well to place the problem of armament expenditure promptly and emphatically before the conference of the International Chamber of Commerce. As was foretold the other day by Mr. Henning, we are to have a good deal of advice from our distinguished visitors as to how the world depression is to be relieved, and the outstanding proposals are all for relief at our expense. We are to cancel our war loans, we are to put our gold reserve at the command of some international committee in which we have one vote, we are to reduce our tariff so as to permit a more easy competition in our home market with our own industries, we are to invest where it will do the most good to Europe according to the opinion of some international agency, and we are to open our gates again so as to permit the unemployed of other countries to join our own.

We have been told frequently in recent years that we are chiefly responsible for conditions in Europe and for the restoration of world prosperity. We have heard little of the responsibility of the European governments and peoples for their own misfortunes. The persistent bellicosity of the wrangling European household, the perpetual war talk, the building up of armies and navies, the erection of trade barriers across economic lines of natural coöperation, the complication of financial and commercial policies with political and military considerations, the fostering of ancient rivalries and rancors—for all these we find no signs of penitence. Uncle Sam is the stubborn malefactor and he must reform—of course for his own good.

In the presence of this admonition the President has done well to invite our monitors to look to their own household. It will have no appreciable effect upon them, but at least it may do something toward checking the tendency of so many of our supposedly practical captains of finance and industry who are impressed with the superiority of European judgment over our own. We hope it will brace up their American self-respect. There is nothing more mischievous in our international situation than the fact that the control of our international activities is largely under the influence if not completely in the control of men in New York and the East who suffer from snobbism and a social inferiority complex with respect to Europe. Constructive coöperation with other nations is desirable and even essential to our own greatest prosperity. But it should be founded on a clear headed regard for the rights and interests of the American people. Too many of our representatives at international conferences seem to feel that in complacently accepting a status inferior to the European members they acquire one superior to other Americans.—CHICAGO *Tribune*.

(2)

No Time to be "Cool"

Though President Hoover is to address the first meeting of the International Chamber of Commerce at Washington to-day, it is carefully explained that our government will abstain from taking any part in it. With it the administration will have nothing to do "officially." Further than that, it is broadly hinted that our government will be distinctly "cool" toward the entire proceedings. Important representatives of banking and commerce and industry and shipping from all over the world have come together to discuss the burning economic and financial questions of the day, but they are notified in advance that this government will stand apart in callous indifference. If they expect to enlist our interest, they are much mistaken. Among the subjects which they will debate are the gold supply, war debts, and especially tariffs. But only to hear of such things appears to be enough to make the American authorities run away in alarm. Debts and tariffs? Why, the very mention of such things ought to be forbidden. Unless we keep religiously away from conferring with these foreigners, they will be asking us to make some "commitment," and what could be more terrible than that?

So far as this attitude has been defined and may be persisted in, it is a willful ignoring of conditions in which we have a greater concern than any other country. The International Chamber of Commerce is to bring to the front matters of truly world-wide interest. The United States is caught in a general misfortune. For us to refuse to do our part to relieve it, or even to consult with those who are planning measures of relief, is worse than a crime, for it is a gigantic blunder. For this nation or this government to be cool or suspicious in the presence of endeavors to help the whole earth out of an international mess is to heap folly upon ignorance. We really ought to have the warmest and most instant sympathy with the whole inquiry, and lend to it every help and countenance. But thus far our official position has been that depression and disasters in other countries are a good excuse, or political alibi, for their having occurred here also. President Hoover has more than once tried to reassure his fellow-countrymen by telling them

> that they are suffering only what has befallen all other people. But when other people come and ask us to reason together with them in order to see if means cannot be devised for aiding the world to its feet again, we ostentatiously decline to have part or lot with them. Nothing like this has been seen since the Pharisee kept very cool and passed by on the other side.—NEW YORK *Times.*

8. Keeping in mind the discussion in this chapter, write an editorial in which you comment on the following address by Mr. Bernard Shaw in May, 1931:

At the present time the press is time-lagging very badly in many ways. Take such a cheerful example as the Russian Revolution. The press has not yet recognized that the revolution has taken place.

Take the French Revolution. I was a grown up person in 1878 during the great French exhibition when Lord Salisbury, English foreign minister, who, for an aristocrat and diplomatist, had an exceptionally intelligent mind, refused to allow England to be represented at that exhibition because France was a republic. He was convinced that the Bourbons, or at least the Bonapartes, would come back and that there would be a return to the old régime. He was nearly a century out of date.

Lord Salisbury probably never did find out that the French Republic had come to stay, and we have not found out the Russian Soviet has come to stay. The consequence is that we have thrown away one of the most magnificent commercial chances any of us can hope to see in our lifetime.

We have not only thrown away a tremendous commercial opportunity, but a political friendship which may be of the greatest possible value to us. All our political friendships in the future will not be with Bourbons, Plantagenets, Valois, and Romanoffs, but with modern republics. They will each involve, like our own country, a very great deal of Communism which we cannot possibly do without for a single week.

Do not write about them like a very old-fashioned governess in a very old-fashioned cathedral town. If you do, time-lag will beat you. You will lose your power over the public mind, and a great deal of that is already passing to the wireless [radio]. . . .

The profession of journalism—God help it!

9. Explain, in the terms used in this chapter, why the naïve scheme of "outlawing" war appeals to so many Americans, whereas they object to a comprehensive scheme, such as the League of Nations, for preserving peace?

10. Read Henri Bergson's *An Introduction to Metaphysics* (Hulme translation) and try to formulate a definition of "insight." Is it possible to formulate a definition of "insight," in terms of metaphysics, which can be reconciled with a definition of "insight" in terms of psychology?

Write out a definition of each of the following terms as it is used by Bergson:

absolute	metaphysics
intuition	intellectual auscultation
analysis	thinking
integral experience	

11. In the light of the materials discussed in this chapter, comment on the following statement:

In a chapter on the "Mental Processes of the Inventor" [in *The Psychology of the Inventor*, by Joseph Rossman] Mr. Rossman declares that the best opinion of those who have experimented with animals indicates that in invention we deal with habit formations or set patterns. From these habit formations and patterns the inventor breaks away to the extent of giving us new arrangements. But the impulse to break the old habit or rearrange the familiar patterns is not yet accounted for satisfactorily.

When we deal with flashes and impulses we also deal with chance. Hence, although inventors often deliberately set out to invent, they may owe their happiest discoveries to chance. It takes an extraordinarily observing and receptive mind to see the significance of a chance occurrence. Goodyear literally fries sulphur and rubber and notes a curious effect which turns out to be vulcanization. Saccharine is discovered because a chemist who happens to eat his luncheon in his laboratory without washing his hands tastes something intensely sweet. Daguerre leaves an exposed photographic plate in a closet which contains an open dish of mercury and thus discovers a necessary photographic developer. Etc., etc.—Waldemar Kaempffert in *New York Times Book Review,* Sept. 6, 1931.

12. Write an editorial suggested by the following generalization:

"Immigrants from overpopulated countries have invariably gone to countries with a higher standard of living than their own, not to underpopulated areas in Africa and Australasia."

Chapter XI

Values

1. What two points of view are reflected by the following editorial, which was published in the Baltimore *News* in 1907? Which point of view—that is, which social end—do you prefer? Embody your answer in an editorial.

> The constitution of the United States is being tugged at nowadays in a way that has not been paralleled since the great struggle of the Civil War. The question of how far the federal gov-

ernment can go in the regulation of the industrial, commercial, and transportation interests of the country, as a consequence of the "interstate commerce" clause of the constitution, is constantly to the front. . . .

The basis of all interstate commerce legislation is to be found in just four words of the constitution. Among the powers granted to Congress by that instrument is included the power to "regulate commerce with foreign nations, and among the several States, and with the Indian tribes." . . .

To prohibit the transportation, in interstate commerce, of goods in the making of which child labor has entered [proposed in the Beveridge bill] is to use the power over interstate commerce simply as a weapon of coercion in the regulation of conditions of industry in the several states. The purpose may be ever so laudable, but the point is that it is a purpose having none but the most accidental—incidental is not a strong enough word—and far-fetched connection with interstate commerce, or commerce of any kind. If the power to regulate interstate commerce be held to justify an application so remote, what is to hinder its being used to prohibit the transportation of goods of any kind from a state in which child labor is allowed, or in which the sale of alcoholic liquors is permitted, or which does not maintain a state university? It may be that between the Beveridge proposal and such fantastic propositions as we have here imagined there is a wide gulf; but the point is that unless it be recognized that the power to regulate interstate commerce is to be construed as having such limitations as a reasonable attitude toward the meaning of written language would impose, we are landed in a situation in which the power of the federal government to coerce the separate states upon any point of internal policy would be practically without limit. And even if it be admitted that the necessity of a great stretching of federal power in industrial and commercial matters is a necessity of the times, it should be borne in mind that the process of changing the constitution by orderly amendment is open to the nation. That this process is only a paper possibility, but is in practice out of the question, is a belief widely entertained, but it is in reality little better than a superstition. It is high time that the question were being seriously considered whether the un-

> limited stretch of the constitution can be justified
> by the unwarranted assumption that legal amend-
> ment of that instrument is an impossibility.

2. In 1918 the United States Supreme Court declared unconstitutional the child labor law which forbade the interstate shipment of products produced by child labor. In 1929 Congress
passed the Hawley-Cooper bill which prohibits the interstate transportation of goods produced by prison labor. Write an editorial
in which you bring out all the aspects of the principle involved.

3. Drawing on your observation of events, write an editorial
suggested by the following statement:

The day of the expert is upon us and his coming has not been an un-
mixed blessing. As the Geneva naval conference showed, he may mag-
nify technical difficulties until there is no possible solution: what is
needed in this complicated world is a philosophical view of the whole.

4. In the absence of adequate data concerning the question of
fair electric light and power rates, do you think President Hoover
was justified in opposing government operation of Muscle Shoals,
an avowed experiment, on the ground that public ownership and
operation of utilities is wrong in principle? Referring to the discussion in this chapter, write an editorial which expresses your
opinion of the President's attitude.

5. Comment editorially on the following statement:

Gradually we are being divested of the right of trial by jury. With
respect to civil cases, the workingman's compensation acts have substituted a state industrial commission for the jury, and in some states a
movement is being promoted to have automobile accident liability cases
heard by a board instead of a jury. In criminal cases, we witness the
use that is being made of the injunction to convict alleged violators
of the Volstead Act without trial by jury, and in contempt cases, the
judge himself constitutes the jury as well as the accuser. The inalienable
right of trial by jury should be preserved at all costs.

6. Comment editorially on the following statement:

The tendency of American reformers is almost never to teach, to
educate public opinion and to convince gradually the citizenry the value
of reform, but it is to secure the passage of prohibitory legislation and
then leave it to the government, state and federal, to carry out the
reformers' ideas. This tendency is not only mischievous but illogical.

7. Referring to the discussion in this chapter, comment editorially on the following statement:

We witness this fault in legislation. The Sherman Antitrust Law,
passed in 1890, is an example. This act was calculated to attain a

specific end—the protection of an individual business from an unfair combination of competitors. But it has also retarded the expansion of certain kinds of business which are important to the nation. Business men are now urging that it ought to be amended in certain respects. They declare that it was adopted before all the consequences of trusts had been discovered by experience.

CHAPTER XIII

Readers' Attitudes

1. Do you agree with the following statement of Elihu Root?

Civilization progresses only by changes within the individual, not by outside compulsion, and improvement of international relations can come only through the elevation of the standards of conduct of the people who compose the nations.

2. Develop in an editorial the full meaning of this statement from Professor C. E. Merriam:

The new world demands scientific knowledge to deal with the new world forces that are being unleashed. Propaganda and pseudoscience will not be able to provide adequate government of the world in a period where stability and order and morale are more important than ever before in the history of man.—*New Aspects of Politics*, p. 18.

3. To what spring of action does each of the following editorials appeal?

(1)

Madison may be a center of culture, but it must parade its appreciation of art and music in a cowbarn.

It is a strange anomaly that a community of Madison's artistic attainments has no auditorium or hall where singers of a national reputation can be comfortable and at their best in a recital.

We wouldn't blame John McCormack if he were to veto any future appearance in Madison. The difficulties and handicaps under which he was asked to appear at the Stock Pavilion last night were such as to discourage any artist. Here was a man with one of the golden voices of the ages and yet he was compelled to sing to the accompaniment of sizzling radiators and chugging steampipes while scores of prospects for Smith Bros. coughdrops were barking against the countless draughts of the big barn.

(2)

Two days ago Mrs. Katherine Post, 56 years old, mother of 16 children, passed through St. Louis from Arkansas on her way to a federal prison in West Virginia. She was in the custody of a United States marshal, and had been convicted of selling whiskey.

Mrs. Post is the wife of a fruit grower living near Altus, Ark. Their home is some 45 miles from Fort Smith. Five of her children are under 18 years of age and living at home. A woman remarkably typical of that sturdy stock which pioneered the United States, Mrs. Post made a profound impression upon all those at the station who witnessed this amazing American tragedy. The institution to which she is going is the Federal Industrial House of Correction. It is at Alderson, W. Va. Conveying this country woman thence, the majestic United States government provided an entourage of one United States marshal and the marshal's mother as matron.

It was charged against slavery in those stirring days before the Civil War that it did more than sell human beings into servitude. It tore the mother from her children, and the husband from the wife. The humane instincts of those who opposed slavery were so fired by these incredible cruelties that they became at length a flaming sword. Yet here we have duplicated in another time those very abominations for which slavery was destroyed. Presumably those who put prohibition above the humanities, as in another time there were those who put slavery above the humanities, can justify the transportation of this woman from Arkansas to West Virginia.

Mr. Lincoln said: "If slavery is not wrong, then nothing is wrong."

To paraphrase that powerful pronouncement, if transporting this woman, for such a petty offense, from her country home down in the Arkansas woods to a federal prison in West Virginia, tearing her away from her family—if that is not wrong, then nothing is wrong.

4. Analyze the various attitudes regarding prohibition.

(a) To what extent is the attitude of some women influenced by a primary wish to preserve the sanctity and security of the home?

(b) To what extent is the attitude of some unstable persons influenced by their desire to protect themselves from the temptation of drink?

(c) To what extent is the attitude of some intellectuals influenced by their philosophy of life which holds that society has no right to make the individual conform to a strict moral code in "nonessentials"?

(d) To what extent is the attitude of some intellectuals influenced by a philosophy of life which holds that society should enforce a strict moral code upon the individual in the interests of society?

5. Write an editorial addressed to some section of the public in which you urge the individuals to do some act for which you hold out a reward.

6. After reading the following description, by Mr. H. N. Brailsford, of the composition of the British Conservative party, write an editorial in which you discuss the possibilities of the Labor party for winning over a part of this section of the public:

The Tory party includes three-fourths of the professional class, of the academic intelligence of the universities, and of the captains of industry. . . . A great part of their clientele requires no new departures in our national life. In spite of the industrial depression, banking thrives and so do most of the distributive trades. "The City's" interests (by which we mean finance) have been well served through all these years of deflation, and behind the City [financial district] is the whole *rentier* class [i.e. bondholders], bigger and incomparably more influential in our older society than it is in America. With it march the solid phalanx of the semi-parasitic population, the big servant class, the purveyors of luxury, and the villagers who still live, half-dazzled, half-intimidated, under the social leadership and the economic despotism of the landlord, and his spiritual lieutenant, the parson. These people ask for no program [of reform]; they prefer inertia; they find satisfaction for their need of romance in the picture of a vast empire, and in loyalty to the throne.

The problem for the Tories, as an election approaches, is to find for this solid main body the support of a fringe of the unorganized and non-political population, the smaller middle class, the women, old and young, and the workers who have not yet come under the influence of the Labour movement. For these one does not cater with intelligence. The schemes of Mr. Lloyd George and the Labour party, even when one reduces them to the simplest terms, demand too much thinking, too much knowledge, some power of imagination, some social altruism. These people are won by bribes or by fear. For the women, who, in this election [1929] will vote for the first time their full strength, the Tories offer two inducements. Mr. Churchill [Chancellor of the Exchequer] has abolished the duty on tea and Mr. Baldwin [Prime Minister] has promised, rather vaguely, some improvement and expansion, apparently by the creation of a free national service of midwifery, of the care which the community offers to the working-class mother. A cruder sort of bribe is offered to the farmer. He is told that for half the year the army and navy will be fed on 50 per cent of British beef and 25 per cent of British wheat.   [Also] agricultural land will be immediately relieved of the whole burden of local taxation. . . .

Fear is a strong motive.   In 1924 the Tories swept the hesitating voter into their net by their use of the almost-certainly forged Zinoviev letter [alleged offer of help from Soviet Russia to British working-class] to discredit the Labour policy of an economic *rapprochement* with Russia.

CHAPTER XIV

Editorial Policy

1. List five principles which you think are worth fighting for.

2. Write an editorial which explains, aside from logical reasons, why the United States has declined to cancel or reduce the inter-Allied war debts since they were funded.

3. If you were an editor, what position would you take with reference to the question of birth control? the passage of laws to make an organized Communist party illegal? the passage of a law to designate October 12 (Columbus Day) as a legal holiday? a declaration of war against Japan? against Great Britain? of an embargo on imports from Soviet Russia?

4. List the six most important social, economic, and political problems which, in your opinion, are the most pressing today.

5. Draft a platform of policy for a newspaper of which you are owner.

6. What is the underlying principle in the political philosophy of Herbert Hoover? of Norman Thomas? of Senator Borah?

7. List one or two recent instances you have observed in which a conflict is taking place on the conflict level (i.e., propaganda level) which ought to be fought out on the level of discussion.

8. Do you agree with the following statement by Louis I. Jaffee, editor of the Norfolk *Virginian-Pilot?*

There are times when a newspaper with a proper sense of its responsibility as an organ of opinion must "go after" some abuse with all its works, but these occasions are few.   The normal weapon of the liberal newspaper, as I see it, is the normal weapon of any other liberal—good, plain, forthright argument, repeated, varied in its presentation, but persistently, relentlessly repeated—repeated so often that it sinks into the consciousness of the readers and helps to shape their social and political outlook.

9. Do you agree with this statement by Walter Lippmann?

It is vain to suppose that our problems can be dealt with by rallying the people to some crusade that can be expressed in a symbol, a phrase, a set of principles, or a program.   If that is what the progressives are looking for to-day, they will look in vain.   For the objectives to which a nation like this could be aroused in something like unanimity are limited to war or to some kind of futile or destructive fanaticism.

10. Debate the proposition of Mr. Mencken that newspapers must correct wrong "by translating all argument for principle into rage against a man."

11. If you were a successful newspaper publisher, what would you do with your surplus earnings?

12. Do you agree with this statement by George S. Johns, editor of the St. Louis *Post-Dispatch?*

When a rich man comes into possession of a newspaper he may not have any background of culture or experience, but he wants to enjoy the prestige and standing of editor. Naturally, he wants to print the kind of newspaper he likes and his rich friends like. He hires talent to do the work to his taste. He doesn't want his newspaper to injure his own or his friends' interests, whatever they may be. He does not want his newspaper to be obnoxious to the roundtable of his club, where he and probably his better paid editors gather. In the mellow atmosphere of his club, it seems foolish to pay attention to the inequities that oppress the common people, or to feed their dissatisfactions and aspirations. It seems foolish to attack the interests of respectable men of wealth and influence who are shrewd enough and strong enough to profit by privilege and exploitation. They are the leaders and pillars of our social and economic system. The money-making game is the chief end of man. Ideals and ethics are the illusions of the irresponsible and unsuccessful!

13. Debate this proposition:

Wherever professional newspaper men have been free to formulate editorial policy, that policy has always been liberal.

14. Prepare a 500-word description of a community conflict with which you are familiar.

15. List those instances which you have observed or read about in which the following groups were involved in a community conflict: a memory group, an occupational group, a religious group, a nationality group, a symbolic group.

Chapters XV to XVII

XV. The Structure of the Editorial
XVI. Editorial Style
XVII. Miscellaneous Types of Editorials

1. Select an editorial from the Baltimore *Evening Sun* and answer the following questions about it. Include quotations when possible.

(*a*) How many words does the editorial contain? Is it longer or shorter than the average editorial in the issue from which it was selected?

(*b*) Is its length proportionate to the importance and the complexity of the subject it discusses?

(*c*) Does the writer waste time in getting under way?

(*d*) Does the writer stop after he has accomplished his apparent purpose?

(*e*) How many paragraphs does the editorial contain?

(*f*) What is the average length of the paragraphs?

(*g*) If you were writing the editorial, would you have the paragraphs longer or shorter than they are?

(*h*) Is the beginning likely to interest the average reader in the subject?

(*i*) Is the beginning annunciatory (i.e., is the editorial hung on a "news-peg")?

(*j*) Does the editorial progress logically, step by step, from the first sentence to the last?

(*k*) Could you change the order of the ideas and thereby make the editorial clearer or more effective?

(*l*) Could any part of the editorial be omitted to advantage?

(*m*) Does the editorial end effectively?

(*n*) Is the ending a summarizing sentence, or does the editorial merely stop?

(*o*) Does the ending help to give unity to the editorial?

(*p*) Is the title concise, interesting, and attractive?

(*q*) Could you improve the title?

2. Examine several issues of the Baltimore *Evening Sun* and the *Christian Science Monitor*. Do you think the same editorial manner is reflected in the editorials? If there is a difference, describe it.

3. Examine several issues of the *Spectator* (London) and the *Nation* (New York). Do you think the same editorial manner is reflected in the editorials? If there is a difference, describe it and try to account for it.

4. Select an editorial from the Milwaukee *Journal* and answer the following questions about it. Include quotations when possible.

(*a*) Are the paragraphs coherent units?

(*b*) Are the paragraph beginnings emphatic?

(*c*) Is the sentence construction firm?

(*d*) How is sentence emphasis obtained?

(*e*) Is the style concise or wordy?

(*f*) Does the style readily yield its meaning to the ordinary reader?

(*g*) Does the style have force? Does it have vigor?

(*h*) Does the editorial contain any epigrams, ironic touches, litotes, or antithetical expressions of any kind?

(*i*) Are specific or general words most often used?

(*j*) Are colloquial words or expressions used?

(*k*) If humor is introduced, what form does it take?

5. What is it that gives this sentence force?

The British have always thought that they could make of natives good House of Commons parliamentarians in a short time.

6. Read several editorials by H. L. Mencken in the *American Mercury*, listing all of the concrete expressions employed and all of the figures of association. Do you think these are effective? Would you make use of them in the editorial page of a daily newspaper?

7. What fault of diction (not arrangement of words) makes this sentence difficult to understand in rapid reading?

There are times and there are some people who look back of the impressive monument of America, the land of equality and liberal progress, to see the betrayal of such creeds of Americanism in a country still steeped in the dyes of age-old prejudice and fanaticism of tradition.

8. Write an editorial based on the following news dispatch:

> Prof. Edward Wilbur Berry, of the department of paleontology at the Johns Hopkins university, has been selected dean and provost to succeed Dr. J. H. Ames, president-elect. Professor Berry, a former salesman and newspaper man; has no college degree and attended college only a short time.

9. Write a "recognition of service" editorial.
10. Write an editorial entitled, "The Year in Retrospect."

INDEX

Values, definition of, 223 *ff.*; conflict of, 224 *ff.*, 226 *ff.*; social, 225 *ff.*; ultimate, 227 *ff.*
Variable factors, 96, 102 *ff.*
Vigor in editorial style, 356, 372

Waddell, Agnes Stewart, quoted, 31 *ff.*
"Wall Street," 211
Walter, John, 327
Ward, Henshaw, 217 *n.*
Washington, George, 25 *ff.*, 176 *ff.*, 187, 292
Watterson, Henry, 319 *ff.*, 320 *n.*
Whately, Richard, quoted, 127
Wheat, dumping of, 59 *ff.*, 211
Whiskey Rebellion, 156

"Whiskey trust," 140
White, William Allen, 359; quoted, 311, 363 *ff.*, 364
Williams, Talcott, 328 *ff.*; quoted, 318, 378
Wilson, Woodrow, 358 *n.*; quoted, 281, 318 *ff.*
Wishes, classification of, 263 *ff.*
Wishful-thinking, 214 *ff.*, 278; value of, 222
"Working principles," 143 *ff.*
World Court, 106, 152 *ff.*, 266 *ff.*

Zimmerman, C. C., quoted, 139
Zimmern, Alfred, quoted, 235 *ff.*, 272 *ff.*

(1)